This one is for two stout-hearted friends:
Julian Thompson and Eric Garner

Robin Neillands

Robin Neillands is 'one of Britain's most readable military historians' (*Birmingham Post*) and the author of several widely acclaimed books on the First and Second World Wars, including *The Battle of Normandy, 1944*; *The Great War Generals on the Western Front*; *The Conquest of the Reich*; *The Bomber War* and, most recently, *The Old Contemptibles*.

Other books by the author

Eighth Army

From the Western Desert to the Alps,
1939–1945

ROBIN NEILLANDS

JOHN MURRAY

First published in Great Britain in 2004 by John Murray (Publishers)
A division of Hodder Headline

1 3 5 7 9 10 8 6 4 2

A CIP catalogue record for this title is available from the British Library

ISBN 0 7195 5647 3

Typeset in Palatino by Servis Filmsetting Ltd, Manchester

Printed and bound by
Clays Ltd, St Ives plc

John Murray (Publishers)
338 Euston Road
London
NW1 3BH

Contents

Illustrations

The author and publishers would like to thank the following for permission to reproduce illustrations: Plates 2, 3, 5, 6, 8, 9, 10, 13, 15, 16, 17, 18, 19, 20, 23, 24, 25, 26, 27, 28, 29 and 30, Trustees of the Imperial War Museum, London; 11, 12, 21 and 22, Hulton Archive; 14, Bettmann/Corbis. Plate 4 is from the author's collection.

Maps

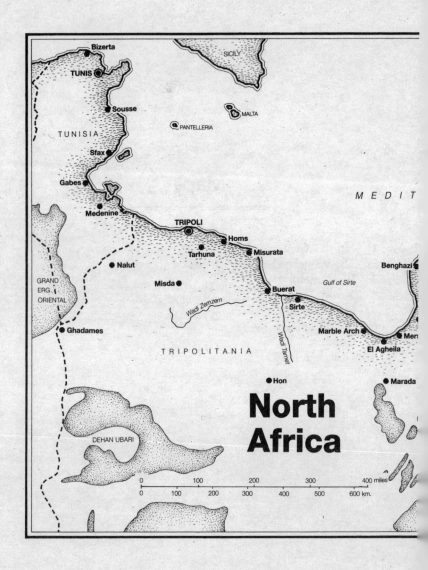

North Africa

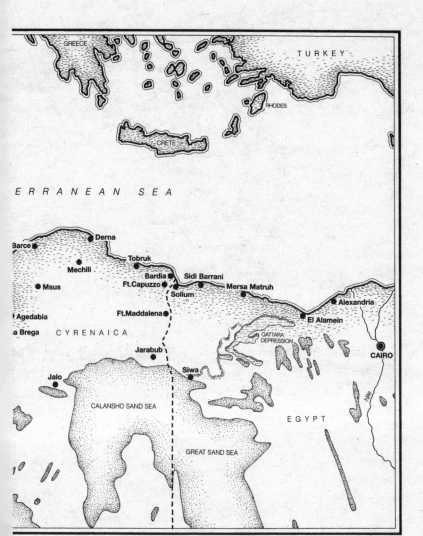

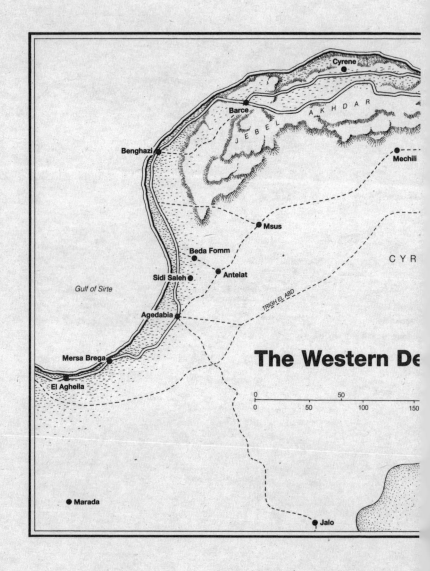

Cyrene

Barce

AKHDAR

Benghazi

Mechili

JEBEL

Msus

CYR

Beda Fomm

Sidi Saleh

Antelat

Gulf of Sirte

Agedabia

TRIGH EL ABD

The Western De

Mersa Brega

El Agheila

0   50
0   50   100   150

Marada

Jalo

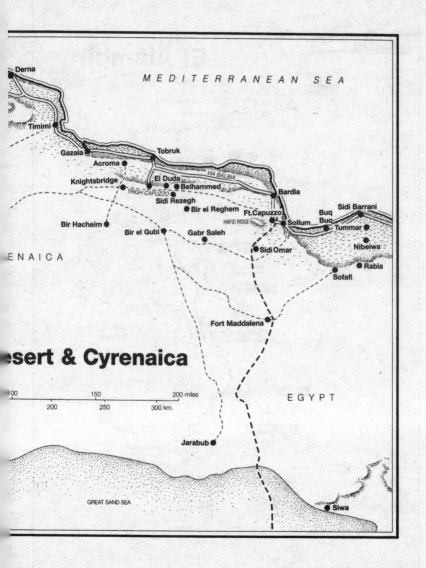

Derna

MEDITERRANEAN SEA

Timimi

Gazala   **Tobruk**

Acroma

Knightsbridge   **El Duda**   **Belhammed**

TRIGH CAPUZZO   *VIA BALBIA*

Sidi Rezegh   **Bardia**

Bir el Reghem   **Ft.Capuzzo**   **Sidi Barrani**

Bir Hacheim   *HAFID RIDGE*   **Sollum**   **Buq**   **Buq**

Bir el Gubi   **Gabr Saleh**   **Tummar**

Nibeiwa

CYRENAICA   **Sidi Omar**

Rabia

Sofafi

Fort Maddalena

esert & Cyrenaica

100   150   200 miles

200   250   300 km.

EGYPT

Jarabub

GREAT SAND SEA

Siwa

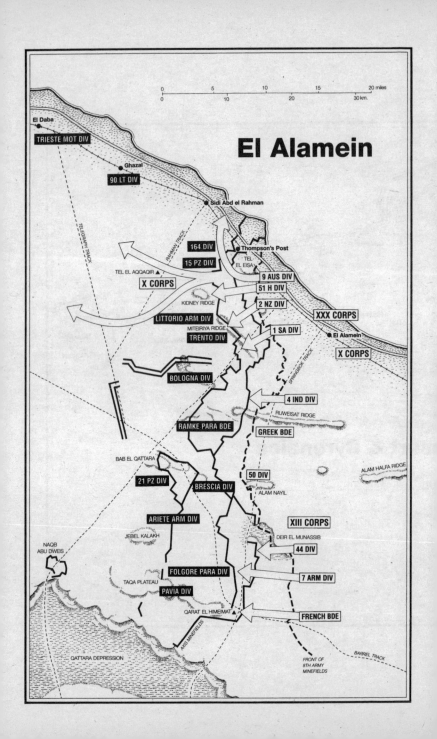

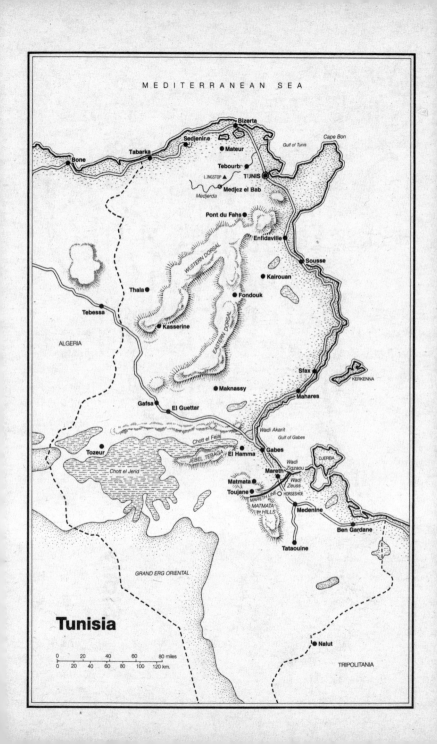

Tunisia

MEDITERRANEAN SEA

Bizerta
Cape Bon
Sedjenine
Mateur
Gulf of Tunis
Bone
Tabarka
Tebourb
LONGSTOP
TUNIS
Medjez el Bab
Medjerda
Pont du Fahs
Enfidaville
WESTERN DORSAL
Sousse
Kairouan
Thala
Fondouk
Tebessa
EASTERN DORSAL
Kasserine
ALGERIA
Sfax
KERKENNA
Maknassy
Mahares
Gafsa
El Guettar
Wadi Akarit
Gulf of Gabes
Chott el Fejaj
Tozeur
JEBEL TEBAGA
El Hamma
Gabes
Wadi Zigzaou
DJERBA
Chott el Jerid
Matmata
Mareth
Wadi Zeuss
Toujane
MARETH LINE
HORSESHOE
MATMATA HILLS
Medenine
Ben Gardane
Tataouine
GRAND ERG ORIENTAL
Nalut
TRIPOLITANIA

| 0 | 20 | 40 | 60 | 80 miles |
| 0 | 20 | 40 | 60 | 80 | 100 | 120 km. |

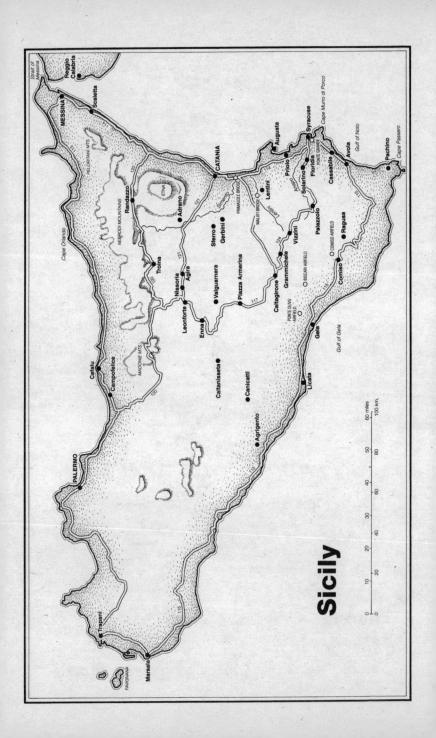

Sicily

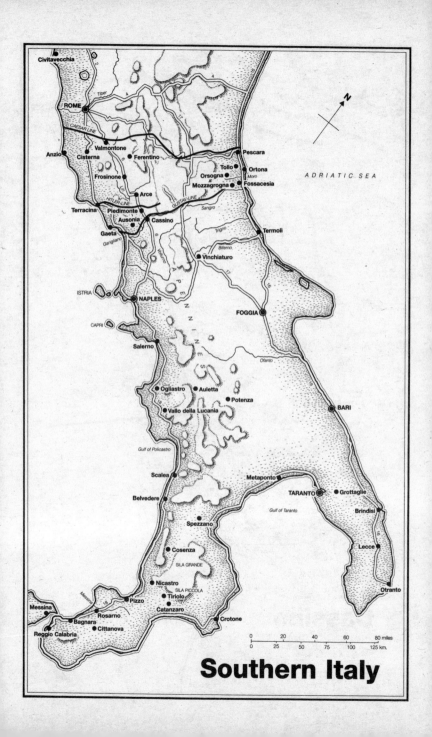

Southern Italy

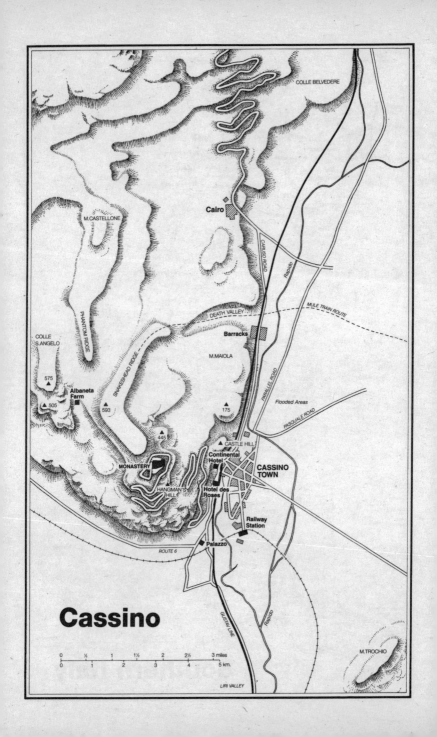

COLLE BELVEDERE

M. CASTELLONE

Cairo

CARISO ROAD

Rapido

DEATH VALLEY

MULE TRAIN ROUTE

COLLE
S.ANGELO

PHANTOM RIDGE

Barracks

M.MAIOLA

PARALLEL ROAD

▲ 575

SNAKESHEAD RIDGE

Albaneta
Farm

▲ 505

▲ 593

▲ 175

Flooded Areas

PASQUALE ROAD

▲ 445

▲ CASTLE HILL

Continental
Hotel

CASSINO
TOWN

MONASTERY

HANGMAN'S
HILL

Hotel des
Roses

Railway
Station

■ Palazzo

ROUTE 6

GUSTAV LINE

Rapido

Cassino

| 0 | ½ | 1 | 1½ | 2 | 2½ | 3 miles |
| 0 | 1 | 2 | 3 | 4 | | 5 km. |

M.TROCHIO

LIRI VALLEY

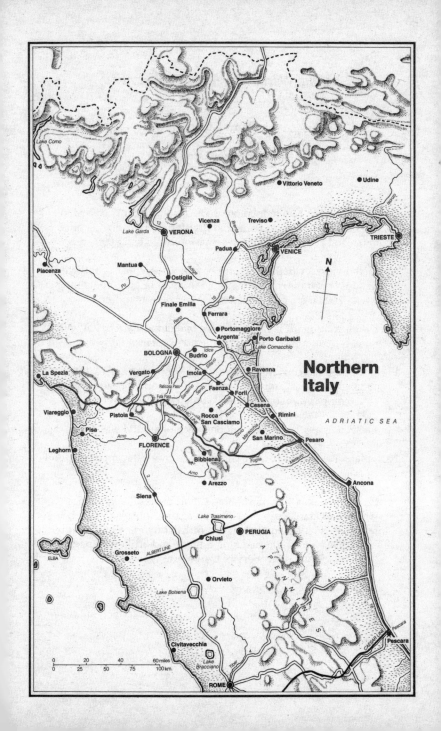

Lake Como

Udine

Vittorio Veneto

Vicenza   Treviso

Lake Garda   VERONA   VENICE   TRIESTE

Padua

Mantua

Piacenza   Ostiglia

Finale Emilia

Ferrara

Portomaggiore

Argenta   Porto Garibaldi

Lake Comacchio

BOLOGNA   Budrio

La Spezia

Vergato   Imola   Ravenna

Raticosa Pass   Faenza

Futa Pass   Forlì

GOTHIC LINE   Rocca   Cesena

Viareggio   San Casciamo   Rimini

Pistoia

Pisa   San Marino   Pesaro

Leghorn   FLORENCE

Bibbiena   Ancona

Arezzo

Siena

Lake Trasimeno

Chiusi   PERUGIA

Grosseto   ALBERT LINE

ELBA

Orvieto

Lake Bolsena

A
P
E
N
N
I
N
E
S

ADRIATIC SEA

**Northern
Italy**

N

Pescara

CAESAR LINE

Civitavecchia

Lake
Bracciano

ROME

0   20   40   60 miles
0   25   50   75 100 km.

Second World War Army Organization

Army Group
|
Two or more armies
|
Each army has two or more corps
|
Each corps has two more more divisions – an infantry division
(*c.* 15,000 men) and an armoured division (*c.* 9,000 men) – plus
attached arms, so an infantry division could be 25,000 men
|
Each division, whether infantry or armoured, consists of three
brigades or armoured regiments, an infantry brigade containing
c. 4,000 men, plus division HQ and divisional troops
|
Each infantry brigade consists of three battalions. Each battalion has
c. 800 men, including attachments
|
Each battalion has four rifle companies, a support company (mortars
and machine-guns, anti-tank and engineers) and a headquarters
company. A company will contain *c.* 100–120 men
|
Each company has three platoons, each of around 30–35 men
|
Each platoon contains 10 men, commanded by a sergeant or corporal

Please note that this information is only for outline guidance.
Artillery and tank units are different again. Note also that a US
infantry regiment is equivalent to a British brigade. Eighth Army
divisions also had an attached tank brigade and artillery, sapper and
Royal Army Service Corps supply units.

History has assigned to it the task of judging the past, of instructing the present for the benefit of ages to come. To such lofty functions this work does not aspire. Its aim is merely to show how things actually were.

Leopold von Ranke

Preface

When this war is over, it will be enough for a man to say, 'I marched and fought with the Desert Army.'

Winston Churchill, speech to the men of Eighth Army, Tripoli, January, 1943.

Now and again the wars produce an Army whose exploits are remembered. Wellington's Peninsular Army during the Napoleonic Wars was one such fighting force. Robert E. Lee's Army of Northern Virginia in the US Civil War was another. These armies fought hard campaigns and won great victories but they are really remembered and justly celebrated because of their spirit.

During the twentieth century another such army was the British Eighth Army, arguably the most famous army of the Second World War. Like the two armies mentioned above, Eighth Army had its ups-and-downs; it was not always victorious, its equipment was often obsolete or inadequate, its generals not always inspired and its command and control systems were not always of the best. And yet, despite all that, Eighth Army had something. What that something was this book will attempt to discover, but the core of Eighth Army – the secret of its enduring reputation and its eventual success – lies, I suspect, in its men.

In researching this book I have met or corresponded with many veterans of Eighth Army. What I gained from them – Australians, Canadians, British, New Zealanders, Poles, South Africans: Eighth Army was a cosmopolitan force – combines into an impression of a shared quality: a sense of humour, comradeship, courage in adversity, above all a willingness to go on in spite of defeat and disillusion, sometimes thinking themselves hard done by, never thinking themselves brave.

The men of Eighth Army went through some difficult times, but those made them what they were – hardship is the school of the soldier. Forged by hardship in the harsh conditions of the Western Desert of North Africa, these men made good soldiers, and between 1940 and 1945 they created a memorable Army. That Army – 'often defeated but never dismayed' – kept on going for thousands of miles across varied terrain, gaining in power and expertise, as it marched and fought from the valley of the Nile to the foothills of the Alps. Eighth Army contributed more than most to the Allied victory in 1945.

The Eighth Army was born in the desert. It was therefore often known as the Desert Army, though it also fought across Sicily in 1943 and up the rocky spine of Italy in 1943–5. Veterans – and pedants – should therefore know that this history of Eighth Army begins in 1940 with the Western Desert Force, more than a year before the Eighth Army as such was created. The Army came first; the name came later.

Eighth Army was also the British Empire at war. The desert campaign up to Alamein was the last time the forces of the Empire campaigned on their own before the arrival of the Americans at the end of 1942. Into the Eighth Army order of battle came some of the great fighting divisions of the war: the 2nd New Zealand Division, the divisions of the 2nd Polish Corps, the 4th and 5th Indian Divisions, the Canadian Corps, the 6th, 7th and 9th Australian Divisions, the South African Divisions, the British 7th Armoured Division – the famous Desert Rats – the 78th Division, the French Foreign Legion, the Greek Brigade, the 51st (Highland) Division, the 50th (Northumbrian) Division and many more. These corps and divisions bore the brunt of the battle for many years; their exploits should not be forgotten.

This book is a narrative history of Eighth Army, starting with its origins as the Western Desert Force and giving full voice to the veterans. That alone has created a very big book, especially when the various conflicts and controversies – and myths – surrounding the Italian campaign and Allied strategy in the Mediterranean theatre are introduced as well. Covering the strategy and the controversies is necessary, both to put the exploits of Eighth Army into context and to explain the quite extraordinary difficulties faced by the commanders in the field.

At this point I must make an apology and a plea for understanding. I am conscious that this book has failed to cover every aspect of the Mediterranean campaign and give full credit to the Desert Air Force, the Mediterranean Fleet, special forces like the SAS and the Long Range Desert Group, and the gallant people and troops of the island fortress of Malta. No offence is intended by such omissions: there simply was not the space to cover all these units or places and the events to which they contributed. I have tried to make it clear that they had a part to play in the main story; to do more was not possible.

Many of the Eighth Army formations have been the subject of other histories, and this book does not attempt to detail the exploits of every Eighth Army contingent on every day of the Second World War. This book concentrates on Eighth Army *as a whole*, and attempts to put it in the context of the campaigns in which it was engaged – not only the strategy and the controversies, but also the politics: matters that might have seemed remote indeed to the soldier in the tank or trench, but which had a direct bearing on his life – or death.

During the war, Eighth Army was famous. Escaping across France in 1943, George Millar, then an officer in the Rifle Brigade and later a hero of the French resistance, recalls how the local people were delighted to help an officer of the '*Huitième Armée*', the army that had given the Germans a bloody nose in North Africa and shattered the Italians at Beda Fomm. Perhaps the subsequent fading of Eighth Army from public attention is because at the end of 1943 it lost its most famous and most controversial commander, General Sir Bernard Law Montgomery. Another reason may be that after D-Day, in June 1944, the Italian campaign in which Eighth Army was then engaged became a sideshow. Whatever the reason, by the time the Second World War ended in 1945 Eighth Army had almost been forgotten.

This later neglect needs to be corrected. From June 1940 to November 1942 – the worst three years of the Second World War – Eighth Army was the focus of the national effort against the Axis powers. It was the only Western Army facing and fighting the enemy – Italian as well as German – on the battlefield and beating them more often than not, albeit usually by a narrow margin and only after a series of defeats at the hands of its highly regarded opponent General Erwin Rommel. In those early campaigns Eighth Army had its problems, but all that changed at Alamein.

'Before Alamein it seems we never had a victory; after it we never had a defeat,' said Churchill in November 1942. This is only half-true: the Western Desert Force shattered the Italians in 1940, most notably at Beda Fomm, and plenty of hard fighting lay ahead after Alamein. But, although the history of Eighth Army is full of battles, this book aims to do more than simply recall the defeats and triumphs of this wonderful army. This is an attempt to catch the spirit of Eighth Army – what it was like to serve in it, and why that North African medal ribbon, with the tiny metal '8' as a clasp, is still a source of pride (and a source of irritation to many Eighth Army veterans, since not every member of Eighth Army is allowed to wear it).

Life in the Desert Army was never dull, but the story of Eighth Army continues after Panzerarmee Afrika surrendered outside Tunis in May 1943. This book follows Eighth Army to Sicily and Italy and on to the scene of more terrible battles as it forced its way up the peninsula, to Termoli and the Sangro, to Ortona and Cassino and the Liri valley, to the Gothic Line and the Po valley, to Comacchio and Argenta and the foothills of the Alps. This is a story that deserves to be told – about an army that deserves to be remembered.

7 Armoured Div.

1

The Western Desert Force
1940

The immortal march of the Eighth Army, from the gates of Cairo along the African shore, through Sicily, had now carried its ever-victorious soldiers far into Italy, towards the gates of Rome.

Winston Churchill to General Montgomery, January 1944

This is the story of an army, and only that Army – not of the many and various corps, divisions and regiments it contained. Their exploits will be covered certainly, but only in passing; the histories of Eighth Army's component parts have been described in many other accounts, both official and personal, and in much more detail than there is space for here. The aim of this book is to tell the story of Eighth Army as an entity and in context, from its beginnings as the Western Desert Force in 1940 to its end as the triumphant army of 1945.

Above all, this book is about the men of Eighth Army: about their five-year march from the arid wastes of the Western Desert to the foot of the Italian Alps, and the many trials and tribulations they endured along the way. Their story is an epic of military history that deserves to be remembered, for no army in the Second World War fought for so long or travelled so far.

The story is not one of continual success. Eighth Army was not always well led, well trained or properly equipped. No man is on oath when writing a eulogy, but Winston Churchill was wrong in that extract quoted above: Eighth Army was not always victorious. It had its full share of defeats, retreats and reverses – and not a few of them traceable to the actions or demands of Mr Churchill himself.

And yet Eighth Army kept moving and kept fighting. The soldiers of this army came from many nations – Australia, Britain, Canada, Greece, India, Nepal, New Zealand, Palestine, Poland, Rhodesia, South Africa, the Seychelles, Mauritius – even Italy – but what they had in common was endurance.[1] This quality proved essential, for these soldiers had much to endure – not least the demands of fighting campaigns in terrain that was never less than rugged, often with inadequate equipment, always against a resolute opponent. In spite of this these soldiers persevered, and in the end they triumphed.

For half its history Eighth Army was better known as the Desert Army, and its story begins in the Western Desert, one of the most arid and desolate regions on earth, stretching some 1,500 miles from the Nile Delta to the frontier of Tunisia. The Egyptian portion of this desert runs for some 250 miles from the Delta to the Libyan frontier and is 150 miles across at its widest point, between the coast and the oasis at Siwa. South of Siwa lies the Great Sand Sea. East of Siwa, running north and east below sea level, growing wider as it moves north, lies the wide salt-marsh of the Qattara Depression, which peters out 40 miles south of the Mediterranean coast – and a little railway station called El Alamein.

The Western Desert was a battlefield with two open flanks: the Mediterranean Sea to the north and the open desert to the south. These flanks provided opportunities for the many special-force units produced by the desert war: the Long Range Desert Group (LRDG), the Special Air Service (SAS), Popski's Private Army, and the commando units of Layforce. These forces carried the war behind enemy lines, striking from the open desert or from the sea at airfields, supply dumps and ports – even at Rommel's headquarters.

At first sight the Western Desert appears flat and empty, a dusty grey expanse dotted with gravel and scrub, but this impression is misleading. There is cover here for tanks and troops, because the desert rolls, with plenty of shallow valleys – *wadis* – long ridges, and expanses of rock or boulder-strewn sand spread thinly over a limestone base. The great physical feature of the Western Desert is the coastal escarpment which begins west of Mersa Matruh and rises to a height of 450 feet in parts, a steep wall that can only be climbed where roads have been cut through, at the Halfaya Pass and Sidi Rezegh. The desert on the escarpment is seamed with camel tracks or *trighs*; during the Second World War some of these were 'barrel tracks' with oil drums marking out the route from place to place, rather like buoys in the sea.

Nor is this desert entirely without people. Stop in the desert for any length of time and the local Arabs will arrive from some lonely encampment – one usually centring on the desert wells or *birs* – bartering oranges and eggs for tea leaves. A less welcome arrival are the flies, a steady torment from dawn to dusk. Other things to endure out here include scorching summer heat, humidity, desert sores caused by sand irritating the smallest cut, bitterly cold nights, either a scarcity of water or torrential rain, and at any season the scourging *khamsin* – the relentless, sand-and-grit-bearing desert wind.

The only advantage of the Western Desert as a place of war is that there are very few towns – and those only along the coast – and no permanent rivers. The desert is a place for mobile, open warfare – a war of movement limited only by the chronic problem of supply. The desert has been described as 'a tactician's paradise and a quartermaster's hell', and there is considerable truth in that comment. There is nothing to sustain an army here; every gallon of petrol, every drop of water, every round of ammunition, has to be carried in. The first point to bear in mind about the war in North Africa from 1940–43 is the chronic problem of *supply*.

The only relief from this grey monotony comes in the rugged hills of the Jebel Akhdar – the Green Mountain – west of Tobruk. This closely cultivated region of small farms is indeed green for part of the year. The only water available elsewhere comes from *birs*, and the only signs of urban life – apart from the large oases in the south of the desert, at Siwa, Kufra and Jarabub – lie along the Mediterranean shore. This coast contains several small towns and some scattered hamlets, and in 1940 it was spanned by a single-track railway running from the British naval base at

Alexandria to the small port of Mersa Matruh, 120 miles to the west. There was also a narrow coastal road – well surfaced as far as Matruh, but becoming a rough track west of there as it ran past Buq-Buq to the Halfaya Pass and the town of Sollum near the frontier with Libya.

These places did not contain much in the way of population: in 1940 Buq-Buq was just a point on the map, and Sollum barely a hamlet, the port of Mersa Matruh possessed only a single jetty. Only Bardia and Tobruk – the latter with a population of around 4,000 – were capable of handling large ships. Nevertheless, given the distances and the paucity of land communications, the best means of supplying a force in the Western Desert was by sea – even though port facilities were scanty and cargo ships were liable to air attack and submarine interdiction.

West of Sollum lies the Libyan frontier. Libya had been an Italian colony since 1912, and its eastern edge was marked by a thick, barbed-wire fence, 12 feet high and 12 feet wide – the Graziani Fence – that ran south from just west of Sollum, past the Beau Geste-style ramparts of Fort Maddalena to the Jarabub oasis. West of this wired frontier the coastal track became a met-alled road – the Via Balbia – built by the Italians along the edge of the escarpment to Bardia and then to the port of Tobruk, the largest town west of Alexandria before the distant facilities of Tripoli, a thousand miles further on.

This terrain and these places are the basic elements of the coun-try where the Western Desert Force – the forerunner of Eighth Army – would fight its campaigns. Any understanding of the events in this book should therefore begin with a careful study of the maps on pages xxii–xiii and xiv–xv, noting the significant ter-rain, the Qattara Depression, the Jebel Akhdar, the towns and tracks, and the various countries and regions – Egypt, Libya, Cyrenaica, Tunisia – through which the desert campaigns would be conducted.

Libya's status as an Italian colony was the fruit of Italy's first attempt to refound the Roman Empire in 1912 and establish itself as a leading power in the Mediterranean. The conquest of Libya before the First World War had been matched later in the century with the founding of further Italian colonies in Somalia and Eritrea, the latter a province of Abyssinia (Ethiopia) where Italy had waged an aggressive war in the late 1930s.

Though ruled by King Victor Emmanuel III, since 1922 Italy had been governed by Benito Mussolini – the Duce – a despotic, totalitarian, Fascist dictator, a friend and associate of the German Führer, Adolf Hitler. In May 1939 these two dictators had signed an agreement, the Pact of Steel, each promising to aid the other in the event of war. But Italy was not ready to fight when Hitler invaded Poland four months later, and as declarations of war flew about Europe, Italy remained neutral, waiting – as in the First World War – to rush to the aid of the victor. This moment seemed to come in June 1940, with the defeat and surrender of France and the evacuation of the British Expeditionary Force from Dunkirk.

Before June 1940 the presence of French forces in Tunisia and Algeria had acted as a check on the Italian forces in Libya. France also occupied Syria, so protecting the Suez Canal against attack from the north, and these French forces, plus the powerful units of the French Mediterranean fleet, were a valuable addition to British strength in the Middle East. With the fall of France, all that was to change.

As France fell, the Duce ordered his forces to invade southern France. Their advance along the Côte d'Azur came to a halt after the new French administration established under Marshal Philippe Pétain – the so-called Vichy government – came to an agreement with the Führer. France was partitioned and the southern half – and France's overseas colonies and possessions, notably in Algeria and Syria – became part of Vichy, effectively allied to Nazi Germany and hostile to the British.

This arrangement freed the Duce's hands for adventures in North Africa. With France out of the war and the Vichy French actively co-operating with the Germans, the Italians could now send considerable forces against the British in Egypt. In 1940 Italy had two armies in North Africa: the Fifth Army in Tripolitania and the Tenth Army in Cyrenaica, a total force of twelve Italian divisions and two Libyan native divisions, well supplied with field artillery and light tanks, but short of training, heavy guns . . . and morale. These forces were backed by an air force equipped with modern machines and supported by the powerful Italian fleet.

Apart from at sea, where the Royal Navy's Mediterranean Fleet was a most formidable force, the British could not match the Italians in either equipment or numbers. When the Duce declared war on Britain from one minute past midnight on 11 June 1940, the situation for the British commanders in the Middle East instantly became critical and the Italian armies began to move east, expecting the early conquest of Egypt and swift possession of the Suez Canal.

Egypt, though an independent state, was largely controlled by the British. The British Army had first come to Egypt in 1882 for the brief, two-month-long, Anglo-Egyptian war. After winning that war the British had taken over the administration of Egypt, then an outpost of the Turkish Empire, and extended their rule into the Sudan – later the Anglo-Egyptian Sudan – after the Battle of Omdurman in 1898. The main reason for this takeover was the Suez Canal, a waterway which became of great strategic importance to Britain from the moment it opened in 1869. The Canal became part of the short-sea route to India, a link in the chain of imperial outposts running from the UK to Gibraltar, Malta, Cyprus and Alexandria, then through the Canal to Aden and on to Singapore, Colombo and Bombay.

Through the Canal in the other direction came tankers bringing oil from the British-owned oilfields in Iraq, and rubber and tin from Malaya. The importance of the Suez Canal to British imperial strategy can hardly be overstated, and the prime purpose of the British Army in Egypt in 1940 was the protection of the Canal. Egyptian compliance with this strategy had been confirmed in 1936 by the Anglo-Egyptian Treaty, under which the two countries would be allies in any coming conflict. This alliance was not an equal partnership: Egypt was an Allied base, but the Egyptians took little direct part in the war.

In 1940 the British High Command in the Middle East was entrusted to a triumvirate of senior officers: the Naval Commander-in-Chief, Mediterranean, Admiral Sir Andrew Cunningham, the Air Officer Commanding (AOC), Royal Air Force, Middle East, Air Chief Marshal Sir Arthur Longmore; and the Army Commander-in-Chief, Middle East, General Sir Archibald Wavell. Since this book is the history of an army, it is with General Wavell and his successors that this story is mainly concerned.

While all these commanders had responsibilities outside the defence of Egypt, Wavell's commitments were especially wide-ranging. He was also responsible for the Sudan, for Palestine – then in the midst of an Arab uprising against the British Mandate and Jewish immigration – for Transjordan and for Cyprus, with further responsibilities in Iraq – where a rebellion was pending – Aden, British Somaliland and the Persian Gulf. In the words of the Army Council Instructions, he also had to 'liaise and co-operate' with his peers, the Mediterranean naval and air force commanders-in-chief, with assorted ambassadors, governor-generals and High Commissioners, and with 'the allies of His Majesty's Government in the Near and Middle East and North Africa'.[2] In 1940 the War Cabinet expanded Wavell's responsibilities still further, adding East Africa and 'any forces that might be sent to Turkey or the Balkans, including Greece'.[3]

To help Wavell carry out these awesome tasks he was given just five staff officers and a total force consisting in 1940 of one ill-equipped armoured division, two brigade groups, two as yet unformed infantry divisions, sixty-four guns of various calibre – 'and a camel corps'.[4] In terms of manpower, Wavell had 36,000 men in Egypt and another 27,500 men in Palestine. Some of these were on internal-security duties, many were still in training; not all their units were fully equipped and much of the existing equipment was obsolescent – some of it, like the armoured cars, of First World War vintage. Not a few units were still on horseback.

Lord Bruntisfield was then an officer in a horsed cavalry regiment, the Scots Greys:

> We were in Palestine in 1940, operating against Arab insurgents in the hills or against villages where no wheeled transport could easily go. You had to move tactically, but so long as you did so and were not casual you were unlikely to get into trouble. We learned to read a map, and the tactics of a horsed regiment – requiring a mixture of movement, communications, offensive and defensive tactics were – strangely enough – exactly the same as afterwards we had to do in tanks. We also learned what was expected of us and to anticipate orders from our commander. The great principle, and it's not a bad one, was that when faced with a problem – when being shot at, or being in doubt over what to do to retrieve a situation – if you did something you might with luck be right, but if you did nothing you were bound to be wrong.
>
> But then in 1941 we lost our horses and went as lorried infantry to invade Syria with an Australian Brigade. This was a short

campaign, and when we got back to Palestine we were told that we were to be an armoured regiment and got three American tanks to train on. Since hardly any of the soldiers could even drive a car, this meant starting from the basics. To this day I have no idea how an engine works, and I travelled in a tank from Alamein to the Baltic.[5]

The main units in Egypt on the outbreak of war in 1939 were the first elements of what became the 7th Armoured Division, which had two brigades rather than its full complement of three, and the 4th Indian Division, which lacked an infantry brigade and most of its artillery. There was also the newly arrived 2nd New Zealand Division – still in training, short of transport and heavy weapons, and currently consisting of only one brigade. More troops, including an Australian division, were training in Palestine.

To support these, the RAF had 96 bombers, mainly Blenheim Mark Is and ancient Bombays, and 75 Gladiator biplane fighters, deployed in Egypt and Palestine. The potential enemy – Italy – was somewhat better endowed with air power. In Libya alone the Italians had 84 modern bombers and 144 fighters, with more on call from Sicily and the mainland of Italy.

A point to note is that there was no 'Supreme Commander' in the Middle East at this time. Fortunately the three service commanders co-operated without undue friction, but while the Army and RAF commanders had their headquarters in Cairo, Admiral Cunningham, when not at sea with the Mediterranean Fleet, had his HQ in Alexandria so communication was not always swift or easy.

Each commander had his own special responsibilities and the Royal Navy was particularly concerned with the defence of its central Mediterranean base, the island fortress of Malta, 800 nautical miles from Alexandria. From Malta, destroyers, submarines and RAF bombers could harry supply ships bringing men and equipment from Italy to the Axis forces in North Africa, and the island was destined to become a thorn in the side of the enemy. Malta was also a vital link on the short sea route from Britain to Alexandria and beyond. If that link failed, the Mediterranean would be closed and supplies for Egypt would have to take the much longer route via South Africa and the Red Sea. Any consideration of the North African campaign has therefore to' consider the need to defend the island. Without Malta, the war in North Africa could not be won; without success in North Africa, Malta could not be held. All these factors provide the context within which Wavell had to command his forces in the Middle East and the Western Desert.

General Sir Archibald Wavell was a typical British general officer of the period, in that there was rather more to him than there appeared. A professional soldier and a fighting man, he was also a poet and a scholar. His headmaster at Winchester said of him that there was no need for Wavell to enter the Army as 'he had sufficient brains to make his way in other walks of life', and during the desert campaigns of 1940 and 1941, when not commanding his armies, Wavell was compiling an excellent anthology of poetry, *Other Men's Flowers*.[6] On half-pay between the wars, he had spent time as a lecturer at Cambridge, and had the Second World War not intervened he might have taken the Chichele Chair of the History of War at the University of Oxford.

Commissioned into the Black Watch in 1901, Wavell had first seen service in the South African War of 1899–1902. He went to the Staff College in 1908 aged twenty-six – most of the other students were in their mid-thirties – and in November 1914 he became a brigade major on the Western Front, losing the sight of his left eye to a shell splinter in 1915. That wound ended his frontline career, and he spent the rest of the war on staff duties – including a spell as Brigadier-General, General Staff (B-GGS) of XX Corps during Allenby's successful mobile campaign against the Turks in Palestine. In the inter-war years he progressed steadily through a varied range of staff appointments – and several periods on half-pay – and when war broke out in September 1939 he was General Officer Commanding (GOC) Middle East, being advanced to Commander-in-Chief, Middle East, in February 1940.

Wavell was a soldier of considerable intellect, but he had one personal flaw. He was gruff, even inarticulate, at meetings and conferences, and this became a problem later when he clashed with the War Minister – and Prime Minister – Winston Churchill, a man who wanted clear and instant answers to complicated questions. However, Wavell's main concern in June 1940 was not with Churchill's demands or with his own wide responsibilities and slender resources, but with the Italian Tenth Army – now rumbling forward in Cyrenaica.

The only British forces available to contain this threat were those under the GOC, British Troops in Egypt, Lieutenant-General Sir Henry Maitland Wilson, a rotund officer known to his intimates as 'Jumbo'. Although their resources were small, Wavell and Maitland Wilson had already elected for a 'forward' policy to confront the Italian threat, and had deployed a force in the Western Desert to defy the Italians and defend the Nile.

The Western Desert Force could muster around 35,000 men, with little in the way of tanks or artillery but support from some RAF bombers of various types and from those obsolete Gladiator biplanes, the forerunners of the Desert Air Force. However, the operations of this air force were hampered by a shortage of airfields: in September 1939 there were just five airfields in Egypt, none of which could accommodate more than one RAF squadron and all of which were in the Delta.[7] Until forward airfields could be built, the troops out in the Western Desert would be very short of air cover. The main support must come from their only armoured unit – the 7th Armoured Division, 'The Desert Rats'.

The British had deployed small armoured forces in the Western Desert of Egypt and Cyrenaica for years. British armoured cars had operated in the Western Desert towards the end of the First World War, and were later used to fend off attacks on Egypt by Senussi tribesmen from Cyrenaica. Cyrenaica, Tripolitania and, in 1936, Abyssinia became part of Mussolini's expanding African Empire, and after the 1938 Munich Crisis the British decided to increase their forces in Egypt, hoping to compensate for a chronic lack of numbers with mobile armoured forces. A 'Mobile Force' was established at Mersa Matruh in early 1939 – the first element of what later became Eighth Army.

The core of this Mobile Force was the Cairo Cavalry Brigade. This consisted of three regiments converted from horsed cavalry – the 7th, 8th and 11th Hussars (this last the famous 'Cherry-Pickers') – and the 1st Royal Tank Regiment (1st RTR). This brigade was supported by the 3rd Regiment the Royal Horse Artillery (3rd RHA), a company of the Royal Army Service Corps (RASC) and a field-ambulance unit. This 'Mobile Force' was the nucleus of what would become the 7th Armoured Division.

The Mobile Force had good men but poor equipment. The 11th Hussars were mounted in Morris and Rolls-Royce armoured cars, the latter of First World War vintage. The 1st RTR had light Mark VI tanks – already obsolescent, and armed only with Vickers .303 medium machine-guns (MMGs). The 7th Hussars were 'mounted' in 15-cwt trucks, also armed with Vickers machine-guns, but these trucks were two-wheel drive and not suitable for desert operations. The 3rd RHA, the only unit with a solid punch, had 3.7-inch howitzers but was short of ammunition and four-wheel-drive transport. This Mobile Force also needed an infantry element, which was eventually provided by the 1st Battalion the King's Royal Rifle Corps (1st KRRC), commanded by Lieutenant-Colonel W. H. E. ('Strafer') Gott, an officer who was to make a great name for himself in the desert war.

The Mobile Force duly set about patrolling the Libyan frontier wire and training in desert warfare, but its enthusiasm was not matched by the powers-that-be in Cairo. Still wedded to the horse, this desk-bound brigade at GHQ – later known as 'The Gabardine Swine' – referred to the Mobile Force as the 'Immobile Farce' and did very little – a euphemism for damn all – to improve or support it. Fortunately, soon after the Mobile Force arrived in Mersa Matruh, a very energetic officer, Major-General Percy Hobart, DSO, MC, arrived from England to take command, and the Force – now called the Mobile Division – started an intensive training programme in the Western Desert.

Percy Hobart was one of the pioneers of armoured warfare in the inter-war years, a man to rank in this field with Major-General Sir Ernest Swinton and General Heinz Guderian, as an officer ahead of his time. During the 1930s Hobart had realized that armoured warfare was the coming thing and that the British Army must master its complexities and give up its long-standing love affair with the horse. Unfortunately, officers with vision do not get far in the British Army. Hobart – 'Hobo' to his fans – was not the most tactful of men, and the combination of being both right and successful was bound to make him enemies – which he soon had in quantity.

'Hobart was single-minded, intolerant and a great trial to his superiors,' said Field Marshal Lord Carver, 'but on the other hand his subordinates adored him and he was probably unequalled as a trainer of armoured forces.'[8] Hobart's own philosophy was encapsulated in the advice he gave Michael Carver when the latter was a young lieutenant. 'The secret of success in the Army', Hobart averred, 'is to be sufficiently insubordinate – and the key word is "sufficiently".' Whether Hobart was capable of taking his own advice remains debatable. He was brilliant but extremely tactless and his explosive outbursts when frustrated by bigots and blind diehards were famous in the pre-war Army.

Hobart's mastery of tank warfare had been demonstrated in the UK when he commanded the Experimental Tank Brigade in the 1934 manoeuvres. Taking his brigade about the countryside at speed, he quickly ran rings round the opposition, showing up the tactical shortcomings of the opposing commanders and giving great offence to his peers. Hobart's methods were studied closely by the German general and tank-warfare strategist Heinz Guderian and influenced the embryo tank – panzer – forces in the newly established Wehrmacht, but they met with no particular praise from the cavalry generals at the War Office, where the horse was still regarded as the king of the battlefield. Neville Gillman, of the armoured-car-equipped County of London Yeomanry, recalled one regular officer complaining, 'Bloody, smelly tanks . . . Give me horses any time' – and this in 1939.[9]

Hobart, in short, was *not popular*, and his views on the organization and employment of armoured forces, frequently and sharply expressed, met with increasing opposition from the War Office. So, when it was decided to expand the Mobile Force into a division in 1938, the War Office moguls saw this as a golden opportunity to get rid of him. Promoted major-general, Hobart duly arrived in Egypt, where his reception was chilly. He was greeted by the then GOC, Lieutenant-General Sir Robert Gordon-Finlayson, with the words 'I don't know what you've come here for, and I don't want you anyway.' After that encouraging start, communications between the GOC Egypt and his principal subordinate took the form of waspish memoranda, while day-to-day routine requests for the necessary men, kit, ammunition and fuel to train and equip the Division for war were met with what the military historian Basil Liddell Hart later described as 'No help and no lack of hindrance'.

Hobart reorganized his Division into three brigades. The Cairo Cavalry Brigade became a Light Armoured Brigade, consisting of the 7th Hussars, 8th Hussars and 11th Hussars in armoured cars, and a Heavy Armoured Brigade, consisting of the 1st RTR in light tanks and the newly arrived 6th RTR in light tanks and A9 cruiser tanks. It will be noted that this 'Heavy Brigade' had light Mark VI tanks mounting a 2-pounder gun and lacked its third regiment – the Mobile Division was still an embryo force. The final brigade in the Mobile Division was the Pivot Group – later called the Support Group – consisting of the 3rd RHA, 'F' Battery of the 4th RHA, and 'Strafer' Gott's 1st KRRC.

The purpose of the Pivot Group was to supply the tanks with artillery and infantry support, but the KRRC – supposedly a motorized battalion – had no transport and no anti-tank guns. The Division was also without a headquarters staff to handle the supply and intelligence functions, but fortunately Hobart had also been given command of the Abbassia Military District in Cairo and was able to co-opt local RASC troops for exercise purposes. Thus organized, in May 1939 the Mobile Division was led by Hobart into the Western Desert to put his ideas into practice.

The Western Desert was a hard place to live and fight in, but many of the troops had served only in horsed regiments and were in sore need of practical training. Tank, infantry and artillery tactics, vehicle maintenance, and desert lore all had to be learned together – in the desert. Fortunately, some of Hobart's units were already used to the wilderness. The 1st Royal Tank Regiment had served in Egypt in 1936, and its then CO, Lieutenant-Colonel J. A. C. 'Blood' Caunter, was still its CO in 1939. Though 1st RTR had built up considerable desert experience, the most desert-wise unit in either the British or the Italian Army was undoubtedly the 11th Hussars, which had converted to armoured cars as long ago as 1928. The 11th Hussars was a distinguished and fashionable cavalry regiment, which had charged with the Light Brigade at Balaclava during the Crimean War. Equipped with armoured cars, the officers and men of this unit eagerly embraced the desert reconnaissance role – and filled it to perfection.

Hobart's aim was to make his division a soundly knit force that felt comfortable in this uncomfortable terrain, able to fight while coping with the heat, the flies, a shortage of water, and chronic maintenance difficulties with its equipment. Time was spent learning desert navigation by the use of the sun-compass, but more time went on routine vehicle maintenance. It was soon discovered that dust and sand played havoc with mechanical and electrical equipment; all vehicles, including tanks, had to be fitted with sand-filters and improved water pumps before they were able to operate in desert conditions – tanks and vehicles could not be operated as soon as they arrived at the Alexandria docks.[10]

The fact that tanks – or certainly not British tanks – could not be driven off the ship and straight into action was a useful lesson learned in these exercises in 1939, but one that the base supply people did not remember even later in the war. Before they could be used, tanks and transport vehicles had to be serviced and checked on arrival, and any newly arrived crews had to be trained in desert techniques. All this took time, but given the right leadership good troops can learn quickly, and under Major-General Hobart the Mobile Division 'got its knees brown' and acquired the skills it needed.

War with Germany began on 3 September 1939. On that day the Mobile Division moved to the Egyptian–Libyan frontier and took up positions along the wire, ready to repel any Italian attack. None came; Italy was not willing to enter this war until the Duce saw which side was winning. In fact the first blow struck against the Mobile Division came from the War Office, when in November 1939 Hobart was relieved of his command.

Hobart's dismissal was not unexpected, and the two officers responsible for removing him – General Wavell and Lieutenant-General Maitland Wilson – were not fools. Maitland Wilson wrote that Hobart was 'self-opinionated and lacking in stability, I do not consider that Major-General Hobart can be relied on to discard his own ideas and carry out instructions from his superiors in a spirit of loyalty or co-operation'. Wavell endorsed this opionion, and Hobart had to go. By the summer of 1940 this difficult but dedicated soldier, a man who understood the basics of mobile armoured warfare and had talents that were sorely needed, was serving his country in the only way then open to him – in the United Kingdom, on the retired list, and as a corporal in the Home Guard.

In 1941 Hobart was rescued from this oblivion by Winston Churchill, and he went on to raise and train two other armoured divisions during the Second World War: the 11th Armoured Division, which did outstanding service in north-west Europe in 1944–5, and the 79th Armoured Division ('The Funnies'), a force of specialized armour which played a great part in the D-Day invasion and the subsequent advance into Germany. General Sir Percy Hobart eventually became Colonel-Commandant of the Royal Tank Regiment.

Hobart's successor in Egypt, Major-General Michael O'Moore Creagh, MC, took command of the Mobile Division in December 1939. Desert exercises continued, and more and somewhat better equipment arrived during the winter of 1939–40, during which time the three original brigades changed their names. The Light Armoured became 7th Armoured Brigade, the Heavy Armoured became 4th Armoured Brigade, while the Pivot Group became the Support Group under the command of Brigadier 'Strafer' Gott. Each tank regiment now had fifty-two tanks, and the Support Group expanded with the arrival of another fully motorized infantry battalion, the 2nd Battalion the Rifle Brigade, riding in trucks and tracked Bren-gun carriers.

Finally, on 16 February 1940, the Mobile Division became the 7th Armoured Division. To mark the event the Division received a new divisional emblem, depicting a leaping desert rodent, the jerboa or desert rat. The original Mobile Division emblem was a plain white circle on a red background, but Mrs Creagh, having inspected a jerboa closely in Cairo Zoo, produced a design of a desert rat that met with general approval from the divisional officers and men, and her outline design was developed into the famous jerboa emblem by Trooper Ken Hill of the 50th RTR. (Trooper Hill was killed later in the desert war, while clearing booby traps from a German tank near Tobruk.)

The men of the 7th Armoured Division adopted the nickname of 'The Desert Rats' with alacrity. It is worth pointing out here that the term 'Desert Rat', though often used to describe any soldier of the Desert Army or the men who fought in Tobruk – the Australians have a 'Rats of Tobruk' Association – should strictly be applied only to the men of the British 7th Armoured Division, whose shoulders or vehicles bore the jerboa emblem.

On 23 April 1940 the 7th Armoured Division moved up to Mersa Matruh, from where the 11th Hussars, still mounted in their elderly armoured cars, went out to reconnoitre the wastes of the Western Desert. The Division formed the major part of the Western Desert Force, which then consisted of just the 7th Armoured Division and the 4th Indian Division, but which would shortly be joined by the first Australian and New Zealand units – the 6th Australian Division and the 2nd New Zealand Division – the first elements of which had arrived in Egypt by February 1940. The Australians were first sent to Palestine, the New Zealanders to Maadi near Cairo; both contingents started training hard, but were in need of modern equipment, automatic weapons and motor transport. The same was true of the 4th Indian Division, which had arrived by brigades during the winter of 1939–40.

Paul Edwards, an artilleryman with the 2/8th Field Regiment, was one of the first Australians to land in Egypt:

> We drew alongside the wharf at Kantara on 18 December 1940 and went to a camp at Kilo 89, near Gaza, before transferring to another camp closer to Tel Aviv. Before we moved we learned a great deal about the skills of the local Arabs. They would steal anything, and could move almost unseen at the dead of night. Their favourite targets were weapons, and we lost one rifle before we learned to take proper precautions. We only had enough rifles to mount a camp guard, and when not in use bolts were removed and the rifles were locked to a central tent pole with a chain through the trigger guard. We soon knew the meanings of the Arabic words *'kliftee bandook'* – 'rifle-thieving bastard'![11]

Another early arrival was Ernie George from New Zealand:

> The first echelon of New Zealand volunteers in late 1939 had been enrolled, dressed in khaki uniforms complete with the well-known 'lemon-squeezer' hats, and been given First World War surplus Lee-Enfield .303 single-shot rifles. Our training at Hopu Hopu military camp went pretty much along the lines of First World War infantry: how to drive bayonets into bags of straw, how to march in threes, and – most important of all – how to salute. My unit, the New Zealand Railway Battalion, left in the third echelon with the 28th Maori Battalion and the 24th Auckland Infantry Battalion, and we got to Egypt in September 1940.

Wavell was in desperate need of troops, and saw that his sprawling Middle East Command must eventually expand to a force of fifteen divisions – say 300,000 men. But where these men and their equipment would come from was currently hard to say. The British people may be warlike, but Great Britain is not an aggressive nation and Britain was woefully unprepared for war when it broke out in 1939. Whatever kit was available or could be quickly produced was both obsolescent and in very short supply, and went to the British Expeditionary Force divisions in France rather than to the then quiet front in Egypt. The British Empire forces in the Western Desert and Egypt were therefore short of all manner of equipment – especially modern tanks and heavy guns – but they were lucky in their commander: a jaunty and indomitable officer, Lieutenant-General Richard O'Connor.

Born in 1889, Richard O'Connor was another fighting soldier. Like Wavell, he had been commissioned into a Scottish regiment – though a Lowland one, the Cameronians (Scottish Rifles). During the First World War O'Connor had won the MC and the DSO (twice) and had been mentioned no less than nine times in dispatches. He could also wear the Italian Silver Medal for Valour, won in action on the river Piave in 1918. At the end of the Great War O'Connor was a lieutenant-colonel commanding an infantry battalion, and it is some indication of how slow promotion was between the wars that, having reverted to his substantive rank of captain in 1918, it was not until 1936 that he again commanded an infantry battalion, the 1st Cameronians.

From then on, however, his promotion was rapid. Promoted brigadier in 1937, by 1939 O'Connor was a major-general, commanding the 6th Infantry Division in Palestine. There was civil unrest between the Jews and the Palestinians at this time, and O'Connor and his colleague commanding the 8th Division – Major-General Bernard Montgomery – saw plenty of active service while 'aiding the civil power'. Montgomery was invalided back to England in 1939, and on regaining fitness he took over the 3rd Infantry Division in October that year and took it to France for the 1940 campaign that ended at Dunkirk. O'Connor stayed in the Middle East and saw no more action until June 1940.

Summoned to Cairo by Maitland Wilson on 12 June, he was ordered up to Mersa Matruh to take command of what on 17 June 1940, officially became the Western Desert Force. Once there, facing the much reinforced Italian Tenth Army across the frontier wire, O'Connor was in a desperate situation. However, he seemed quite unperturbed, and his first task, having inspected his troops, was to take a close look at the ground.

Three weeks after O'Connor arrived at Matruh, an officer of the 11th Hussars, patrolling well behind the Italian lines west of the wire, was amazed to find the commanding general coming towards him in a staff car – from even further west. When the Italians finally moved, O'Connor would be ready to oppose them; the problem was, what with?

The 7th Armoured Division, with its obsolescent tanks and armoured cars, was virtually O'Connor's entire force. The only other troops available were an infantry brigade currently garrisoned at Mersa Matruh. Other forces – infantry from India, Australia and New Zealand – were training in the Delta or in Palestine, but desperately short of equipment. For air support O'Connor's force had just one RAF unit in the Western Desert, No. 208 Squadron, flying light bombers, Lysander reconnaissance aircraft and some Gladiator fighters: there were no airfields for any more. For the moment the defence of Egypt in the Western Desert rested on O'Connor's small force of deserttrained troops in 7th Armoured Division. Against this single division the Italians could deploy Marshal Balbo's Italian Tenth Army, now consisting of six divisions and containing more than 300,000 men.

This was the situation at one minute past midnight on 11 June 1940, when Italy entered the Second World War. Later that night patrols of the 11th Hussars, which had been probing the Italian positions for months, crossed the Libyan frontier wire and went in search of the enemy.

XIII Corps.

2

Sidi Barrani and Beda Fomm
June 1940–February 1941

*Approaching Buq-Buq we came upon a sight that seemed too unreal, too
wildly improbable to be believed. An entire Italian division was marching
into captivity . . . first in hundreds, then in thousands, the stupendous
crocodile of marching figures stretched way to either horizon.*

Alan Moorehead, *African Trilogy*, p. 61

Wavell and O'Connor could have been dismayed by the numerous difficulties confronting them when Italy declared war in June
1940, but fortunately these generals were not subject to dismay.
Wavell had made his dispositions and he ordered O'Connor to
attack the Italian Army before it could advance into Egypt – a
task that O'Connor and the Western Desert Force took on with
considerable relish.

Nor were the desert soldiers alone in this aggressive stance:
the RAF and the Royal Navy also hastened into battle. One hour
after the Italian declaration, Admiral Cunningham took the
Mediterranean Fleet to sea in search of the enemy. The battleships *Warspite* and *Malaya*, the aircraft carrier *Eagle*, seven
cruisers and nine destroyers trailed the White Ensign along the
Libyan coast and to within 120 miles of the heel of Italy, daring
the Italian fleet to come out and fight. The only reaction came

from Italy's submarines, one of which torpedoed and sank the cruiser HMS *Calypso*.

A response to this loss was provided by the bombers of No. 202 Group, RAF, which attacked the Italian cruiser *San Georgio* in Tobruk harbour and set her on fire. Further air attacks followed. Soon after daylight on 11 June, Blenheims of Nos. 45, 55 and 113 Squadrons attacked the El Adem airfield outside Tobruk, destroying enemy aircraft on the ground. The air and naval operations along the North African shore cannot be detailed here but must not be forgotten for they provide a background to O'Connor's operations: the Western Desert Force fought hard in 1940, but it did not fight alone.

The desert war began with patrol actions. During the night of 11/12 June, the 11th Hussars shot up Italian posts at Sidi Omar and took 70 prisoners. On 14 June the Italian frontier forts at Capuzzo and Maddalena were captured by the 7th Hussars and the 11th Hussars. On 17 June an ambush on the coast road – again by the 11th Hussars – killed 21 Italians and took a number of prisoners, including the engineer-in-chief of the Tenth Army, General Lastucci. The Tenth Army was now concentrating in Cyrenaica, ready to cross the wire into Egypt, while the Italian Fifth Army was currently facing the French forces in Tunisia.

On 17 June an 11th Hussar reconnaissance squadron detected a large number of Italian tanks and infantry near Nezuet Ghirba and reported this fact back to Division. The Italians were promptly attacked by a cruiser-tank squadron of the 7th Hussars and 'J' Battery, RHA. In this action the British killed or captured more than 100 Italians, together with all their artillery, light tanks and trucks; there were no British casualties. The object of all these attacks, by the Army or by the Royal Air Force, was the same: to convince the enemy that the British forces in Egypt were both more numerous and better equipped than they actually were. This aim was achieved. In operations from 11 June to September the Italians suffered 3,500 casualties to the British 150. The main problem affecting the Western Desert Force at this time was the constant deterioration of its equipment; by the end of June some 20 per cent of 7th Armoured Division's tanks had been returned to the workshops for repair.

The 11th Hussars took part in all these early harassing operations west of the frontier wire. To this day the veterans of the 7th

Armoured Division freely admit that the 11th Hussars was a most remarkable unit, but the greatest compliment to the energy and expertise of this distinguished regiment was to come later in the war and from their most professional and distinguished opponent, Field Marshal Erwin Rommel of the German Afrika Korps. Chastising a subordinate for some error, Rommel rounded off his rebuke by stating, 'The 11th Hussars would never have made an error like that.'

On 28 June Marshal Balbo, the Italian commander-in-chief in Libya, was killed when his aircraft was shot down by Italian anti-aircraft batteries over Tobruk. Balbo was well known in the pre-war aviation world and Air Chief Marshal Sir Arthur Longmore had a note of regret dropped on to El Adem airfield. Balbo was replaced by Marshal Rodolfo Graziani, a veteran of the 1936 Abyssinian campaign.

There was still time for chivalrous gestures, but the war in North Africa took a serious turn on 17 June 1940 when, following the collapse of Belgium, the French government asked the Germans for an armistice and the British forces in France withdrew to Dunkirk. The armistice with Germany was granted on 22 June, and was followed on 24 June by an armistice with Italy. This French surrender to the Axis powers altered the strategic situation in the Middle East by removing any threat of a French attack on the Italians from Tunisia.

The French surrender also added to Wavell's burdens with the establishment of a hostile French force in Syria after the French commander there, General Mittelhauser, followed the commander in Algeria and Tunisia, General Noguès, in supporting Marshal Pétain's collaborationist Vichy government. These actions would cause chronic problems for General Wavell in the coming months, but the most immediate concern was the disposal of the French Mediterranean fleet.

The powerful units of this fleet could not be allowed to fall into German hands, and German assurances that they would be decommissioned after surrender failed to convince anyone. On 24 June the commander of the French naval squadron in Alexandria, Admiral Godfroy, was ordered by the French Minister of Marine to leave Egypt at once and sail for Toulon. Admiral Cunningham then had to make it clear to Godfroy that the French squadron would not be allowed to leave Alexandria.

Godfroy reluctantly complied, but on 3 July units of the British Mediterranean Fleet under Vice-Admiral Sir James Somerville were obliged to open fire on French warships anchored at Mers el Kebir, near Oran in Algeria, to prevent them from falling into German hands. Several French ships were sunk, others were damaged, and 1,297 French sailors were killed.

Winston Churchill was right to describe this action as 'one of the most disagreeable and difficult tasks that a British admiral has ever been faced with'. Though very necessary, deeply regretted and undertaken only after various alternatives had been rejected by the French commanders, it was bitterly resented by the French, drove many Vichy forces firmly into the German camp, and made French-held Syria another hostile front, close to the Suez Canal and Palestine.

On the other hand, the sinking of French warships demonstrated to the world, not least to the United States, that a new and necessary element had entered this war – a degree of ruthlessness in the direction and conduct of affairs without which wars cannot be won. After the years of appeasement, such action was surprising and long overdue; the only regret is that this ruthlessness had to be deployed against a former ally rather than a constant foe.

The elimination of the French fleet may have lessened the strategic problems, but it did not help the Western Desert Force. This was faced with a rapid increase in enemy strength as more Italian units moved east from Tunisia into Cyrenaica. Balbo's successor, Graziani, was willing to engage the British, but a rapid survey of the troops at his disposal convinced him that their equipment was inadequate and their training lamentable. Graziani was also misled by O'Connor's tactics. The harassing operations mounted by 7th Armoured, plus the bombing of Italian convoys and airfields by the RAF, continued throughout June; they did not prevent the steady build-up of the Tenth Army or the recapture of Fort Capuzzo, but they slowed the Italians down, gave Graziani the impression that he was facing superior numbers, and made him cautious.

Graziani requested an increase in motor transport and aircraft, but Mussolini – anxious for a success to lay before Hitler – insisted that the Italian Army in Libya should advance upon the British with the considerable forces already at its disposal. Had Graziani done so, Wavell's position might have been extremely difficult, but fortunately the Italians made no move to invade Egypt for another three months, and in that time the British position in the Western Desert improved somewhat. More equipment arrived – tanks, guns and mines – and more units came forward to join the Western Desert Force, easing the manpower situation, if not the shortages in equipment. These shortages, and the limitations of what was available, were unavoidable. After Dunkirk, the war factories in Britain were busy re-equipping the Home Army against the possibility of invasion; there was not much kit to spare for the Middle East.

There was time for Wavell to fly to London, brief the War Cabinet about the situation in the Middle East, and put in claims for more equipment, for the situation was critical. The 7th Armoured Division had only 65 cruiser tanks instead of 220, and not all of those available were operational.[1] There were only 12 Bofors anti-aircraft (AA) guns in Egypt, all deployed around the naval base at Alexandria. The 4th Indian Division had very little artillery, and the Australians and New Zealanders needed Bren guns and anti-tank guns.

Wavell's stark account appears to have produced results. A number of units – three armoured regiments – and a quantity of kit including 20 Bofors and 500 Bren light machine-guns were readied for dispatch to Egypt. Actually getting them there, down the Mediterranean via Malta in the teeth of air and submarine attack, would be quite another matter, and in the end this resupply convoy took the slow route via the Cape. The Air Force was also reinforced with Hurricane fighters and Wellington twin-engined bombers – a most useful addition, though not enough to tilt the balance in the air.

A slightly less welcome arrival was a long 'General Directive' from Churchill to Wavell. This missive, containing the Prime Minister's views on the conduct of the war in the desert and requesting Wavell's comments, arrived in Cairo on 22 August. It went into great detail on the tactics to be employed when the Italians moved on Egypt, even describing how wells might be polluted, verges mined and roads destroyed. The Official History of the war in the Mediterranean and Middle East comments that this indicates 'the Prime Minister's concern with the Middle East theatre.'[2] It also indicates a close interest in details that Wavell could surely have worked out for himself.

Wavell replied in similar detail, pointing out that the current problem was one of *matériel* rather than manpower, that the enemy would soon attack with large armoured forces and that the forces which must repel him were currently short of 250 field guns, 34 medium guns, 230 anti-tank guns, 1,100 anti-tank rifles and 500 Bren-gun carriers – and more armoured troops were essential.

The Official History records tactfully that this 'general exchange of views helped, no doubt, to focus attention on essentials', but adds that 'this was the first of a long and remarkable series of telegrams from the Prime Minister to one or other of the Commanders-in-Chief in the Middle East'. It also adds that 'some were exploratory, some advisory, some expressed generous praise, some were frankly admonitory. Some must have been more welcome than others. Almost all required answers.'[3] The Prime Minister was clearly determined to 'play general', adding yet another burden to Wavell's broad but overloaded shoulders as the Italian offensive developed.

Operating well behind the enemy lines, the 11th Hussars sent back a constant stream of reports on the Italian dispositions, and General O'Connor was aware of what was happening across the wire before the Tenth Army began to advance towards the Delta in mid-September 1940. Following three days of attacks by the bombers of Italy's Colonial Air Force, Graziani advanced into Egypt at dawn on 13 September. Knowing what was about to happen did not enable O'Connor or his scanty forces to prevent it, but this first Italian advance did not last long.

The Italians advanced as far as the town of Sidi Barrani in the face of fierce opposition from RAF bombers and the 7th Armoured Division, which fell back slowly along the coast, destroying the road as it did so. Apart from a thrust along the coastal escarpment, which was halted by a small detachment consisting of 'C' Squadron of the 11th Hussars, the Royal Horse Artillery and a battalion of the Coldstream Guards, the main Italian advance came directly along the coastal road. Arriving at Sidi Barrani on 16 September, Graziani halted and the Tenth Army was still there – its communications and supply routes harassed by the RAF and by bombardments from the Royal Navy's Inshore Squadron – when the British struck back in January 1941.

These skirmishes in the first six months of the desert war

proved useful to the British, who discovered that their equipment – inadequate and obsolescent though most of it was, was
still better than that of the Italians. They also discovered that,
while the Italian troops were gallant enough – the Italian artillery
always stood to its guns – they had no taste at all for the bayonet,
disliked fighting at night, were easily confused, and tended to
stick to the coast road and to fixed positions. This left plenty of
scope for skirmishing, raiding and outflanking movements by
the British troops, utilizing the open desert flank.

Elsewhere in the Middle East the British position was deteriorating. Malta was being heavily bombed and although units of
the Mediterranean Fleet were constantly at sea and harassing the
Italian supply convoys, Cunningham was steadily losing ships to
Italian submarines and air attacks. The situation in Greece and
the Balkans was also becoming critical. On 12 October 1940,
Mussolini decided to invade Greece, and a series of incidents
were created to justify this aggression. These culminated on 28
October, when the Italians presented an ultimatum to the Greek
government, demanding access to certain strategic centres in
Greece for the Italian Army.

The reply from General Yanni Metaxas, the Greek Prime
Minister, was brief: 'Οχι' – 'No.' A few hours later Greece and
Italy were at war, Italian troops were over the frontier, and the
British were offering to aid the Greek government with arms and
men. The Greeks declined this initial offer of ground forces, and
at first British aid consisted of some naval units and the dispatch
of RAF bombers and anti-aircraft guns to Athens and Crete. But
it was clear that British ground forces would probably be
required if the Italian advance continued, and Wavell's resources
in men and *matériel* would then become dangerously stretched.

To balance this looming threat in the Balkans, the Royal Navy
scored a victory at sea. On 11 November Fleet Air Arm Swordfish
torpedo bombers from the Mediterranean Fleet attacked the
Italian fleet at Taranto, sinking or damaging several ships. This
attack put half the Italian fleet out of action for months; the
remaining vessels fled west, lifting the threat of naval interference with the British convoys between Athens and Alexandria.
Meanwhile it was time to attack in the Western Desert.

By December 1940 the Western Desert Force had received substantial reinforcements. These included three armoured units

from the UK: the 2nd RTR and the 7th RTR, both equipped with heavily armoured but painfully slow Matilda 'infantry' tanks, and the 3rd Hussars, equipped with cruiser tanks. A number of Rhodesian troops and a squadron of RAF armoured cars had also joined the 11th Hussars. These reinforcements enabled O'Connor to have a cruiser-tank squadron in every tank regiment, equipped with 2-pounder guns capable of knocking out the main Italian battle tank, the M13.

These first months gave the British unit commanders and their troops valuable experience in desert warfare, not least in the all-important skills of maintaining their weapons, tanks and vehicles in a desert environment. With little reference to any-one above brigade or divisional level, they developed a form of free-range soldiering that came to be called 'column warfare', in which small mixed groups of tanks, armoured cars, infantry and artillery – 'Jock columns' – roved the desert at will to harry the enemy, supported by their own 'B' echelons to bring up sup-plies of food, fuel and ammunition.

This activity seemed sensible at the time, and succeeded in its intended purpose of deceiving the enemy about British strength. It was also highly enjoyable – the unit diaries are full of accounts of good times spent 'swanning about in the Blue'. But this lack of concentration by the armoured brigades, this willingness to indulge in small, ad-hoc operations, had unfortunate effects later. When the Germans came on the scene they presented O'Connor's forces with an enemy that could not be lightly brushed aside – and one which attacked the British brigades in divisional strength and rapidly overwhelmed them.

The Italian attack on Greece greatly increased the strain on Wavell. For the moment the Greeks were doing well and holding their own, but Wavell decided to attack the Tenth Army before either the Italians attacked him or the situation in Greece became critical and required a major transfer of troops and equipment. O'Connor was therefore instructed to smite the Italian Army in the area of Sidi Barrani and Sofafi and around the salt pans of Buq-Buq, using the heavily armoured Matilda tanks against the Italian forts. Supported by RAF bombers and fighters, the Western Desert Force began this attack on 9 December 1940.

The Italians had gone over to the defensive since September, and the Sidi Barrani position was protected by a string of fortified camps. Three of these – Nibeiwa, Tummar East and Tummar West – lay just south of Sidi Barrani and were manned in strength by Italian infantry, tanks and heavy artillery. O'Connor estimated that the Italians had six divisions around Sidi Barrani with some 120 M14 tanks and 200 guns of various calibres, supported by 250 bombers and 250 fighters. (The actual totals were 140 bombers and 191 fighters.)[4] To match this, he could field the 7th Armoured and 4th Indian Divisions, amounting to 25,000 men with 275 tanks, including the Matildas, and a number of the new and highly effective 25-pounder field guns for his artillery.

O'Connor's plan for his attack – known as Operation COMPASS or the Battle of Sidi Barrani – called for 7th Armoured to sweep west and cut off the Tummars and Sidi Barrani from the main Italian army around Tobruk. While it was doing that, 4th Indian Division with 7th RTR supporting in Matildas would drive north to overrun the Tummar camps and take Sidi Barrani itself. The attack was carefully rehearsed throughout November, and on 9 December O'Connor's advance began – and kept on going.

Operation COMPASS was originally planned as a raid, but it quickly turned into something much more than that. On 9 December the 4th Armoured Brigade of 7th Armoured Division got astride the coast road west of Sidi Barrani while the 4th Indian Division attacked the Tummar camps and moved on Sidi Barrani from the east. The Italian collapse came swiftly. The Indians overran the Nibeiwa position and both the Tummars while 7th Armoured, driving hard to the west and north, cut the coast road down which the garrison of Sidi Barrani was now in full retreat. Among the men attacking this town was Doug Denton of the 3rd Battalion, The Coldstream Guards:

> Sidi Barrani can hardly be described as a town. It was scarcely more than a small village, but Mussolini described how he got the tramcars running after its capture by Graziani; it is doubtful if the inhabitants back in those days knew what a tramcar was. On 18 December we were told that the battalion would make an attack on Sidi Barrani that night, moving out at 2000 hours and being in position by 2300 hours. We were to be part of Selby Force, and make a diversionary frontal assault with naval gunfire support while the main attack went in on the Italian right flank.
>
> It was a cold still night and there was moonlight, and at exactly 2300 hours the first salvo of projectiles from the Fleet passed

overhead, bound for the Italians with the Admiral's compliments. The sound of their passing was frightening, and the enemy, having endured the first salvo, had no intention of waiting for the second one. They beat a hasty retreat, and as far as I remember when our company arrived at their camp it was deserted.

We regrouped, and during the next morning moved towards the main Italian positions. I was a battalion signaller, riding in the rear of the company commander's truck. We drove along the tarmac coastal road towards the summit of a ridge, but were stopped by a military policeman who said to the OC, 'The enemy are just beyond that ridge and if you go over it you'll be shot up.' The OC said he intended to contact another company, and told the driver to press on.

We crossed the ridge and were promptly greeted by a hail of fire, so we withdrew, debussed, formed into our three platoons, and began to advance. We had not gone far before we were pinned down by machine-gun fire. This was early afternoon, and we had to remain there until it got dark. During this time we were shelled frequently, but the Italian shells seemed very ineffective – they dug into the ground, but did not fragment much. After dark we moved to the top of the ridge and dug-in, but we only had a few picks, the ground was rocky, and it took us all night to accomplish this task, digging trenches about 18 inches deep.

At dawn we came under fire from a machine-gun across the valley on our right front, which kept it up until the afternoon, when a Vickers medium machine-gun of the 2nd Cheshires came up and put it out of action. During this time my comrade had to lie on top of me; every time he moved, bullets thudded into the earth we had piled up in front of our trench. But he had a packet of twenty Players and shared them with me.

In the middle of the afternoon we heard a shout from a gunner that the enemy was showing white flags. Should he continue firing? We took a look and it was like washday out there: whites were showing everywhere, and the Italians were climbing on each other's shoulders to show white flags. So we moved on and took them prisoner.[5]

At the frontier wire there was more resistance, but a storm of 25-pounder shells from the field guns of the RHA and the grinding, unstoppable advance of the 7th RTR's Matildas soon cracked the defences at Nibeiwa. Many of the defenders fled – but not all of them. The Italians could fight when they wanted to, and the

Italian commander at Nibeiwa, General Malatti, emerged from his tent to engage the British tanks with a light machine-gun and continued firing at the approaching British tanks until he was killed, his son falling wounded at his side.

The Cameron Highlanders then swept through Nibeiwa camp at the point of the bayonet, killing several hundred Italians and taking over 4,000 prisoners. This Highland attack on the Tummars was reinforced by the drivers of the No. 4 Motor Company of the New Zealand Army Service Corps, who charged in with the British infantry, issuing competitive cries of 'Come on, you Pommie bastards!' – a fine example of the élan that the New Zealanders were to demonstrate so frequently thereafter.

By the evening of 10 December over 5,000 prisoners had been taken. When the 7th Hussars finally blocked the Italian retreat at Buq-Buq, the Italian prisoners became so numerous that, unable to count them, a country-bred 7th Hussar officer came up on the radio to report: 'As far as I can see, we have captured about 20 acres of officers and about 100 acres of men.'

By 11 December some 38,000 Italian prisoners had been taken in the battles around Sidi Barrani; British and Indian losses totalled about 624, killed, wounded and missing. More might have been achieved in following up this triumph had not the two brigades of the 4th Indian Division been recalled to Cairo on the second day of the battle – 10 December – and sent to East Africa, where another Italian army had taken the field from Italian Somaliland, so opening yet another drain for Wavell's scanty forces.

This loss of a crack division left the mopping-up and pursuit phase of the battle around Sidi Barrani to the 7th Armoured Division, which swept on to secure the Rabia and Sofafi camps, which had been abandoned by the Italians and fell – inevitably – to a troop of the 11th Hussars on 10 December. O'Connor decided that in spite of the reduction of his forces the pursuit should continue. The Italian Army was now in full retreat, harried by 7th Armoured's Support Group and the roving armoured cars of the 11th Hussars and the RAF. Shedding men and equipment, the Italians fled back into Cyrenaica, leaving a vast quantity of kit behind, including 237 guns and over 70 M14 tanks.

Having chased the Italians out of Egypt, the British paused on 15 December, six days into this offensive, to count their gains and reorganize, though taking Sollum on 16 December. Having decided that the entire 4th Indian Division must go to East Africa, Wavell replaced it with the 6th Australian Division, brought down hurriedly from its training ground in Palestine. This decision brought to the Desert Army one of its most famous and resolute formations.

The 6th Australian Division had already done a great deal of travelling. Australia declared war on Germany in September 1939. Full mobilization was ordered, followed by some debate in the Australian parliament on whether Australian forces should be sent overseas or be kept for the defence of Australia should Japan enter the war. There was also the problem of equipment: Britain had barely enough arms for her own forces, and Australia could produce only rifles, Vickers medium machine-guns and anti-aircraft guns, but these debates did not last long. To both the Australian government and the Australian people, the issue in 1939 was simple. War had been declared on Britain, the 'Old Country' was in danger, and the Australians should be there.[6] On 15 September Robert Menzies, the Prime Minister of Australia, announced that a force of one division plus ancillary units – 20,000 men – would be raised for service either at home or abroad as circumstances dictated.[7] This force became the nucleus of the 6th Australian Division, which, to indicate continuity with the Australian Imperial Force raised to fight in the First World War (1 AIF), numbered its battalions 2/1st, 2/2nd, and so on.

The same course of action was followed in New Zealand, where 6,000 volunteers were called for in the first days of the war. Also in Canada, where on 28 September 1939 the government in Ottawa announced that 'a division of troops was being prepared for service overseas'. Even in India, where the Viceroy aroused fury in the Congress Party by announcing war without consulting with it first, more than 1 million Indian volunteers flocked to the colours. So it went all over the British Empire: the Dominions and colonies were rallying to the defence of the 'Mother Country', and many of the troops raised would eventually serve in Eighth Army.

On 13 October 1939 command of the 6th Australian Division went to Major-General Thomas Blamey, a regular army officer aged fifty-five. Blamey had been chosen in place of the other obvious – and somewhat younger – candidate, Major-General Gordon Bennett, largely, says the Australian Official History, because some senior officers felt that Bennett lacked 'the tactfulness needed in the commander of a Dominion force which had to co-operate closely with British and Allied Armies' – a prescient judgement, which those British and Allied commanders who met Bennett in Singapore two years later would have heartily endorsed.

Blamey had served at Gallipoli in the First World War, and by 1918 he was a brigadier-general on the staff of Lieutenant-General Sir John Monash, the Australian commander in France. After the war Blamey had been the Australian representative at the War Office in London, and then commissioner of police for Victoria. Since then he had been on the unattached list, awaiting further employment. The only gap in his armour was a lack of command experience in the field. In France between 1916 and 1918 he had commanded a battalion for three weeks and a brigade for six; otherwise his service had been on the staff.[8] But this was no bar to his current appointment and Blamey would eventually become commander of the entire Australian contingent in North Africa, with the command of the 6th Australian Division passing to Major-General I. G. Mackay.

The 6th Australian Division would consist of three brigades, each of four battalions, its establishment totalling 16,528 officers and men, which meant that it would be substantially larger, by more than 3,000 men, than a British infantry division, which only had three battalions to the brigade. The Division would also have the addition of an armoured cavalry regiment equipped with 44 Bren-gun carriers and 28 light tanks. When fully equipped and trained, the 6th Australian Division – the first division of the 2nd Australian Imperial Force (AIF) – would be a formidable addition to the strength of the British Army in the Western Desert.

Perhaps with an eye on the future, the Australian Official History – published in 1952 – speculates on why so many Australians were then ready to fight in a war zone half a world away. Nine out of ten of the AIF recruits had been born in Australia, of Australian parents, and were intensely proud of their country and its independence. The Official History, while acknowledging this, and adding that the Englishman (the 'Pom') was 'as puzzling to the Colonial as the Colonial was irritating to the Englishman',[9] suggests that the two nevertheless shared a common history and culture and democratic values.

The letters received from Australian veterans for this book

reveal a number of other reasons. In some cases they went because their friends were going and they did not want to be left behind. In many cases their fathers had served with the Anzacs in the First World War, and they felt a need to follow in their footsteps. Others saw the war as an adventure, as an opportunity to get away from a boring job or a chance to travel and see the world. All these reasons existed, but there was another one, only rarely or briefly expressed but underpinning all the rest: like their comrades from Britain and the other countries of the Empire, most of these young Australian soldiers volunteered to fight Fascism because they thought it was the right thing for decent men to do.

On 9 January 1940, the 16th Brigade, the first unit of the 6th Division, marched through the streets of Sydney and on to their troopships, the liners *Otranto*, *Orcades*, *Orford* and *Strathnaver*, and sailed for Palestine. The convoy arrived at Ismailia in the Canal Zone on 12 February, and the troops were sent to Julius, 35 miles south of Tel Aviv, where they were joined by the 4th New Zealand Infantry Brigade and welcomed by the Scots of the 2nd Battalion The Black Watch and the 1st Battalion The Hampshire Regiment, both of the Palestine garrison.

The 6th Division then started intensive training in the various schools run by the British Army – Bren-gun carrier training, cipher courses, desert acclimatization and training with their new weapons, the 2-inch mortar, the Bren light machine-gun and the 2-pounder anti-tank gun. W. H. Jenkins of the 2/1st Battalion recalls this time:

> I joined up in Sydney on 22 October 1939 and sailed for Egypt in February 1940. In September that year the decision was made to form the 16th Anti-Tank Company with a platoon from each rifle company, and the same was done in the 17th and 19th Brigades. We had nine 2-pounder guns in the company, but not all the other anti-tank companies had that many to begin with. Then we went up the desert for the push up to Bardia.[10]

While other Australian divisions – the 7th, 8th and 9th – were forming in Australia, the 6th Australian Division made itself ready for war, and by the time the Italians joined that war in June 1940 the 2nd Australian Imperial Force had expanded, at least on paper, to four divisions. Only one brigade of the 6th Division was in Palestine at this time, and when the other two brigades, the

17th and the 18th, were on the sea in the spring of 1940 they were stopped at Colombo until the growing Italian threat had been assessed. Then came the German attack in the Low Countries and Dunkirk, after which was decided that part of the Division – Brigadier Leslie J. Morshead's 18th Brigade, with its supporting units – should sail for Britain. The Brigade arrived in the UK on 17 June 1940, and received, says the Official History, 'warm hospitality' from its British hosts.[11] This brigade did not finally arrive in the Middle East until December 1940, when it formed the nucleus of the 9th Australian Division.

General Blamey had therefore to sort out his forces in Palestine. To replace the missing 18th Brigade, the 19th Brigade was incorporated in the 6th Division. In November most of the 7th Division arrived, the remainder arriving in December together with troops for the embryo 9th Division. Blamey could then hope that his Australian Corps – until then just one incomplete division – would soon have its full complement of three: the 6th, 7th and 9th. (The brigades of the 8th Division, formed in Australia, were used to reinforce units in the Middle East, and the 24th Brigade of the 8th Division was duly transferred to Egypt.)

In October the 6th Division – less the 19th Brigade, which arrived only in November – moved west of Alexandria, where it took the 1st Polish (Carpathian) Brigade under command. Here the Diggers had their first taste – literally – of the Western Desert. 'Dust such as we have never known before; you breathe, eat and sleep in dust,' wrote one Australian soldier.[12]

Their training had lasted a full year, and now it was over. When the 4th Indian Division left for East Africa and the fighting in Eritrea, the time had come for the Australians to move up to the front and show what they could do. It soon appeared that they could do a great deal.

During the rest of December, following the attacks at Nibeiwa and the Tummars, both sides held their positions while the 6th Australian Division and the 7th Armoured Division prepared for the next phase of the advance, the assault on the small Libyan port of Bardia, 75 miles east of Tobruk – a town held by Lieutenant-General Annibale Bergonzoli, an officer known to soldiers on either side as '*Barba-Electrica*' or 'Electric Whiskers'. To defend Bardia, Bergonzoli had a garrison of 40,000 men and over 400 guns, all in well-prepared positions – though these positions were subject to British bombing and periodic shelling from the Royal Navy in the shape of the monitor HMS *Terror*. On 17 December *Terror* was joined by the gunboat HMS *Aphis*, which entered Bardia harbour and within the hour, according to the captain of HMS *Terror*, 'was having a good time', great clouds of black smoke coming from burning shore installations and anchored shipping. Bardia was now under siege by sea and land, but the garrison showed no sign of surrender.

With Bardia under siege, the advance elsewhere continued. On 16 December the Italian position at Sidi Omar fell to the 7th Hussars and the 2nd RTR, supported into battle by the guns of the 4th RHA – an action in which Captain Hobart of the 2nd RTR was seen, 'steel helmet on, shooting away over the top of his turret cupola with a pistol'.

That noted, a real problem during December was the ongoing battle of supply, the root of this being a shortage of suitable ports. Those that existed had few docking facilities, and there was only one coastal road down which supplies could move forward. Add a lack of adequate air cover against the Italian bombers – the main Allied fighter in the middle Western Desert at this time was still the Gloster Gladiator biplane – and it will be seen that the need for constant replenishment of food, ammunition and, above all water and petrol, threw a great strain on the rear echelons and in particular on the drivers of the Royal Army Service Corps, the unsung heroes of the desert war.

The RASC drivers drove hundreds of miles, often by night, over open desert to find and replenish the forward units, only to discover on arrival that half their supplies had literally run into the sand. The inadequacies of British equipment were not confined to tanks and guns. Petrol, oil and water were conveyed to the forward troops in 2- or 4-gallon cans, rightly called 'flimsies', which cracked their seams and leaked during these rough desert journeys, often losing half their contents. The desert *birs* were an inadequate source of water – they were often salty, and were sometimes polluted with oil by the enemy to prevent them being used. Water was therefore always short, only half a gallon per man per day for all purposes – which included replenishing vehicle and tank radiators, cooking, washing and shaving, so reducing the amount available for drinking to about a pint. Fresh food was rare, and bully-beef stew pepped up with tomato purée captured from the Italians was the usual fare. Meals were brewed up on a 'tommy-cooker', a tin can cut in half and filled with petrol-soaked sand.

Ernie George of the New Zealand Railway Battalion, charged with operating railways in the desert, recalls their efforts to improve the supply situation:

In September 1940 the 16th Company was paraded to be addressed by Colonel Sage, the battalion commander. After the usual well-rehearsed baloney about being the sons of the Anzacs and upholding the traditions of our forefathers that we had heard so often prior to our departure from New Zealand, he finally concluded the sweet-talking and got down to business.

The time had arrived, he told us, when we were about to commence the job for which we had been well trained and equipped – 'I refer of course to the operation and running of trains in the Western Desert.'

A small advance party had been chosen to proceed to Mersa Matruh, the railhead, checking engines and facilities on the way, and on 20 September 1940 Sergeant Flannery and his carefully selected team slipped away quietly on their train, taking with them their Lee-Enfield .303 rifles and their ration of five rounds of ammunition. 'That's all you get mate,' said the quartermaster-sergeant. My rifle must have seen less use than the others, as it was date stamped '1918'.[13]

Lyndon Evans, a colleage of Ernie George, takes up this story:

New Zealand construction companies, with Indian labour, constructed 92 miles of railway by October 1941 from 10 miles east of Mersa Matruh to about 20 miles south of Sidi Barrani and eventually to Belhammed, south of Tobruk, by December 1942. That's 407 miles from Alamein, and we could then shift 4,200 tons of supplies to the railhead in 24 hours. The railway war was continuous, as the Luftwaffe declared open season on the desert railway and obtained a good bag of hits. I remember that an airfield over the escarpment was the home of several First World War-type biplanes – Gladiators – and the arrival of a lone Hurricane fighter caused great excitement. Two mates and I walked over to the airfield to inspect this fantastic machine, and were approached by an Australian officer who said he did not mind us looking at his pride and joy but 'For God's sake don't steal the bloody thing.'[14]

'Desert supply lines are particularly vulnerable,' writes Douglas Hodge, an officer in the 19th (Wellington) Battalion in the New Zealand Expeditionary Force, 'and ultimately the victor in the desert would be the side which got the most and best supplies in the shortest time.'[15] He quotes Rommel's comment that 'Supplies are the basis of the battle and must be given priority protection.'

Apart from the chronic supply difficulties, not all these troops were in the best of health. It was now winter in the Western Desert; this reduced the number of flies but the desert nights were often freezing. Some troops had not received their warm battledress tunics, blankets were in short supply, and there was a considerable amount of sickness. Irritated by sand, cuts and grazes swiftly became deep, suppurating ulcers known as desert sores, while jaundice was common and for some reason particularly prevalent among the officers. Winter in the Western Desert was hard, even without the bombing and shelling.

On 27 December the Australians moved up to the Bardia defences. For the attack on Bardia the 6th Australian Division was supported by 120 guns of the Royal Artillery (RA), the 7th RTR, with 23 serviceable tanks, and the medium machine-guns of a British infantry unit, the 1st Battalion the Royal Northumberland Fusiliers. Before the attack, the town was also heavily bombed by Wellingtons and Bombays of Nos. 70 and 216 Squadrons. On New Year's Day 1941 the Western Desert Force was renamed XIII Corps, and on 3 January Bardia was attacked by the 6th Australian Division and the 7th Armoured Division. Among the troops was W. H. Jenkins, an Australian anti-tank gunner:

> On the first day of the battle, Arthur Pickett of our battalion destroyed six Eytie tanks that had the 2/3rd Battalion in trouble. Arthur got the DCM, and those of his crew that survived got the MM. Thence to Tobruk where the Eytie tanks disappeared when we came into view so we used HE [high-explosive] shells on enemy gun posts with great effect, our guns being used mainly off the portée – a 30-cwt truck with no sides, hood or rear; it could be dug in or fired off the wheels, come what may. We went on with the 19th Brigade to Derna and Benghazi, and after the clean up there we were left behind when the 6th Division went to Greece and Crete.[16]

This attack at Bardia forged one of the most formidable desert combinations: the tanks, armoured cars and artillery of the British

7th Armoured Division and the infantry of the 6th Australian Division. The attack began at 0530 hours, the tanks moved in at 0700 hours, and by 0830 hours the 16th Australian Infantry Brigade had taken 8,000 prisoners and suffered very few casualties. By now Bardia was under fire from the 15-inch guns of two battleships, HMS *Warspite* and HMS *Barham*, and seven destroyers. At 1130 hours the 17th Infantry Brigade opened its advance, and the 19th Brigade put in its attack early on the following day. Bardia fell on the evening of 5 January and when the Australians counted their prisoners – which, to their disappointment, did not include General 'Electric Whiskers' Bergonzoli – they found they had taken 40,000 Italians, more than 400 guns and some 130 light and medium tanks. Australian losses in this three-day battle came to just 426 men, killed, wounded or missing.

Ernie George encountered the aftermath of this fighting:

I saw this great cloud of dust over a mile long moving slowly towards Mersa, much too slowly for vehicles. Debating on whether to take off in the opposite direction, I waited a little longer until I saw a soldier in an Australian slouch hat followed by an Italian soldier carrying the Aussie's rifle for him. When they came nearer I made the obligatory wisecrack to the Aussie about being a lazy so-and-so, too tired to carry his own rifle. He told me to point the way to the nearest water tap or he would hit me over the head with it.

There must have been *thousands* of these Italian prisoners following that Aussie soldier, and I spent some hours filling their water bottles from what I knew to be the sole water point in that area. The Italians, many of whom spoke English, made it quite clear that they did not want any part of this war and made derogatory comments about Mussolini, their great leader. They were very happy and relieved to be prisoners.[17]

While the Australians were counting their prisoners, the 7th Armoured Division was on the move again, thrusting along the coast road towards Tobruk. When the 19th and 16th Australian Infantry Brigades came up to join it, 7th Armoured had already surrounded the Tobruk defences, which contained around 20,000 men and 200 guns – roughly half the number of men as at Bardia with twice the front to defend. This in itself was not much to reckon with, but the problem for XIII Corps was still one of supply. The troops and tanks were running low on food, fuel and ammunition, and fresh supplies had to come up from Egypt before the attack went in.

When Tobruk had been surrounded and the road west to Derna had been cut by the 7th Armoured Support Group, the Australians came up from El Adem to assault the defences. This attack went in on 21 January. Half the defences had fallen by nightfall, and at dawn on 22 January the garrison surrendered, yielding another 25,000 prisoners and a vast haul of booty – though yet again General Bergonzoli had slipped through the net. British and Australian losses in the taking of Tobruk came to just over 400 men.

What these Australian and British troops were now achieving in the Western Desert was a great feat of arms – and an astonishing victory. A corps of two divisions, with obsolescent equipment and advancing at the very limits of its supply lines, was inflicting regular defeats on a well-equipped force ten times its size. With the capture of Tobruk, Wavell was able to pour equipment and supplies in by sea or up the coast road, intending to complete the rout of the Tenth Army, which was now in full retreat through Derna and Barce, towards Benghazi, a major town with a population in 1940 of some 65,000.

Benghazi lies on the north-eastern shore of the Gulf of Sirte, over 180 miles to the west of Tobruk by the coast road, but only 120 miles by the direct route across the open desert and the hills and rocks of the Jebel Akhdar – the Green Mountain. This region of hills and cultivated, rock-strewn fields runs up to a height of 3,000 feet, fits snugly into the north east coastline of the Gulf of Sirte, and was a formidable barrier to any rapid advance south of the coast road. A further problem was the dilapidated state of 7th Armoured's 50 remaining cruiser tanks, which were long overdue for an overhaul and well over their recommended track mileage.

Since the Anglo-Australian combination of armoured hook and infantry assault had proved so successful at Bardia and Tobruk, O'Connor intended to employ it again, sending a 7th Armoured force across the Jebel to cut the coast road south of Benghazi at Beda Fomm, while the Australians attacked Benghazi. If all went well, the Australians would drive the Italian Army out of Benghazi and into an ambush further south –

provided 7th Armoured could cross the Jebel Akhdar and get to Beda Fomm in time.

This would not be easy. The Jebel Akhdar was largely unmapped and, according to the British Official History, the going varied from good to vile.[18] Even so, this was the course of action Wavell ordered: the pursuit must continue across the Jebel, and 7th Armoured must advance until it could advance no longer, striking south-west across the desert, through Mechili and Msus and Antelat, emerging to block the coast road somewhere between Sidi Saleh and Beda Fomm. Led as usual by the 11th Hussars, on 3 February the 7th Armoured Division struck into the hills.

As expected, the going was terrible – 'the worst yet encountered in the desert', according to the British Official History,[19] with steep wadis and rocks. Before long the advance of the tank regiments had slowed to the point where progress was being measured in hundreds of yards per hour. Brigadier Caunter of the 4th Armoured Brigade therefore decided to send the faster vehicles and the infantry of the Rifle Brigade forward in their Bren-gun carriers to join the 11th Hussars, who were ranging ahead. This composite force of armoured cars, light tanks and infantry was placed under the command of Lieutenant-Colonel John Combe of the 11th Hussars, and was therefore called Combeforce.

Combeforce consisted of the 11th Hussars reinforced by a squadron of the King's Dragoon Guards, the RAF Armoured Car Squadron, the 2nd Battalion the Rifle Brigade with its 2-pounder anti-tank guns, and 'C' Battery of the 4th RHA. With this force of some 2,000 men, Colonel Combe hurried to cut the coast road. Speed was vital, for the Italians had already been bundled out of Benghazi by the Australians and were coming south as fast as their transport could carry them.

Combeforce reached Msus, north-east of Beda Fomm, on 4 February and was on the coast road near the village of Sidi Saleh by about noon on 5 February. The infantry barely had time to dig shallow trenches and take up their positions when the first column of Italian lorries came hurrying down from the north and ran into rifle and Bren-gun fire from 'A' Company of the Rifle Brigade. The battle of Beda Fomm was on with 2,000 soldiers of Combeforce standing in the path of a desperate army.

With support from the artillery and 'C' Squadron of the 11th

Hussars, the riflemen soon brought the Italian column to a halt. As their trucks and tanks began to create an enormous traffic jam, the Italians fanned out to the west of the road, moving towards the sea and probing south around the road block, but they were quickly engaged by more of Combe's scanty forces. By early afternoon fighting was taking place astride the road and it continued throughout the day. In spite of increasing Italian pressure – and a growing shortage of ammunition – the 11th Hussars, the gunners and the riflemen continued to block all escape to the south. When the rest of 4th Armoured Brigade came up that evening to strike the enemy in the flank at Beda Fomm, the Italian rout was complete.

This was no easy victory against a weak foe. The Italians were desperate, and pressed home their attacks with considerable resolution. They also had the advantage of numbers and an apparently inexhaustible supply of ammunition. Brigadier Caunter repeatedly asked for more supplies and for the urgent support of 1st RTR from the divisional reserve now mustering at Antelat, 40 miles to the south-east, but this regiment did not arrive until the battle was nearly over.

Much of the tank-versus-artillery fighting was around a feature called The Pimple, just east of the coast road at Beda Fomm. After the battle, Colonel Binks of 4th Armoured Brigade described the scene here as 'An extraordinary sight, a two-mile area of knocked out tanks, abandoned tanks, ditched tanks, burned-out vehicles, and dead or dying Italians, many roving about trying to surrender.'

With more units arriving, the 7th Armoured Division pounded the Italian Tenth Army for two days at Beda Fomm, and by 1100 hours on 7 February it was all over. White flags began to appear, the Italian Chief of Staff surrendered to the HQ of 4th Armoured Brigade and General Annibale Bergonzoli – 'Electric Whiskers' himself – came in a little later. After that, all that was left of Tenth Army laid down its arms; 20,000 men (including six generals) and a vast quantity of weapons, tanks, transport and supplies – including a fully staffed mobile brothel – fell into British hands. The cost of the Battle of Beda Fomm to 7th Armoured Division was 9 men killed and 15 wounded.

This indeed was victory. In ten weeks since the attack on the frontier forts, General Wavell's forces – never more than two divisions, with limited air support – had advanced over 500 miles and destroyed an entire army, capturing 130,000 prisoners and over 400 tanks. Australian, British and Indian losses in this campaign came to 500 killed, 1,373 wounded and 55 missing.[20] However, this was a victory against a foe with no great stomach for the fight; the Official History is being kind when it says that 'perhaps the most charitable and not the least accurate view of the attitude of most of the Italian junior leaders and soldiers is that they had no heart for this particular war'.[21]

The jubilation was considerable, but the campaign was not over. As soon as the Italians surrendered at Beda Fomm, the 11th Hussars set off south for Agedabia and El Agheila. This was mainly a reconnaissance, for the rest of the 7th Armoured Division was unable to follow. The Division had now been in action for eight months and its tank strength was reduced to just 12 A13 cruiser tanks and 40 Mark VI light tanks, all in need of repair. It was therefore withdrawn to Egypt and replaced by the first elements of the 2nd Armoured Division, newly arrived from the UK.

This need to re-equip brought the advance to a halt. General Wavell was eager to advance into Tripolitania, take Tripoli, and drive the Italians out of North Africa, but at this critical point his other responsibilities intruded. The Italians had already ordered their forces in Eritrea to take the field and draw off some of Wavell's forces, and calls for help were now coming from Greece, where the invading Italians had just been given another beating by the Greeks. This might have been encouraging, but in their despair the Italians had called for help from Hitler, and German forces were now taking the field in the Balkans.

Orders from London therefore compelled Wavell to halt the Desert Army south of Beda Fomm and to send many of his men and equipment across the Mediterranean Sea to help the Greeks. The tough and now experienced 6th Australian Division – victor of Bardia and Benghazi – was sent to Greece, together with the 2nd New Zealand Division (currently just two brigades), a full tank brigade of 2nd Armoured Division, and most of the Desert Air Force. The defence of the newly conquered territory in Cyrenaica was left to one armoured brigade, the Support Group of the 2nd Armoured Division, and another new arrival, the 9th Australian Division. Their task was to go over to the defensive west of Benghazi and hold the ground already gained. The possibility of a final victory over the Italians in North Africa, gained at Beda Fomm, was thrown away by these diversions to Greece.

Worse was to follow. Up to now the desert war had largely gone Britain's way. In spite of a shortage of men – and a spirit of daring and regimental élan more than made up for any shortage of numbers – British equipment and training had proved more than adequate to overwhelm the Italians. All this was about to change. On 14 February 1941, an armoured car patrol of the 11th Hussars was strafed on the open desert by a flight of fighter air-craft – German Me 109s – attacking at low level with cannon and machine-guns. This attack was pressed home with great skill and persistence.

These aircraft came from a German Luftwaffe unit, Flieger-korps X, the first part of a new force, the Deutsches Afrika Korps (DAK). Consisting of the 15th Panzer Division and the 5th Light Division, this strong and mobile corps was already coming ashore at Tripoli. As in Greece, the Germans had again been obliged to come to the aid of their Italian ally, and this obligation introduced a new phase in the desert war. It also introduced a new and most formidable foe in the person of General Erwin Rommel, and after Rommel took up his command in Tripoli, on 12 February 1941, life became increasingly difficult for the British commanders in North Africa.

Australian Imperial Force

3

Tobruk
May–December 1941

The defences of a city are its men, and not its walls.

Thucydides (*c.* 455–*c.* 400 BC), *History of the Peloponnesian War*

According to Adolf Hitler, the commitment of German troops to North Africa was necessary 'for strategic, political and psychological reasons'.[1] The Italians must be supported, Tripolitania must be held, the attack on the Suez Canal must be renewed. These aims were encapsulated in Führer Directive No. 22, on 11 January 1941, and the DAK began to arrive in North Africa a few weeks later. The first unit to arrive was the 5th Light Division, which had a tank unit, the 5th Panzer Regiment, as its main striking force and was soon followed by the powerful 15th Panzer Division.

Before the arrival of Rommel and the DAK, all seemed to be going well for the British in North Africa. Their forces in the Delta were growing in numbers and equipment, while the advance to El Agheila had secured Egypt's western flank and given Wavell control of Cyrenaica as a buffer against any counter-attack. The British also acquired the ports at Benghazi and Tobruk to ease, if not eliminate, the chronic problem of supply. This advance also overran a number of airfields and so reduced the number of air attacks from Italian aircraft in Cyrenaica against British convoys to Malta. The Italians had been soundly defeated at Beda Fomm, and would surely be defeated again when Wavell moved west into Tripolitania.

This view, while accurate, offers a somewhat narrow view of the situation in the Middle East. General Wavell's responsibilities included Greece, and that commitment was to prove the last straw, the added burden that broke the back of his always over-stretched resources. When the Italians invaded Greece in October 1940 the Greeks quickly proved more than a match for Mussolini's forces and brought their advance to a halt. The Germans were therefore obliged to come to the aid of their ally and send troops into Yugoslavia and Greece. These advanced rapidly through the Balkans towards Turkey – and Egypt.

This German advance into the Balkans began in February 1941 – for Adolf Hitler an irritating if necessary diversion from Operation BARBAROSSA, the German invasion of Soviet Russia, already planned for June. The British government was in turn compelled to send troops to Greece, and these forces could only come from Wavell's command – which obliged Wavell to halt any further advance into Libya. The brief Greek campaign in the early months of 1941 ended with the expulsion of Allied forces on 29 April. A further expensive debacle then followed in Crete, with an evacuation from that island on 1 June. Both campaigns cost Wavell a great deal of equipment and a number of excellent troops.

If all this was not a sufficient distraction, in April 1941 Wavell was faced with a revolt by nationalist forces in Iraq, a country that provided much of Britain's oil. On the orders of Prime Minister Rashid Ali, Iraqi forces laid siege to the RAF base at Habbaniya and threatened the oil port of Basra. Military action became necessary, and continued until the end of May, when Rashid Ali fled to Persia (now Iran) and the revolt collapsed. No sooner had this been settled than French Vichy forces in Syria gave further cause for concern and that country too had to be invaded and occupied. The one bright spot in all these events of spring 1941 was the defeat of the Italian fleet at the Battle of Matapan on 28 March, Cunningham's ships sinking two Italian cruisers and damaging the battleship *Vittorio Veneto*.

These brief campaigns in Greece, Crete, Iraq and Syria – and also in Abyssinia and Eritrea, where the 4th and 5th Indian Divisions were engaged against the Italians – fall outside the main scope of this book, but they illustrate the many problems confronting Wavell at this time: the Western Desert was his main concern, but far from the only one. These diversions of British strength also provided Rommel with a breathing space in which to muster his forces and plan his campaign against Wavell's thinly held western line at El Agheila.

The need to fight in Greece and Crete – and the resulting failure to finish off the Italians in Libya – was entirely due to Prime Minister Winston Churchill. On 12 February he wrote to Wavell:

> We should have been content with making a safe flank for Egypt at Tobruk and we told you that thereafter Greece and/or Turkey must have priority but that if you could get Benghazi easily and without prejudice to European calls, so much the better. We are delighted that you have got this prize three weeks ahead of expectation but it does not alter, indeed it rather confirms, our previous directive, namely that your major effort now must be to aid Greece and/or Turkey . . . we should try to get in a position to offer the transfer to Greece of the fighting portion of the Army which has hitherto defended Egypt.

Poor Wavell. It is arguable that had he been permitted to send 'the fighting portion of the Army which has hitherto defended Egypt' west of El Agheila immediately after Beda Fomm, it could have taken Tripolitania, destroyed the Italian presence in North Africa, provided a great strategic victory for Britain – and denied Rommel any base from which to mount his counter-attack. That done – and done quickly – aid could have then been sent to Greece or Crete. By leaving the North African task half-done and diverting scanty – and in the event inadequate – resources to another theatre, Churchill was easing Rommel's task. Rommel did not hesitate to grasp this opportunity.

Erwin Rommel was born in Württemberg in 1891 and began his military career in 1910, serving in the First World War as an infantry officer and commander of mountain troops. Between the wars he was one of the 4,000 officers permitted to stay in the German Army by the Treaty of Versailles, and he wrote a book, *Infanterie Greift An (Infantry Attacks)*, that sold no fewer than 400,000 copies[2] – a best-seller by any standards, and a work that brought him to the attention of Adolf Hitler. A captain in 1933, he was a full colonel by 1937 and was promoted to major-general in August 1939, serving at Hitler's HQ with special responsibility for security. Rommel's view of Hitler at this time was not untypical of that of other Germans of his background: he admired the Führer, but was dubious about the aims and ethics of Hitler's entourage.

Hitler liked Rommel. In May 1940, just in time for the offensive in France and the Low Countries, Rommel obtained command of the 7th Panzer Division, and with it he stormed across France in a fashion he was to repeat in the desert, coming to a halt only at Saint-Valéry at the mouth of the river Somme, where he took the surrender of the British 51st (Highland) Division. In this campaign Rommel established a style of leadership that was to stand him in good stead in North Africa.

Basically, Rommel led from the front. Although this can pay off in terms of troop morale and quick responses to events, this method of command is not always desirable in general officers. Generals and commanders at every level should be concerned with their command as a whole and not get sucked into the details of particular actions, which are best left to trusted subordinates. It can also be risky: forward command works only if the communications are good, so that contact can be maintained with headquarters and other units in the field. In North Africa, Rommel managed to exercise command – in general and in particular – by travelling with a tactical headquarters, getting about in a staff car or a half-track vehicle or a small Storch monoplane, and keeping in touch with events elsewhere by radio. Whenever there was trouble, whenever a unit got 'sticky' or failed to push on, Rommel would appear, assess the situation, and give clear orders based on the situation before him.

Rommel's method of command was very suited to the mobile warfare of the desert campaign, and superior to the more ponderous command methods then current in the British Army. However, no general is without fault, and Rommel possessed two characteristics that were to limit his early successes: he was remarkably intolerant of delay and tended to push his forces up to and beyond their limits, and he tended to ignore the orders of his superiors – orders which on occasion were very sensible and worth noting. Nevertheless, these were minor faults: Erwin

Rommel was a superb commander, fighting in a theatre that gave full scope to his talents. For the next year and a half the British could find no way to cope with him – a point made by Winston Churchill to the House of Commons in January 1942, 'We have a very daring and skilful opponent against us – and may I say, across the havoc of war, a very great General.'

Rommel's first task in North Africa was to retake Cyrenaica. For this task he would have two German divisions – the 5th Light Division and the 15th Panzer Division, together making up the Afrika Korps – plus four Italian infantry divisions and two Italian armoured divisions – a force soon to be known as Panzergruppe Afrika, but, since this was an Italian theatre, Rommel would be under Italian command – at least in theory. Sparing no efforts to get the German units ashore, he was soon ready to attack and on 31 March he struck the British line at El Agheila.

Australian anti-tank gunner W. H. Jenkins again:

> After the rest of the 6th Division went to Greece we were attached to the British and the King's Dragoon Guards (KDGs) and did a lot of patrols with them well beyond El Agheila. At this time we only had one gun in action as we only had one portée in use, the other two trucks having broken down. The first contact with the Germans came on 20 February, when one KDG armoured car and one portée of our 16th Anti-tank, commanded by Corporal Jim Duncan with yours truly as the gun layer, were well past Agheila when we watched their tanks go past the fort and return in the same manner.
>
> We had the only gun that could cause these German tanks any trouble, as the armoured cars were not well armed. I had a shot with my sights set well over the distance and it still landed short, but the next round went over the barrel of the first tank so we were the first Aussie troops to engage the Huns on the ground. They had their revenge later that day when two Messerschmitts flew down and found Fred Mahwer and me behind a small hillock and spent all their ammunition on us – but missed. I won't forget those first days around Agheila – the Pommie infantry from the Tower Hamlets, the Northumberland Fusiliers and the Royal Horse Artillery. Had we had some aircraft we could have given Rommel the big KO.[3]

From the spring of 1941 to after Alamein in October–November 1942, Allied accounts of Axis activity in the desert refer not to the relevant German or Italian units but to 'Rommel'. It is always 'Rommel' who is advancing, or moving up, never the unit concerned. In recent years Rommel's reputation has come under attack from revisionist historians and he is now sometimes portrayed as an opportunist or as a general who just happened to be lucky. If so, then this quality has some precedents; Napoleon, himself no mean commander, regarded luck as an essential requirement in any general.

In certain respects, Rommel *was* lucky. He was lucky that his equipment, especially his tanks and anti-tank guns, was far superior to that of his opponents. The Afrika Korps was equipped with the latest Panzer Mark III and Mark IV tanks. The Mark III weighed 20 tons, carried a crew of five, now mounted a 50-mm gun and two 7.92-mm machine-guns, and had frontal armour 30 mm thick. The Mark IV was still more formidable: also weighing 20 tons and with a similar amount of armour it mounted a 7.92-mm machine-gun and a 75-mm gun, which outranged any British tank gun then in service.

German tanks were also more sophisticated than the current British machines; they came with wide turret rings which enabled the hulls to be fitted with larger turrets and so be easily upgunned – there was no need for a complete redesign in order to improve their firepower. To these technical advantages can be added mechanical reliability and the activities of the German tank-recovery units, which roved the battlefields during the action, removing knocked-out tanks from the battlefield and restoring them to service. The Afrika Korps also had good anti-tank guns, including a small but significant number of the formidable 88-mm guns, a weapon capable of engaging both tanks and aircraft – the finest artillery piece of the Second World War. In short, Rommel's force was small, professional, well-integrated, well-equipped and supported by the modern fighters, bombers and dive-bombers of Fliegerkorps X. The decisive factors, however, were leadership, training and morale – numbers and kit, while important, are not everything

Rommel arrived in Tripoli on 12 February 1941. He was followed by transports bringing a crack Italian armoured division – the Ariete – and part of the German 5th Light Division, soon followed by the 15th Panzer Division. The 5th Light Panzer Regiment was equipped with 70 light tanks, eight-wheeled armoured cars and half-tracks and 80 Mark III and Mark IV panzers; this was no 'reconnaissance' formation. The 5th Light Division contained anti-tank units equipped with the excellent Pak-50 anti-tank gun and a few of the much feared 88-mms. From 1941 until the end of the war, Allied accounts of tank fighting never failed to mention the 'whip-crack' sound of the high-velocity 88-mm shell, a projectile that was perfectly capable of blowing a tank apart or setting it on fire. Most of this force had disembarked at Tripoli by 11 March 1941, and was ready for action by the end of the month.

Further east, General O'Connor had handed over command of XIII Corps – actually the Cyrenaica Command, for there was no Corps headquarters – to Lieutenant-General Philip Neame, VC, and had returned to Cairo for a well-earned rest. The forward positions of XIII Corps were now occupied by scattered elements of the British 2nd Armoured Division, deployed at the Mersa Brega gap, between the desert and the coast just east of El Agheila, while the 6th Australian Division had been replaced by the as yet unblooded 9th Australian Division. The 2nd Armoured Division was in a lamentable state, equipped with worn-out tanks and very little else; the Division actually amounted to no more than one weak armoured brigade and the ill-equipped Support Group.

Nor was General Morshead's 9th Australian Division in much better shape: two brigades of this division had been sent to Greece and replaced by two less well-equipped brigades from the 7th Australian Division, and the 9th Division was also very short of support weapons, signalling equipment and transport. Neame drew these deficiencies to the attention of General Wavell, but nothing could be done about them: British resources were currently overstretched everywhere although more British and Indian units were en route to the desert war.

This XIII Corps organization set the pattern for British formations in the desert war: industrialized Britain (and later the USA) would provide the armoured forces and the specialized arms, the artillery, signallers and engineers; the Dominions would provide much of the infantry, though there were British infantry units in the desert – the Royal Northumberland Fusiliers, the Kings Royal Rifle Corps and the Cameron Highlanders have already been mentioned, and these were just three of nearly 40

British battalions which were to serve in the North African campaign. There were also Australian and New Zealand artillery and anti-tank units. The Desert Army was never a homogeneous force and this division of tasks and functions caused problems; individually the divisions were excellent, but they had yet to be welded into an army.

All the formations in North Africa – Australian, British, Indian and New Zealand – had been stripped of much of their transport, ammunition and guns to equip the forces sent to Greece. Basically, Wavell was responding to Churchill's demands by gambling: he hoped that Rommel would not attack until his new units could be trained and reinforced. Writing to Churchill, Wavell gave his reasons for this calculation:

> Tripoli to Agheila is 471 miles and to Benghazi 646 miles. There is only one road and the water is inadequate over 410 miles of that distance; these factors, together with a lack of transport, limit the present enemy threat . . . he may test us at Agheila with offensive patrolling and, if he finds us weak, push on to Agedabia in order to move up his advance landing grounds. I do not think that with this force he will attempt to recover Benghazi.[4]

Wavell was wrong. Rommel moved fast, pushed hard, and kept on pushing. The cutting edge of Rommel's advance on 31 March was just 50 tanks, but these were Mark III and Mark IV panzers. Supported by 200 bombers and fighters of the Luftwaffe, these forces smashed through the British defences like an armoured whirlwind, rapidly driving XIII Corps back towards Benghazi. On 2 April the Support Group of 2nd Armoured was driven out of Agedabia and fell back to Antelat and then towards Benghazi, many units being overrun in the retreat. This exposed the flank of the 9th Australian Division, which fell back on 4 April covered by the remains of 2nd Armoured's Support Group. In three days Rommel had got the British on the run, and by 10 April, 'convinced that the British were collapsing and must be vigorously pursued . . . Rommel let it be known that his objective was now the Suez Canal'.[5]

The British became convinced that he was attacking in overwhelming strength, and by concentrating all his tanks into one force Rommel reinforced this impression. In fact only a part of his force had as yet come ashore at Tripoli. He attacked only because –

for the reasons already explained – the British seemed reluctant to advance any further into Tripolitania. This smacked of hesitation and, thus encouraged, Rommel took the initiative, compensating for his current lack of strength with increased mobility.

Wavell's forces were inadequate, but Rommel's success was compounded by the fact that the British forces were well scattered around El Agheila. Advised by Ultra intelligence decrypts on German movements from Italy – information which they were receiving daily, though in no great quantity, from England – Wavell and Neame had assumed, not unreasonably, that Rommel would wait until all the Afrika Korps had arrived before attacking.

This assumption reveals one of the snags with Ultra intelligence: it revealed only what the Germans were doing or about to do or what they said they would do; it did not say what they might *actually* do in the immediate future, for, like much intelligence, it was out of date by the time Wavell received it. From the basic information coming via Ultra, assumptions were made by XIII Corps and Army Intelligence that were not always correct – and that would be even less correct when they were made about Rommel, who tended to go his own way and rarely did what his opponents, or his superiors, expected.

Nor was there an adequate amount of Ultra coming from the Government Code and Cypher School at Bletchley Park. According to F. H. Hinsley, in April 1941, well into Rommel's advance into Cyrenaica, the number of Ultra decrypts sent from Bletchley to Wavell's HQ in Cairo averaged fewer than one per day.[6] Most of the available Ultra was based on decrypts of the Luftwaffe Enigma, which recorded the number of ships, and separated tankers from those carrying dry stores, but gave no other information on cargoes.

Information on the make-up and state of the Afrika Korps was not forthcoming through Ultra until November 1941, when Bletchley broke the German Army Enigma for North Africa, code-named Chaffinch, and even then breaking Chaffinch took time. Peter Calvocoressi, another Bletchley Park historian, states, 'I do not believe that Chaffinch was often broken in less than 48 hours.'[7] Lacking precise information, the British therefore underestimated the strength of Rommel's thrust at Tobruk and Egypt in March.[8]

Nor was Rommel without accurate, up-to-date intelligence; he too had a source – the US military attaché in Cairo, Colonel Bonner Frank Fellers. Colonel Fellers had carte blanche to roam about the British lines in the Western Desert, and was welcome at many headquarters. The Australian war correspondent Alan Moorehead recalls meeting him during the battle at Sidi Rezegh in November 1941:

> My party had blundered into the British armoured division head-quarters and the first officer I saw there was the welcome figure of Colonel Bonner Fellers, the US Military Attaché. Bonner Fellers was often in the desert. He liked to gather his facts at first hand and in the Wavell campaign we used to see him buzzing about from place to place in an ordinary civilian car. And now, here he was again, looking quizzically across to the east where quick heavy gunfire had suddenly broken the quiet of the afternoon. I called across to him, 'What's happening?' and he just had time to reply, 'Damned if I know', when we had to duck for shelter as two Messerschmitts came over, ground strafing.[9]

Following these forays, Colonel Fellers would return to Cairo and send detailed reports on XIII Corps strength, equipment, positions, intentions and morale to his superiors in Washington. Unfortunately for Colonel Fellers – but even more unfortunately for the British commanders in the Western Desert – the Italians had broken the US diplomatic 'Black Code' which Fellers was using to send these dispatches. Rommel's HQ was therefore receiving copies of Feller's information direct from Rome on a daily basis. Rommel and his staff officers refer to the use of this information constantly in their diaries and memoirs, and this 'Good Source' was most useful when Rommel was planning his offensives.

Aided by Fellers's information and having made his own assessment of the British forces to his front, Rommel attacked with what forces he had at the end of March – and took the British completely by surprise. By 3 April the British were in full retreat, abandoning stores which the Germans and Italians were able to use to alleviate their supply problems. Picking up petrol and transport from the retreating British, Rommel decided to press on across Cyrenaica and drive them out of Libya. Reports of this time indicate 'considerable confusion' in the British lines.

Units coming up to join the fight were overrun by the advancing Germans, tanks ran out of petrol and had to be abandoned, ammunition dumps were blown up, food stores were left to sustain the enemy. Everywhere the Afrika Korps swarmed forward, capturing a quantity of men – and even some generals.

On 6 April a German motorcycle unit, scouting one of the desert tracks, captured a staff car containing Lieutenant-General Sir Philip Neame, the current commander of XIII Corps, General Sir Richard O'Connor, the victor of Beda Fomm, and Brigadier John Combe, until recently CO of the 11th Hussars. On the following day the commander of the 2nd Armoured Division and what was left of his command surrendered at Mechili. On 11 April, falling back along the coast road, the 9th Australian Division and British artillery units withdrew into Tobruk, where a brigade of the 7th Australian Division had already been brought in by sea. The Germans had advanced 450 miles from El Agheila in 12 days.

So it continued, the DAK retaking all the ground abandoned by the Italians in the campaign of the previous winter. The Germans captured Bardia on 12 April – turning a big gun, known as 'Bardia Bill', on the defenders of Tobruk. Sollum and Fort Capuzzo fell on the following day, and on 14 April Rommel's forces arrived at the Egyptian frontier. In two weeks Rommel had swept the British out of Libya, and of all their recent conquests only the fortress of Tobruk remained. It was held at first by the 9th Australian Division and then, after that division was withdrawn, by the British 70th Division, a Polish brigade and a Czech battalion, the garrison being supplied by sea while pounded from the air.

The siege of Tobruk will always be remembered as another epic of the desert war. The defences occupied by the Australians were largely those constructed by the Italians. A double ring of concrete defence posts – 128 in all, each capable of holding an infantry section or a machine-gun team – were arranged in two rows, the outer posts being 600 to 800 yards apart. Between the posts were barbed-wire fences some 5 feet high and an unfinished anti-tank ditch about 12 feet wide. This defence line was situated 8 miles outside the town, forming a defence perimeter of some 30 miles. The outer defences, mostly wire and anti-tank ditches, were in a poor state when the Australians moved in, the wire rusted and fallen, the anti-tank ditches filled with drifting sand. The 24th and 18th Australian Infantry Brigades set to work to improve these, while the other two brigades, the 20th and 26th, remained in the desert, defending the port while this work went on.

Support was limited, but professional. The anti-tank artillery in Tobruk consisted of two regiments: one British, one Australian. There was no field artillery but an assortment of 75 light and heavy anti-aircraft guns. There was a British tank brigade, the 3rd, made up of 26 cruisers, 15 light tanks and just 4 Matilda infantry tanks. The British contingent in the garrison at this time also included a machine-gun battalion from the Northumberland Fusiliers, signallers, sappers and anti-aircraft units; in all, Tobruk was defended by some 36,000 men. At the start of the siege, in April, the main force consisted of the 9th Australian Division – three infantry brigades holding the perimeter, with the 18th Infantry Brigade in reserve. Continued resistance by the Tobruk garrison depended on the 'Spud Run' – the nightly arrival of Royal Navy ships from Alexandria, largely vessels from the Inshore Squadron, bringing in supplies and reinforcements, and evacuating the wounded.

The defence of Tobruk can be divided into three phases. The first is the defence by Morshead's Australian division – a unit that came to relish the title 'the Rats of Tobruk'. With its supporting British units, the 9th Division held Tobruk from April to August 1941, after which it was gradually withdrawn. The second phase covers the actions of the British 70th Division, the Polish Carpathian Brigade and a Czechoslovak battalion, which continued until the end of the year. The last phase covers the actions of TobForce during the breakout from Tobruk in early 1942, in support of Operation CRUSADER. Both these phases will be covered later. The total duration of the Tobruk siege was eight months.

General Leslie J. Morshead of the 9th Australian Division – 'Ming the Merciless' to his troops – was placed in command in April and was tasked to hold the town for eight weeks until a relief could be organized. Morshead elected for an aggressive defensive policy, telling his commanders bluntly that 'There'll be no Dunkirk here. If we should have to retreat we will fight our way out. There is to be no surrender and no retreat.'[10] The policy was implemented every night with strong fighting patrols moving into enemy territory. There was no 'No Man's Land' around Tobruk. Where the German and Italian lines ended, the Australian line began, at bayonet point.

The first task was to occupy the former Italian defences, restring the wire, dig the sand out of the anti-tank ditches, and beat off Rommel's attacks on the perimeter when he attempted to overrun Tobruk before the defence could be organized. The first of these attacks came in on 10 April and was beaten off with loss, General von Prittwitz of the 15th Panzer Division being killed in the attack. Further attacks by tanks and infantry followed on 13–14 April; in beating off one of them, Corporal Jack Edmondson won Australia's first VC of the war – sadly a posthumous one – in hand-to-hand fighting around the perimeter.

The fighting around the perimeter went on for the rest of the month, but the Germans were unable to break in. Resolute defence by the infantry, close support from the tanks and guns, the gradually improving defences – all combined to bring the German offensive to a halt. Even so, their efforts continued with another major attack at the end of the month, and on May Day a breach was made in the perimeter and a small salient was created. Lieutenant Gerhart Schorm, a German panzer officer, left an account of this attack:

1 May 1941. General Rommel has ordered that we take Tobruk. This will be our fourth attempt on the town. Up at 0330 hours and move at 0430 hours. We lose touch in the pre-dawn darkness and clouds of dust, but regain contact by radio. We file through the gap where many of our troops have fallen and deploy on the left side of 6th Company. On the right are 7th and 8th companies – altogether about 80 tanks.

English artillery open fire on us at once. The attack has commenced, but no troops are sent out to reconnoitre. Tier after tier of guns boom out from the fortifications before us. I prepare to move when the 6th company commander informs me that his tank has been hit on the track. Things are happening fast, a fearful crash on my front and right. A shell? No, a mine. An order is received to turn, but too late – I hit a mine underneath and to the left. I am unable to move. What the hell are the storm pioneers doing? This area was supposed to be clear. We clamber out and on to tank 623 and back though the artillery fire, about 100 metres.

The attack has failed, We are ordered back over the heights and to safer ground. Crew members of mined tanks turn up; morale is at rock bottom. Now it is the enemy's turn. His tanks are negotiating the minefield, because they have mine-location maps, but they don't go far as our artillery hits the area. Lieutenant Rosskol's tank returns and he tells us that the company has lost 9 heavy Mark IVs and 3 light Mark III tanks. What a field day for the enemy!

Suddenly a wireless message. Enemy infantry are on the attack. Are they crazy? No, it's actually true. Two Australian companies are leaving their lorries and forming skirmishing lines. All sorts of Very lights are going up – green, red and white. The flares hiss down by our machine gun posts. It is now getting too dark to aim at anything. Italian trucks with flame-throwers move up to clear a triangle of fire. Long streaks of oil with filthy smell prevent any advance by enemy infantry, and all action gradually winds down. At 2300 hours we have retired through the gap and commence our journey back to base. At 0300 hours some rations beside the tank. I and a few crew members have terrible cramp. To sleep.[11]

Try as he would, pounding the garrison from the air and with artillery, putting in armoured and infantry attacks, Rommel found himself unable to subdue the dauntless defenders of Tobruk, some of whom should now have a say.

Henry Tranter was a signaller with the 9th Australian Division:

The general opinion among Australians was that anyone in the British Army with rank treated lower ranks like dirt. Their type of discipline did not appeal to us, and we did not think highly of their senior officers. This feeling was mutual, for they thought Australians undisciplined.

We found the Pommies quite generous, and they generally liked the Australians. About the first morning after the retreat to Tobruk, two linemen and I were either laying a line or on a recce when we came across a group of Poms, sitting around a fire enjoying a hearty breakfast. We absolutely drooled, and I wondered aloud if the Poms would give us some tea and suger. One of the mates said, 'They wouldn't give us anything', but I thought it would do no harm to ask and the response was immediate. 'Of course, Aussie. What can we put it in?' They found an old canvas rifle cover and filled it to the brim with tea and sugar and we had enough for days – and could not believe our good luck.

The only Poms I had much contact with were a machine-gun company of the Northumberland Fusiliers, who were attached to our brigade in Tobruk. Many thought the Australians were great and intended to emigrate to Australia after the war . . . Before the big battle at Alamein we were really pleased to learn that we had Scottish Highlanders on our left flank. I am sure we would not have been so happy with anyone else, other than the New Zealanders.[12]

Alf Curtis of Billinga, Queensland, and the 9th Division Ammunition Company, recalls one Australian contribution to the resistance:

William Joyce, the British traitor called Lord Haw Haw, referred to our commander as Ali Baba Morshead and his Twenty Thousand Thieves, living like rats in holes and the scum of the earth. When the war ended Joyce was hanged, but the Rats of Tobruk have become part of Australia's heritage. The enemy had armour, heavy guns and aircraft, but could not match the Royal Horse Artillery, which played a significant part in the defence.

We had at our disposal quite a number of captured Italian artillery pieces with an almost inexhaustible supply of shells. The sights had been removed and the guns were dangerous to use, but by attaching a lanyard to the trigger and retiring behind a sangar or a sandbag the risk of serious injury was reduced. The troops who manned these weapons were known affectionately as the Bush Artillery.[13]

Another account of these unorthodox gunners recalls that their favourite method of aiming was to sight along – or through – the gun barrel, and that the fire order consisted of the cry 'Let 'er go, mate!'

As for the Twenty Thousand Thieves, that title too was gleefully adopted, as this verse from a poem sent in by Ron Culbert, a Tobruk veteran, makes clear:

Old Jerry had us on the run, the news was far from hot;
He had his feet in Egypt and the Sphinx was on the spot.
The GOC, despondent, sent signals out in sheaves,
'Send me Ali Baba Morshead and his Twenty Thousand
    Thieves.'[14]

Garth Suthers was an officer in the 2/9th Infantry Battalion of the 18th Infantry Brigade:

I was a platoon commander when we arrived in Tobruk, disembarking from a destroyer, and I saw a great many Australian nurses embarking on the ship we had just left. Several of them were weeping with disappointment, and one of them remarked to me, 'We enlisted to do a job where we are needed, and the first time it looks a bit dangerous we are evacuated out of harm's way.'

On that first day in Tobruk our battalion had only one map, but we set off from the wharf about 1000 hours and marched for most of the day. At about 0200 hours that night the adjutant said to me, 'I'm buggered. Take your platoon on a bearing of x degrees – I forget which – for about 600 yards and when the stench of enemy dead is overpowering you will have arrived at your position, post R57.' This turned out to be on the extreme left of the battalion line and the point where the 6th Division had broken through the defences some months earlier and were in too much of a hurry to bury the enemy dead.

Incidentally, a Salvation Army welfare officer, Brigadier Arthur McIlveen – a brigadier in the Salvation Army, that is – was attached to our battalion throughout the siege. He was a remarkable preacher, and we never had any trouble getting the men out for church parade. Among the many hymns we always sang 'Sunshine on the Hills', and after the war until just a few years ago, now that our ranks have thinned, we always sang 'Sunshine on the Hills' when one of our number died, at the funeral service, regardless of the religion of the deceased. The padre's gramophone, which he played to the wounded at the 2/4th Field Hospital, is now on display at the War Memorial in Canberra. After the war the Rats bought him a cottage on his retirement – he called it Tobruk – and when he died he received a military funeral, gun carriage and all.[15]

A number of Tobruk veterans have urged some mention of the 'Spud Run', the nightly convoys run into Tobruk by the Royal Navy. Among those who arrived that way was a British anti-tank gunner, Bill Armitage of the 149th Anti-Tank Regiment:

Shortly after 2200 hrs the speed slackened and we nosed up to a wooden jetty in Tobruk harbour. It was pitch black and we were quickly ashore and climbing into dilapidated trucks to our destination, the echelon areas of the 2/3rd Australian Anti-Tank Regiment and 3rd Royal Horse Artillery. After a short rest and breakfast we relieved their front line gun crews and found out what life in Tobruk was like: sand, flies, heat, very little water, and tea which when made looked like coffee and tasted like sulphur. We learned to keep a very low profile as any movement was made uncomfortable by enemy artillery but as the days passed we became self-reliant, tough and glad we were not in the harbour when the Stukas went over to bomb – and there we stayed until the breakout in November.[16]

John Sinclair was a stoker on HMS *Kipling*, a Royal Navy destroyer:

We took part in the battle for Crete, when Mountbatten's ship HMS *Kelly* and HMS *Kashmir* were lost and many brave men with them. After that we on *Kipling* were based at Alexandria and found ourselves taking part in the desert war, on what we came to call the Tobruk Run. What we did was take in food, medical supplies, ammunitions, clothing, everything you can think of – so much that it was difficult to get along the deck on watch, as every inch of space was crowded with goods for our troops. We also took in troops to replace those wounded, sailing from Alexandria harbour at nightfall. This was all supposed to be 'hush-hush', as the locals were not to be trusted.

So, in the middle of the night, no lights showing, we would arrive off Tobruk and come in slowly to dock. Then, in the next ten minutes or so, everyone – and I mean everyone – turned to, dropping the guard rail and sending the goods ashore, hand to hand, as the wounded and sick were brought on board and down to the mess decks. We also evacuated German and Italian prisoners. Then in half an hour, certainly under an hour, we were ready to sail again, under air attack back to Alexandria.

We had the task of trying to help the forces in Tobruk, and we were delighted to do so. HMS *Kipling* did this trip up three times before the siege ended. *Kipling* was sunk by air attack on 12 May 1942 with the loss of 30 men, mostly engine-room personnel. In fact of our entire 5th Destroyer Flotilla only HMS *Kelvin* survived the war.[17]

Ned Maxwell of the 2/12th Battalion of the 24th Infantry Brigade – a 9th Division veteran from Tasmania – recalls the RAF at Tobruk:

Our position was at Eagle Corner at the junction of the Bardia, Derna and Fort Pilastrino roads, near the big food dump. It was not a healthy place to be, because the Stukas came in to bomb the town and always made the food dump one of their targets. Many a Bren magazine we fired at them, but on one particular day the RAF Hurricanes went up to intercept them. I think there were only about three fighters left to defend Tobruk, and they were all shot down a few days later. Those fighter pilots were exceptionally brave men; you could see wave after wave of Stukas and escorting Messerschmitt 109s coming in, and yet they would still go and try to break up the bombing formation. Each British plane would be pounced on by two or three Germans, and they didn't have a chance. I saw one Hurricane shoot down two Jerries before another German shot him down and there were three blazing planes falling to earth – a sight not often seen.[18]

Edward Butler from Queensland:

Can I make some reference to the medical services in Tobruk? Basically this was just the regular regimental aid posts (RAPs) and the field ambulance, and they had a hard job and of course it was a bit rough and ready. I remember having a couple of teeth taken out, sitting on a crate in the open, no painkiller and the dentist clad only in a pair of shorts. Apart from wounds and other sicknesses, like jaundice, there were desert sores, dysentery and of course a sprinkling of self-inflicted wounds.

The only hospital was an underground cave near the harbour, which made it easier to ship the sick and wounded out to the destroyers that arrived every night to discharge supplies and reinforcements and take the sick back to Alexandria. There were no female nurses and precious few other staff, and little equipment apart from stretchers and blankets – the atmosphere down there was pretty fetid. Being on the harbour it was also in range of a big gun, a large howitzer we called Bardia Bill, which regularly lobbed its missiles around the area. Lying in the hospital we could hear all this, and it was interesting that you heard the sound of the gun firing before you heard the 'woosh' of the arriving shell.

And, yes, the Royal Navy destroyers need a mention, because the story of these destroyers is a great – fantastic – epic that has never been properly told. The trip up from Alex was bad, but the return journey was worse as it had to be done in daylight, fully exposed to enemy planes. Sometimes, on account of the lack of space, some of the sick and wounded had to remain on deck, and it did happen that in the zigzagging to avoid the bombs some were washed overboard.[19]

Jack Wilkinson was in Tobruk with the 9th Division Cavalry (Mechanized):

We sailed from Australia on 10 April 1940 and were sent into Syria to deal with the Vichy French while the rest of the 9th Division were in the desert with the rest of the British forces pushing back the Italians. Then the Germans came and drove us back to the little port of Tobruk, where we stayed to fight. We waited for General Rommel, and we had not long to wait, but he never managed to push us out of Tobruk. We were supplied by several small ships of the Royal Navy and General Rommel made many attempts to drive us out, but he always failed. It brings a lump to my throat to think of those brave soldiers who held Tobruk.[20]

Lloyd Tann of the 2/5th Australian Field Ambulance was among the Australians shipped out of Tobruk on HMS *Jervis*, and he recorded the trip in his diary:

It is 0615 hours and we think we are back in Tobruk again, because all hell has broken loose. The ship is vibrating madly, her guns blaze madly. A sickening thud hits her broadside on, dull and metallic. We heel over sharply. We don't like this at all; cooped up below as we are, we wonder what is going on. All's well that ends well, and soon the action is over and we are allowed on deck.

Then mid-morning and it is on again! Sailors race to action stations, gun crews elevate their guns, and once more we are herded below and instructed to stay put. The harassed *Jervis*, her engines racing, changes course violently; her pom-poms blast into action. This action is short-lived, however, and we sail on and somewhere ahead lies Alexandria.

Many ships are at anchor when we get there, and an officer informs us that we are to 'Dress ship', lining up along the rail as we sail in down a line of ships from all the Allied navies, all the crews dressed in whites also lining the rails. As we reach the first ship, a Britisher, the crew take off their white caps and give us a hearty cheer and the ship siren blasts. This occurs right along the line as we pass each ship, and in other parts of the harbour other ships join in – cargo vessels, tankers, old tramps. Never before have the troops been paid such an overwhelming tribute, and the Rats stand there and take it. It is the proudest moment of my life.

We don't know what the future will hold for us, but, together with the officers and men of the British and Australian navies

who by their gallantry along the Spud Run made the withstand-
ing of the siege possible, we can look back on our sojourn in
Tobruk with quiet satisfaction.[21]

Ned Maxwell recalls another attack on the Tobruk perimeter:

This attack began on 17 May. They got a footing on the S9 defence
post, and Post S10 was overrun and our post, S8, was cut off for
two days, but because 12th Platoon held S8 and S10 was regained
by the rest of the battalion the door to Tobruk was slammed shut
in Rommel's face. Murray Steele, Tom Berry and myself were in
the forward gun pit of S8 when the attack started; also there was
Death, his scythe over his shoulder.
    At the time I thought a mortar bomb had landed among us, but
I later assumed it must have been a stick grenade. It had plenty
of punch, for it blew the sandbags down and punched holes in
the water jacket of the Vickers big enough to poke your fingers in.
I was firing at a group of enemy, and I must have cut the grenade
thrower down just as he threw it for no more came in.
    Some time later a stretcher bearer came round to look at Tom,
but said he could do nothing for him: he had taken the full blast
of the grenade, and it was only a matter of time. Murray went off
to get his head bandaged, and I returned with a Thompson sub-
machine-gun and some grenades as our gun had been knocked
out. Tom was in agony, kicking and groaning something awful,
and when Murray returned I told him what the stretcher bearer
had said and, since I could not bear to see him in such agony, I
was going to finish him off.
    I had placed the muzzle of my .38 revolver against Tom's head
and was about to pull the trigger when Murray said something
and did something I will remember for the rest of my life. He put
his hand on my wrist and said, 'Ned, we are mates, for my sake,
please.' There was something in his voice that touched me, so I
put the pistol away. Murray never mentioned this again and neither did I, but now, years later, there would be only a handful of
us left from S8 so it does not matter as much now as then.
    Tom died before morning, and we covered him with a blanket.
We could not shift him anywhere, and he lay in the hot sun all day.
We could not risk taking the dead back for burial that night, so
after dark I went out a few yards from our gun pit and dug a grave.
It took me a fair while, as the ground was rocky, and I could only
get down a couple of feet. Then I got one of the lads to help me
carry Tom out and sent him back inside in case we copped a burst.

Standing there alone in no man's land, I tried to think of the padre's burial service but all I could remember was 'Yea though I walk through the shadow of the Valley of Death'. After that I could think of no more, so I took off my steel helmet, lowered my head, and recited the Lord's Prayer all the way through.[22]

Fortunately for Wavell, after investing Tobruk, Rommel's offensive stalled on the frontier wire – not through any sudden resurgence of British resistance, but because the Axis forces had outrun their supply lines. Had Tobruk fallen and its abundant stores passed into Rommel's hands, it might have been a different story. This pause was a great relief to Wavell, who now had forces closely engaged in North Africa, Greece, Syria and East Africa. German troops had invaded Greece and Yugoslavia on 6 April, Vichy French forces in Syria looked likely to support the German side, and there were stirrings of the Rashid Ali revolt in Iraq. Only in Abyssinia were the prospects brighter, the capital, Addis Ababa, falling to British and Indian forces on 5 April.

Another bright corner could be found at sea, where the Royal Navy, advised by Ultra, was getting to work against the Axis convoys to North Africa. On 16 April a convoy of five Italian supply ships, escorted by three destroyers, was attacked en route to Tripoli by four British destroyers. One British destroyer was lost, but all five Italian ships went to the bottom, half the German troops on board being drowned. On that day, in view of the situation in the desert, Wavell ordered that the dispatch of the 7th Australian Division and the Polish Brigade to Greece should be postponed – thus effectively ending British participation in the Greek campaign. Hard though it was, this was the right decision: any available reinforcements must go to the Western Desert. The British had been pushed back below the Halfaya Pass, but they still held positions on the coastal escarpment to the east, from where they could perhaps prevent any further German advances into Egypt. To do that Wavell needed more men and more tanks.

Help – of a kind – was at hand. On 12 May a convoy codenamed 'Tiger' docked at Alexandria. This convoy consisted of five ships which had fought their way through the Mediterranean escorted by two battleships, an aircraft carrier, four cruisers and seven destroyers, bringing with them Winston Churchill's 'Tiger Cubs': 135 Matilda tanks, 82 of the new, 2-pounder-gunned, Mark VI Crusader tanks, 21 light tanks, and 43 modern Hurricane fighters for the Desert Air Force. On the face of it this was a considerable force; closer inspection revealed the operational and technical snags.

The Hurricane II was no match for the Me 109F that the Luftwaffe was now using, and the RAF pilots were outnumbered. The Crusader was a good-looking tank with frontal armour 40 mm thick and a top speed of 26 m.p.h., and at first the crews were very glad to get it. Only when they began to use it did they discover that the Crusader had a number of serious technical defects. The 2-pounder armed Crusader was undergunned and mechanically unreliable, with a water pump that caused continual trouble; this last was a serious defect in the desert, where water was always in short supply. It was also discovered that, without considerable maintenance and the fitting of sand filters, these tanks were not fit for desert operations.

Getting the tanks operational took time, but unfortunately for Wavell the arrival of the 'Tiger Cubs' in Egypt led Churchill to make fresh demands for action. Now, or so it seemed to the Prime Minister, XIII Corps had the strength for an immediate and devastating attack on Rommel, pushing him back and relieving Tobruk. On the day the tanks arrived at Alexandria, Churchill sent a cable to Wavell, asking how soon they could be used. That cable crossed with one from Wavell to the Chief of the Imperial General Staff (CIGS), General Sir John Dill, saying that the next attack was at least a month away and could not possibly be mounted before 7 June. The tanks had to be checked and serviced – which revealed a crop of problems caused by various factory and shipping failings – and then prepared for the desert, and the crews had to be trained in their use. Wavell put back the date of his attack to 15 June – an action that caused Churchill 'terrible anxiety and anger'.[23]

Churchill's anger was directed at the wrong man. Though typical of the types of weapon the British Army was supposed to fight with in 1941–2, these tanks had deficiencies and defects that should have been seen to years before. During trials in 1937 the cruiser tank prototype was found to have 47 separate mechanical flaws; the engine dated back to one designed in 1915, the gearbox gave out after 70 miles, the brakes after 130 miles; the carburettor and distributor had to be redesigned, fresh tracks and stronger components had to be introduced – the list of necessary modifications goes on for pages.

Design faults were not eased by poor workmanship during manufacture. When the production models of this tank arrived in Egypt in 1941, the bolts on the chassis were found to be only hand-tight and the engines were found so unreliable that Wavell soon realized that he needed a reserve of at least 25 per cent simply to cover tanks awaiting repair in the workshops – not counting the reserve of tanks needed for battlefield losses, which amounted to another 25 per cent.[24]

A later investigation by Middle East HQ revealed that shipping arrangements often compounded these failings. In December 1941, reporting to Churchill on two Churchill tanks sent to the desert for trials, General Sir Claude Auchinleck reported that

> These vehicles were stowed on the forward well-deck, unsheeted and unlocked, exposed to sea water. When received these tanks had water on floors and showed rust markings nine inches up the walls; considerable damage to electrical and wireless gear, requiring fourteen days work before tanks can run. Method of stowing and despatch most unsatisfactory. All American tanks are despatched with all crevices and doors pasted up with masking tape.

None of this carelessness and inefficiency helped, but the basic fact was that almost all the British equipment, with the exception of the 25-pounder field gun and the .303 Bren gun, was inferior to that of the Germans – and the Bren was no match for the belt-fed German Spandau. The 2-pounder anti-tank shell bounced of the panzers' frontal armour, and the British tanks were underpowered, unreliable, under-gunned and thinly armoured. The Matilda infantry tank had better armour than the rest – though not enough to resist an 88-mm shell – but was slow and mounted only the 2-pounder-gun. And yet men had to fight in them.

Eric Garner of the Royal Engineers describes an incident with one of the new – and equally useless – Valentine tanks in 1942:

> We were on exercises with a group of Valentine tanks in wooded country and our task was to ambush them. Being slightly mad,

like all sappers, we decided to make things more interesting by putting a small quantity of ammatol explosive in a milk can with a detonator and about 5–10 seconds of safety fuse, and as the Valentines appeared we lobbed these milk tins in their direction.

Within 30 seconds we had three tanks out of action, one with a broken track, one where the explosion of a small charge on the engine hatch stopped the engine, and one where a tin had exploded underneath and the tank simply refused to go. These charges were nothing like as powerful as the normal anti-tank grenade, but we sappers were not too popular with that tank regiment from then on. But if just playing around on an exercise could do that to them, what were they like in action? We only had one casualty, a piece of milk tin in the arse of one of my sappers – so at least they learned to keep more than their heads down.[25]

Urged on by Churchill, Wavell decided to attack the enemy positions at Sollum and Fort Capuzzo, partly to clear the ground for a further attack, partly to push Rommel back from the frontier and perhaps relieve the forces penned-up in Tobruk. This attack, Operation BREVITY, went in on 14 May and was well named, for it lasted just two days. The British forces, under Brigadier 'Strafer' Gott, consisted of the Support Group of 7th Armoured Division, the 11th Hussars and the motorized 22nd Guards Brigade, supported by artillery and Hurricanes of No. 274 Squadron, plus the 2nd RTR from the 7th Armoured Brigade equipped with reconditioned A9 and A10 cruiser tanks and the 4th RTR equipped with the heavily armoured Matildas – a total of some 55 tanks. None of these were Tiger Cubs: the latter had arrived only on 12 May, and no amount of urging from Downing Street would make them ready for action in two days.

The 22nd Guards Brigade and the 4th RTR opened the offensive with an assault up the Halfaya Pass. At first they achieved complete surprise; then they were held up by the Italian gunners, who knocked out seven Matildas before being overrun. This sound of this battle alerted the Germans further south at Fort Capuzzo, who greeted the advancing tanks of the 4th RTR with a hail of shells. The fort fell, but was quickly recaptured by a German counter-attack. Gott's forces continued to press forward during the night, but on 15 May with the opposition steadily increasing, he decided to pull back and defend the Halfaya Pass, which was being held by a squadron of the 4th RTR in

Matildas and the 3rd Battalion the Coldstream Guards. There they stayed, and BREVITY was over.

Doug Denton of the 3rd Battalion the Coldstream Guards took part in BREVITY:

> The attack reached the old fort at Capuzzo and came to a stop as usual, again demonstrating how superior the German tanks and weapons were. Digging trenches was impossible, so we had to build rock sangars with walls about two and a half feet high and we had a Bofors gun, manned by Australians, in another larger sangar further down the slope. During the day we were bombed at regular intervals by the Luftwaffe, and although our fighters arrived they never seemed to be there at the same time as the German bombers.
>
> Just behind us was the mortar platoon's 30-cwt truck, loaded with bombs, and standing beside it, jawing away, were two of the officers. When the bombers came back everyone took shelter except these officers. I saw three bombs falling on our position – you could see them all the way down, and the front rims of our helmets were digging into the ground as we saw them heading straight for us. Then there was a tremendous explosion, one on our right and then another behind us. One bomb had landed right at the side of the sangar and the other on the mortar truck, which had disappeared along with the two officers. A call went out for a sandbag to collect the remains, but all we could find of them was a hand severed at the wrist and two fingers.
>
> This bombing continued throughout the day, and on the following morning we began to pull out, with vehicles of all descriptions rushing back across the frontier – a real flap. The only things left between us and the Germans were about ten Matilda infantry support tanks, but the only way to stop the enemy was to fire 25-pounder guns at them over open sights – at very short range. This was HE, for at that time the 25-pounders had no armour piercing ammunition and the 2-pounder anti-tank gun was absolutely useless.
>
> These Matildas were about 800 yards west of us, and our way out was along a track along the edge of the escarpment that runs from Sollum to the Halfaya Pass. But there was an enemy strongpoint there, from which they could not be ejected, and Bardia Bill, a big gun the Italians had at Bardia, was dropping shells on the track at this time. One amusing sight was a captured Italian truck with about 40 prisoners, which had sunk up to the rear axle in soft sand and was immovable. The Scots Guardsman driving it

jumped out and got away on another truck, but the Italian prisoners, after a heated discussion, also jumped out, heaved their truck free by sheer manpower, and drove furiously after him. We pointed out to them that in a few minutes they would have been back in their own lines, but they said, 'No thank you . . . we are your prisoners, and prisoners we are going to stay.'

Eventually we retired to Buq-Buq, where our brigade regrouped. Incidentally, in the fighting around Sollum our company – 90 strong – lost 58 men, killed, wounded or missing, and the battalion casualties totalled 173. Yet Richard Dimbleby, the BBC correspondent, described this action as 'increased patrol activity on the frontier'.[26]

The British Official History rightly calls BREVITY a failure;[27] it had failed either to relieve Tobruk or to destroy significant amounts of enemy equipment. Indeed, with their superior skills in tank recovery, the Germans soon recovered most of their own tanks and captured or destroyed many British tanks which had been knocked out or had run out of fuel and been abandoned by their crews. Churchill, however, seems to have been happy with BREVITY, telling Wavell that 'Without using the Tiger Cubs you have taken the offensive, advanced 30 miles, captured Halfaya and Sollum, taken 500 German prisoners and inflicted heavy losses in men and tanks. For this twenty "I" [infantry] tanks and 1,000 or 1,500 casualties do not seem to be at all too heavy a cost.' This eulogy concludes, however, with 'What are your dates for bringing Tiger Cubs into action?'

The British held the Halfaya Pass until 27 May, when Rommel sent three battle groups to push them away – at which Churchill's satisfaction promptly evaporated. With the British once again back across the wire, Rommel proceeded to fortify the Libyan frontier with more wire and minefields, covered by Pak-50s or 88-mm guns. That done, he sat down to build up his supply base, integrate the units of the 15th Panzer Division which started to arrive on 20 May, and await the next British assault, Operation BATTLEAXE.

BATTLEAXE had a firmly stated aim – 'The destruction of Rommel's forces and to achieve a decisive victory in North Africa' – and the launch of this offensive depended on how quickly the 7th Armoured Division could be re-equipped. The operation was an ambitious undertaking, but the attack might at least relieve the stout-hearted defenders of Tobruk, and orders to that effect were passed to the new commander of XIII Corps, Lieutenant-General Sir Noel Beresford-Peirse.

Beresford-Peirse had never commanded an armoured force before, and his three-phase plan lacked originality. Basically a rerun of BREVITY, it called for the capture of the frontier posts at the Halfaya Pass, Fort Capuzzo and Sollum in the first attack – an attack that must surely be expected and would fall on a strongly defended sector of the German line. The attack would be made by Major-General Frank Messervy's 4th Indian Division, with Matilda tanks of the 4th Armoured Brigade in support. The 7th Armoured Division, flush with Tiger Cubs, would then come forward, join with the 4th Armoured Brigade, and break through to Tobruk. Finally, with that much achieved, 7th Armoured, reinforced by the Tobruk garrison, would push on and secure a line between Derna and Mechili.

That was the plan, but there was a serious snag with it: the vital matter of reserves. Wavell's forces were now scattered all over his vast command, and his reserves were at best scanty. Rommel could reinforce his front at Halfaya and Capuzzo with the 15th Panzer Division and the Italians, but what could the British do to keep their attack moving in the event of success? General Creagh, now the 7th Armoured Division's commander, wrote later that 'The answer was difficult since it depended on which side could reinforce the quicker . . . the Germans could reinforce with their second armoured division from Tobruk, only eighty miles distant, while *as far as I knew* [my italics] we had no means of reinforcement at all.'

The 'as far as I knew' is revealing; the clear implication is that the British attack was a desperate gamble. If it failed, there were no reserves to bolster the front against a German counter-attack; if it succeeded there was no means to follow it up and ensure a German retreat.

Wavell estimated that Rommel had some 13,000 men and 100 tanks close to the frontier wire at Capuzzo, and another 25,000 men with another 130 tanks around Tobruk, 80 miles to the west. He therefore hoped to defeat Rommel's forces on the frontier before German reinforcements could arrive from Tobruk. The operation began on the night of 14/15 June 1941, the British advancing in three columns to Halfaya and the wire.

Wavell had overestimated Rommel's tank and anti-tank strength – if not the quality of his forces. The British had some 300 assorted tanks to Rommel's 200 – of which only about 100 were the gun-armed Panzer Mark IIIs and IVs. However, aided by information from his Good Source, Rommel had ample time to prepare for this attack and, following BREVITY, he had expected another British move to relieve Tobruk. He had therefore moved all his anti-tank guns forward to Halfaya; these included the 88-mms, against which even the thick armour of the Matilda tanks would prove totally inadequate.[28]

The attack on the Halfaya Pass began badly, soon after first light – the troops and tanks running directly into mines, machine-guns and anti-tank positions. The 4th RTR, supporting the 2nd Cameron Highlanders, found their tanks confronted by 88-mms with only their muzzles visible above stone-built sangars. The German artillery commander at Halfaya was a Captain (Haupt-mann) Bach, who, among his other considerable talents was a Protestant pastor – and 50 years old. Bach and his men stood to their guns – just five 88-mms and some Pak-50s – engaging the Matildas over open sights and blowing them to pieces.

The 'C' Squadron commander in 4th RTR, Major Miles, was last heard on the regimental wireless net reporting that the 88-mms were 'tearing my tanks apart'. Even so, the attack was pressed and the fight at Halfaya went on until about 1000 hours, when 'C' Squadron was down to one Matilda and one light tank. The Camerons were then forced to withdraw by infantry counter-attacks covered by machine-gun fire, and fell back down the pass with great loss.

Other squadrons of the 4th RTR continued to keep the enemy busy while the centre column, led by the 7th RTR, captured Fort Capuzzo, losing five tanks in the process. Meanwhile, the main force of the 7th Armoured Division was preparing to hook round the German southern flank, led by the 7th Armoured Brigade, which had been re-equipped with the new Crusaders. To keep the new tanks as a surprise, this column was led by the 2nd RTR in A9 and A10 cruisers. The first phase of this advance, to cap-ture the Hafid Ridge, went well, but prior reconnaissance had failed to reveal that the Hafid Ridge was actually three ridges, all prepared for defence.

The advance of the 2nd RTR secured only the first ridge at

Hafid; then the attack stalled while Rommel hurried more tank and anti-tank gun reinforcements forward from Tobruk. The Crusader tanks of 6th RTR were then engaged by Panzer Mark IIIs and Mark IVs – and seventeen Crusaders were quickly knocked out or broke down. The Crusaders displayed an alarming tendency to catch fire when hit, and by the end of the first day, 7th Armoured Division's tank strength had fallen by half. Rommel's forces were still largely intact and now rapidly increasing as the 5th Light Division came up from Tobruk.

On the second day of BATTLEAXE Creagh decided that the 7th Armoured Division advance should be renewed with another assault on the Hafid ridges, this time by the Matilda tanks of the 4th Armoured Brigade; these had been recalled from assisting the 4th Indian Division, since most of the Crusaders had broken down. The Support Group and the 7th Armoured Brigade would remain in reserve, either to reinforce the success of the 4th Brigade or to smash any attempt by Rommel to hook round behind the 4th Brigade near Sidi Omar.

Unfortunately for this plan, Rommel attacked first. The 15th Panzer Division counter-attacked around Capuzzo overnight, while the 5th Light Division made a hook around the British left with the aim of reaching the Halfaya Pass and cutting off both British divisions from either supply or escape down the escarpment. This move by 15th Panzer forced General Messervy, commanding 4th Indian Division, to tell General Creagh that he himself must retain the 4th Armoured Brigade to support his division at Capuzzo. BATTLEAXE was falling apart. The dawn attack on the Hafid ridges was therefore called off, but the 7th Armoured Brigade was heavily engaged by Rommel's 5th Light Division, and by nightfall it was down to just 25 tanks.

Two of the Royal Tank Regiments – the 2nd and the 6th, the latter with only nine of the new Crusader tanks still running – had been forced to fight separate engagements all day and were then driven back east of the wire to refuel and rearm. Rommel took the withdrawal of these two units as an indication that the left flank of the British advance was crumbling. That night, 16/17 May, he concentrated the 5th Light and 15th Panzer Divisions on his right flank and struck hard at the exposed left flank of the 7th Armoured Division. This attack went in at 0430 hours and made good progress – a process helped by some kinks in the British command system. Creagh had by now withdrawn his divisional HQ to Alam el Fakhri, 25 miles east of the wire and well behind his forward units. From there he contacted Beresford-Peirse on the radio, suggesting that the XIII Corps commander – who was even further back – should come up and look at the situation on the divisional front.

Their talk was intercepted by German listening posts. Rommel's diary records, 'It sounded suspiciously as if the British Commander no longer felt capable of handling the situation.' Thus encouraged, the 15th Panzer and 5th Light Divisions struck north, cutting through 7th Armoured Division's now extended lines and heading for the crux of the battle at the Halfaya Pass. The advance of these German divisions was checked for a while by the depleted Matilda squadrons of the 4th Armoured Brigade under Brigadier Alec Gatehouse, but the BATTLEAXE offensive had clearly failed. By dawn on 17 May the British were in full retreat, screened by the RAF, which flew constant sorties against the German formations, the bombers concentrating on the German columns while the RAF and South African Air Force fighters kept the German bombers and Stuka dive bombers away from the retreating British.

By mid-morning on 17 June 7th Armoured Division – or what was left of it – was back at Sofafi, 30 miles east of the wire, the position it had left three days before, and morale was not good. Fewer than 1,000 men were reported as killed, wounded or missing, but 91 tanks had been lost and nearly 80 per cent of the British tanks were out of action by the time the three-day operation ended. The RAF had lost 33 fighters and 3 bombers. German losses amounted to 93 killed and 585 wounded or missing; 12 tanks were lost and about 50 were disabled or broke down, all of which were eventually recovered. The Luftwaffe lost 10 aircraft.

Clearly, Rommel had out-guessed and out-fought the British, and had proved as adept in fighting on the defensive as in mounting attacks. The tactic of drawing the British tanks on to the anti-tank guns, notably the 88-mms, and then counter-attacking with his panzers had proved decisive during BATTLE-AXE, and would do so again in the future. The British Official History comments that 'it is doubtful if they (the British commanders) fully appreciated the German conception, which was that the primary use of tanks was to deal with the troops and soft-skinned transport and that the task of destroying the enemy's tanks was largely one for the anti-tank guns'.[29]

The British troops felt, with some reason, that their attack had not been well handled. The Germans always managed to appear in overwhelming strength, the 'new' Crusaders were clearly inadequate against the 88-mms and 75-mms, and Rommel had run rings around the British commanders. As the Royal Tank Regiment's history bitterly records, 'BATTLEAXE became a byword for blundering' – an accurate assessment of the entire operation, which should have led to a full inquiry and some improvements.

One of the problems was certainly the kit. The battle of quality versus quantity was clearly displayed during BATTLEAXE, and the British assault at Halfaya simply provided Matilda tanks as targets for the 88-mms. Rommel had only a dozen of these high-velocity guns, but they could shatter even a Matilda at 2,000 yards or more and after BATTLEAXE the desert soldiers were always wary of them. The Germans also had large numbers of the almost equally effective Pak-50s, a long-barrelled 50-mm anti-tank gun with excellent sights and a range of 1,000 yards or more. This superiority in the quality of weaponry, matched with the tactical deployment of anti-tank guns, was to be a feature of Afrika Korps actions throughout the desert war. In terms of numbers, however, the British forces exceeded Rommel's – and there are no reports at this stage, as there were later, that the British 2-pounder (40-mm) tank gun was in any way inferior in hitting power to the 50-mm mounted in the Panzer Mark III, although it was out-ranged by the 75-mm.

Churchill was bitterly disappointed at the failure of BATTLEAXE, and particularly by the loss of the tanks sent out on the 'Tiger' convoy. He was already discontented with General Wavell, whose taciturn temperament did not match that of the ever-optimistic Prime Minister. Studying the Ultra decrypts, counting up the number of British troops in Egypt, Churchill could not see why the Desert Army did not sweep Rommel back from the Egyptian frontier and out of Africa. He concluded that the fault lay with Wavell, and he therefore decided that the General must go. On 21 June 1941 General Sir Archibald Wavell was told that he was to be relieved of his command and sent to India, being replaced in North Africa by General Sir Claude Auchinleck, who was previously the Commander-in-Chief in India.

Given the continued run of defeats since Rommel's arrival in Africa, Wavell's dismissal was probably inevitable, but it would be unjust to blame him entirely for all the troubles of his command. Many factors – some of them created by Churchill, including those detailed in the previous pages – combined to make his task difficult and limited his operations in the Western Desert. Wavell simply had too much to do, and not enough to do it with. But this was war; Churchill also had his problems, and if his commanders did not deliver results they must expect to be poleaxed.

However, the change of commander in Cairo did not lead to the immediate attacks and sweeping victories that Churchill had expected. Five months were to pass after BATTLEAXE before the British attacked again. Meanwhile, away to the west, the garrison of Tobruk continued to hold out – still defiant, still full of fight.

Eighth Army

4

CRUSADER: The Battle for Sidi Rezegh
June–December 1941

The fighting about Tobruk and Sidi Rezegh, which began on 21st November and lasted with a few pauses for three days, was the fiercest yet seen in the desert. Round Sidi Rezegh airfield in particular, the fighting was unbelievably confused.

The Mediterranean and Middle East, vol. 3, p. 44

Between BATTLEAXE in June 1941 and the next British attack, Operation CRUSADER, in November, both sides received considerable reinforcements in men and *matériel*, though both experienced great difficulties with supply. Rommel's Italian lifeline, from Naples to the port of Tripoli, was open to harassment by the RAF and by submarines from Malta, both alerted to the supply convoys by Ultra. The British convoys had the choice of either forcing a passage through the Mediterranean from Gibraltar, under air attack the whole way, or taking the safer but longer haul round the Cape and up the East Coast of Africa to Suez. This battle, the battle for supply, was as vital a part of the struggle for North Africa as were the other campaigns fought in the Middle East in the middle of 1941.

Having evicted the British from Greece, the Germans followed this up with an airborne assault on Crete which began on

20 May. This ended with an evacuation on 1 June and cost the Australian, British and New Zealand forces some 15,000 men; German losses came to around 7,000 – most of them in the airborne forces. The concurrent Rashid Ali revolt in Iraq went on until British forces took over the country and a new Iraqi government was formed on 4 June. Four days later, following Ultra reports that Luftwaffe units were using bases in Syria to mine the Suez Canal, British and Free French forces invaded Syria.

The invasion force, commanded by General Sir Henry Maitland Wilson, included the 7th Australian Division, a brigade of the 4th Indian Division, and some commando troops from Layforce, the commando brigade under Brigadier Robert Laycock now deployed to the Middle East. The Vichy forces resisted strongly, and the fighting in Syria went on until mid-July, when the French commander asked for an armistice. British losses in Syria amounted to another 3,300 men.

These subsidiary campaigns greatly increased the strain on resources, but on the whole the British did rather better than the enemy in the build-up phase from January to July 1941, their equipment increasing in quantity if not in quality. They also received another three infantry divisions and another ten armoured regiments, reinforcements totalling another 115,000 men, though none of these was desert-trained or fit for immediate operations. These units included the 50th (Northumbrian) Division, the headquarters of what would become X Corps, the rest of the New Zealand Division and the 7th Australian Division, the completion of the 9th Australian Division, and part of the 2nd South African Division. The only problem with this build-up was that it increased the demands of Prime Minister Winston Churchill for an offensive, and led, as we have seen, to General Sir Claude Auchinleck replacing Wavell on 5 July. This pressure to attack now began to fall on the new commander, Auchinleck, who, to Churchill's annoyance, was equally determined not to put in another attack on Rommel's forces until he was ready to do so.

Auchinleck was a soldier's soldier, brave, competent, astute – but unlucky. Those who write on the desert war are unfailingly favourable in their accounts of Auchinleck's period in command – and correspondingly harsh in their judgement of his successor at Eighth Army, Bernard Montgomery. There are good reasons for such favourable opinions, and assessments of

Auchinleck by Correlli Barnett and others must command respect; many of the problems that beset Auchinleck were beyond his capacity to remedy, and he was unlucky in lacking sound commanders who should have provided him with the support he needed in the field. That said, Auchinleck made some unfortunate choices in selecting field commanders, and was eventually obliged to take the field command himself.

Claude Auchinleck was born in 1884, the son of a colonel in the Royal Artillery. At Sandhurst he qualified for the Indian Army, which took the cream of the crop, and was sent to the 62nd Punjab Regiment on the North-West Frontier. On the outbreak of the First World War, Auchinleck's battalion was sent to Egypt. There it became involved in early skirmishes with the Turks, before joining the expedition up the Tigris to Baghdad, where fierce fighting and disease quickly reduced the 62nd Punjabis to just 247 men. When the colonel was wounded, Auchinleck took command of the battalion, and he spent the rest of the Great War in Mesopotamia.

During the inter-war years Auchinleck's career followed the usual Army pattern, appointments to the staff alternating with periods of field duty, notably in command of the Peshawar Brigade during the Mohmand campaign on the frontier in 1935. Auchinleck then became Deputy Chief of the General Staff, India, a job that was mainly concerned with the replacement of British officers with Indian officers as a step towards eventual self-rule and independence. On the outbreak of war in 1939 Auchinleck, now a major-general, was given command of the 3rd Indian Division, but in January 1940 he was posted back to the UK and given command of IV Corps, which was then in training. This appointment did not last long and Auchinleck was then sent to command British troops at Narvik during the Norway campaign, staying there until the troops were evacuated in early June 1940.

On returning to England Auchinleck was first given command of V Corps and then promoted lieutenant-general and appointed GOC, Southern Command. V Corps, which formed part of Southern Command, was commanded by Lieutenant-General Bernard Montgomery, and the two men never got on, disagreeing on many aspects of command, training and policy. These disputes ended when Auchinleck was promoted full general and sent to

India as commander-in-chief, where one of his first tasks was to
send a force to Iraq to crush Rashid Ali. Now he was in Egypt,
facing another 'soldier's soldier' – Erwin Rommel.

In May 1941 Rommel received two more units, the 15th Panzer
Division and the 90th Light Division, both short of armour and
transport. Constant pleas for more 88-mm guns raised Rommel's
total to just 35 by the opening of the CRUSADER operation, but most
of his anti-tank units now had the Pak-50, itself no mean weapon
in trained hands. By September 1941 Rommel had 158 anti-tank
guns, of which 98 were Pak-50s.[1] The battle-hardened 5th Light
Division received more Mark III panzers and changed its name
to 21st Panzer Division.

With that and the arrival of three Italian divisions, Rommel
had to be content, his total forces – now named Panzerarmee
Afrika – peaking at three German and five Italian divisions. From
July 1941 Panzerarmee Afrika consisted of the Afrika Korps – the
15th and 21st Panzer Divisions – under General Ludwig Crüwell,
the 90th Light Division, the Italian Savona Division and the
Italian XXI Corps of four divisions – Trento, Bologna, Brescia and
Pavia. Two more Italian divisions, the armoured Ariete and the
motorized Trieste, were in command reserve.

Unlike many British soldiers and commanders, Rommel did
not despise his Italian troops. His dispatches record that they
always did more than he asked of them, and he always gave due
credit to the courage and tenacity of the Italian private soldier.
The Italians had many good units, most notably the armoured
and artillery regiments, and could fight well on the defensive;
the problem lay with the officers, who often failed to provide
their soldiers with the necessary leadership and support.

Panzerarmee Afrika was a decent-sized force, but Rommel's
lengthy supply lines were a constant problem. The smaller ports
in Axis hands, Buerat and Sirte, were not adequate and were
under regular bombardment by the RAF and the Royal Navy,
while the overland distance from the large facilities of Tripoli to
Tobruk was over 1,000 miles – plus another 100 miles to the frontier wire. The petrol consumed in simply getting supplies,
including fuel, to the forward units was a considerable drain on
Rommel's slender resources. It therefore seemed to his superiors
in Rome and in the German High Command (the OKW) that
Rommel had already gone too far east and was courting disaster

if, or rather when, the British attacked. On 27 April the OKW sent General Friedrich von Paulus to Rommel's HQ in an effort, according to General Franz Halder, the Chief of the General Staff, 'to head off this soldier gone stark mad'.[2]

Paulus was charged with making an assessment of the entire North African situation and finding out exactly what Rommel intended to do. He was also to impress on Rommel that, with the Russian campaign looming, the OKW had very few troops, tanks or supplies to send him. Paulus duly carried out these instructions and reported to OKW that all ideas of advancing to the Delta had been abandoned. Rommel's present intention, said Paulus, was to take Tobruk and then take up a defensive position in Cyrenaica on the line Siwa–Sollum and defeat the British when they came forward again. Taking Tobruk was clearly going to be difficult. The defences were getting stronger all the time, and could he afford to ignore the build-up of British forces in Egypt as forces flowed in from Britain and the Empire?

By the summer of 1941 the Desert Army had become a very cosmopolitan force. Apart from the various nations and regions of Britain, it now contained soldiers from Australia, France, India, Poland, South Africa and New Zealand – all marked by the desert, all retaining their individual style. After he had taken over Eighth Army, Montgomery, himself given to casual dress, was to say that he did not much care what his soldiers wore as long as they could soldier, which may have been an acceptance of the inevitable: new uniforms were in short supply, the days were hot and the nights cold, and men dressed as best they could to cope with these extreme conditions.[3]

The soldiers of the Desert Army – most notably the British soldiers and their officers, especially the cavalry officers – had by now evolved their own style of dress: a mixture of battledress, khaki drill and civilian clothing. The officers tended to sport fly-whisks and moustaches and to wear corduroy trousers and civilian shirts, set off with Paisley silk scarves. In 1941 Captain Clay, an Old Etonian officer in the 2nd Royal Gloucestershire Hussars, was captured by the Italians wearing 'no badges of rank, but a golf jacket, a pink shirt into which was tucked a yellow silk scarf, a pair of green corduroy trousers and an expensive pair of suede boots'. The Italian reaction to this colourful apparition is not recorded.

Bizarre though it may sound, much of this dress was sensible. Battledress soaked up sand, which scratched at the neck and wrists and created desert sores. Tropical kit – khaki drill, or KD – was not warm enough for the desert nights. As a rule, the commanders did not care how the men dressed, provided their equipment functioned and their weapons were clean. This popular desert attire was eventually recognized, if not officially, then tacitly by the Army at large, through a popular series of cartoons by Jon, featuring 'The Two Types' – a pair of languid army officers dressed much like Captain Clay. This attire may have raised eyebrows among the more regimental arrivals, but they were usually quick to adopt it.

Apart from colourful dress, the Desert Army tolerated a number of colourful characters. Among these was Admiral Sir Walter Cowan, KCB, DSO and bar, who had first come to the Middle East as a young naval lieutenant commanding a Nile gunboat during Kitchener's advance to Khartoum. He earned his first DSO during the subsequent battle against the dervishes at Omdurman in September 1898. In August 1941 the Italians captured this elderly gentleman – now aged seventy-four – in the open desert while he was engaging their oncoming tanks with his service revolver. A few days later they returned him to the British lines with a polite note judging him 'of no further use to the British war effort'.

The Italians could not have been more wrong. Sir Walter promptly attached himself to No. 8 Commando in Layforce, the commando brigade that had recently arrived in the Middle East, and took part in a number of raids along the North African shore. Major Milton of No. 7 Commando recalls the Admiral taking part on a raid on Bardia in April 1941:

> We were accompanied on this raid by Admiral Cowan, a real fire-eater about 5 foot 3 inches tall. He was a friend of Sir Roger Keyes, and with Lieutenant Evelyn Waugh – the novelist, then an officer in 8 Commando – had embarked for the raid in my LCA [landing craft, assault]. When we arrived off the port and went to boat stations on the *Glengyle*, it was quite rough. In those days the first assault wave climbed into the LCAs in the davits at deck level and were then lowered into the water. For some reason on this occasion our bow davit lowered quicker than the stern davit and we hit the water bows first, smashed into the side of *Glengyle*, and

damaged our starboard engine. Therefore, though supposedly the lead craft, we limped ashore slowly on one engine.

About 100 yards from the shore we ran on to a sandbar and Admiral Cowan ordered our coxwain, Sub-Lieutenant England, 'to lower the door'. He complied, and the Admiral and Lieutenant Waugh dashed out – and promptly disappeared under the water. Relieved of their weight, the LCA lifted over the sandbank and the rest of us made a dry landing on the beach.[4]

When the North African campaign was over, Admiral Cowan departed to the Adriatic and the war with the Yugoslav partisans with the 2nd Commando Brigade, winning a second DSO there, more than forty years after the first one, and remaining in (largely unofficial) service until the end of the war.

New tanks, armoured cars and guns were now arriving in the Delta. The 'Valentine' was a slight improvement on the A10 cruiser, though armed only with the inadequate 2-pounder gun, while the 4th Armoured Brigade was re-equipped with the fast American 'General Stuart' tank, known to the British as the 'Honey'. The Honey had a good turn of speed – 36 m.p.h. on roads, and perhaps half that on the desert – and a high-velocity 37-mm gun. Another reinforcement for the 7th Armoured Division was the Territorial 22nd Armoured Brigade, which consisted of the 3rd and 4th County of London Yeomanry (CLY) and the 2nd Royal Gloucestershire Hussars, all three regiments being equipped with the fast but unreliable Crusader tank.

The 11th Hussars were re-equipped with Humber armoured cars and were joined in the 7th Armoured Division by the King's Dragoon Guards and the 4th South African Armoured Car Regiment, so providing each armoured brigade with a reconnaissance unit. The British also received a number of 3.7-inch anti-aircraft guns – a weapon which, had it been supplied with armour-piercing ammunition, might have proved as devastating an anti-tank weapon as the dual-purpose German 88-mm. In addition, the British could now put 700 aircraft into the air, compared with the combined German and Italian total of 320. With all the advantages seemingly lying with the British and revealed to him by Ultra, Churchill was naturally insistent that Auchinleck should attack soon, not least because the Wehrmacht had launched Operation BARBAROSSA – the invasion of Russia – in June 1941 and was already making great advances. If only to aid the Russians by forcing the Germans to divert men and *matériel* to Rommel, Auchinleck must attack.

Auchinleck refused. He explained patiently and many times that tanks had to be prepared for desert conditions and that troops must be carefully trained in desert warfare before either were of any use in the field; neither could come off the ship and go straight into battle. This attitude, while eminently correct, did not find favour in Downing Street. Churchill had replaced Wavell for failing to attack, and now here was Auchinleck with the same story. It does not seem to have occurred to the Prime Minister that, if two intelligent and well-regarded generals reached the same conclusion, there might be some merit in what they said.

Auchinleck's eventual autumn offensive, code-named CRU-SADER, had two aims. First, to trap and destroy the enemy forces in eastern Cyrenaica. Second, to occupy Tripolitania and drive the enemy out of Africa. These moves would also ensure the relief of Tobruk. The forces tasked to do all this were now commanded by Lieutenant-General Sir Alan Cunningham – a brother of Admiral Sir Andrew Cunningham, who commanded the Mediterranean Fleet.

Lieutenant-General Sir Alan Cunningham is one of the tragic figures of the desert war. He was appointed to command XIII Corps on the basis of the reputation he had recently gained in his campaign against the Italians in East Africa, where he marched out of Kenya with four infantry brigades and shattered the Italians at the Juba river. That done, he kept going and captured Mogadishu, the capital of Italian Somaliland. He then decided to march into Abyssinia – another 750 miles – driving the Italians before him, and on 6 April 1941 his forces paraded triumphantly into Addis Ababa. Two months later Cunningham placed Haile Selassie, the Emperor of Abyssinia, back on his throne.

So, when the time came to find a new commander for XIII Corps, Alan Cunningham, the man of the hour, was the obvious choice. In August he arrived in the desert to take command of a force which on 18 September 1941, finally became Eighth Army.

Cunningham was aware of the task before him: 'I arrived in August,' he wrote, 'and was told that there would be an offensive in November. I therefore had two months only in which to form and train an army. Some of the divisions were not there.

Apart from 4th Indian Division and 7th Armoured Division, most of the troops were quite untrained. Time was so short. That was my trouble.'[5]

That was not his only trouble. The real problem was that Cunningham was faced with a much larger task than anything he had encountered before. He had commanded a strong division of four brigades; now he must form and command a full army, made up of divisions from many nations. He had fought the Italians; now he must fight the Germans – an entirely different proposition. He had commanded infantry in the mountains; now he must command armoured forces in the desert. Cunningham's character – open, outgoing, vigorous – was ideal for the task. The problem lay in his experience and his professional ability.

Perhaps the quotation given above also reveals a character defect, a tendency to pessimism, for the situation confronting Cunningham in the Western Desert was nowhere near as black as he paints it. Most of the divisions for Eighth Army were already in the desert or the Delta, training hard, and the troops were of superb quality. Certainly he had to form an army, but equipment – somewhat better equipment than hitherto – was arriving in quantity, and he had adequate air cover. Compared with the situation that O'Connor and Neame had faced in the previous year, Cunningham had much to be thankful for – and yet he seemed uncertain.

The Eighth Army consisted of two Corps; XIII Corps, under Lieutenant-General Alfred Godwin-Austen, and the new XXX Corps, under Lieutenant-General C. W. M Norrie. It was unfortunate that, like Cunningham, neither of these corps commanders had any desert experience – Goodwin-Austen had previously served in East Africa, and Norrie had just come out from the UK. Since it was recognized that the desert presented unique problems that called for a great deal of training and experience, it might have been better to promote some of the tried and tested divisional commanders to Corps command – Morshead and Bernard Freyberg, of the 2nd New Zealand Division, come to mind – rather than bring out senior officers from the UK or from theatres with different conditions.

In XXX Corps for CRUSADER were the 7th Armoured Division (under Major-General Gott), with the 7th, 4th and 22nd

Armoured Brigades, and the 1st South African Division (under Major-General G. L. Brink), with two brigades. The South African Division was to protect the communications of 7th Armoured and later to attack the Sidi Rezegh ridge. There was also the 22nd Guards Brigade, charged with protecting the supply dumps and landing grounds around Gabr Saleh.

In XIII Corps were the 4th Indian Division of three brigades under Major-General Messervy, the 2nd New Zealand Division – three brigades under Major-General Bernard Freyberg – and the 1st Army Tank Brigade. This corps was to cut off the German troops on the frontier and then push west towards Tobruk. To back up these desert formations, other units were training in the Delta or resting in Palestine and Syria. These included the 2nd South African Division in Eighth Army reserve and the 9th Australian Division.

The 'Rats of Tobruk' – the 9th Australian Division and the 18th Brigade of the 7th Division – had gradually been withdrawn from Tobruk in August and September, the last units leaving in October. After a well-earned rest in the Delta, the 9th was sent on garrison duties to Syria; they would remain there until the next setback in the desert caused the commanders to send for them again. Only one battalion of the 9th Division, the 2/13th, had remained in Tobruk throughout the siege. The other Australian divisions, the 6th and 7th, had been returned to Australia after Japan entered the war in December 1941, but the 9th Australian Division was to make its mark again in the desert war, at Alamein. With the evacuation of the 9th Australian Division, the Tobruk garrison now consisted of the 70th Division, the Polish Carpathian Brigade and the 32nd Army Tank Brigade, which together formed 'Tobforce'. The CRUSADER task for Tobforce – commanded by Major-General R. M. Scobie – was to make a sortie from Tobruk when ordered to do so.

The final element, far out in the desert, was Oasis Force, a detachment of infantry, armour and artillery tasked to secure Jarabub at the southern end of the wire fence, protect the forward landing field No. 125, and take the Jalo oasis.

The main part of CRUSADER required XIII Corps to attack and pin down the enemy along the frontier wire, from the Halfaya Pass to Sidi Omar, while XXX Corps, with the nine armoured regiments of the 7th Armoured Division as its cutting edge, would hook around the desert flank and destroy the German armour before relieving Tobruk, from which the garrison would foray to meet them, aiming to reach El Duda as XIII Corps arrived. In the first phase of the attack the main task of 7th Armoured was to capture the airfields at Sidi Rezegh and El Adem on the escarpment above Tobruk. There was no particular originality in this plan; it depended mainly on the application of superior force – which the British appeared to have. By the end of October, Cunningham had 770 tanks – 170 of them Matildas – 600 field guns, 200 anti-tank guns, 900 mortars and 240 anti-aircraft guns of various calibre.[6] But Auchinleck was still not happy with Eighth Army's kit, and he was right to express doubts: he only had one armoured division and he needed two, and his equipment was still inferior to that of the enemy.

Nevertheless, one fact was recognized and stressed: the need to keep this armour concentrated. In his orders for CRUSADER Auchinleck stated: 'It is essential to concentrate the strongest possible armoured force. Any subsidiary movement which might require detachment of tanks, other than I tanks, for local protection against possible attack by enemy armoured units must be foregone in the interests of ensuring the strongest possible concentration of fast armoured units for the decisive battle.' It could hardly be clearer: the infantry must rely on their own anti-tank weapons and the support of the slow Matilda infantry tanks, while the armoured units were kept together to take on the German and Italian armoured divisions – and by so doing prevent them from ranging at will among Eighth Army's infantry.

At the start of CRUSADER the available British tank forces outnumbered the Germans and Italians by a ratio of nine to four: an inferiority in quality was balanced by a superiority in numbers. Even if only gun-armed German panzers are taken into account, the British had a superiority of four to one. But unfortunately the Germans also had superior tactics – and Erwin Rommel. One of the ironic post-BATTLEAXE jokes going round Eighth Army at this time was that Hitler had telephoned Churchill, offering to remove Rommel from his command – provided Churchill left all the British generals in place. Rommel was highly thought of on both sides of the wire – so much so that, before CRUSADER began, General Auchinleck thought it necessary to issue a Special Order to his commanders on the subject of the enemy general:

To: All Commanders and Chief of Staff
From: Headquarters, BTE [British Troops, Egypt] and MEF [Middle East Forces]
There exists a real danger that our friend Rommel is becoming a kind of magician or bogey-man to our troops, who are talking far too much about him. He is by no means a superman, although he is undoubtedly very energetic and able. Even if he were a superman, it would still be highly undesirable that our men should credit him with supernatural powers.

I wish you to dispel by all possible means the idea that Rommel represents something more than an ordinary German general. The important thing now is to see to it that we do not always talk of 'Rommel' when we mean the enemy in Libya. We must refer to 'the Germans' or 'the Axis powers' or 'the enemy' and not always keep harping on Rommel.

Please ensure that this order is put into immediate effect and impress upon all Commanders that, from a psychological point of view, it is a matter of the highest importance.

C. J. Auchinleck
General
Comm-in-Chief, MEF

The effects of this order are not recorded, but it is unlikely that the troops paid any attention to it; Rommel was the best general in North Africa, and everyone knew it. The only way to knock him of his pedestal was to defeat him in battle – and everyone knew that as well.

The CRUSADER offensive duly began on 18 November 1941, when Eighth Army began to roll east, one solid, impressive mass of infantry and armour, apparently unstoppable. Then, a few hours into the advance, this army began to break up into its component parts: first into corps, then into divisions, and finally into brigades – and the basis for all the future problems of CRUSADER had been laid. This point was made clear by Brigadier Howard Kippenberger of the 2nd New Zealand Division:

The great approach march will always be remembered by those who took part in it though the details are vague in memory. The whole Eighth Army, 7th Armoured Division, 1st South African Division and the 2nd New Zealand and 4th Indian Divisions moved westward in an enormous column, the armour leading. The Army moved south of Sidi Barrani, past the desolate Italian

camps of the previous year, along the plateau south of the great
escarpment, south of the frontier wire into Libya, south of the
enemy garrisons in the Sidi Omars, and wheeled north. Then, just
as we were rejoicing in the conception of a massive move on
Tobruk, disregarding the frontier garrisons and crushing everything in our path, the whole Army broke up and departed in different ways.[7]

General Messervy's 4th Indian Division of XIII Corps began the
assault, attacking across the wire north of Sidi Omar, while the
three tank brigades of 7th Armoured hooked north-west, around
the southern flank, intending to await the inevitable German
counter attack at Gabr Saleh, east of Bir el Gubi. This British attack
pre-empted the assault Rommel intended to make on Tobruk on
23 November, and for a while Rommel chose to regard this British
thrust as a feint. Even so, this move towards Tobruk gave him one
great advantage: when he finally decided to engage Eighth Army,
the 15th Panzer Division and the 90th Light Division were in just
the right position to thwart the British attack.

On the XXX Corps front, 7th Armoured's advance was made
in heavy rain and by brigade column. On the first day the
advance went well, the tanks refuelling and rearming at two
field maintenance centres, Nos. 63 and 65, which had been established west of the wire, south-east of Gabr Saleh. Then, with no
enemy tanks appearing, the three armoured brigades were sent
to find them. The 22nd Armoured Brigade, on the left, was the
first to engage the enemy, meeting the Italian Ariete Division
around Bir el Gubi, putting in a spirited attack – and promptly
losing 40 tanks before the enemy's dug-in anti-tank guns. The
heaviest losses fell to the 2nd Royal Gloucestershire Hussars,
whose tank strength fell to just 19, their Crusader tanks showing
an unfortunate tendency to catch fire when hit. Here again,
superior tactics paid off: when attacked, the Axis tank forces
simply fell back slowly, luring the British on to a screen of dug-
in guns.

The 7th Armoured Brigade, in the centre column, overran the
airfield at Sidi Rezegh, the 6th RTR destroying a number of
German aircraft. Then matters started to go awry. By the time the
7th Brigade moved up to the escarpment overlooking the plain
before Tobruk – on which stood the tomb of the Muslim saint
Sidi Rezegh – the enemy had brought up infantry and anti-tank

guns to bar the only track and greeted the British tanks with 88-mm shells.

Meanwhile the 4th Armoured Brigade, the right-flank column, which was protecting the inner flanks of both corps, was advancing north towards the Trigh Capuzzo, where it was attacked by a German panzer battle group, Battle Group Stephan, a force of 100 tanks formed from 21st Panzer Division and supported by infantry.

All three brigades of 7th Armoured were in action, but were widely separated when these strong German counter-attacks came in on 20 November. This last attack, on 4th Armoured Brigade, should have been anticipated, for at 1100 hours on 20 November Norrie was informed that two panzer divisions were about to fall on 7th Armoured. This intelligence was more interesting than useful, for Norrie now had no means to stem this powerful attack – his division had split into widely separated brigade columns, which were about to be shattered one by one.

The right-flank column, the 4th Armoured Brigade, had been in action almost from the start. This brigade had the dual task of protecting the flanks of the centre column (the 7th Armoured Brigade) and that of XIII Corps as it advanced further north. The 8th Hussars were attacked by Battle Group Stephan and lost 20 tanks before dark, knocking out only three on the German side, and this was only the first of several attacks that were to come in against the scattered brigades of the 7th Armoured Division. On 20 November – Cambrai Day, the anniversary of the Tank Corps's first great battle in 1917 – the enemy counter-attacked at Sidi Rezegh airfield. A confusing tank and anti-tank gun battle then developed, the 7th Brigade hanging on to the airfield with great difficulty until the Divisional Support Group, commanded by Brigadier Jock Campbell, came up that evening. By this time the great armoured battle of Sidi Rezegh was well under way.

The airfield and the dominating El Duda and Belhammed ridges were the vital area in the long fight for Sidi Rezegh. For the British, holding this area would give access to the garrison of Tobruk. For the Germans, this area was the choke-point on the roads up to the frontier; unless it could be held, their units at Halfaya and Sollum would be cut off.

The battle around the airfield at Sidi Rezegh grew in ferocity throughout 20 November. The whole weight of the 15th Panzer

Division fell on the left of the 4th Armoured Brigade, which by sunset was down to just 98 tanks. The Germans had lost just seven tanks in the last two days, their recovery teams finding and repairing many damaged or broken-down tanks each night. The 7th Armoured Brigade and Campbell's Support Group still held the airfield, but the Germans were mustering quantities of tanks and anti-tank guns to the west of the airfield and preparing to renew the fight at first light on 21 November.

This fight for the Sidi Rezegh airfield and the ridge north of the airfield would decide the outcome of the battle, because whoever held the ridge at Sidi Rezegh controlled the Trigh Capuzzo track – and so dominated the plain before Tobruk. The 1st KRRC and the 6th Field Regiment Royal Artillery, with 25-pounder field guns, took up position just south of the airfield and were in action for most of the day. At midday on the 21st, General Cunningham instructed the 22nd Armoured Brigade to turn east from Bir el Gubi and help the embattled 4th Armoured Brigade, which had returned to refuel and re-arm near Gabr Saleh. This help came too late; 22nd Armoured Brigade was short of fuel and could not reach the 4th Brigade position, south of Sidi Rezegh, until nightfall.

Rommel had now realized that CRUSADER was not simply an attempt to relieve Tobruk but an all-out attack with the aim of driving him out of Cyrenaica. He therefore decided to delay his assault on Tobruk and drive a wedge between the two British corps, striking at their junction around Sidi Rezegh. Therefore, disengaging from the battered 4th and 22nd Armoured Brigades at dawn on 21 November, the 15th and 21st Panzer Divisions were sent to attack the Support Group and the 7th Armoured Brigade, which still held the airfield.

This British force was preparing to assault the German forces on the ridge north of the airfield when two panzer divisions fell on their rear and a whirling tank and infantry battle then broke out around the airfield and the ridge. The 7th Hussars were overrun and almost wiped out by 21st Panzer, while the anti-tank guns of 15th Panzer eliminated the tanks of the 2nd RTR, which were attempting to protect the soft-skinned transport of the Support Group and the 7th Armoured Brigade. When the 1st KRRC, supported by a company of the 2nd Rifle Brigade and the 6th RTR and artillery, attacked the Sidi Rezegh ridge, they suffered severely from machine-gun and anti-tank fire. The 2nd Rifle Brigade and the 6th RTR took a terrible beating at Sidi Rezegh, but they also took the ridge – though the German tanks were able to destroy a great deal of transport and equipment on the airfield before the 22nd Armoured and 4th Armoured Brigades, hurrying up from the south, were able to intervene and drive the panzers away.

The 1st KRRC was on the ridge by noon, and British artillery then began to engage enemy traffic along the Trigh Capuzzo. Unfortunately, Lieutenant-Colonel de Salis, CO of the KRRC, lacked the men to hold all of the ridge and had to concentrate around the only high point, Point 167, where the battalion hung on as German tanks and infantry reoccupied the rest of the escarpment. In this action, Rifleman Beeley of the KRRC won a posthumous Victoria Cross attacking an enemy position.

All mobile battles tend to be confusing, but the battle at Sidi Rezegh was more confusing than most – not least because the situation remained fluid.[8] The battle at Sidi Rezegh was actually a series of separate encounters, with little co-ordination; units simply engaged the enemy to their front or flank and fought on until they ran out of ammunition, when they either pulled back to find more or were overrun. There was fighting all over the Sidi Rezegh area this day, but the man in the thick of it was Brigadier Jock Campbell of 7th Armoured's Support Group, whose exploits appear in many accounts.

The full weight of the two Afrika Korps armoured divisions was now concentrated on the 7th Armoured Brigade and the Support Group, mustered to the south of the airfield. Fifty German tanks attacked the 7th Hussars and some 2nd Rifle Brigade companies, their attack being preceded by artillery fire and Stuka dive-bombers. During this engagement Lieutenant Ward Gunn of the 3rd RHA fought his battery to the last round, with the battery commander, Major Pinney, and the battery NCO, Sergeant Grey, acting as loaders; for this action Lieutenant Gunn was awarded a posthumous Victoria Cross.

By 1600 hours on 21 November 7th Armoured Brigade could muster only 40 tanks. The weight of the battle therefore fell on the Support Group and scattered elements of various regiments and battalions, constantly mustered and remustered by Brigadier Campbell, who led his men back into the attack again and again, standing up in his staff car and waving them on.

By dawn on 22 November the various units of the 7th Armoured Division were deployed as follows. The division's Support Group was holding the airfield, with some tanks of the 6th RTR to the north, east and west. Two miles to the south lay the remaining 79 Crusader tanks of the 22nd Armoured Brigade. The 4th Armoured Brigade lay 6 miles further to the south-east, near Bir el Reghem. Nothing was left of the 7th Armoured Brigade except 12 tanks of the 2nd RTR and 9 tanks of the 7th Hussars, all of which were under the control of Brigadier Campbell's group on the airfield. All these tanks were very short of ammunition and fuel.

During the night of 21/22 November the German forces withdrew to the north-west, to reorganize and replenish their petrol and ammunition before another thrust against the airfield. As dawn broke on 22 November the Support Group could see a large group of enemy vehicles, including about 80 tanks – Panzer Mark IIIs and IVs – mustering to the north. These tanks were engaged by the 25-pounders of the 60th Field Regiment RA, urged on by Brigadier Campbell. The enemy were then attacked by the 12 remaining tanks of the 2nd RTR – an attack led, yet again, by Brigadier Campbell in his staff car, 'waving flags and encouraging the tanks on'.

The enemy met this assault with heavy fire and brought it to a halt – and no sooner had the British withdrawn than heavy firing broke out all around the airfield. Enemy tanks had come up from the west and were engaging the Support Group while German infantry attacked from the escarpment to the north. This assault took the Support Group by surprise, and it took strenuous efforts to stave off the German advance. At one point during this engagement Brigadier Campbell was seen alone 'loading and firing an anti-tank gun at the advancing enemy, with the crew dead or wounded around the gun'. For his gallantry and leadership day after day in the battle at Sidi Rezegh, Brigadier Campbell was later awarded the Victoria Cross. Few men ever did more to earn it.

The fight between the Support Group and the tanks of the 21st Panzer Division spread across the airfield and the ridges north and south. Sidi Rezegh was now a litter of burning aircraft, knocked-out tanks, shattered guns, and dead or wounded infantry – British, South African, German and Italian. The smoke and dust of battle concealed events from the 22nd Armoured

Brigade, which, with what remained of the 4th Armoured Brigade, was now ordered to assist the Support Group. Their attack came in against a screen of German anti-tank guns and, in spite of Brigadier Campbell's efforts to sort matters out, confusion reigned as lone tanks and small groups of men roamed about in the smoke and dust, seeking to engage the enemy or locate their own units.

The failure of British tank tactics was fully exposed by these actions at Sidi Rezegh. Numbers and gallantry were of no avail if the tactics were faulty, and the tactics employed at Sidi Rezegh were very faulty indeed. As Rommel remarked later to a captive British officer, 'What difference does it make to me if you have two tanks to my one, if you send them out and let me smash them in detail? You presented me with three brigades in succession.'

This view is confirmed by another German officer, Major-General F. W. von Mellenthin; when writing of the CRUSADER offensive and the struggle at Sidi Rezegh, he says:

> The commander of the 7th Armoured Brigade decided to leave the 6th RTR with the Support Group on Sidi Rezegh airfield and took the 7th Hussars and the 2nd RTR to meet the advancing Panzer divisions. This was typical of British tactics at this time – their commanders would not concentrate their tanks and guns for a co-ordinated battle. In a short while most of the tanks of 7th Hussars were on fire and 15th and 21st Panzer had reached the high ground overlooking the airfield from the south. The Afrika Korps then attempted to overrun the airfield by launching attacks from the south-east. These attacks failed owing to the magnificent resistance of the 7th Support Group and 6th RTR commanded by Brigadier Campbell. The British Artillery was the best trained and best commanded element in the British Army and the quality of these gunners was fully proved in the desperate fighting at Sidi Rezegh on 21 November.

On the late afternoon of 22 November some order was at last restored to the British units around Sidi Rezegh. The remnants of the three armoured brigades and the Support Group gradually withdrew to a ridge south of the airfield which some elements of the 22nd Armoured Brigade had occupied that morning, and at about 1700 hours two regiments, the 3rd and 5th RTR, were ordered back to the airfield to cover the removal of the

25-pounder field guns, which were being threatened by enemy infantry advancing from the edge of the escarpment.

The diary of the 5th RTR states that this effort 'proved futile'. Their light Honey tanks were outgunned by the German panzers, and while they were away from the southern ridge the 4th Armoured Brigade endured a further blow when 15th Panzer came up and struck its rear, scattering the 8th Hussars and killing most of the staff of Brigade HQ. After an hour of intense fighting the 8th Hussars were left with just 8 Honeys fit to fight, the Germans having destroyed no fewer than 35 tanks in this sudden onslaught. Those remaining were withdrawn into a close, protective leaguer which was then attacked by German tanks and infantry.

While the 7th Armoured Division was hotly engaged at Sidi Rezegh, the other units of Eighth Army had not been idle. Tobforce was now on the move. Its task during CRUSADER was to break out 'when ordered to do so' and join with XIII Corps for the push west. Its breakout from Tobruk began on the night of 20/21 November, when gaps were cut in the wire and the minefields and the advance towards El Duda began. The way had to be forced through the German lines and a series of fortified positions, one of which, the Tiger position, was the objective of the 2nd Battalion, The Black Watch. Unknown to the Scots, the Tiger position was defended not by Italians, but by a German machine-gun battalion, supported by mortars and artillery.

The advancing battalion was therefore greeted by intense machine-gun fire and driven to ground – the accounts describe the fire as 'a hailstorm of lead', and the men crouched under it, seeking what cover they could on the open ground, until they were rallied and brought to their feet by one of the company officers – some accounts say the battalion adjutant – who rose to his feet among the bouncing tracer and cried out to his soldiers, 'Isn't this the Black Watch? Then come on . . .'

What got the soldiers to their feet that night was something elemental – regimental pride. The Highlanders rose among the confusion and carried the enemy position at the point of the bayonet, played on to the objective by their regimental pipers. Pipe Major Roy continued to play and was wounded three times before he fell, when Pipe Sergeant Mc'Nicol went forward with the attack. One officer of the battalion records that he 'heard the pipes playing "Highland Laddie" as I lay in the enemy's JILL position, and that was what got me up and got us advancing again'.[9] By the end of the day, having taken two German positions, the 2nd Black Watch, which had left the Tobruk perimeter with 32 officers and 600 men was reduced to just 5 officers and 160 men. This indeed was the Black Watch.

The last Australian battalion in Tobruk, the 2/13th, also took part in the breakout, during which Bert Ferrers from New South Wales was awarded the Military Medal:

> On 29 November, a freezing cold night, we moved out to support an attack on Sidi Rezegh by the New Zealanders, being heavily shelled as we went forward. We were in column of platoons, and the odd shell landed among our leading platoons so we were a platoon short when the leading companies put in a bayonet charge aimed at the El Duda ridge. We had to wait a while as British Matildas and German tanks argued for about three hours over who had the ridge, and hugging the ground we got a worm's eye view of a night tank battle – lots of tracer and the splash of solid shot on armour. They were firing at ranges of 400–500 yards, and one or more of the German tanks caught fire, illuminating the battlefield. By now it was about 0130 on 30 November when we were ordered to move on the enemy, supported by these British tanks on the flanks.
>
> It was a classic bayonet charge, starting with the walk up, firing from the hip with rifle and Bren, then a screaming and yelling run at the enemy. As the extreme left-hand man on my line, with a Bren gun, I seemed to do more than my share of running and met more than my share of Germans, who did not know whether to keep firing, run, or surrender, so with the help of my section I rounded up as many as I could. Altogether 167 Germans were captured – 7 more than the attacking force.
>
> When dawn came, an amazing sight was revealed: German troops marching about, trucks, tents, field kitchens, looking more like a camp than a battle group. But the Royal Horse Artillery put paid to that. We were heavily shelled all day and threatened by some 40 tanks, but endured for the next four days until relieved by the Border Regiment. Tobruk was finally relieved on 7 December – the day of Pearl Harbor.[10]

Breaking through the enemy lines at Tobruk took most of the day, but by mid-afternoon the 70th Division had opened a gap about 2 miles wide and 2 miles deep and had broken out of the Tobruk perimeter. General Scobie then decided to hold the ground taken, since there seemed little chance of any of the Eighth Army units awaiting the 70th Division at El Duda as the German counter-attacks continued.

So far XIII Corps had had a comparatively quiet time in this battle. The 4th Indian Division and the 2nd New Zealand Division moved forward on 19 November led by New Zealand infantry and some Matilda infantry tanks. They too achieved some successes, for on the night of 22/23 November the 6th New Zealand Brigade overran the Afrika Korps HQ, capturing most of the staff, though not General Crüwell or his astute chief of staff, Colonel Fritz Bayerlein. XIII Corps continued to push to the west, towards the Belhammed ridge north-east of El Duda and 7 miles outside the Tobruk perimeter, where it was due to link up with Tobforce. As German resistance stiffened at Belhammed, the advance slowed.

John A. Black was a machine-gun crew private in 3 Company of the 27th Machine Gun Battalion in the New Zealand Division:

Our first action at Sidi Rezegh came on 23 November. We arrived on top of the escarpment, and small-arms fire and machine-guns were spitting all around us. I asked my mates Bun and Saint where they wanted me to stop, and they replied, 'Right here', and that is where they were both wounded – hit in the buttocks. They struggled to their feet, linked arms, and went off to the RAP. The MG fire was very heavy, and my thoughts were 'If this is action, I do not have long to live.' I do not recall any fear, but our company casualties that day were five killed – including my platoon commander, Lieutenant Tom Daly – and four wounded.

The next evening we dug a MMG gun position on the plain. The Germans were digging in about 200 yards away, but I had found a tommy gun abandoned on the track and a couple of bursts kept them busy while our gun team dug in. We were pretty tired by this time, having had no sleep for 36 hours.

On the morning of 24 November we had to contend with shelling and small-arms fire and our No. 8 Platoon was pulling out. No point in staying – we would have been POWs in no time, so at 1100 hours, under heavy fire, we retreated, leaving our guns behind. Eric Heaps, a No. 1 gunner, was mortally wounded at this time. On the way out I asked the CO of the 26th Battalion if our guns could be pulled out by his Bren-gun carriers – a big request, but our guns were brought back next day. At Sidi Rezegh, we had a good night's sleep, but the panzers rounded up two of our battalions in the wadis below.[11]

The 2nd New Zealand Division had a very rough time at Sidi Rezegh, as these diary extracts from Staff Sergeant James Huston of the 5th Field Regiment of the Royal New Zealand Artillery make very clear:

23 November (Sunday)
Up at daybreak and cleaned up etc. Had a long talk with Major Grigg, MP, who was our 2 i/c, and when we shook hands I never thought it was the last time I would see him. (He was killed a few days later.) When he was killed he was actually firing the gun. A fine chap. In fact when I said 'Cheerio' to all the boys I had no idea that in a few days they would all either be killed or taken prisoner. This is the outfit that ran into trouble, and Brigadier Hargest, Brigadier Miles, Colonel Fraser and several other senior officers were captured. Heard that the 27th Battalion and Maoris had left the Brigade and gone north. As it turned out they were the lucky ones, as they had a victorious time and their casualties were very light compared with the rest of the Brigade.

24 November
Move several times and get shelled on and off all day. Pass through a battlefield where the tanks had met, and what a mess. The poor devils must have had H . . . There were disabled tanks lying everywhere, both British and German, and these Jerry tanks were huge things. Also bodies lying everywhere – mostly British. Had a look in several tanks and it must have been awful, just charred remains inside.

25 November
On move again, spot convoy, and get ready to have a go at it. They fire at us and we return fire, but they are too big for us and we beat it smartly. Water getting low, but plenty of grub. Shaving is out of the question, a cup of tea is more important. At daybreak we are to make a dash for safety and we are to move in orderly fashion, 21st leading and my nine trucks making up the rear. I have seen a stampede of horses on the screen, but nothing like this. The Jerries peppered us all the time, and the trouble started when some trucks tried to get ahead – dinkum rabble. We came

across some boys who had been protecting us with a machine-gun and found they'd been run over and there was nothing we could do for them. Don't know who was to blame for this she-mozzle, but I know one of my chaps who was as much to blame as anyone. He was one of those mouth-almighty chaps, full of talk and no brains or guts.

It was out of frying pan into fire as a German artillery battery opened up on us from less than 2 miles and they had a wonderful time as we had nothing to fire back; two trucks hit and several of my chaps hit. We had to set off again, and this time the boys kept in good order. I'd threatened to shoot them if they didn't, and the only one to play up was the one I mentioned previously.

27 November

A tank battle raging in the distance a fine sight. The little British tanks look like terriers having a scrap with an Alsatian. They nip in and have a shot at a big tank and go like hell the other way while another tank nips in and has a go. Trucks and bodies every-where – all Tommies – and we buried them in our lines. By this time I have a box full of identity tags and pay books from chaps we'd buried. There was an 8-ton truck nearby, and several of my chaps had had a look and beat a hasty retreat. The driver was all in one piece and had been killed by concussion, not a mark on him. The officer, who was standing on the seat with his head and shoulders through the trapdoor, had been blown in half. It was an awful sight, the bones of his thighs were showing and all his guts had run out.

1 December

The worst day of my life. We stood to at dawn. The 6th Field had 24 guns, and with our 8 it made a total of 32, which were formed in a square, 8 on each side, and in the centre were about 200 ve-hicles. At around 0730 we noticed a huge convoy on 'C' Troop's front. Had a look and thought they were the South Africans, who were said to be coming up, but we began to feel uneasy.

Sure enough they opened up on us and 'C' Troop opened on them, followed by 'F' Troop. About the third round hit Ernie Higgins fair and square in the side and blew him to bits. We could feel the rounds hitting the water truck, and practically all the trucks were write-offs. Had a look at 'F' Troop, who were firing flat out with Harry Crawford Smith directing them. Ted Little waved with his usual grin, and I waved back. I have not seen him since, as he was captured. 'C' Troop were having a rough time;

Captain Roy Hume was killed while firing a gun – the crew were hit and short-handed, so Roy took a place in the crew and he stopped on, as did Alec Sinclair. The tanks were now getting closer and closer and things look hopeless – 'C' only had one gun still firing. Not much point in staying now; boys were still intact, so told them that we'd better get going – the tanks were now only a few hundred yards away. I tried several times to get on a truck but they were full up, so I gave up and kept going as far as I could on my feet, sitting down a mile or so from the battlefield.

What a fight the boys had put up! From the start we had no show, but that did not stop the boys standing to their guns till it was finished, or rather we were. It was a terrible affair but at the same time a great experience – one that only comes once in a lifetime.

10 December
Set off early and got to Mersa Matruh. Found the remains of our battery and found Harry Crawford Smith. Saluted and said that the remains of the party from Tobruk had arrived. A great welcome we got, and one chap told me he had reported seeing me dead alongside Ernie Higgins, but admitted he was running so fast at the time he could not stop to make sure. It was great to be back among such friends.

In XXX Corps, dawn on 23 November found the 7th Armoured Division in considerable disarray. The 4th Armoured Brigade was scattered, 7th Armoured Brigade was reduced to 15 tanks, 22nd Armoured could muster just 34 Crusaders, and the Support Group had been virtually wiped out. During the day General Norrie attempted to reform XXX Corps behind the southern ridge at Sidi Rezegh, screened from the enemy by the 5th South African Brigade, the 22nd Armoured Brigade and the 1st South African Infantry Brigade, which was now coming up. But Rommel had no intention of ending the battle or of permitting XXX Corps to regroup. He sent 21st Panzer to hold the escarpment to the north, while 15th Panzer with the Ariete Division circled to the south-east and came into the flank and rear of XXX Corps from Bir el Gubi.

More confusion here led to another heat of the 'November Handicap', a hurried flight east of the South African transport and the forward elements of the 1st South African Infantry Brigade. This left the 5th South African Brigade and the 22nd Armoured Brigade to take the main weight of the German assault, and neither was in any state to resist for long. By night-fall on 23 November the 5th South African Brigade had been anni-hilated and the 22nd Armoured Brigade was down to its last 20 tanks. During the night of the 23rd/24th great efforts were made by both sides to repair tanks left on the battlefield, but when day-light came on the 24th the victory seemed to lie with Rommel.

The Germans gradually drew out of this mêlée and rallied to the south-west, where they attacked and scattered the remnants of the 5th South African Brigade. This brought on another whirl-wind engagement when the remaining Crusaders of the 4th County of London Yeomanry and a squadron of the 2nd Royal Gloucestershire Hussars went to the South Africans' assistance. The 22nd Armoured Brigade, to which these units belonged, had now been reduced to a composite regiment, but it swept in to the attack again and again. This held the panzers off, but by night-fall the 5th South African Brigade had disintegrated, having lost over 3,000 men and most of its equipment.

That night, what was left of the three armoured brigades of the 7th Armoured Division leaguered near the airfield at Sidi Rezegh while the Support Group mustered at Gabr Saleh. And matters were not going well elsewhere. In XIII Corps the New Zealanders had sustained heavy casualties in the battle for the Belhammed ridge, having been ordered to advance along the Trigh Capuzzo track and link up with Tobforce.

On 24 November a decisive victory lay within Rommel's grasp – and then he threw it away. Rommel now had two sound options available. First, he could move on Tobruk with a good chance of success, since the 70th Division was now outside the perimeter and heading for El Duda. Second, he could continue smashing away at the British forces around Sidi Rezegh and complete the destruction of Eighth Army. He did neither. Having given XXX Corps a caning, he slipped past XIII Corps and made a dash for the Egyptian frontier. On 25 November leading elements of the Panzerarmee Afrika crossed the wire and entered Egypt.

Rommel clearly believed that if he did this Eighth Army would collapse. He had some reason for this opinion, for most of XXX Corps's soft-skinned transport was now withdrawing rapidly to the east, the retreating British and advancing Germans were all in glorious disorder, 'the desert was covered with scores of vehicles, all moving east at their best speed', while Brigadier Campbell and the 11th Hussars roved among the scattered groups and transport convoys, attempting to bring infantry, tank squadrons or parts of squadrons back together again and form a coherent force.

However, Cunningham gained an advantage here, for Rommel's thrust at the wire reduced the pressure at Sidi Rezegh and left the British astride the Axis communications, and able to inhibit, if not fully prevent, the forward movement of supplies. There was also time to recover tanks abandoned at Sidi Rezegh and restore the three armoured brigades of XXX Corps to some sort of order. Rommel's speed and aggression – or impetuosity – was telling against him. Order was being restored to the British forces on all parts of the battlefield on the 25/26 November, tanks were being repaired and refuelled, and stiffening resistance plus the exhaustion of his men and a shortage of supplies forced Rommel to fight his way back to the west.

By some fortunate mischance, Rommel's troops failed to discover either of the two British field maintenance centres, Nos. 62 and 63, south of Gabr Saleh. These had been stocked with food and petrol, and would have provided all the supplies he needed to continue his advance. The main result of Rommel's brief appearance in Egypt was the sacking of General Sir Alan Cunningham, who was relieved of his command on 25 November, seven days after the start of CRUSADER. He was replaced – at first on a temporary basis – by Major-General Neil Ritchie, Auchinleck's deputy chief of staff.

Apart from General Maitland Wilson, currently commanding British Troops Egypt, there was no one else available, but Ritchie was not a wise choice. He had been serving on Auchinleck's staff, but he lacked experience of desert command and he was a major-general commanding lieutenant-generals. Some have argued that either Norrie or Godwin-Austin might have been a better choice. It is noteworthy that for the first ten days after Ritchie's appointment Auchinleck stayed at Eighth Army Headquarters in the field, effectively commanding the Army with Ritchie as his deputy. It might have been better if Auchinleck had taken direct charge of Eighth Army at this time and moved Army HQ forward from Fort Capuzzo and closer to the fighting, which was now building up to a climax.

One of the notable features of the desert war was the resilience displayed by both sides; both showed a remarkable ability to recover from a defeat. For example, the 4th Armoured Brigade, scattered and low in reserves on 23 November, had reorganized and received 36 new tanks by 26 November, bringing its tank strength up to 77. A scouring of the battlefield by tank recovery teams led to the discovery and repair of no fewer than 70 broken-down or lightly damaged tanks, and the tank strength of 22nd Armoured Brigade rose to a useful 50.

On that day Rommel returned from his foray into Egypt and took up the fight again at Sidi Rezegh. General Scobie, realizing that the New Zealanders were still held up at the Belhammed position and Sidi Rezegh, decided to move the 70th Division forward and take El Duda himself. The El Duda ridge was taken by the 1st Battalion, The Essex Regiment and the 32nd Tank Brigade, and during the battle Captain J. J. Jackman of the Royal Northumberland Fusiliers won the Victoria Cross. That night the 6th New Zealand Infantry Brigade took Sidi Rezegh and the 19th New Zealand Battalion made contact with the troops from Tobruk, briefly ending a siege that had lasted eight months. This relief was short-lived: 15th Panzer and 21st Panzer were back from the frontier and moving west along the Trigh Capuzzo, coming in against the New Zealand infantry, and before long the Tobruk garrison was isolated yet again.

The CRUSADER operation was still far from over, but, since few battles can be so confusing as those around Sidi Rezegh, it would be wise to look at the state of affairs on 30 November, two weeks into an operation that still had nearly a month to go. In XIII Corps, the 4th Armoured Brigade was supporting the 2nd New Zealand Division and the 1st South African Infantry Brigade near Bir el Reghem, where they engaged the Ariete Division and destroyed 19 tanks. Meanwhile the New Zealanders had scored another success, capturing General Johann von Ravenstein, the commander of 21st Panzer, which, with the Ariete Division and 15th Panzer, was assembling west of Sidi Rezegh for another thrust at Belhammed and El Duda. Rommel had now realized that his troops were reaching the end of their strength and that the crux of this battle was at El Duda. He was also determined that Tobruk should not be relieved. To prevent that he must destroy the New Zealand Division at Belhammed.

Attacks against Freyberg's positions at Point 175, just south of the Trigh Capuzzo, went on throughout 30 November and 1 December, destroying one brigade and driving the others back. When the much reduced New Zealander infantry was finally forced to withdraw, 15th Panzer reoccupied both the Belhammed ridge and Sidi Rezegh. Some of the New Zealander units crossed the Trigh Capuzzo and made their way back into Egypt; others joined the garrison of Tobruk. The Official History notes a comment from General Norrie: 'I was much impressed by the discipline of the New Zealand troops, in spite of the rough handling they had had.' Had this fine division been properly supported, especially with tanks and anti-tank guns, its losses would have been smaller and it might well have been able to hold on and complete the relief of Tobruk.

However, by 30 November Rommel had decided that the battle at Sidi Rezegh had become a battle of attrition.[12] He also realized that essential supplies of food, petrol and ammunition were not getting to his forward units. Though he had retaken much of the ground lost in the early stages of the battle, and Tobruk had been sealed off again, El Duda was still in British hands. With more Allied troops coming up and the Desert Air Force making constant raids on the German positions, his position was becoming untenable. Realizing that Rommel must be at the end of his resources, General Ritchie elected to renew the attack. XIII Corps was to hang on to the ground already won, and XXX Corps – with 7th Armoured, two South African brigades and the 4th Indian Division – was tasked to seize El Adem.

Losses were mounting in Eighth Army as men were killed, captured or wounded. Here are accounts from three such people.

Corporal Arthur Smith of 'A' Squadron 8th RTR was killed at Sidi Rezegh on 27 November 1941, soon after writing this letter:

> I am still OK but may not be in a few day's time. Tonight the move to the last stage of a journey that has taken such a way. I am afraid the photo of Gillian that I desired to see may not catch me for a long time, or maybe I shall never know the joy of seeing the face of our child. By the time you read this all the world will know about the coming battle and I sincerely hope and pray that we have been victors and beaten the Germans at last. All the troops are confident that we will push Jerry out of [censored] this time and everyone is just waiting for the word to go. Trim will be with

me on my left and Maxie is the Major's driver now and he will be with us in the struggle.

Three and a half years later, in June 1945, Arthur Smith's widow received another letter:

Dear Mrs Smith,
I have been wanting to write to you for the past three and a half years about your husband. I have been unable to do so as I was taken prisoner a few days after he was killed.

He was in my Troop the whole time I had it and drove my tank. I could not have wished for a better man and considered myself lucky to have him. It was a great blow to me when he was hit. I felt I had lost more than a Corporal-driver, I suffered a severe personal loss that day. A large shell burst right under the tank just where he was sitting By the time I recovered from the shock of the explosion and the smoke had cleared off he had passed away. I do not think he suffered much. We got him out of the tank and gave him a Christian burial the next day; his grave is just south of the Trigh Capuzzo, south-east of Gambut.

I hope I have not opened up old wounds by writing to you about him; but I felt you would like to know how he gave his life and I also wanted you to know how much I valued and respected him as a soldier. Please let me know if I can help you in any way.
R. D. Read, Lieutenant, RTR[13]

Lieutenant Eric Eastwood of the 2nd New Zealand Division was taken prisoner at Sidi Rezegh when the Germans overran Brigadier Hargest's brigade:

Thursday 27 November
40 tanks and 200 MT [motor transport] reported at 0715 to be advancing from NE. We started as POWs, 46 officers and 650 o/rs, to march to Bardia, about 22 km away. No food or drink from Jerry. Managed to scrounge a few tins of bully and fruit before we left.

Friday 28 November
Italian guards searched us, finding only a few rounds of ammunition and a camera from one of us. Treatment quite decent except that at 1400 hrs no sign of food and only one beaker of water brought along. We divided a tin of bully and a tin of Heinz beans among six of us. This scarcity of food is a good sign – they must

be feeling the pinch through sea and road blockade. The Brigadier was allowed to bring nothing so I lent him my razor every morning. Those who haven't simply borrow from those that have.

Tuesday 4 December
I am writing this some 200 ft below the surface of the Mediterranean, in an Italian submarine, making the journey from Bardia to Benghazi. It is 0900 hrs and we have breakfasted on biscuits and coffee. The captain of the submarine came through to see how we are; he is a charming young man, married to an Auckland or Hamilton girl – the submarine is the *Admiral Millo*.[14]

Eric Eastwood spent three and a half years as a POW.

G. H. Levein was a major in the Royal New Zealand Army Medical Corps:

With my medical truck I was on the flat of the Trigh Capuzzo, along with two ambulances and several open trucks filled with wounded. The battalion, together with the 4th and 6th Brigades, were under attack from the Afrika Korps and our line was broken by tanks and the troops fell back from the ridge, hotly pursued.

Shells and anti-tank shot followed us, and a mile or so along we stopped to assess the wounded. One man was in agony; a piece of shrapnel, the size of a walnut, had entered his hand and lodged just under the skin on the web between thumb and finger, pressing on the nerves. We were under fire, but some action was needed and there was no time for anaesthetics to work. I took a scalpel, made an incision over the lump, and with a long and strong pair of bullet forceps, recently acquired from a burnt-out German truck, I hauled out the piece of metal. The poor man almost fainted, I was none too happy, but the excessive pain was gone – a field dressing was applied, morphia obtained, and off we went out of range – and I still have the forceps.[15]

The medical services were often in the thick of it – sometimes in 'friendly fire' incidents – as this account of Private Maurice Muir reveals:

At the end of November Maurice was with the 24th Battalion, New Zealand Infantry, setting up an RAP in a hollow at Sidi Rezegh. Brigadier Barraclough ordered six Valentine tanks to the Belhammed ridge, and these tanks headed north through the lines of the 24th Battalion, where they opened fire on their own troops. A section of Bren gun carriers was chased towards Battalion HQ and there was a difficult situation until Maurice, suddenly grasping that the tank crews had not realized their mistake, ran across 30 yards of open ground sprayed by tank bullets, climbed on one of the Valentines, and put a stop to the fire. The tank commander got out and was very upset when he learned what had happened, though luckily no one was hit.[16]

This exploit was witnessed by the padre, Keith Watson, and as a result of his report Maurice Muir was awarded the Military Medal.

So this grinding battle continued south and east of Tobruk, until on 8 December, with his men and machines worn out and his supplies of petrol and ammunition almost exhausted, Rommel began a slow retreat to the west, reluctantly abandoning the German forces at Bardia and Pastor Bach's force at the Halfaya Pass, which surrendered on 17 December. The siege of Tobruk finally ended on 10 December and the Axis forces elected to withdraw from Cyrenaica, moving back around the shores of the Gulf of Sirte to El Agheila.

On 19 December Rommel was reinforced by 45 tanks, but his retreat continued until 27 December, by which time the German forces had been moved – one can hardly say driven – back inside the boundaries of Tripolitania. CRUSADER had been a very close-run thing but Rommel had withdrawn as far west as Agedabia and the Tobruk garrison was once again linked to the rest of Eighth Army. The cost had been considerable. The British had lost 17,700 men, killed, wounded or missing, to the Axis 38,000 – though the latter total is inflated by the 13,800 German and Italian prisoners taken at Bardia and Halfaya.

The Official History devotes several pages to an analysis of the CRUSADER battles.[17] It concludes that – although some blame can be placed on the equipment – tactical and command deficiencies made the most significant contribution to the failure to gain a more decisive victory. However, Rommel had been driven back and Tobruk was again behind the British lines. By constant fighting throughout the CRUSADER operation, General Auchinleck and his soldiers could claim a victory – albeit a very narrow one.

1 Armoured Div.

5

Gazala
January to June 1942

Worse still, what was the matter with British arms?

The Mediterranean and Middle East, vol. 3, p. 274

What *was* the matter with Eighth Army in 1941 and 1942? That something was the matter seems undoubted, for success remained elusive. CRUSADER had been a very narrow and expensive victory, which saw a great deal of courage but no great feats of generalship on the British side. By 1942 it seemed all too possible that North Africa in this war would match South Africa in the Boer War as a graveyard of military reputations. It was increasingly obvious to all – from Winston Churchill to the lowest private soldier – that Erwin Rommel, with smaller forces and at the end of a long supply route, was able to run rings about Eighth Army whenever he wished, and questions on why this should be had now to be addressed.

Rommel clearly enjoyed certain advantages. He commanded a relatively homogeneous force, and his troops – especially his German troops – were well trained and aggressive in action. And, whereas the British and Dominion forces seemed to require months of training and acclimatization, his troops were apparently able to go into battle as soon as they stepped off the ship.

The Afrika Korps also had much better equipment than Eighth Army. Even though much of it was in short supply, the kit that Rommel had was reliable and could be used when it arrived without weeks of modification in the workshops. Rommel also had the backing of strong Italian forces, which, although despised by many Allied soldiers, could fight well on occasion, especially on the defensive. Added to this, Rommel was a commander of genius when fighting the kind of battle – a mobile battle – for which his talents were especially suited. So, in the critical areas of troops, training, equipment and command, the Axis forces – certainly the German element – had a clear advantage. Rommel also had that vital intelligence information on Eighth Army, supplied unwittingly by Colonel Bonner Fellers. But none of this fully accounts for the British Army's constant balancing on the knife-edge of defeat in the Western Desert.

Eighth Army certainly had problems. It was made up of many nationalities, and contained units which arrived in the desert in various states of training. Although many divisions were of high quality, these troops and their units had to be welded into a homogeneous whole – an integrated army; it was not possible to send a British tank brigade to an Australian division and expect them to work in perfect harmony. They had to learn to work together as a team, using equipment – especially tanks and artillery, but including infantry support weapons and even platoon weapons like the Bren light machine-gun and the 2-inch mortar – that many had not seen and few had had the chance to train with before they arrived in Egypt. In many ways Eighth Army was untrained and had to learn on the job – at any time an expensive process.

Then, as already noted, much of the equipment was inadequate. The tanks were unreliable, thinly armoured and undergunned. The untracked transport was unsuited to desert conditions – two-wheel-drive transport tended to bog down in the sand and became hopelessly stranded when it rained. Even small items were inadequate – like the British 4-gallon petrol tins, which were a great drain on scanty fuel resources. 'My late father served with the 1st Armoured Division in North Africa,' writes Charles R. Butt, 'and envied the Germans their superior and more practical equipment. One of his favourite examples was the "jerrican", sturdily made and with an open or shut spout, which was far superior to our poorly designed and flimsy square petrol tins, which were ever liable to crack and leak and most inconvenient to use.'[1]

John Statham was a sergeant in the 11th (HAC) Regiment, RHA:

At the beginning of the Second World War we were militarily four years behind the Germans – and a dictatorship can move twice as fast as a democracy, so Germany's lead amounted to eight years. To us in the Western Desert in 1942 that meant that we had to abandon vehicles because our petrol cans leaked, and our tanks had to close to within 500 yards of the enemy before they even had a chance, while the German tanks could sit back and knock out our tanks at 1,500 yards and our 2-pounder anti-tank guns were a joke. In spite of these disadvantages we had to attack continually in order to hide our lack of resources. Our commanders were in no way to blame for what happened.[2]

E. J. (Ted) Smith was also in this regiment:

The HAC – Honourable Artillery Company – was part of the 2nd Armoured Brigade, which was made up of three tank regiments, with artillery – ourselves, an AA Bofors regiment and an anti-tank (A/T) regiment with 2-pounders mounted on portées – plus an infantry battalion. Each of the HAC's three batteries of eight 25-pounders was assigned to give close support to a tank regiment, and my battery – 'A' – was with the Queen's Bays. Our good times and bad were to be closely linked.

The 2nd Armoured Brigade was one of two brigades in the 1st Armoured Division, newly arrived in North Africa after Beda Fomm, and we crossed into Libya moving west about 20 miles into the desert. Most of the tanks were on transporters, as it was pretty rough going, and as we moved forward we found plenty of derelict tanks and vehicles – evidence of hard fighting and the realities of warfare. By Christmas Day 1941 we had progressed 500 miles or so and were about 40 miles south of Tobruk, where the garrison had recently been relieved. Most days we continued moving west through the desert, with almost all the other activity confined to our long supply convoys going west to establish supply bases and returning empty. With the railhead near Mersa Matruh in Egypt and only one road, it was a major problem getting supplies up to the front. For example, our main RASC vehicle was the 3-tonner, which could carry 240 rounds for our 25-pounders. When we were busy, our guns might easily fire off this amount in 15 minutes. With a return journey of perhaps two weeks, the RASC needed an awful lot of drivers to keep the supplies flowing.

With a few reservations, I loved the desert. What appealed to me was the changing colours and the forms of the landscape: mile after mile of salt flat where we could make good going; stretches of low ridges and soft sand giving endless variations where the horizons were near or far. In the desert there was always a sense of remoteness. If ever there was a place for men to be tested in war, this was it.[3]

In matters of support, the tanks and infantry were well served by the artillery and by the Desert Air Force, but the RAF did not have full control of the desert skies. The Luftwaffe had plenty of aircraft, its fighters were more than a match for the British and South African machines then in service, and its Stuka dive-bombers were a menace to static forces on the ground.

There are therefore a number of good reasons why Eighth Army was not performing well – even when its soldiers were fighting well – but these reasons do not excuse the general and chronic failure to get a grip on the smaller Axis forces and drive them back to Libya and beyond. To explain that, one must look at the area of command.

Here too there are reasons for failure. Wavell's command had always been far too big, and he had been forced to weaken his desert forces and call off successful campaigns in order to send troops and kit to other areas: to Greece and Crete, where losses had been high, and to Syria and Iraq and Eritrea, where victory had been achieved only at a considerable cost in time, equipment and manpower. Wavell – and now Auchinleck – had too much on his plate, and this vast command should have been split.

There was also continual interference from London. Winston Churchill – War Minister as well as Prime Minister – was always urging attacks before the desert commanders were ready to make them. Churchill had good reasons for urging action – pressure of events elsewhere, not least in the House of Commons – and the Allied commanders had good reasons for delay – a need for more training and a shortage of equipment. But such considerations and such interference do not seem to have deterred Rommel, who was equally plagued from on high.

Rommel was subject to calls from OKW – usually urging caution or restraint, for, with the Russian campaign under way, OKW regarded the desert war as a sideshow. Rommel was also subordinate to the Italian commander in North Africa and the Comando Supremo in Rome – at least in theory, though provided he was successful, and kept the support of Adolf Hitler, in practice he was able to fight his campaigns much as he wished. That said, the reasons for Rommel's successes lie as much with failures in the British command as with his own undoubted talents.

First, in this respect, there is the matter of tactics. The normal rules of attack and defence did not often work in the desert, where there were only a few positions – the Alamein Line, the Halfaya Pass, some of the ridges and high ground as at Sidi Rezegh – where the terrain permitted a defensive line with fairly secure flanks. As a rule, any position could be outflanked, so desert battles were rather like fleet engagements at sea. The outcome depended on which general could keep his force together and under control; each side aimed to split the opposing force and destroy it in detail, rather as Nelson split the Franco-Spanish fleet at Trafalgar.

One other tactic, deployed so often and so successfully by Rommel, was to create a defensive line using anti-tank guns. The British tanks were lured on to the enemy anti-tank-gun positions time and again – and aided their own destruction by deliberately splitting their force, enabling Rommel to bring his forces against them and defeat them in detail. The way to deal with such a situation was simple in theory, though often more difficult in practice. On running against an anti-tank position, the tactic was to hold back out of range and pound the anti-tank gunners with field artillery using high-explosive charges; once the anti-tank gunners had been killed or dispersed, the tanks could move forward. Tanks, anti-tank guns, field artillery and infantry had to work together. But the need to fight the 'all-arms' battle was not grasped at this time. Douglas Hodge, an officer in the 2nd New Zealand Division, is quite correct when he states that 'the main reason why the British Army bungled hopelessly in its tank battles was its pernicious habit of scattering its resources and denying the tank units proper artillery support'.[4]

Again, part of the problem may have been with the kit. The British tanks were out-gunned and out-ranged by the German tanks and anti-tank guns, and the British 25-pounder – an excellent piece of field artillery – was not used well and was frequently out-ranged by German artillery. The finest gun on the battlefield was the German dual-purpose (anti-aircraft and anti-tank) 88-mm, and it remains a matter of wonder that the British did not equip their own anti-aircraft gun with anti-tank ammunition.

This action was certainly contemplated: in July 1941 Lieutenant-General Alan Brooke, then a corps commander, attended a meeting with Beaverbrook 'concerning the production of A/T ammunition for our 3.7 and 3-inch AA guns, to deal with large tanks should they be landed'.[5] One reason for failing to proceed with this idea – apart from a chronic shortage of anti-aircraft guns – was that the 3.7-inch had been designed for high-angle fire, in which most of the recoil shock is taken by the ground. When fired horizontally, the shock of recoil tended to shake the gun mountings to pieces – though this defect could surely have been rectified.

The British commanders had not yet grasped the basics of armoured warfare in the desert: the need to match mobility with a concentration of force at the crucial point in time and space.[6] For CRUSADER, Cunningham, in defiance of Auchinleck's clear orders, had first split his two corps, then split the divisions of XXX Corps, and finally split the brigades of 7th Armoured Division into three brigade columns. Whatever good reasons he must have felt he had for this at the time, this dispersion ignored a basic military rule – that a force should not be split in the presence of the enemy – and it enabled Rommel, who *had* concentrated his forces, to descend on the British brigades at Sidi Rezegh and elsewhere and crush them in detail. When such concentration was important, one has to ask why Auchinleck did not insist that his order to concentrate was obeyed.

The handling of the armoured forces was particularly poor. The British concept seems to have involved groups of tanks, even single regiments like the 8th and 7th Hussars, cruising about in flotillas, seeking and engaging enemy tanks where found. Since the German tanks had better armour and guns with greater hitting power and longer range, this tactic rarely worked to the British advantage. For their part, the Germans preferred to fight tanks with anti-tank guns, and, since the German anti-tanks guns were both numerous and effective, they were able to wreak great damage on the British armoured forces without great loss to themselves – and such losses as they did sustain were reduced by the work of their excellent tank recovery and repair teams. The overall impression is that British amateurs were fighting German professionals and taking regular beatings while they learned their trade.

On the infantry front there is less to criticize – which again points the finger at the kit, since there is no reason to suppose that armoured soldiers were less proficient or less gallant than infantry soldiers. The Germans had to rely mainly on Italian infantry, which was no match for the Australian, British, Indian or New Zealand infantry, which was outstanding and – except in anti-tank guns – well equipped. Nevertheless, there were some problems here, for this wonderful infantry lacked mobility and needed more transport – and reliable tank support. However, when push came to shove on the battlefield, the British and Dominion infantry carried the day – usually with the bayonet. But this, alas, was achieved at considerable cost, and did not in itself prove enough to compensate for the other failings.

Finally there is the matter of 'grip'. 'Grip' is one of those military qualities that are hard to define but most noticeable when absent. 'Grip' is best imagined as a tight control of events and units. From Beda Fomm in 1940 until the battle at Alam Halfa in mid-1942, there was a distinct lack of 'grip' in the higher echelons of British command in North Africa. A 'well-gripped' military formation knows the presence of command because things work. The soldiers are conscious that the powers-that-be know what they are doing and are working to some logical, strategic plan – one that allows for unforeseen emergencies. Such 'grip' was lacking in the British Army and all too apparent in the German Army – all the British soldiers recognized that Rommel had 'grip'.

So much is obvious, but the larger question is, Why should this be? What was the root of these continued failures? It is possible that one reason for this lack of 'grip' – apart from the distractions listed above – lay in the command structure of the pre-war British Army. This tended to be slow, ponderous and confined by routine. Everything had to be done by 'The Book' – by existing laid-down rules and procedures – and the old service adage that 'The Book is for the guidance of wise men and the obedience of fools' seems to have been forgotten; the book became the Bible. The generals, or most of the generals, were trying to use systems of command that were simply too slow for the fluid conditions of modern war in the desert.

Radio communications in the desert were poor, and the commanding generals did not help matters by placing themselves well in the rear – Cunningham was at Fort Capuzzo, 60 miles from his army, when it went into battle at Sidi Rezegh, and was unable to come up quickly or keep a grip on the situation as it developed. This 'staying back' was normal procedure: according to The Book, a general must stay out of the detail in order to understand and control the big picture. Though a valid doctrine, this procedure simply did not work in the desert in 1941–2. The forces were too evenly balanced; the army that moved first and fastest and was the more tightly commanded would usually carry the day.

Nor – see above – was there any real understanding of the armoured or all-arms battle at the corps or army level. The pre-war British Army was too small to provide the commanders with any experience of command above the divisional level, and British training areas were too small to permit the deployment of large forces for tactical manoeuvres; the hindrances imposed on Hobart's attempts to train up the Mobile Division in the desert before the war have already been recorded. The Germans, on the other hand, had the vast plains of Prussia and north Germany in which to test their tactics, and many of their commanders had direct experience of modern warfare, either in the Spanish Civil War of 1936–9 or in the 1939–40 campaigns in Poland and France, where speed and mobility were the paramount factors. These German officers seemed to be highly professional soldiers with flexible minds, and they had the backing of Adolf Hitler, who wanted a large, well-equipped and well-trained professional army before he went to war – and was prepared to pay for it.

Although this was of no comfort to the officers and men, Britain's pre-war neglect of its armed forces was perhaps understandable. Hitler was a dictator, planning an aggressive war and the subjugation of Europe. Much of what was wrong with the British armed forces in the early years of the Second World War can be attributed to the fact that the British, while apt for war when provoked, are not aggressively inclined and had no desire to occupy the territory of their neighbours. The price of appeasement in the 1930s was paid by the British soldier in the 1940s.

Rommel either did not have a 'Book' or had thrown it into the bin on arriving in North Africa. He led from the front, he appeared in the line at the crux of any battle, and his orders – given on the spot – were swiftly executed. In the British Army, situation reports and requests for help or orders were relayed up the line – to battalion, brigade, division and corps – and the resulting decisions were often out of date before they had been relayed back down the line and implemented.

Nor was this fault apparent only among the high command and regimental officers; the training of German NCOs stressed the importance of taking immediate action, not only acting on orders provided from above, as in the British Army. The German aim was to take decisions as close to the action as possible, which usually led to a swift and decisive response. The desert war was a new kind of war, and British command and control systems, evolved pre-war, were simply not fast enough to cope with it. That lesson was not learned at Sidi Rezegh, and that failure paved the way for Eighth Army's next setback, under its new commander, Major-General Neil Ritchie.

Like Wavell, Ritchie had been commissioned into the Black Watch. He had served in the Middle East in the First World War, but his main task so far in the Second World War had been to form the second 51st (Highland) Division, after the first one had been destroyed by Rommel at Saint-Valéry-sur-Somme in 1940. He had then come to the Middle East and served on the staffs of Wavell and Auchinleck. Before his sudden transfer to field command he had been the Deputy Chief of the General Staff in Cairo. Ritchie was a competent commander, but had been promoted above his level of ability – which was division or corps level – and should have been replaced as soon as CRUSADER was over. That he remained in post reflects badly on Auchinleck's choice of subordinate commanders.

Before continuing with this story it is necessary to put the desert events in context and look briefly at what was happening elsewhere. In June 1941 the Germans had turned on their former ally Soviet Russia by launching Operation BARBAROSSA. This brought Britain a new if demanding ally, but was of little help to

Eighth Army. Indeed, aircraft and tanks which Auchinleck could have used were diverted to help Stalin's armies stave off the first German onslaught. The war at sea continued, and their advance into Cyrenaica gave the Germans possession of airfields from which to attack convoys sailing to Malta from Alexandria and Port Said; by the end of the summer of 1941, Malta was in desperate straits. Eighth Army's push forward towards Tripolitania was therefore welcomed by the naval commanders, as the advancing troops overran a number of German airfields. The Mediterranean Fleet had suffered losses to its capital ships during an attack on Alexandria by Italian human torpedoes.

On Sunday 7 December 1941 the Japanese attacked Pearl Harbor and the USA entered the war. This event was to prove a decisive factor in the eventual outcome of the war, but the more immediate effects were less positive for the British in the Western Desert. On that Sunday the Japanese also attacked Malaya and other British possessions in the Far East, so further scant resources in men, tanks and modern aircraft were diverted away from the desert to shore up the defences of India and then Australia – which last requirement led to the eventual departure from North Africa of the splendid Australian divisions. The equally splendid 70th (British) Division and 7th Armoured Brigade both went to Burma and vanish from this story, while another Middle East-bound reinforcement from the UK, the 18th Division, was diverted to Singapore – and Japanese captivity. In short, in spite of this accretion of distant allies in Soviet Russia and the USA in 1941, the situation of Eighth Army in the Western Desert remained perilous.

As we have seen, at the end of CRUSADER, the Germans and Italians withdrew as far as Agedabia. There were constant clashes during the pursuit, with a considerable tank battle north of Agedabia between the two German panzer divisions and 90 tanks of the 22nd Armoured Brigade; the British lost 37 tanks, the Germans 7. Another engagement, on 30 December, cost the British 23 tanks, again to 7 panzers. In spite of these disproportionate losses the British still outnumbered Rommel in both men and tanks.

On 5 January Rommel received another 55 tanks, from two supply ships, the *Ankara* and the *Monginevro*. This shipment brought the Afrika Korps's tank strength up to a grand total of just 111 machines, Panzer Mark IIIs and IVs. However, 19 of these Mark IIIs were the new (J) Specials mounting a long 55-mm gun, which had a penetration 50 per cent better than the short 55-mm. These tanks reached the front on 14 January. One point that will strike the reader at this point is how *small* Rommel's resources were; throughout the desert war Rommel never enjoyed overall superiority in manpower or equipment, but this small reinforcement – plus his usual confidence and aggression – enabled him to mount a counter-attack against the British forces on 21 January, driving them back to Gazala, west of Tobruk.

Before that attack came in, Eighth Army had reorganized somewhat. After CRUSADER had petered out, the 1st Armoured Division, which was short in tanks and training, had come forward from Palestine to relieve the worn out 7th Armoured Division, which returned to Cairo to refit. While in Cairo, the Support Group of 7th Armoured – which soon afterwards became the 7th Motor Brigade – held a parade for the presentation of Brigadier Jock Campbell's VC, awarded for his inspiring leadership at Sidi Rezegh. Campbell was then promoted to major-general and was due to succeed Gott as commander of the 7th Armoured Division while Gott went to command XIII Corps. Two weeks later, however, Campbell was killed in a motor accident. His death was a great loss to Eighth Army and his place in command of 7th Armoured was taken by General Messervy, formerly commander of the 4th Indian Division.

When Rommel renewed the offensive after so short a time it took the British commanders completely by surprise. There seems to have been no adequate intelligence from Ultra or the Long Range Desert Group – or if there was it was ignored. The War Office Intelligence Summary for the week of 21–8 January 1942 states that 'a build-up of troops in Italy as possible reinforcements for North Africa was a defensive measure by the Germans to prevent possible disturbances in the event of a complete Allied victory in TRIPOLITANIA, or even to meet a British attack on Sicily'.[7] It seems that the British were blissfully unaware of any German intention to advance in North Africa, happy to gloat on the possibility of defeating the Germans and invading Sicily.[8] General Auchinleck also believed that CRUSADER had done enough to give Rommel pause, even stating in a dispatch that it was 'highly unlikely' that Rommel would attack again in the near future.

" Pass the sand, old man!"

Sand and flies, the extra ingredients in any Desert Army dish

A Valentine tank advances through loose sand in 1942. The need for sand traps to keep the engine working is evident

Crusader tanks at dusk in the Western Desert, 1942. The dawn and dusk 'stand-to' marked the beginning and end of every day

Italian m-14 tank. Many captured Italian tanks, though under-gunned and thinly armoured, were employed by Desert Army units in 1941–2

A 6-pounder anti-tank gun is moved into position. The 6-pounder was a useful gun, a great advance on the previous 2-pounder

Soldiers of the 51st (Highland) Division clean their weapons. Keeping equipment clear of sand and in working order was a constant task in the Western Desert

" —— and precisely what do you mean by improperly dressed?"

The sensible – if eccentric – dress worn by many Desert Army officers was not always approved of by the authorities

An Australian sergeant in the Western Desert: beer of any kind was always welcome and in very short supply

Desert Army humour: a blood transfusion point in the Western Desert

'Brewing-up': boiling water for a quick cup of tea was a Western Desert art

Claude Auchinleck, a fine general who led the Desert Army in some hard battles before his dismissal in the summer of 1942

Erwin Rommel, 'The Desert Fox': a German officer regarded on both sides of the line as the finest general in North Africa . . . until Montgomery arrived

Left General Montgomery before a Grant tank, Western Desert, 1942: vain and arrogant, but a highly professional soldier

Below Churchill at Montgomery's headquarters with some of his generals: (*left to right*) Lieutenant-General Sir Oliver Leese, Commander of XXX Corps; General Sir Harold Alexander; Prime Minister Winston Churchill; General Sir Alan Brooke; Lieutenant-General Bernard Montgomery

British infantry charge past a burning German tank; the results of anti-tank gunfire are clearly visible

The opening barrage at the start of Operation LIGHTFOOT: 25-pounder guns in action at El Alamein, October 1942

Glad to be out of it, November 1942: after Alamein Italian prisoners come in by the thousand. No guards are necessary

The rain arrives and the Western Desert becomes a swamp slowing Eighth Army's pursuit

However, German reconnaissance and Colonel Bonner Fellers's helpful cables to Washington had revealed that 1st Armoured Division was repeating the usual British error of dispersing its component units about the desert, and on the first day of his offensive – 21 January 1942 – Rommel struck these scattered units hard. Two days later his armour attacked the three regiments of the 2nd Armoured Brigade, each of which came into action separately and was – as usual – defeated separately, losing over half the Brigade's tanks. Rommel then burst through the 201st Guards Brigade and reached Msus, the British falling back before him in some disorder – 'in complete confusion' according to the war diary of 15th Panzer. Total disaster was averted only by the constant sorties of the Desert Air Force, which attacked Axis columns wherever found and held off the dive-bombing Stukas.

On 28 January Rommel took Benghazi, capturing a huge quantity of petrol and ammunition that had been laboriously stockpiled there for the next British attack – Operation ACROBAT, a continuation of CRUSADER – due in mid-February. By 4 February Rommel's hustling tactics had levered the British back to Gazala, 150 miles north-east of Msus and 30 miles west of Tobruk. Many British units arrived at Gazala in considerable confusion, although Rommel had already stopped advancing and was resting his forces at Benghazi.

This reverse did no good to Ritchie's reputation – and Auchinleck's deputy chief of staff, Major General Eric 'Chink' Dorman-Smith, on whose advice Auchinleck relied, was already urging the Commander-in-Chief to appoint another commander to Eighth Army – probably Gott. However, Auchinleck was reluctant to have yet another change in command so soon, telling Dorman-Smith that 'I have already sacked one army commander. To sack another within three months would have effects on morale'.[9]

Ritchie was therefore still in post when Rommel advanced again in May 1942, so pre-empting any British counter-offensive. Before that, one departure from Eighth Army was Lieutenant-General Godwin-Austen of XIII Corps, who asked to be relieved of his command on 2 February as General Ritchie had apparently lost confidence in him – during the retreat to Gazala, Ritchie had issued orders to Godwin-Austen's subordinates over his head. Losses in the January retreat had not been severe: 1,390 men, killed, wounded or missing, plus the loss of 72 tanks and 40 field guns. The worst aspect of this reverse was that, as Auchinleck wrote to Churchill, 'personnel of the Royal Armoured Corps are losing confidence in their equipment'.

Churchill had other worries at this time – not least the situation in Malta, which was under heavy attack and in danger of starvation. One result of the recent setbacks in the Western Desert was that the Luftwaffe could use the airfields of Cyrenaica to attack the island. Churchill wanted action, partly to take the heat off Malta by pushing the Luftwaffe from those airfields, but Auchinleck was again unwilling to go forward until he was ready – probably not before June. The rising tensions between London and Cairo came to a head on 10 May with a blunt cable from the Prime Minister:

> We are determined that Malta shall not be allowed to fall without a battle being fought by your whole Army for its retention. Its loss would involve the surrender of 30,000 men . . . give the enemy a clear and sure bridge to Africa with all the consequences flowing from that . . . severing the air route upon which you and India depend for a substantial part of your air reinforcements . . . Compared with the certainty of these disasters we consider that the risks you set out for the safety of Egypt are definitely less, and we accept them.

That was laying the situation on the line. As the Official History points out, Auchinleck was faced with the stark option of attacking or resigning.[10] On 19 May he replied to this ultimatum, telling the PM that he would attack with the primary intention of driving the enemy out of Cyrenaica and destroying his army; more than that he could not do. Unfortunately for General Auchinleck, Rommel attacked first.

During the three-month pause after their retreat from Agedabia in January and February, the British had been busy creating the so-called Gazala Line, 30 miles west of Tobruk. This line consisted of a series of self-contained fortified brigade 'boxes', running from Gazala on the coast to Bir Hacheim in the south, a distance of some 45 miles, but had no secure southern flank. In laying out this line, the British commanders repeated on the defensive the mistake they had already made while on the offensive – a failure to concentrate. In the Great War – Western Front – sense the Gazala Line was not a 'line' at all. For example, there was a 15-mile gap between the Free French Brigade at Bir Hacheim (Free French units had been serving with the British in North Africa since 1940) and the box occupied by 150th Brigade of the 50th (Northumbrian) Division further north, and the screening minefields, not being covered by artillery or machine-guns, could be quickly cleared.

The Eighth Army's two corps were now as follows: Gott's XIII Corps had the 50th British Division and the 1st and 2nd South African Divisions, plus the 1st and 32nd Army Tank Brigades, equipped with Matildas. Norrie's XXX Corps had the 1st and 7th Armoured Divisions, the latter including the 29th Indian and 1st Free French Brigade Groups. In army reserve were the 5th Indian Division and 'Dencol' a small force composed of various detachments.

Each box was manned by a full infantry brigade, supported by artillery and surrounded by thick belts of wire and mines – a 'mine marsh' in the jargon of the time. The idea was that these boxes were to be mutually supporting, the gaps and minefields between them would be covered by fire and patrolled by roving armoured units from the two armoured divisions, 1st and 7th – the latter having returned from the Delta. In fact, as Rommel's attack soon revealed, these boxes were too far apart for mutual defence, the minefields could quickly be cleared, and the covering armoured forces to the rear were too dispersed to come to the aid of the boxes before the Germans could outflank them and screen them off. As with the armoured brigades at Sidi Rezegh, Rommel would crush the Gazala boxes in detail.

There had been some changes in the composition of the two British armoured divisions. Auchinleck had recast them, and each was now more like a panzer division. An armoured division would now consist of three armoured brigade groups, each with a motorized infantry battalion and a regiment of field artillery, and a motor brigade group, with three motorized infantry battalions and an artillery regiment. The armoured divisions were also now getting supplies of the new American Grant tank, a great improvement on the Crusader. Infantry divisions would retain their traditional organization and consist of three infantry brigades, each of three battalions, plus field and anti-tank artillery regiments. These anti-tank regiments would have the new 6-pounder gun, of which 112 had arrived in the desert, while the infantry and motor battalions had still to put up with the 2-pounder. Even so, tank and anti-tank kit was getting better with the Grant and the 6-pounder. Whether the tactics were getting better was another matter.

Auchinleck had also to stress, yet again, the great lesson of Sidi Rezegh; the need to keep the armour concentrated and avoid the 'Jock Column' philosophy. He told his commanders that 'Jock Columns' were to be used only sparingly and only for raids or harassing tasks, never for major attacks or in defence. It is curious that these facts still had to be pointed out to his commanders.

Apart from these additions to the armour, there had also been some improvements to the infantry kit. The motorized infantry battalions, in Bren-gun carriers, had been re-equipped with the Vickers medium machine-gun and had 2-pounder anti-tank guns in their support companies. On balance, if not yet ready to start an offensive, the British were well placed to withstand an attack – or so it seemed.

Aware that Rommel might attack again, Auchinleck anticipated either a thrust at the centre of the Gazala Line or one round the southern flank. Whatever happened, the brigades of XIII Corps were to hold the boxes, and the armoured divisions of XXX Corps were to attack the enemy wherever he appeared. 'I consider it to be of the highest importance', he wrote to Ritchie 'that you should not break up the organization of the armoured divisions. They have been trained to fight as divisions, I hope, and fight as divisions they should. Norrie must handle them as a Corps Commander and thus be able to take advantage of the flexibility that having two formations gives him.' This is a clear direction, but that 'I hope' over the training of these divisions is worrying. Since fighting in divisions was fundamental to success, why did Auchinleck not *know* that the divisions had been trained to carry out this order and would do so when the battle began?

Another point raised in Auchinleck's instructions was that, in the event of Eighth Army being driven back from the Gazala Line, Tobruk was not to be held. If the enemy seemed able to invest it effectively, Tobruk would be abandoned and the Army would fall back to the frontier.[11]

Rommel's eventual attack was expected, but its strength was

surprising. Bletchley Park had now cracked the Chaffinch Enigma used by German forces in North Africa, but no tank-strength returns were sent to Rome or Germany. However, in April Chaffinch provided much useful information: that Rommel intended an offensive in mid-May – code-named VEN-EZIA – and would receive another 80 tanks before it began.[12] It should have been apparent that this attack would be powerful, that Rommel had rebuilt his forces and would handle them with his accustomed verve and skill. What was not revealed was Rommel's precise plan: where he would attack and in what for-mation – battle plans were rarely sent over Enigma.[13] All the boxes therefore prepared to resist a direct assault.

The most vital of these Gazala boxes (see the map on pp. xiv–xv) was at Bir Hacheim in the south, the pivot point for any enemy hook round the British front. This box was held by the 1st Free French Brigade, largely composed of Foreign Legionnaires and commanded by Brigadier-General M.-P. Koenig. To their north, but 15 miles away, lay another box held by the 150th (British) Infantry Brigade, while 12 miles to the east, behind the 150th Brigade box and on the Trigh Capuzzo, lay the Knightsbridge box, held by the 201st Guards Brigade. (This unit was the former 22nd Guards Brigade, now renumbered to pre-vent confusion with 22nd Armoured Brigade.) The area between the 150th's box and the Knightsbridge box would become known as the Cauldron. Other brigade boxes, manned by British and South African units, continued the Gazala Line north to the sea.

The Gazala Line was too long and too thin. The essence of defence is depth, and the Gazala Line had very little depth. The system of boxes, designed to make the most of Ritchie's avail-able forces and cover the entire front, actually split his forces into separate positions, none of them strong enough to withstand a sustained attack and not close enough together either to support their neighbours or to present a solid front. Success would depend on the two armoured divisions, once the German inten-tions became clear.

Rommel was still outnumbered, in both men and tanks. Panzerarmee had about 560 tanks for this thrust at Gazala, but only 240 were Panzer Mark IIIs and only 38 Mark IVs; the rest were the obsolete Italian M13s. The British had some 800 tanks available, including 167 of the new American Grants, which had a 37-mm gun in the turret and a 75-mm gun in a sponson on the side of the hull. The Grant would have been a much better fighting machine had these guns been the other way round, for to use the 75-mm gun the tank had to be fully exposed. It was, however, a powerful machine, and the British tank crews were anxious to try out the 75-mm gun on the German panzers.

The 7th Armoured Division was deployed to cover the open flank and, in order to support the French at Bir Hacheim, lay some miles further south than 1st Armoured.

Rommel's tactics for the Gazala battle were to pin the British armour down with a frontal assault in the north – a feint between Gazala and the Trigh Capuzzo – and then send his tanks hooking round the desert flank. His main advance began on the evening of 26 May 1942, while demonstrations by tanks, bombing and artillery attempted to keep Ritchie's attention in the north. That night Rommel led a strong hook by four divisions – the Ariete, 90th Light, and 21st and 15th Panzer of the Afrika Korps – moving round the southern flank below Bir Hacheim, then heading east and north towards Sidi Rezegh to begin the series of actions later known as the battle of Gazala. These actions were to last a full month.

Rommel's advance was immediately successful. Soon after first light on 27 May a huge German tank force was spotted by crews of the 4th South African Armoured Car Regiment, moving around the southern flank below Bir Hacheim. Here the Germans were engaged by 'C' Squadron of the 8th Hussars, commanded by Major J. W. ('Shan') Hackett, while news of the advance was reported back to division, corps and Army HQ, Brigadier Filose of the 3rd Indian Motor Brigade in 7th Armoured Division telling General Messervy that he was up against 'a whole bloody German armoured division'.[14]

The reaction to this news at 7th Armoured's HQ seems muted, even casual. Filose was actually facing the Italian Ariete Division and part of 21st Panzer, and the Indian Brigade was quickly overrun, losing over 400 men and most of its equipment in under an hour. From then on matters deteriorated rapidly. At about 0830 hours German armour and infantry overran 7th Armoured Division's advance HQ, scattering the 7th Motor Brigade (the old Support Group) and capturing Messervy and several of his staff officers. Messervy quickly removed his badges of rank and fell in with the private soldiers as the Germans rounded up their prisoners. When a German officer inspecting the prisoners came up to ask, 'Aren't you a bit old to be an ordinary soldier?' Messervy fervently agreed, and he remained undetected in the ranks until dawn on the following day, when he was able to escape and return to his division. The news that the divisional commander had been captured did not reach Norrie's corps HQ for another 12 hours – shortly before Messervy turned up again – so communications were clearly chaotic.

As for the 1st Armoured Division, in spite of Auchinleck's orders, that was already splitting into its various brigades. The 22nd Armoured Brigade was ordered to move south and engage the enemy, but ran into two panzer divisions and lost 30 tanks and a number of guns. This brigade then fell back towards Knightsbridge with the enemy in pursuit as the 2nd Armoured Brigade came in from the flank; together they managed to hold off the panzers, supported at Knightsbridge by the 1st Army Tank Brigade of XIII Corps.

The Germans were now pushing hard between the boxes, and the 4th Armoured Brigade – also of the 7th Armoured Division – fought all day in an attempt to stem their onrush, the 8th Hussars being caught before they could move out of their leaguer and suffering accordingly. By mid-afternoon on the 27th the Germans had scattered the 7th Armoured Division and were in position to assault the 201st Guards Brigade in the Knightsbridge box. One report recalls the Germans as 'a black mass of tanks, beginning in the region of the Knightsbridge Box and stretching south as far as the eye could see'. It will be noted that the Knightsbridge box was 12 miles behind the front-line 150th Infantry Brigade box; Rommel's attack had now got into the rear of Eighth Army, and was threatening its supply lines.

In spite of all this, according to the Official History, 'the day ended with the British higher command more satisfied with the day's fighting than General Rommel'.[15] If so, it is hard to see why. Rommel had stopped only for lack of fuel. He had lost a number of tanks, but he had gained a lot of ground and was sure to come on again once the fuel trucks came up. Once more the British had made the mistake of committing their armour piecemeal. They may have had little choice in the face of Rommel's rapid advance and the disruption caused by the loss of the 7th

Armoured divisional HQ, but beyond GHQ the British commanders clearly never had any intention of fighting their
armour in one solid force. In his papers, Rommel writes:

> The sacrifice of the 7th Armoured south of Bir el Harmat [south
> of Knightsbridge] served no tactical purpose whatsoever since it
> was all the same to the British if they met me there or on the Trigh
> Capuzzo [east of Knightsbridge], where the remainder of their
> armour [1st Armoured Div] entered the battle . . . *their aim should
> have been to bring all their armoured forces into battle at the same time*
> [my italics]. Their units were fully motorized and able to cross the
> battlefield at great speed to wherever danger threatened.

Even without the benefit of hindsight, it is easy to see that
Rommel was right: the defence against the German tanks should
have come from anti-tank guns, while the armoured divisions,
instead of dispersing to cover the boxes, should have been held
back to engage the enemy in strength once his position and
intentions were clear. Above all, they should have been kept in
close formation; Auchinleck's instructions on this point to both
Ritchie and Norrie had clearly been ignored.

On the evening of 27 May, to shorten his supply route, which
currently ran around Bir Hacheim, Rommel cleared two paths
through the minefields on either side of the 150th Infantry
Brigade box. Since these minefields were not covered by fire, this
task went ahead rapidly. Fuel and ammunition now came forward, and 15th Panzer – low on fuel and ammunition – stopped
near Knightsbridge to guard these gaps while the advance was
taken up by 21st Panzer, the Ariete and 90th Light.

One surprise that day was the capture of General Crüwell,
commander of the Afrika Korps during CRUSADER, who was shot
down in his Storch; his command was briefly taken over by Field
Marshal Albert Kesselring, who was on a short visit to Rommel's
HQ and clearly relished the chance of field command. And the
loss of Crüwell was not the only German setback; the RAF was
in action over the battlefield, attacking fuel trucks and soft-
skinned transport, and by nightfall on 29 May the entire German
advance had stopped, again largely through fuel shortages.

Rommel himself had been obliged to head back to hurry up
the supply columns – one of the problems with his direct method
of command was that even he could not be everywhere. He went

where he was needed, and the need now was to concentrate his forces and build up supplies of fuel and ammunition for the British counter-attack.

Rommel's forces were therefore concentrated in the desert east of Knightsbridge when fuel supplies arrived on 29 May. To the British this position seemed to present an opportunity, a chance to push the Germans back into the minefields. In fact the Germans were now using the British minefields to cover their flanks while waiting in the gaps for the British tanks to waste themselves against the Axis anti-tank gun screen. On 29 May the 4th and 22nd Armoured Brigades were in action against all three Axis divisions – 21st, 15th and Ariete – while the RAF continued to pound the enemy supply lines west of the boxes. Fortunately for the tank units of Eighth Army, this Axis attack was hampered by a sandstorm and did not fully develop. The main point, however, is that Rommel now had his forces established behind the brigade boxes, which now faced attack from the east, with their supply lines cut.

Rommel concentrated his forces in the minefields near the 150th Infantry Brigade box, and the second phase of the battle began with an assault on this box, supported by Stuka dive-bombers. There was intense fighting in this area for several days, and it rapidly became known as the Cauldron – a boiling region of smoke, shellfire, bombs, tracer and burning tanks. The attack on the 150th Brigade box was followed by an assault on the French box at Bir Hacheim, where the French and Foreign Legionnaires, completely surrounded, put up a magnificent defence for the next few days. Rommel came up to lead some of the attacks there, and wrote later that 'Never in Africa was I given a stiffer fight than at Bir Hacheim.' The fact that a number of the Legionnaires were German refugees from Hitler may have contributed to the stiffness of the resistance.

The 150th Brigade box fell at noon on 1 June, most of the defenders breaking out to the east before it fell. The fighting now began to open out between two widely separated boxes, that held by the Free French at Bir Hacheim and that of the 201st Guards Brigade at Knightsbridge, with various armoured units – British, German and Italian – engaged between and around these positions. Rommel was striking out in all directions from his defensive position in the Cauldron, while the British were putting in attacks against the Germans where encountered – and running time after time into their anti-tank-gun screen. As General G. L. Verney recalls in the 7th Armoured Division history, 'Very many tanks were lost and the effects on the enemy were less than had been hoped.' In fact the evidence suggests that these attacks had no effect on the enemy whatsoever, though they cost the British a great number of tanks. The Official History describes the attacks on 1/2 June as 'a fiasco'[16] – the 'feeling of general satisfaction' recorded for 28 May[17] had not endured.

When General Ritchie counter-attacked again, on 2 June, his assault on the Germans in the Cauldron was marked by the usual errors, while the Luftwaffe devoted itself to pounding the garrison of Bir Hacheim with Stukas. Here the RAF scored a victory, shooting down 16 enemy aircraft; General Koenig sent a signal to Air Vice-Marshal Arthur Coningham, the commander of the Desert Air Force, 'Bravo, Merci pour le RAF', to which Coningham replied, 'Merci pour le sport.' Elsewhere, however, there was little to celebrate.

The British counter attack was too slow, the place chosen was too obvious, and units attacked in scattered formations and were promptly repulsed, often sustaining heavy losses before the enemy anti-tank gun screen. It almost became a routine; Rommel's forces would wait until the British tanks emerged from their artillery smokescreen and then open a devastating fire with their Pak-50 and 88-mm anti-tank guns. The attack by the 32nd Army Tank Brigade on the Sidra ridge was repulsed with the loss of 50 of the 70 Matildas that went forward.

Nor were the divisions co-operating with each other. The Official History records that 'the Tactical Headquarters of 7th Armoured and 5th Indian Divisions were each occupied with their own problems and there was nobody in sole command to co-ordinate their actions'.[18] Auchinleck, knowing that the bulk of Rommel's forces was east of Gazala, contemplated sending the 1st South African Division west towards Bir el Temrad, but the South Africans would need tank support, which was not available. Besides, the main task now was to keep up the pressure in the Cauldron, with a fresh attack on 5 June. This attack began well, but then, as too often before, went awry in the face of German artillery and anti-tank fire.

By the evening of 6 June the British tank strength – 700 on 27

May – had fallen to 170. Then Rommel attacked again, scattering 7th Armoured's brigades for the second time in ten days. The day concluded with what the Royal Tanks' history records as 'delays, misunderstood orders, counter-orders, and disorder' – yet more evidence of poor command and a breakdown in communications. The Official History records that 'on the XXX Corps front there was no single commander, for General Norrie had delegated the command to Generals Briggs and Messervy in turn and they worked out their parts as best they could'.[19] A better recipe for chaos could hardly be imagined.

Ted Smith of the 11th Regiment RHA, recalls the end of the Gazala battle:

The overall position was that the Regiment had been in action for every day of the three weeks or more of the Knightsbridge and Cauldron battles, but after some early successes Eighth Army's position had steadily deteriorated and most of the infantry from the north part of the Gazala Line had been withdrawn.

'A' Battery had deployed early that morning with 'Charlie' Troop a few hundred yards on 'Don' Troop's left. (This was long before the days of 'Able', 'Baker', 'Charlie', 'Dog', never mind 'Alpha', 'Bravo'.) To our front there were a dozen of so tanks of the Bays, supplemented by perhaps 20 RTR tanks, all hull down on our side of the ridge. I was 'Don' Troop's wireless operator and was soon busy passing fire orders to the guns from the OP [observation post] officer's Honey tank. Everything was proceeding normally when a captain appeared beside me and explained that he was the OP of a 6-inch gun battery and as he had only a soft-skinned vehicle he did not want to go any further forward and could we provide his battery with targets? I relayed this message to our battery commander, Major McDermid, stating that some 'Big Bugger' – our term for anything bigger than our own 25-pounders – was requesting targets. We had plenty of targets for them, and after a short pause I was reporting their fall of shot as well as our own so that this captain could give corrections to his guns.

During this time there were, at all too frequent intervals, thick plumes of smoke to our front as our sparse tank numbers dwindled. Passing messages was a problem, as we in 'A' Battery no longer tried to establish field-telephone lines, which were simply chewed up by tank tracks. Because our guns were going to be very exposed when the German tanks came forward, Major McDermid hastily worked out a way for the 6-inch guns to put down a barrage on the ridge to our front as the panzers came on, commenting 'This should give them hell.' The code for our own battery fire was 'Damnation'.

As our handful of tanks began to limp back through our positions there was a lull in our firing, but it soon began again, with the range dropping steadily. Then, as both our troops and the 6-inch gun battery had fired, I received the signal 'Damnation' in my headset and, giving the call signs, said 'Don shot, Charlie shot, Big Bugger shot, Damnation, Damnation.' Maybe this was not the most peculiar signal of the Second World War, but it must have ranked high.

The postcript to this is that we delayed the panzer advance to allow our remaining tanks to get out successfully. 'C' and 'D' Troops then gave each other covering fire as they leapfrogged to the rear. We lost one gun of our eight as the panzers came over the ridge and down the slope with guns and machine-guns firing, but we still managed to get away with fewer casualties than in some other cock-ups.[20]

With the British now in considerable disarray, Rommel sent his panzers south to attack the French at Bir Hacheim, where strong German attacks on 7 and 8 June were stoutly resisted. On the 9th, what was left of the 4th Armoured Brigade was sent down from Knightsbridge in an attempt to relieve the pressure on Bir Hacheim, but its attack was swiftly blasted apart by the 88-mms. On the evening of 10 June the Germans finally broke into the French defences, and on the following night the remnants of the Free French were withdrawn, leaving much of their equipment behind. Two days later, on 12 June, Rommel pinned the 2nd and 4th Armoured Brigades between the 21st and 15th Panzer Divisions, and on the 13 June he cut off the 201st Guards Brigade in the Knightsbridge box. Richie's Gazala Line was being chewed to pieces.

The Germans attacked the north side of the Knightsbridge box on 14 June, overrunning the Scots Guards' position. The 4th and 22nd Armoured Brigades – with their remaining tanks – counter-attacked during the afternoon and evening, losing another 22 tanks, and that night the Knightsbridge box was evacuated, the Guards battalions withdrawing down a corridor kept open by the tanks. This left two divisions, the British 50th and the 1st South African, holding boxes to the north of the Trigh Capuzzo and the Cauldron, their garrisons cut off by panzer forces swinging north towards Tobruk.

Jim Sewell was at Gazala with the Royal Army Service Corps:

> Most of our work was supplying ammo to the guns or petrol to the tanks. We seldom worked the coast road, and in two-wheel-drive transport we often got bogged down in soft sand. Sometimes our work took us through the sites of tank battles, the desert littered with burnt-out tanks and wooden crosses telling the story.
>
> About this time I met a mate of mine who was driving a Chevrolet truck with a 2-pounder gun on the back – a portée. He said that in battle they drove in, swung round, fired a few rounds, and beat a hasty retreat. I don't know if he was telling it straight, but we were hopelessly out-gunned and it was not until we got the Sherman tank and the 6-pounder anti-tank gun that we had anything decent to fight with.
>
> We were then attached to the Rajputs in the Indian Division, and on 13 June my diary says that we were bombed and an Indian sergeant was killed. I also remember seeing a camel step on a mine – a bang and a camel, intact, about 20 feet in the air before disintegrating.
>
> We were bombed and strafed regularly, and my diary reads that on 7 July we were taking ammo up to the guns and stayed the night – they were 25-pounders, and we formed up in a column headed, I think, by the Long Range Desert Group, for imagine my surprise when we set out through the Qattara Depression, a sea of supposedly impenetrable sand. We were about 20 miles behind the German lines at this time and shelled the German aircraft landing at El Fuka before making our way back to our own lines.[21]

The 50th and 1st South African Divisions were ordered to break out before Rommel could send 15th and 21st Panzer to cut them off, but on 14 June Rommel could tell the Comando Supremo that 'the battle has been won and the enemy is breaking up'. This report was all too accurate, and Rommel's original target and long-term ambition, Tobruk, was now within his grasp. The 90th Light Division was ordered to advance on El Adem, and 21st Panzer headed for El Duda, its tanks crushing the wreckage of the previous November's battle.

The weary and much depleted armoured brigades of Eighth

Army managed to stave off the German tanks for a while, and most of 50th Division's units were able to escape towards the east. Cyril Brian was well forward with No. 6 STC, one of the RAF's supply and transport columns, transporting fuel and ammunition to the forward airfields:

By 13 June, Eighth Army was in full retreat and we were ordered to the rear. We had fallen back a long way, but at 0630 on 14 June I was up and made a sand and petrol fire as we had just enough water for a brew each. Then, as it got light, we saw a large gap in the escarpment to our right and two German staff cars, with officers staring though field glasses down towards the coast road. Behind them were about eight German soldiers with tommy guns. They were only a few hundred yards away, and all this took only a couple of minutes. We flung the tea down, jumped into the truck, and were away. There was no fire after us, and either the dust cloud must have saved us or we were not important enough. We got to the Bardia railhead and the CO turned up and saw we were all there and we again headed east, running into some New Zealand gunners – they thought at first we were German and could not understand that we were RAF. From there we posted on to the Alamein Line, where the Eighth Army was already digging in, and stayed here for a while, only 20 or so miles from Alexandria.[22]

The 1st South African Division, withdrawing along the coast road – the Via Balbia – towards Tobruk, lost only its rearguard at this stage and was able to get within the Tobruk defences, but Eighth Army was now in full retreat across the frontier, heading towards the elusive safety of the Alamein Line. John Johnson was an officer in the Royal Corps of Signals:

We were in a truck chased by one of those German eight-wheeler armoured cars. It opened fire, and one shot hit the jerrycan of water we had in the back – I can recall the water flying in the air. So we stopped, and a German got out of the armoured car and counted us – there were eleven of us: myself, three British soldiers, and seven Indians. The German took my revolver and told us to wait while they went after the rest of the party. I saw no future in that, and said to the men that I intended to make a run for Fuka, which was our original destination, and anyone who wanted should take a water bottle and come with me. The three

British soldiers agreed; one was a lance-corporal and I heard him say, "E made me a lance jack, so I gotta go wiv 'im, didn't I?'

We ran towards a small group of camel-thorn bushes and lay on the ground while an Italian tank collected the rest of the party. We expected the tank to fire in our direction, knowing there were four men short, but eventually it moved off and we started walking. Then another, smaller, armoured car appeared and we went to ground, but out got a man in a white shirt and grey flannel trousers. This could only be an Eighth Army officer, so we got up and went forward, telling him there was an eight-wheeler German armoured car just over the hill. He was very keen to have a go at it, but I don't think he would have had a chance as his car only mounted a 2-pounder gun. We therefore went looking for other British vehicles, and came upon a mixed collection. There was at least one gun portée, the odd water truck and several 15-cwt trucks, and we took a few of these and drove off.

After two or three days we popped up at the coast and found it occupied by the enemy, and so we popped back into the desert again and eventually arrived at El Alamein. There I found most of the unit, and they were congratulated because they had brought back all their wirelesses.[23]

On 20 June the Germans rolled over the defences of Tobruk, and on 21 June the Tobruk garrison, now commanded by Major-General H. B Klopper of the 2nd South African Division, surrendered. At 0200 hours that morning Klopper had promised to resist until, 'the last man and the last round',[24] but the port fell into Rommel's hands a few hours later. This capture provided him with 32,000 prisoners, most of them from the 2nd South African Division, and a great quantity of useful booty, including 2,000 serviceable trucks, 2,000 tons of fuel – about 1.5 million gallons – and a large amount of food and ammunition. The cost of this triumph to the Panzerarmee Afrika since the Gazala offensive began on 26 May was 3,360 officers and men, killed, wounded or missing.

With the loss of Tobruk the British disaster at Gazala was complete – and far away in Palestine the soldiers of the 9th Australian Division were furious. Dr Bob Douglas of the 9th Division wrote of the news in his diary:

The news of Tobruk is but three days old and the division as a whole takes a poor view of it. This was the division mainly

involved in the siege, but I have heard very little said against the
Tommies by these men. They all realize how difficult a place it
was to hold, especially against a full-scale attack by armoured
forces. Many of them left their best friends buried up there in the
blue. I dare say there will be a lot of criticism of the Tommies in
Australia, especially by the armchair critics. Make no mistake, the
Tommies are a jolly fine lot and good soldiers too. So are the
South Africans. They would never have surrendered unless completely overwhelmed.[25]

Alf Curtis was also in the 9th Australian Division:

After we came out of Tobruk we went to Palestine for a rest. This
was a great relief, not only from enemy action but also to enjoy
the basics of normal living and we had a good Christmas 1941
and a New Year before we went up to Syria. The 7th Australian
Division had been withdrawn and was homeward bound, and
we replaced it as the security force in that area, being confident
that, with it gone, our turn for home would follow.

But our hopes were dashed and we were devastated when we
heard that Rommel had at last got his prize. It was a major loss
strategically, and our losses in men and equipment were cata-
strophic. The urgency of the situation called for immediate
action, and in July 1942 we were bundled into trucks and sent
non-stop to Alexandria. Within days we were in a coastal position at El Alamein.[26]

For Winston Churchill, the loss of Tobruk was a devastating
blow. He was dining with Roosevelt in Washington when an
aide handed the President a message. 'Roosevelt read it and,
without a word, handed the message to Churchill. The message
read, "Tobruk has surrendered with 25,000 men taken prisoner."
For a moment, no one spoke. The silence was broken by
Roosevelt who asked only, "What can we do to help?"'[27]

Returning to Britain, Churchill was faced on 2 July with a
House of Commons motion expressing 'No confidence in the
central direction of the war'. This motion was defeated by 475
votes to 25 after a Conservative MP had made the fatuous suggestion that the direction of the war should be entrusted to the
Duke of Gloucester, a scion of the royal family who currently
lacked employment. This proposal produced gales of laughter in
the House and saved the day for Churchill. Even so, the fall of

Tobruk was widely seen as a disaster – and one that meant the eventual downfall of General Auchinleck.

Tobruk fell for several reasons. Auchinleck had long since decided that there was no point tying-up troops there for another costly siege if Rommel came on again. The defences had been allowed to decay, tank ditches had filled with sand, and minefields had been stripped to provide mines for the Gazala 'mine marsh'; the 2nd South African Division had done little or nothing to remedy these deficiencies. Finally, Rommel's onslaught, supported by strong Luftwaffe attacks, was devastating. But these facts did little to soften the blow – it should surely have been possible to hold Tobruk for more than a day and so delay Rommel's advance into Egypt.

The Official History records that the fall of Tobruk was 'a staggering blow to the British cause'.[28] This it was – and one intensified by the fact that the town had held out so successfully for eight months in the previous year. Units among the garrison of Tobruk were particularly stricken; some battalions hastened to destroy their weapons and equipment, and numerous parties, including 200 men of the 3rd Battalion the Coldstream Guards, simply refused the order to surrender and made their escape before the Germans moved in. At least two units, the 2/7th Gurkha Rifles and a battalion of the Cameron Highlanders, held their positions and fought on in spite of Klopper's command to surrender – the Gurkhas until the evening of 21 June, the Camerons until the morning of 22 June.

Major Eric Schmidt was in Tobruk at this time with the 570th Corps Field Park Company, Royal Engineers:

> We were ordered to surrender by General Klopper of the South African Division. This we refused to do, and we formed a fighting column with Major Sainthill of the Coldstream Guards. We left the Tobruk perimeter and headed south for about 30 miles before turning east and joining up with Eighth Army HQ. When it was decided that the Sollum dump should be destroyed before we retreated into Egypt, I was appointed Rear Guard Commander and our company (570) carried out this task. We destroyed 180,000 gallons of petrol, 9,000 anti-tank mines, 5,000 lb of gelignite and I fired all the dumps inside ten minutes. At no time were we short of volunteers, and we all knew we would be striking back before long.[29]

Among all the tactical errors that contributed to the defeat at Gazala and this resulting collapse at Tobruk, one major question stands out. Why were the British, yet again, surprised by Rommel's advance, let alone by its speed and weight? They had Ultra, they had the LRDG patrols, they had air reconnaissance, they had an ear to the Italian and Afrika Korps wireless traffic. None of this seems to have made any difference: 7th Armoured Division HQ was surprised and overrun even though it was getting constant reports on the German advance from one of its own patrols throughout the first night of the attack.

Lieutenant Fletcher of the South African Armoured Car Regiment was on patrol well inside the German front line on the night Rommel attacked, and detected two large tank formations, panzers of the 15th and 21st Divisions, clanking over the desert, moving in a south-easterly direction for a point south of Bir Hacheim.

Fletcher signalled this information back to 7th Armoured and continued to shadow the German formations all night, sending in up-to-the-minute accounts of their progress. Keeping slightly ahead of the enemy, he led the two panzer divisions round Bir Hacheim and continued to report on the enemy until daylight when his armoured car was spotted against the eastern skyline and came under shellfire. The warnings resulting from this gallant and highly professional piece of work seem to have been totally ignored by 7th Armoured's HQ – why else was Messervy captured?

Rommel's successes at Gazala were due to his tactics and skilful generalship rather than to superior force, and his practice of leading from the front again paid great dividends during these fluid battles. He was on the spot to see what was happening, and had the authority to order instant changes in the direction of his forces or the conduct of the battle. This enabled him to concentrate his forces, and during any pauses in the fighting he brought his tanks and vehicles behind an impenetrable anti-tank gun screen.

This tight command and the local use of strong forces made all the difference, and Rommel knew it. 'What is the use of [the British] having overall superiority,' he wrote, 'if one allows each formation to be smashed piecemeal by an enemy who is able to concentrate superior forces on every occasion at the decisive point?' Writing of the Gazala battle, Michael Craster states, accurately, that 'the Army Commander [Ritchie] was often wildly out of date and, because of the problems of communications, command and control, found himself quite unable to grip the battle.'[30]

The veterans agree with this. 'You are absolutely spot on when you say there was something seriously wrong with the higher command of Eighth Army in the direction of CRUSADER and again in the Gazala and Cauldron battles in early 1942,' writes Major Eric Schmidt.

General Cunningham had been a brilliant leader in East Africa but he completely lost control in the tank battles at Sidi Rezegh, when he was all for cutting his losses and pulling back to the Egyptian frontier. Auchinleck quite rightly would have none of it and relieved Cunningham of his command. At Gazala we were once again appalled that General Ritchie apparently made no effort to concentrate his armour, with the result that our tanks were destroyed piecemeal on 12/13 June – hence the loss of Tobruk.[31]

Ted Smith of the 11th Regiment RHA recalls this time:

After six months of advance and retreat over many hundreds of miles and only a week or so after the huge tank battles at Knightsbridge, in which the 11th Regiment played a formidable part, the Regiment found itself cut off with its back to the sea just east of Mersa Matruh, in a rearguard action to delay the Axis advance on the Delta.

We were in this position because after the fall of Tobruk, a few days earlier, our regiment had been pulled out of the 3rd Armoured Brigade and ordered to join a rapidly gathered collection of units of less than brigade strength with, as far as I could see, no tanks. The area we occupied was a shallow depression and could hardly have been worse; the sea was to the north, and an escarpment to the south provided the enemy with good firing and observation positions. During the first day there, increasing fire from all around indicated that the Germans were building up their strength, so we were glad when we were told that we were to break out after dark.

When the time came we limbered up and the whole force, in several columns, moved off and climbed the escarpment to reach the open desert, where the Germans were in leaguer for the night.

We soon came under fire, which we returned, and had halted about 10 miles into the desert when we were told to about-turn and go back to our original positions. I expect the Germans were even more astonished by this than by our breakout. We returned successfully through their leaguers with more tracers and fireworks, and bedded down in our previous position, not without some pithy comments – to put it mildly – on what devious plans, if any, the High Command had in mind.

At first light our guns moved into position and a section of the Coldstream Guards gave us cover during the day when we were directing fire from the troop's guns on the ever increasing German forces. Before the sun was quite down Captain Pearson was called to HQ for orders, and quite soon we set off to repeat our breakout of the previous day. I did not think our chances were good, as we moved off too early and the Germans, unlike the day before, would still be in their positions along the escarpment.

We went in low gear, but as we crossed the escarpment we came under heavy machine-gun fire at close range. I could see the muzzle flashes through the canvas, and our truck stopped instantly, its engine riddled. We scrambed over the tailboard, and five or six Germans were already on us and I heard, 'Hands up, Tommy, for you the war is over.' My combat days were indeed over, but many hardships and dangers lay ahead.

I was rapidly searched by one infantryman, who dropped the ammunition clips and a Bren-gun magazine I was carrying on to the sand, but in the other pouch I had a few tubes of sweets taken from an abandoned canteen wagon near Matruh. He pulled these halfway out, then dropped them back into the pouch. Heartened by his attitude, I pointed to the back of our vehicle and made the gesture of putting on a coat. He nodded, and I pulled out my greatcoat – a great asset, as the nights were very cold.

My mate Jock and I were taken off, but we had only gone a few yards when a German soldier called over to our guards and led us to where a badly wounded British sergeant was lying near a knocked-out truck. Jock and I carried him for a short distance, but then we heard more of our trucks approaching and the Germans clearly wanted to get back to their posts. They indicated that we should leave the sergeant, but before doing so I covered him with my greatcoat. We were taken back some 200 yards to their company HQ, and spent the rest of the night there under guard.

From time to time in the next few hours there would be heavy firing as our vehicles tried to break through at various points. In what proved to be the last incident, a staff car was shot up as it crashed through at high speed into the depression in which 20 or so prisoners had been gathered. All the occupants were killed and I took a senior officer's sleeping roll, which proved a real boon over the next few months. The more distant firing died down, and it was not long before I was sound asleep. Next day we were soon heading west in open vehicles under guard, before being handed over to Italian control.

As the years pass, I sometimes think of the impeccable conduct of those Afrika Korps soldiers who shot our truck up and took me prisoner. They were good soldiers, and good men – I hope they survived the war.[32]

After the Gazala battle and the advance to Tobruk, Rommel's forces were very tired and much reduced. His three German divisions had very few tanks, with no more than 44 ready for action. The two Italian divisions – the Ariete and the Trieste – had just 14 tanks, and both the German and the Italian infantry were exhausted by two weeks of continuous fighting. Nor had they enough transport to continue the advance: most of Rommel's infantry and support units were now using captured British trucks, as their own were worn out. But they were now within striking distance of Alexandria – and, as a reward for taking Tobruk, Rommel was promoted to Field Marshal.

Auchinleck reversed Ritchie's first decision after the fall of Tobruk – to stand and fight at Mersa Matruh – and ordered a further withdrawal to the secure line now being prepared between the Qattara Depression and El Alamein. Finally, on the night of 25 June 1942, Auchinleck relieved Ritchie of his command and took over direct control of Eighth Army.

In spite of the depleted state of his forces, Rommel kept on coming – believing that this was the time to conquer Egypt. On 26 June he launched another attack on Mersa Matruh and El Daba and sent more British transport hurrying to the rear, where its sudden arrival spread still more alarm and confusion. Mersa Matruh fell on 27 June, after which confusion became general and on that day the Western Desert was full of British, Italian and German units, all heading east into Egypt.

In some places the advancing Germans were ahead of the retreating British, but with both sides using each other's transport it was difficult to tell. Rommel wrote of 'a wild mêlée . . . the RAF bombed their own troops and German units fired on each other'. This pell-mell retreat into Egypt entered Desert Army folklore as the 'Gazala Gallop', and so, gloriously intermingled, the two armies came back together – and collided again among the defences of the half-completed Alamein Line.

2 New Zealand Div.

6

First Alamein to Alam Halfa
July and August 1942

General Auchinleck, who had meanwhile taken over command at Alamein,
was handling his forces with very considerable skill . . .

Field Marshal Erwin Rommel, 2 July 1942

Another commander, having achieved such a sweeping victory,
might have paused at Tobruk for a mild celebration, but not
Field Marshal Rommel. At 1030 hours on 21 June, as his prisoners were formed into columns and marched west, he ordered
Panzerarmee Afrika to 'reassemble and prepare for a further
advance'. By noon his troops were out of Tobruk and hurrying
after the retreating British Army, where chaos was still reigning.
Much of the confusion gripping the British commanders was
over the question of whether to hold on to El Adem, the airfield
south of Tobruk. According to General Messervy of the 7th
Armoured Division:

> 29th Brigade was in El Adem and I got via Corps an order: on no
> account was El Adem to be evacuated – they were to fight it out
> to the last. It was already surrounded. I was told by Norrie that
> these were the Army Commander's personal orders. Then I had
> a message: it might be evacuated if I thought it could not be held.

I said I was quite sure it could not be held for long; then I was told
to pass this message to 29th Brigade. Then I got another order –
the Army Commander says it must be held. Then yet another;
that it was to be evacuated – if the Brigade could get out. I passed
this on to Denis Reid (the Brigadier) and they got out. This was
an example of what was happening all the time.[1]

There is an Army expression for this sort of thing: 'order, counter-
order, disorder'. In such circumstances it is hardly surprising that
Eighth Army continued to fall back in disarray.

Auchinleck had decided to stand at Mersa Matruh, where the
western perimeter of the town was protected by a wide minefield. He hoped to hold the line between the coast and the
escarpment with the 2nd New Zealand Division, brought down
hurriedly from Syria. This division would be backed up by elements of X Corps, mainly the 10th Indian Division, positioned on
the coast, with what was left of Gott's XIII Corps on the escarpment. These troops were to hold while XXX Corps went back to
the Alamein Line and began to dig in and regroup. On 25 June,
the day on which Auchinleck dismissed Ritchie and took over
Eighth Army himself – which at least had the advantage of
shortening the chain of command – he cancelled the decision to
stand at Matruh and ordered an immediate withdrawal to the
Alamein Line.

Before the forces at Matruh could withdraw, Rommel struck
again. On 26 June, with just 62 tanks and a total force of fewer
than 3,000 German infantry, he routed the two corps at Matruh –
as ever, widely dispersed – and sent them hastening back down
the coast road to Alamein – a resumption of the Gazala Gallop.
Correlli Barnett states that the German victory at Mersa Matruh
marked 'the consummation of a colossal moral ascendancy of
Panzerarmee Afrika over Eighth Army'.[2] This comment seems
all too accurate. The generals of Eighth Army were on the back
foot, and their soldiers had nowhere to go but backwards – to
Alamein.

The soldiers themselves seem to have taken this latest reverse
philosophically. Everyone knew that Rommel was a genius, and
no one was too surprised – or greatly dismayed – that he had yet
again come off best. The New Zealanders, having made another
epic stand on the Minqar Qa'im ridge, south of Matruh, prised

their way though 21st Panzer with the bayonet, and most of the other units of X Corps and XIII Corps, having fought for a while, also managed to make their escape. In this breakout, Captain Charles Upham of the 2nd New Zealand Division won his second Victoria Cross, adding a bar to the VC he had won on Crete. The New Zealand Division marched into the British lines on 28 June, having sustained 800 casualties in three days, and Rommel could add another 6,000 prisoners and a quantity of tanks and guns – the booty of Mersa Matruh – to the lavish spoils of Tobruk. If he could repeat this success at Alamein the British cause in the Middle East would be lost.

Lord Bruntisfield – then Lieutenant John Warrender of the Scots Greys – took part in this withdrawal:

> I was a troop leader in 'A' Squadron, with two Lees and one Grant tank in the long retreat back to Alamein from the Gazala battles, in which we were largely in reserve. I fought our first hard battle with these tanks when we stopped the rout with 22nd Armoured Brigade about 40 miles from Alex. Then I went to 'B' Squadron, the Light Squadron, with Honeys (Stuart tanks), first watching over the minefields on the southern end of the Alamein Line near Himeimat. Incidentally, it was here I first met General Montgomery. We were on a ridge, hull down [i.e. with only the turret visible], watching the enemy line and doing some crew maintenance, when this staff car arrived and out got the CO, the Brigadier and a little man with very white knees wearing an Australian bush hat covered with regimental badges.
>
> I had no idea who he was, and while I was talking to the CO he went over and talked to my fitter, but their talk did not go too well. The officer asked this Glaswegian, 'Who is the finest general in the desert?' The soldier looked him up and down and said, 'You hav'na been here long, have ye? The best general is yon Rommel – everyone here knows that.' Apparently, when they were driving away, Monty asked my name and commented that my men seemed in need of some further instruction. None of us had heard of Monty at that time, but that was to change.[3]

The defensive position at Alamein was already in the course of preparation when Eighth Army came back from Matruh. Work had been started by X Corps and Egypt Base Area troops long before the Gazala battle began, and this line was a much stronger position than any yet found to the west. As at Gazala, the Alamein Line consisted of a number of defended boxes. But, unlike Gazala, the Alamein Line had secure flanks. It rested on the sea at El Alamein in the north, and could not be out-flanked to the south because it terminated after 40 miles at the Qattara Depression which was impassable to tanks. Given good fortune – and a change of attitude – the Alamein position could probably be held.

Even so, Auchinleck was not wedded to a final stand at Alamein. His prime aim – a sound one at the time – was to keep Eighth Army in being. If Alamein fell he would move east to the Suez Canal and fight again – and go on fighting, right up the Nile if need be, keeping his army in being, keeping the Germans away from the Persian and Iraqi oilfields. For the moment, he elected to stand on the Alamein Line and deal the enemy a 'stop-ping blow' when he came up. Auchinleck was also determined to keep his forces 'mobile and fluid, and strike at the enemy from all sides'. Every infantry division was to organize itself into 'bri-gade battle groups' formed around a core of field and anti-tank artillery, with tank and infantry detachments. The aim of this, said Auchinleck, was to provide the wherewithal for either static defence or mobile operations. Even without the problems then affecting the army, there must be some doubt if units so com-posed could be suited for both purposes, static defence and fluid operations. The Official History also expresses reservations on this point:

> Whether these fluid tactics were appropriate to the occasion or not they were certainly new and entirely unpractised. *The British tactical doctrine for a withdrawal had for many years insisted that any-thing in the nature of a running fight must be avoided* [my italics]. Thus Eighth Army was facing a bewildering number of changes. Its Commander had been replaced; it was retreating before a thrusting enemy; it had barely prepared itself for one kind of battle when it was ordered to fight another and in the midst of all this it was told to change its organization and its tactics. But before anything could be done in the way of reorganization, the enemy put an end to one uncertainty by starting to attack.[4]

Rommel arrived at the Alamein Line on 30 June, but found that this last advance was just too much for his exhausted and much depleted units. His German units, the backbone of Panzerarmee, had been in action for two months without a break and were down to around 30 per cent of their former strength. The Italian units, if stronger, were equally exhausted. His forces had been constantly harried by the Desert Air Force in their advance from Tobruk, and, although he had acquired plenty of British transports, spares were short and air attacks were taking a steady toll of these recent assets. Although this book necessarily concentrates on ground operations, the vital contribution of the Desert Air Force to Eighth Army's performance in advance and retreat was inestimable and should not be forgotten. This contribution was recognized in Auchinleck's subsequent dispatch:

Our Air Forces could not have done more than they did to help and sustain Eighth Army in its struggle. Their effort was continuous by day and night and the effect on the enemy was tremendous. I am certain that had it not been for their devoted and exceptional efforts, we should not have been able to stop the enemy on the El Alamein position and I wish to record my gratitude and that of the whole of Eighth Army to Air Chief Marshal Tedder, Air Marshal Coningham and the air forces under their command.[5]

The essence of the situation at this time is that Rommel's men were not capable of putting in an immediate attack on the Alamein Line. Auchinleck's men began working hard on the Alamein position, deploying reserves, rounding up and reorganizing the retreating units, laying a quantity of mines, digging in the artillery and anti-tank guns for the attack they knew was coming. The basic calculation was that to hold the Alamein line would require two infantry divisions and a great deal of armour, spread around three defended localities – or 'boxes' – and a study of the map on page xvi would be helpful at this point.

The ground at Alamein was split in two between XIII Corps and XXX Corps at Bab el Qattara, 15 miles north of the Depression and 25 miles from the coast. Apart from the 'boxes', the troops in the Alamein Line were organized in mobile brigade groups of lorried infantry supported by tanks and artillery. Apart from the minefields, the Alamein defences were not continuous. Auchinleck had no intention of repeating the tactics of Gazala: the idea was that the three defended localities should act rather like breakwaters, splitting the enemy's forces, which would then be taken on in detail by the British mobile forces as they flowed past.

Auchinleck opted for defence in depth, but left the southern side of the line, beyond Bab el Qattara, more open. The aim was to tempt Rommel into attacking here – the most obvious place anyway – and counter him further east, on Alam Halfa Ridge, which ran west to east, south of Ruweisat Ridge. This was a shrewd use of ground and of the enemy's probable intentions, given the nature of the terrain and Rommel's well-honed tactic of getting across Eighth Army's communications with a hook round the southern flank.

If Rommel came in on the southern flank, he had two choices. First, he could press on east across the open desert towards Alexandria and the Canal. If he did that, his communications would become extended and open to attack from undefeated British forces remaining in his rear. The obvious alternative to this risky procedure was to turn north once through the British line and head for the coast road. To do that he must take Alam Halfa Ridge, which Auchinleck proceeded to put in a state of defence with mines, anti-tank guns and a great deal of field artillery. Perhaps the greatest step forward taken by Auchinleck at this time was the grouping of the artillery into one powerful group and a concentration of the armour as more tanks became available. What he needed most of all was time to reorganize and retrain, but on 1 July his time ran out.

Rommel was very short of men and tanks. On 1 July he had around 60 tanks and about 6,000 infantry, of which only 1,500 were German, but he could wait no longer. He intended to make his main thrust along the axis of Miteiriya Ridge, between the two northern boxes, the northern one held by the 1st South African Division and the one held by the 18th Indian Brigade, 6 miles further south. Having broken through there, his forces would then swing north to isolate the Alamein position and cut the coast road. This should bring on the kind of mobile battle at which Rommel was a master, and this attack – usually referred to as 'First Alamein', though it has no official designation – began on 1 July. First Alamein was to last for most of the month and be both hard fought and extremely confusing.

Although Rommel's army was in high spirits it was extremely tired, and the attack did not go too well. At first light on 1 July the

Desert Air Force appeared and bombed the advancing German formations, the DAK and the 90th Light Division, and this caused a delay. Then the 21st and 15th Panzer Divisions ran into heavy shelling and stout resistance from the 18th Indian Brigade at Deir el Shein, on the western end of Ruweisat Ridge. Then they were attacked by the 3rd South African Brigade Group.

None of this had been anticipated. Rommel had believed that his forces would be opposed only by the much reduced elements of the 50th (Northumbrian) Division. The Indians at Deir el Shein held out all day, 90th Light could not get round the Alamein box, and these delays put Rommel's entire strategy out of joint – and cost his force about a third of its remaining tanks.

At dusk on 1 July Auchinleck could look back on a rare event: a day that had actually gone well. The main problem was the tanks of the 1st Armoured Division, which had failed to engage at Deir el Shein, but this mistake would now be rectified – and this in turn would still the cries of alarm coming from Cairo. With Rommel attacking Alamein and the Mediterranean Fleet obliged to move from Alexandria down the Canal into the Red Sea, panic had spread among the General Staff in the Delta. A rain of ash was falling on Cairo from bonfires lit to destroy confidential papers at GHQ; in future years Wednesday, 2 July 1942 would be referred to in Eighth Army as 'Ash Wednesday'.

Up in the desert, Auchinleck remained calm. He was pleased with the day's events and, mustering his forces to renew the battle at first light, gave precise, unequivocal orders to Gott and Norrie. XXX Corps would continue to resist Rommel's pressure, while XIII Corps would drive into his right flank and cut his communications by reaching the coast. With luck, this could result in the complete destruction of Panzerarmee, at worst it would give Rommel a long-overdue bloody nose. Eighth Army was at last getting that essential touch of 'grip', and had XIII Corps had an adequate number of tanks and men this plan might have succeeded.

On 2 July the 4th Armoured Brigade moved against the flank of the 15th Panzer Division, promptly losing a number of tanks to the 88-mms. However, the main thrust of the Afrika Korps, east of Deir el Shein, in an attempt to reach the coast road and cut off the Alamein position, was hindered by the sudden appearance of 50 tanks of 22nd Armoured Brigade which clashed with

21st Panzer. It should be noted that the Afrika Korps's two divisions now had a combined strength of only 26 tanks.

Rommel's advance had not started until the middle of the afternoon – because the Desert Air Force had appeared at first light and bombed his supply trucks – and at dusk his forces halted and went into leaguer, having made little progress. On the other hand, he had not been cut off or further punished: the British attack had been too slow, and the 22nd Armoured Brigade, which should have cut around the Afrika Korps, had collided with it and taken losses in a fierce tank battle. On balance, however, the day was Auchinleck's – Rommel had been halted.

In this continual July fighting, much of the credit on the British side must go to the Desert Air Force. The pilots flew some 15,400 sorties in the July battles, an average of over 500 attacks a day. On 3 July Rommel reported to OKW that his divisions were down to brigade strength and that the constant air attacks were reducing his supplies to a dangerous level, leaving him with no option but to halt his attack, at least for the time being.

Auchinleck therefore took up the initiative, sending his troops forward to probe the enemy positions and prepare for a follow-up if the enemy looked like withdrawing. Rommel proceeded to regroup his forces and switched his attention to the southern end of the Alamein position with the intention of attacking the 2nd New Zealand Division, which, he noticed, had edged a little forward. Destroying the New Zealand Division would have been a very good move: this outstanding division was a constant thorn in the flesh of Panzerarmee Afrika – resolute in attack, stubborn in defence, ably commanded by Freyberg and his brigadiers.

Rommel's plan was thwarted on 8 July by another push by Auchinleck in the north. This attack was mounted by XXX Corps, now commanded by Lieutenant-General W. H. Ramsden, and had the aim of capturing Italian positions on the Tel el Eisa and Tel el Makh Khad ridges, west of the Alamein box. The task of taking the Tel el Eisa ridge was given to the 9th Australian Division, which had just arrived from Syria, while the 1st South African Division was to capture Tel el Makh Khad; both attacks would be made with tank support, and they began in the early morning of 10 July.

The attacks went well, and both positions were taken by midday. Then the Germans began to react, sending in a battle group of 15th Panzer against the 26th Australian Brigade, and pounding both ridges with artillery and mortars. The fighting here went on until 14 July, when, having attracted some German units to the north, Auchinleck mounted another attack on the Italian and German positions around Deir el Shein, along the axis of Ruweisat Ridge.

It will be seen from this series of attacks that, under Auchinleck's command, Eighth Army was far from being either passive or defensive; it was constantly attacking the Axis lines and writing down the enemy forces in a series of small but well co-ordinated attacks at various points along the line. Eighth Army was finding its feet – and greatly enjoying the sensation.

The attack along Ruweisat Ridge lasted three days, from 14 to 17 July. It was only partly successful and somewhat costly, especially to the New Zealand Division, which, with the 5th Indian Infantry Brigade, provided the infantry for this attack. The New Zealanders were in trouble from the start, largely owing to communication failures, and were to compound these problems by failing to completely clear the enemy positions they overran. This led to the 22nd New Zealand Battalion being attacked by tanks of the 8th Panzer Regiment – a brief skirmish in which the New Zealanders' anti-tank guns were quickly knocked out and the unprotected infantry, caught in the open with only platoon weapons, had the option of death or surrender; 350 men of this fine battalion were hustled into captivity. This event was observed by Brigadier Kippenberger, who went in search of some British tanks, hoping to prevent such a catastrophe from happening again. Kippenberger found the tanks 4 miles from the ridge, their crews watching the battle through field glasses.

In every turret, someone was standing gazing through glasses at the smoke rising from the Ruweisat Ridge, four miles away. I found and spoke to the regimental commander who referred me to his Brigadier who received me coolly. I did my best not to appear agitated, said I was commander of 5 New Zealand Infantry Brigade, that we were on Ruweisat Ridge and were being attacked in rear by tanks when I left an hour ago. Would he move up and help? He said he would send a reconnaissance tank. I said there was no time. Would he send his entire brigade? While he was patiently explaining some difficulty, General Lumsden drove up.[6]

Major-General Herbert Lumsden, then commanding the 1st Armoured Division, was not much help either. While his tanks were being located, the remnants of the 22nd Battalion located an Italian position and a platoon led by Sergeant K. Elliot put in a bayonet attack, taking the position and 200 prisoners. Wounded three times in this attack, Sergeant Elliot was awarded the Victoria Cross.

The problem for the New Zealanders and Indians here was caused initially by a failure to mop up – enemy units held out in small pockets behind the Allied advance and prevented more troops coming forward and the wounded being evacuated. And this was fatally compounded by the failure of the armour to provide close support. There was then another German tank and armoured-car assault, this time on the 4th New Zealand Brigade, in which the brigade headquarters were overrun and 380 men were taken prisoner, including the redoubtable Captain Charles Upham, VC and bar. This three-day battle on Ruweisat Ridge in mid-July cost the 2nd New Zealand Division no fewer than 1,405 officers and men and left the survivors extremely aggrieved by what they saw as the neglect of the armoured units they should have had in support.

The Australians were also in action at this time, as this account from Bill Sutherland of 'D' Company 2/23rd Battalion confirms:

'D' Company were allocated a forward defensive position on the slopes of a hill, Tel el Eisa, on the railway, forward of the main Alamein position. This was close to a railway cutting which the Germans had already occupied, so we had to build sangars and were pinned down most of the day, only getting about at night. On 16 July we were ordered to attack the cutting – we had about 130 men and we went in with the bayonet at around 0500 hours, taking around 400 prisoners and holding the cutting for around four hours until we were obliged to come back to our former lines. By then we were down to about 70 men and we had lost the company commander and most of the officers. We were then told that we were to attack the cutting again on the next night, with the 16th Platoon going into the cutting from one end, the 17th from the other and 18th Platoon chucking grenades from the top on to the enemy in the middle.

We heard these orders with disbelief and then with resentment, and there was a bit of a mutiny since we were going to our deaths if this went forward and in the end 13 men refused to advance and the attack was called off. These men were put under arrest and were brought before the CO, Colonel Bernard Evans. He would not accept their arguments or their suggestion that they would make the attack if the CO would lead them in person. When the attack went in it was discovered that the Germans had evacuated the cutting, but had it gone in when first planned it would have been suicide.[7]

The following splendid account, illustrating the confusion of battle, comes from the diary of Max Parsons, then an artillery observer with the 2/12th Australian Field Regiment:

On 17 July 1942 I was a forward observation officer, advancing in a Bren-gun carrier with the infantry. 0330 hours and it is still dark. I wear KDs, mainly to protect my legs from the hot engine, plus taking a haversack, my shorts and my .38 revolver. Zero hour is 0500 hours, and except for some shelling all is quiet. Tanks, guns and trucks everywhere. Some delay and I am exchanging repartee with the infantry in their trucks while Fid and Streety are already having trouble with the wireless. We move below the ridge and the 2/23rd Infantry Battalion starts moving over the crest into direct view of Jerry. As soon as the leading 25 men advance in dispersed formation, the shelling commences.

Infantry now advancing in open formation with rifles at the trail. Jerry is landing shells among them – why do men just walk into what looks like certain death as though they were walking across a football ground? Several of the infantry have gone down when shells land 5 or 6 yards away. Some have stayed down, and the stretcher bearers will move out in a few minutes. All those who have not been blown down are still moving forward – after that shelling nothing will stop them.

Up to now we have met only defensive artillery fire, but now an 88-mm is on to us, also anti-tank fire from the right flank, and tanks add some nasty crossfire. We have 12 Valentine tanks with us, and they move on until we reach a minefield. The infantry are advancing firing from the hip. Major Feitel is now with us and we watch as one after another the Valentines blow up in the minefield – the mines are obvious, so why? The minefield extends far to the right and left; the infantry move through, but the vehicles cannot. Enemy medium guns, possibly 105s, now start shelling and are bursting all around us. A line of mines is cleared and a jeep goes through. We try in the carrier, mines just

6 inches away on my side, Don says they are closer on his – on we go.

We step on the gas and speed through a shelled area to where the infanteers are rounding up prisoners of war from a couple of posts and sending them back in batches. A staff captain comes up and tells me I must take an urgent wounded back to ambulance, and we help a man aboard with his arm blown off close to the shoulder. As he climbs aboard the exposed arm bone rises up as though the missing arm is trying to help – I remember the overwhelming smell of meat and the flies on his shattered shoulder. Stretcher-bearers did a wonderful job, but most of his arm is raw.

We move back to the 'ambulance', which turns out to be a derelict truck. Don spots vehicles over there and we go that way only to find they are anti-tank guns flat out in battle. Over come airbursts, MG fire and anti-tank – what a racket! We will never make it. I huddle down in my seat and my tin hat is too small, but I try to cover my whole body with it. Air bursts are exploding 50 feet above the carrier – we can feel the heat of the exploding TNT. Occasional ground bursts, and we hear MG fire splatting off the side of the carrier.

We reach a slightly covered area with infantry on the ground firing away with rifles. A sergeant sits up and yells, 'Get to hell out of here!' We swerve away and reach the main casualty area, nearly running down a casualty in the scrub. During all this our casualty has been very game – never complained. I don't know how he got on, but I fear the worst as I've known so many die from shock after such a traumatic loss of a limb and delay in hospital treatment. The ambulance man was very considerate and helped him down from the carrier, saying in a gentle voice 'What have they been doing to you, laddie?'

I get into the blood-covered front seat and explain to Don that Major Feitel had told me that the infantry were going to retreat so we'll have to race back and pick him up, choosing a rough course to keep out of the path of MG and anti-tank fire. In the middle of the shelled area our petrol runs out. Don and I hop out and put in a 4-gallon tin of fuel and off we go again – flat out. The carrier has taken a lot of punishment. As we approach the gap in the minefield I am looking out for mines when I see men jump from a vehicle and run like hell to the left. I shout to Don, 'Swing left and go like hell, the tanks are coming.' But Don looks behind and says, 'It's a bombing raid, you silly bugger – get out.' I looked around and saw a dozen or so planes zooming down on us and bombs dropping from the leading Stuka. The first bombs burst before I knew what was what, so I crouched down on the floor of the carrier as the bombs came closer and closer. Fortunately they missed by yards. The planes continued strafing away from us, so we carried on.

Italian prisoners gave us a chuckle: there were hundreds of them – some with a couple of our walking wounded looking after them, some with no escort at all. Jerry began to deliberately shell these groups of prisoners, and I saw many killed.

Instead of going back through the minefield, I saw Major Feitel coming back with the battalion commander, so we drove to him. We took up position near a knocked-out armoured car OP and decided to stay there and direct our guns on to the advancing Germans while our infantry retreated through us. The OP officer from the armoured car turned out to be a South African, and he had a nasty hole in his head. He joined us and with a towel pressed against his wound, directed the fire of his guns. Fid and Streety did a great job transmitting his orders in between our calls for fire to our regiment.

Only four Valentine tanks remained between us and the enemy when our carrier received a direct hit from an enemy anti-tank gun. We had to leave both carrier and SA armoured car and walk. I was all in favour of leaving everything and dashing off, but Major Feitel ordered that we grab all the equipment – even coils of wire from the carrier – and take it with us. So, laden with all this salvage, we staggered off.

That walk was something to remember – it seemed that every enemy gun on the front was aimed at my backside, but somehow we made it. When we were about halfway to our lines a jeep raced out and picked up Major Feitel and the wounded South African and the rest of us walked back to our lines. One of my mates, Signaller George Wardle, was aware that we might be in trouble and without permission came out looking for us to lead us in – he said he was worried that we might be lost: such is mate-ship. You must remember that this was written by a 22-year-old and I was rather impressed by the magnitude of the action that day.[8]

Serious as these steady losses were to the British side, Panzerarmee Afrika was in no better state. On 21 July Rommel wrote a gloomy view of the situation to OKW, stating that his armour was now reduced to just 26 tanks and his men were exhausted by weeks of constant fighting. Facing fresh British forces, his tank strength gone and the Italians a constant anxiety,

Rommel's forces could do no more. Auchinleck, on the other hand, well aware of this situation via Ultra, continued to urge his men forward, though they too were tiring.

Rommel's problems were compounded at about this time by the loss of his Good Source; the leak of information via Colonel Bonner Fellers had finally been discovered and stopped. How this happened remains unclear, but Feller's information would have been sent to Rommel by Enigma and it is possible that an Ultra decrypt finally revealed what was going on. Perhaps the information came from an Italian source in Rome, but one possible explanation is the overrunning of an Italian radio link in the desert by an Australian fighting patrol, which returned to Eighth Army with prisoners and a quantity of documents. Whatever the reason, in mid-July Fellers was hastily called back to Washington and Rommel's most useful source of intelligence information dried up.

The fight for the Alamein Line continued for the rest of the month, but in a somewhat feeble fashion. The opposing forces were like two exhausted boxers, flailing away at each other in the final round, neither strong enough for a knockout blow, each hoping to score some last-minute points. The 9th Australian Division in XXX Corps and the 2nd New Zealanders in XIII Corps added to their existing reputations, but the battle was inconclusive. Each side attacked in turn, only to find that the other had grown a little stronger in the interval – and holding Rommel at First Alamein had not helped Auchinleck's reputation in London.

The critical situation at Alamein and the successes of General Rommel throughout the early summer – successes which had brought the enemy to within 60 miles of Cairo – now brought Winston Churchill to Egypt. General Alan Brooke, the CIGS, wanted to go alone, but Churchill insisted on accompanying him. He found the troops of Eighth Army 'brave but bewildered, but still cheerful, confident and proud of themselves'. The Prime Minister was less happy with General Auchinleck, and extremely critical of his decision not to attack again before September. If there was one constant in Churchill's attitude to the desert generals it was his wish for frequent attacks on the enemy, and his irritation when his commanders declined to deliver them.

Churchill felt that he had supplied this general – and all the previous desert generals – with a great deal of *matériel* and hundreds of thousands of men and yet *still* the enemy was triumphant and *still* there were excuses and further delays. The difficulties facing Auchinleck – and the previous generals – some of them caused by Churchill himself, quite escaped the Prime Minister's attention. When Churchill arrived in Egypt on 4 August he had already decided that Auchinleck must go.

At the time and since, some have felt that Churchill's decision was unfair, not least because in the fighting at First Alamein Auchinleck had 'magnificently redeemed his errors. Thus the military case for relieving him was much weaker than it had been.'[9] This may well be so – but this point admits that there *was* a case for relieving him, albeit a weak one. What finally doomed Auchinleck was, first, the fall of Tobruk and, second, his decision, however correct, not to attack Rommel again until September.

There was clearly some breakdown in communications between Auchinleck and Churchill. Even before Gazala, Auchinleck had announced that, should Rommel again threaten Tobruk, he – Auchinleck – had no intention of defending it. And yet, when the news of Tobruk's fall reached Churchill in Washington, he recalled, it was 'a bitter moment', and he added, 'Defeat is one thing; disgrace is another.' Churchill even had difficulty believing that the news could be true.

The fall of Tobruk came just a few months after the equally humiliating fall of Singapore and was perhaps the final break of the ever tenuous accord between Churchill and the desert generals. Churchill had probably had enough of the endless delays in taking the offensive. He had heard too many reasons for delay – however justified – and found that, in the event, these reasons were never justified by any subsequent success.

Nor does everyone consider Auchinleck's dismissal unfair. Writing in 1979, Field Marshal Lord Carver, a staff officer in Eighth Army in 1942, clearly disapproved of Montgomery's cavalier treatment of Auchinleck on taking up the command of Eighth Army, but added, 'This does not, in my opinion, mean that it was wrong of Churchill to have replaced Auchinleck by Alexander when he did . . . far from it. Of course, it was a bitter blow for Auchinleck just when he thought he had restored the situation but after the defeats and failures of the summer of 1942, it is inconceivable that he could reasonably have expected to stay in command.'[10]

On arriving in Egypt, Churchill interviewed many of the Eighth Army commanders down to brigade level and inspected many of the units. Then, having reviewed the situation on the spot, he acted. First he took the long-overdue step of cutting the Middle East Command in half, splitting affairs in Persia and Iraq from those in the Mediterranean and the Western Desert. He then refused to accept Auchinleck's objections to any renewal of the offensive before September. On 6 August Churchill proposed that the War Cabinet replace Auchinleck, currently both Commander-in-Chief and GOC, Eighth Army, with General Sir Harold Alexander becoming C-in-C Middle East, and the command of Eighth Army going to Lieutenant-General 'Strafer' Gott. Churchill was anxious to retain Auchinleck in some capacity, and he was offered the new command in Iraq – a post that Auchinleck declined.

Gott did not want command of Eighth Army. He had been in the desert since 1940, having arrived as a lieutenant-colonel in the KRRC, and he frankly admitted that he was now completely tired out and in sore need of rest. In Gott's honest and freely expressed opinion, some fresh thinking was needed in the desert and new men should be appointed to command, but when pressed he reluctantly agreed to accept the appointment.

Gott never had the chance to command Eighth Army. On 7 August, when he was flying back to Cairo to take up this post, his aircraft was shot down by German fighters. Gott survived the crash and escaped from the aircraft, but was killed when he returned to the burning plane to rescue men trapped inside. His death was a great blow to the Desert Army. He was the last of the desert warriors, a veteran of campaigns which had already seen the loss of so many good officers – great fighting men like Jock Campbell and Richard O'Connor. His sudden death marks another turning point, for at last it brought to the desert a man who was to prove a match for Erwin Rommel: Lieutenant-General Bernard Law Montgomery, the famous 'Monty', who took over command of Eighth Army on 13 August 1942.

Montgomery had just been appointed as the British commander for Operation TORCH, the Anglo-American landings in Algeria which were then being planned, but on Gott's death

Brooke decided that Montgomery was the man to change the fortunes of Eighth Army – and, as it transpired, Brooke was right.

Soon after arriving in North Africa on 12 August, Montgomery became deeply engaged with his parallel career – making enemies. This process began on the day after his arrival when he decided to take over command of Eighth Army with immediate effect, without having the courtesy to inform the existing commander, General Auchinleck, who had intended to stay in post until 15 August. Montgomery then informed Churchill that, on taking command, he had discovered that Auchinleck had intended to retreat to the Delta. He added that, while visiting the troops, he had discovered that 'Many were looking over their shoulders for their place in the lorry, and no plain plan of battle or dominating will power had reached the units.'[11]

This is not to say that Montgomery's comments were entirely baseless. In his memoirs, Kippenberger recalls a meeting with Gott:

> Gott was in his armoured command vehicle (ACV), the first I had seen. He got out at once and handed me a letter. It was a short note from General Corbett, then Auchinleck's MGGS [Major-General, General Staff]. I remember very clearly the opening sentence, 'The Chief has decided to save Eighth Army.' The note then went on to say that the South Africans would retire through Alexandria and the rest of us down the desert road to Cairo.[12]

Kippenberger then recounts Gott explaining that 'a general retirement and evacuation of Egypt was being contemplated and he supposed that we – the New Zealand Division – would go back to New Zealand. I protested', writes Kippenberger, 'that we were perfectly fit to fight and that it was criminal to give up Egypt to 25,000 German troops and a hundred tanks. Gott replied sadly that the NZ Division was battle-worthy but very few other people were and he feared the worst.' Kippenberger concludes that 'in the evening a provisional order for our retirement arrived from XIII Corps. It certainly envisaged the abandonment of Egypt.'

So there appears to be some basis for Montgomery's allegation. But it was both wrong and quite unfair of Montgomery to imply that the troops of Eighth Army were demoralized after the battles of Mersa Matruh and First Alamein.[13] Kippenberger, who saw the Eighth Army units come back from Matruh records, 'Eighth Army poured back through us, not looking at all demoralized except for the black South African drivers, but thoroughly mixed up and disorganized. I did not see a single formed fighting unit, infantry, armour or artillery.'[14] Evidence from the veterans – including, most usefully, extracts from diary accounts written at the time – indicates not that the troops were demoralized but that they were completely fed-up with the continual reverses and wanted someone to take a grip on Rommel and give them a fair chance of victory.

This meeting between Gott and Kippenberger took place on 30 June, and a lot had changed in the weeks since then, but the abandonment of Egypt had clearly been contemplated. Nor was all well within Eighth Army after the July battles. Kippenberger, then commanding the 5th New Zealand Brigade, pulls no punches in his assessment of Eighth Army at this time: 'There was throughout Eighth Army and not only in the New Zealand Division, a most intense distrust, amounting almost to hatred, of our armour. Everywhere one heard tales of other arms being let down; it was almost axiomatic that the tanks would not be where they were wanted.'[15]

Other accounts confirm this view. Kippenberger makes it clear that he understood the difficulties the armoured troops were facing – not least a grisly fate when their tanks were hit and burst into flames – and states that he did his utmost to counter the distrust among his men, but the fact that it existed at all is significant.

Lord Bruntisfield of the Scots Greys describes life as a tank troop commander:

> One got very fond of one's crew. In a battle they would read books, usually Westerns, sitting quietly underneath one, where they could see nothing of what was going on, glancing up at one's face if there was an unusual noise. If you grinned at them and showed no concern they went back to reading, quite unworried. Standing in the turret, I used to have trembling knees when I was frightened, which I could not control, so I used to sit on the turret seat and try to conceal this from the men for fear of worrying them. They soon spotted it, and used to tease me about it.
>
> I never closed the lid of my tank turret. For one thing one simply had to see out to deal with what was going on, and if the tank was hit and caught fire you had to be very quick in baling

out. There was no time to waste opening the hatch, and it might have got stuck through distortion and you were in the turret with three men below you trying to get out of the flames through a very narrow opening. Very often one saw the remains of men all jammed together in the turret and stuck, unable to move. Fire was the great danger, and we wore very few clothes.

About our tanks? Throughout the war our tanks were always grossly under-armed and -armoured compared with the German tanks, and we never caught up let alone surpassed the German models. Our tanks were designed like sports cars, the German tanks like agricultural machines, which of course a tank is. Our tanks were demanding on maintenance, and broke down if treated roughly. On the other hand, we had many more tanks than the Germans, but we never beat them until we learned to copy their tactics. Our commanders always tried to fight tanks with tanks, while the Germans used their tanks to shepherd us on to their anti-tank guns, especially the 88-mm which could brew us up at ranges of 2,000–3,000 yards. In the desert we could only engage their tanks at ranges of about 300 yards – hopeless! Not until Alam Halfa did we follow the German practice.[16]

Inter-arm relations were not good in Eighth Army in mid-1942. Many units – and some national contingents – felt that they themselves were pulling their weight but were being constantly let down by others. The general atmosphere was not encouraging and Montgomery's comments therefore deserve some consideration, though the general tenor of his remarks about Auchinleck is as unpleasant as the comments themselves are unkind.

Montgomery's memoirs also contain some quite unnecessary remarks about Lieutenant-General Gott. 'It is now clear to me', he wrote, 'that the appointment of Gott to command Eighth Army at that moment would have been a mistake. I had never met him; he was clearly a fine soldier and had done splendid work in the desert. But from all accounts he was completely worn out and needed a rest. He himself knew this.'[17] The fact that these views are quite accurate and confirm Gott's own view does not make them any more palatable. Montgomery had no reason to write about Gott at all, but these remarks are typically 'Monty': even the dead are not beyond criticism and must not be allowed to stand in the way of Monty's glory – a glory that will shine all the brighter if the situation before his arrival can be depicted as a shambles.

Montgomery met Auchinleck briefly on 12 August, and the meeting was not a success. The two men had served together in 1940, when Auchinleck had been GOC Southern Command and Monty a divisional general. They had detested each other then, and Monty – on the day he arrived in Egypt – was scathing about Auchinleck's intentions. According to Montgomery's account (see above), these were based on the belief that, whatever happened, Eighth Army must be preserved, even if Egypt was abandoned.

'If Rommel attacked in strength and broke through,' says Montgomery, 'Auchinleck intended to fall back to the Delta and if Cairo and the Delta cannot be held the Army would retreat to the Nile or Palestine, or southwards up the Nile. I listened in amazement to this exposition of his plans', says Monty, 'and asked one or two questions but quickly saw that he [Auchinleck] resented any questions directed to immediate changes of policy about which he had already made up his mind. So I remained silent.'[18]

Montgomery should have remained silent for his version of Auchinleck's plans in mid-August was soon disputed. Auchinleck's current plan was, in fact, the one confirmed by General Alexander and swiftly adopted by Montgomery – to hold the area between the sea and Ruweisat Ridge and to threaten any advance south of the ridge from a strongly defended position on Alam Halfa Ridge. 'General Montgomery,' says Alexander's Alamein despatch, 'now in command of Eighth Army, accepted this plan in principle, to which I agreed.'

There were in effect two plans: the one outlined above and Auchinleck's 'Plan B', the one described by Gott to Kippenberger, for what would happen if the Alamein Line fell – as so many other lines had done – and Eighth Army was forced back yet again. Montgomery had no 'Plan B'. He decided, rightly, that if the Alamein Line fell all was lost for the British in the Middle East. This being so, the logical conclusion was that the Alamein Line *must not* fall. He therefore turned his attention to ensuring that it held. That task must begin with the officers and men of Eighth Army.

Monty's first move was to clear out Auchinleck's staff and senior commanders, starting with Major-General 'Chink' Dorman-Smith, the deputy chief of staff, who seems to have had many enemies in the Army at this time; Dorman-Smith's dismissal from Eighth Army was effectively the end of his career. Fresh

generals were then imported from England: Lieutenant-General
Sir Oliver Leese took over XXX Corps, Lieutenant-General Brian
Horrocks took over XIII Corps, and both proved good appoint-
ments. Monty was also obliged, albeit reluctantly, to accept
Major-General Herbert Lumsden, the commander of the 1st
Armoured Division, as GOC of X Corps.

Montgomery had intended to bring his old friend 'Simbo'
Simpson out from the UK as his chief of staff, but after arriving
in the desert he decided to retain Brigadier Francis ('Freddie') de
Guingand, formerly Auchinleck's Brigadier General Staff,
whom Monty knew well. De Guingand told Monty that Eighth
Army needed 'gripping and a clear lead', which Montgomery
proceeded to apply. On 13 August, two days before Auchinleck's
term was due to end, Monty sent a signal to Cairo assuming
immediate command of Eighth Army and another to the unit
commanders: in the event of an enemy attack there would be no
withdrawal – 'we would fight on the ground we now held and
if we could not stay there alive we would stay there dead'.[19]

This blunt statement went down very well with the troops,
and Brigadier Kippenberger recalled his own reaction:

> The new Army Commander made himself felt at once. He talked
> sharply and curtly, without any soft words, asked some searching
> questions, met the battalion commanders and left me feeling very
> much stimulated. For a long time we had heard little from Army
> except querulous grumbles that the men should not go about
> without their shirts on, that staff officers must wear the appropri-
> ate arm-bands and things of that sort. Now we were told that we
> were going to fight, that there would be no question of retirement
> to any reserve positions or anywhere else. We were delighted and
> the morale of the whole Army went up incredibly.[20]

Having given his army a shake-up, Montgomery studied his
maps and the Alamein defences and decided on his strategy for
when Rommel next came on. With Eighth Army on the defensive, no one doubted that Rommel *would* attack again and make
yet another bid for the Delta. Should he do so, certain possibilities had to be taken into account. The first was the most likely
one: that Rommel would repeat his Gazala tactic, breaking
though the British line with his armour in the south and then
turning across the rear of the British position to cut the lines of

communications with the forward units, destroy the defensive boxes, and bring on the kind of sprawling battle with the British armour in which his anti-tank guns and powerful armoured units could wreak their usual havoc.

Preparations to deal with this situation had been laid by Auchinleck and although the argument over who was responsible for the tactics and dispositions for the next battle is still being argued about sixty years after the event, it appears that both Auchinleck and Montgomery can share the credit for the subsequent engagement at Alam Halfa. This is not to say that Montgomery did not attempt to hog all the credit; on the other hand, had these tactics failed, Montgomery would have received all the blame.

Auchinleck had disposed his forces along the Alamein Line from the coast to Bab el Qattara, some 15 miles north of the Qattara Depression. The ground from Bab el Qattara to the edge of the Depression was covered by the mobile forces of the 7th Armoured Division – the 7th Motor Brigade and the 4th Armoured Brigade – and by a thick belt of mines. When Rommel came it was more than likely that he would cut through in the south and turn north, but at Alamein he would face a problem. First of all, the minefields and the mobile forces, backed by plenty of artillery and the Desert Air Force, would slow him down and cost him casualties and tank losses, as at First Alamein. Second, any advance towards the coast would have to cross the Alam Halfa Ridge, which Auchinleck had intended to defend, 'refusing' his left flank to deepen his defences while offering a tempting approach route for Rommel's panzers. Alam Halfa lies some 15 miles behind the centre of the Alamein line and, running south-west to north-east for some 12 miles, offered the perfect defensive position against any thrust from the south towards the vital coastal road and railway line. Panzerarmee Afrika would be held here, blasted by artillery and pounded by the Desert Air Force until the British armour drove into its flanks.

This was the basic plan. It was a good one, and it was Auchinleck's. Montgomery had only to build on it, but he also introduced a few successful amendments – principally that the enemy should not be greeted with counter-attacks by tanks but should be allowed to come on and waste himself against the British lines. Mobile defence by roving armoured units was out;

the British would now play to their defensive strengths and beat off enemy onslaughts from static positions, using artillery and hull-down tanks, fighting, as the current saying went, 'on ground of their own choosing' behind a screen of dug-in tanks and anti-tank guns backed with artillery. Montgomery saw this encounter with Rommel as an unavoidable trial of strength, a preliminary to the offensive he was already preparing. One current task was to form a *corps de chasse*, X Corps, for the eventual pursuit, and he told Horrocks that 'on no account' was the British armour of XIII Corps, the 7th Armoured Division, to be written down in the next German attack. The 7th Armoured Division, the veteran desert formation, was to be kept for the pursuit.

Having decided on a defensive battle at Alam Halfa, Montgomery proceeded to thicken his defences, bringing up the newly arrived 44th Division from the Delta to Alam Halfa Ridge and backing up the New Zealanders and 7th Armoured Division to the south with tank brigades and artillery. This move was completed just in time to repulse Rommel's attack, which came in on the night of 30/31 August, beginning with a tank thrust through the southern part of the Alamein Line and then turning – as anticipated – up to Alam Halfa.

The 90th Light Division, the Ariete and Littorio Divisions of the Italian XX Corps and the DAK came through the minefields south of the New Zealand positions at Bab el Qattara and turned north, intending to roll across the British lines of communication behind the Alamein Line and cut the supply lines feeding the forward divisional boxes. Rommel did not have the fuel for a sustained offensive but, he wrote later, was relying on 'the slow reaction of the British command, which from experience we know takes time to reach decisions and put them into effect'. He had only 200 tanks, but half of these were Panzer Mark IIIs equipped with the long 50-mm gun and the rest were Mark IVs equipped with the new long-barrel 75-mm.

Rommel's attack on Alam Halfa has strong echoes of Gazala. He intended to smash through the minefields, pass between the two brigades of 7th Armoured – 4th Armoured Brigade and 7th Motor Brigade – and then fan out, having the various Panzerarmee divisions facing north by dawn. His problem here was that Ultra and RAF reconnaissance had revealed his intentions days before and Eighth Army was ready for him. Nor could his attack move fast: a dust storm, mines, constant bombing by the Desert Air Force, and the stout resistance put up by the British armour and artillery slowed his advance considerably.

As they swung north, Rommel's forces were promptly subjected to artillery fire from the guns of the 2nd New Zealand Division and the 7th Armoured Division. By dawn on 31 August the panzer forces had advanced only 8 miles towards Alam Halfa Ridge, and they were held there by fire from artillery of the 44th Division and tanks of the 22nd Armoured Brigade mustered in force on the forward slope of Alam Halfa around Point 102, as well as by more bombing from the Desert Air Force. The 22nd Armoured Brigade consisted of the 3/4th CLY, the Scots Greys, the 2nd Royal Gloucestershire Hussars, the 6th and 5th RTR and two artillery regiments. This brigade was currently commanded by Brigadier G. P. 'Pip' Roberts, and was largely equipped with Grants.

Before long the Panzer Mark IVs were taking a heavy toll of the Grants, and only the arrival of the Scots Greys stopped the German attack breaking into the brigade position. The Greys' tanks came roaring down the ridge slope from Point 102, urged on by Pip Roberts with a typical cavalry exhortation: 'Come on, the Greys. Get your whips out!' The leading panzers were also engaged by the 22nd Armoured Brigade positioned on the forward slope of the Alam Halfa Ridge, which the enemy did not reach until the evening of 31 August, having used up a lot of fuel and lost the commander of 21st Panzer, General Georg von Bismarck, in the process. By dusk the Greys and the CLY had succeeded in halting the German advance. Bombing by the Desert Air Force continued all night by the light of flares as the German tanks gradually withdrew to refuel.

A shortage of fuel reduced the German effort on 1 September to a small-scale attack on Alam Halfa by 15th Panzer Division. Rommel then came up to see what was going on, his staff car being bombed six times on the way. The 15th Panzer Division put in an attack about 0630 hours, but by 0830 hours it too had been driven off, holding back the 8th Armoured Brigade's pursuit with its anti-tank-gun screen, but unable to advance itself through another shortage of fuel. Rommel then elected to hold the ground taken, but bombing continued all that day and all the next night and, since no more fuel could be brought up, the panzers withdrew on 2 September. This was a step-by-step withdrawal – not a rout – but it was still a welcome sight to the weary soldiers of Eighth Army.

Monty has been criticized for not immediately counterattacking Rommel's forces on 3 September, perhaps by sending the New Zealanders south to cut off their retreat. This view fails to consider Montgomery's overall plan for a big offensive and the current state of Eighth Army: to risk another defeat after the Army had seen the enemy pulling back was a risk Montgomery was not prepared to take. Monty's critics also ignore the fact that he ordered his forces to harass the enemy all the way back, and ordered Freyberg's New Zealanders to attack the German flank. Three armoured brigades – the 23rd, 22nd and 8th – were to engage the front and flanks of the panzers, while the 2nd New Zealand Division was to work its way south from Alam Nayil in the Alamein line and close the gaps Rommel had forced in the minefields.

Lieutenant-Colonel Kelly Brown, DSO, commanded a New Zealand infantry company in the Alam Halfa battle:

On the night of 3/4 September 1942 I was company commander of 'C' Company, 18th NZ Battalion, in the 6th NZ Brigade. We had replaced the 24th Battalion in that brigade after they had sustained heavy casualties on the Ruweisat Ridge on 22 July. I have often been asked, 'What is it like in action?' or 'What is a company attack like?', and this may give some idea.

On 1 September Rommel had placed Germans and Italians in battalion strength about 800 yards in front of 'C' Company, to protect his operation turning point at the southern end of the German line – this feature was known as Deir el Angar. It was decided that the New Zealand Division would put in an attack due south to upset Rommel in his withdrawal, and the 5th Brigade and the British 44th Division were to push south to the Alinda Munassib depression.

Our start time was 2300 hours for the attack on Deir el Angar, and our company strength was about 75 men – not the 138 we should have had, so everyone went in except the company clerk, who had to keep the records, and two cooks, who had to cook a hot meal for those who got back. Then, two hours before H-Hour, the orders changed. This was to be a raid and we were to return when we had done as much damage to the enemy as possible.

We filed over to the 'B' Company area in the dark and found

that they had not cleared a gap in the minefield and a 2-pounder anti-tank gun had hit a mine. This blocked the track and caused delay. This gap was partly cleared and 'B' Company had started through when a rifle shot was heard close by. Someone had lost his nerve and shot himself in the foot. Stretcher-bearers were called for when the 'B' Company sergeant-major roared, 'No! Leave him. The stretcher-bearers come with us on the attack.'

Here was another delay, and I was getting worried about the start time and the artillery barrage. It is necessary to get your troops hard up against the barrage to get its full help as you enter the enemy position. We then had to leave our Bren-gun carriers behind, as we could not get them through the gap, and the enemy must now have realized something was up as they started shelling, mortaring and machine-gunning the area.

Our artillery fire had commenced and once through the gap there was no time to shake out or organize on the start line. The platoons simply ran out, turned left, and headed south. After we had gone about 500–600 yards the enemy ahead started firing at us. It was the heaviest small arms concentration I can remember throughout the entire war.

Between the start line and our objective there was a dip in the ground of about 5–10 feet and this saved us from much of the enemy fire which went over our heads. Some men hit the ground, but after I had kicked a few bottoms and roared they got going again. We reached the enemy in reasonable formation and battled with them hand to hand.

'B' Company had mainly hit the rear of the enemy, many of whom had hurriedly retired. They worked through the area, cleaning out and collecting some prisoners. 'C' Company hit the front line troops and had a lively time against small-arms fire and hand grenades. We did a lot of damage, but took heavy casualties in the process.

It soon became obvious that the momentum of our attack had spent itself and the enemy were getting more active. With the possibility of a counter attack, I put up a Success signal with a Very light and organized a withdrawal, getting our troops through the minefield and home. I had difficulty getting our (52) prisoners organized, but eventually this was accomplished and they were handed over to the battalion.

Back in the 'C' Company lines the men settled back into their section posts. The CSM had done a wonderful job, mothering the lads back, getting them a hot meal, and looking after the wounded. All the wounded had been brought back, and we had lost no prisoners. The company clerk then gave me the casualty list: we had lost 26 killed or wounded, including two out of three officers killed and the other one wounded. I was the only officer left, and we did not have a company 2 i/c. As we checked each section post and asked 'Are you all right?' I got the usual answer, 'We're OK, boss.' Their wonderfully calm behaviour made me very humble.

I reported to the CO and apologized for the untidy start. The CO replied, 'Don't worry – the important thing is that you won.'

When 'C' Company left Syria for the desert in late June 1942 it was at full strength: 5 officers and 133 ORs. In action, we received 101 reinforcements at Alamein, which is a total of 239 men, including 18 officers. When we came out of the line on 13 September we had just 1 officer and 44 ORs. Of our 194 casualties I am unable to give details of the numbers killed, wounded, captured or evacuated sick.[21]

The Germans were, as ever, fighting well. The New Zealanders' attack cost their brigades 275 casualties, killed, wounded or missing, and the supporting British infantry brigade almost 700, in its first battle. On 1/2 September 15th Panzer's anti-tank guns taught the 8th Armoured Brigade another expensive lesson, but by the morning of 2 September, after two days of bombing and shelling, Panzerarmee had withdrawn to the western edge of the British minefields. Rommel went over to the defensive, and Montgomery was content to see the Panzers retreat, wisely unwilling to take risks until he had the hang of this new kind of warfare.

By 6 September the Battle of Alam Halfa was over and there was time to examine the results. Eighth Army lost 1,750 men and 67 tanks – almost half of them Grants. Panzerarmee lost 2,900 men and 49 tanks. Constantly in action over the battlefield, the Desert Air Force lost 68 aircraft to the German and Italian 41. Seen in the context of the desert war and of later engagements, Alam Halfa might be regarded as little more than a skirmish and the result at best a draw, but that is not how it was seen at the time nor how it has come to be regarded by historians of the desert war. Alam Halfa is generally regarded as both a turning point of the entire campaign and an essential preliminary to the Alamein offensive.

The repulse of the German armour at Alam Halfa did much to

restore the confidence of the British Army, which was one of Montgomery's objectives. The exact state of the soldiers' morale had never been in doubt; evidence that morale was poor before Alam Halfa is hard to find. However, there was certainly some well-merited dissatisfaction with much of the kit, with the organization and tactics of the Army, and with the higher command. Now it appeared that much could be achieved if sensible arrangements were made and the commanders played to the strengths of their forces rather than dancing to Rommel's tune. Above all, it was apparent that Rommel was not invincible.

In fact Rommel had now passed his peak, and the decline of his formidable power had already begun. This decline was due to a large number of factors. There was the continued existence of the submarines and aircraft based in Malta, hacking away at his supplies, and the growing power of the Desert Air Force across the front line. The increase in the amount and performance of British armour, with the arrival of the Grant and the 6-pounder anti-tank gun, helped reduce the effectiveness of the Axis forces, which were overstretched and growing tired. That apart, Rommel was ill. He had driven his soldiers hard, but had been no less hard on himself, and was now suffering from a range of ailments. He was no longer the man he had been, and was less certain of German victory, less sure of Hitler's wisdom.

None of these factors was apparent to the soldiers in Eighth Army. They knew only that something strange and wonderful had happened at Alam Halfa. Rommel had been driven back and, rightly or wrongly, the credit for that event was given entirely to the new army commander, Lieutenant-General Bernard Law Montgomery.

4 Indian Div.

7

Alamein
October–November 1942

*Your prime and main duty will be to take or destroy, at the earliest
opportunity, the German–Italian Army commanded by Field-Marshal
Rommel . . . together with all its supplies in Egypt and Libya.*

Directive to General Sir Harold Alexander from the Prime Minister,
Winston Churchill, 10 August 1942

At this point in the story of Eighth Army three elements come
together: Bernard Law Montgomery, the Eighth Army and the
Battle of El Alamein. In the popular imagination, these three are
linked to each other for all time. When the time came to select a
title for his peerage, Bernard Montgomery became Field Marshal
Viscount Montgomery of Alamein. When the Eighth Army veterans held reunions after the war, the 'Alamein Reunion' was the
name they gave them. The battle at El Alamein is the definitive
event in the story of Eighth Army.

This connection is strong and well established, but the link is
slighter than it appears. Alamein was a narrow and controversial victory, and Montgomery commanded Eighth Army for
only 16 months. The Eighth Army fought many other battles
before Alamein, and would fight others after it – some much

harder. And yet it is Alamein for which this army and its most famous general are best remembered.

Lieutenant-General Sir Bernard Law Montgomery was and remains the most controversial British military figure of the Second World War. No one is indifferent about Monty: it is love him or loathe him. This is curious, for Montgomery was in many ways a highly conventional soldier and came from the kind of background that has been supplying officers to the British Army for generations. Born in 1887, the son of a London vicar, he was always determined to be a soldier. He entered Sandhurst in 1907, and was commissioned into the Royal Warwickshire Regiment in 1908. Sent to the 1st Battalion on the North-West Frontier of India, he served against the Pathan tribesmen in the frontier campaign and stayed in India until 1912, before returning to the UK and going to France with his battalion in August 1914.

In November 1914 Lieutenant Bernard Montgomery was severely wounded when leading an attack on the village of Meteran during the First Battle of Ypres. For this action he was promoted captain and awarded the DSO – a rare distinction for a platoon commander. On recovering from his wounds he was appointed to the staff and spent the rest of the war in a series of appointments, first as brigade major, then on the staff of a division and finally at a corps HQ, ending the war as GSO1 (chief of staff) of an infantry division.

The First World War was the training ground for many of the senior officers who commanded British armies in the Second World War, and in that first war Montgomery learned three lessons he never forgot. First, that the task of a commander is to select and maintain a clear aim for his battles and then keep command in the inevitable chaos of war, by careful planning and meticulous staff work. Second, that his soldiers must not be committed to battle until they are well trained and fully ready and enjoy every possible advantage that their commanders can provide. Finally, that his soldiers' lives must not be thrown away by pressing on with attacks which offer no further possibility of gain. Those who denigrate Montgomery tend to ignore the principles that guided his military thinking – and fail to note that criticisms of him rarely come from those who were under his command.

After the First World War Montgomery became an instructor at the Staff College at Camberley – where Alexander and Auchinleck were among his students – and served in a series of staff appointments interspersed with regimental duty. In 1927 he married, and he enjoyed ten years of great happiness before his wife died suddenly in 1937. Many of the problems that emerged later from Montgomery's complex personality have been dated to this sad event. His wife had provided Montgomery with the affection he needed and a range of interests outside the narrow military world; while she lived, Monty was a human figure. It was only after her death that the 'other' Monty appeared – critical of his peers and superiors, abrasive, self-regarding, arrogant, increasingly intolerant of failure in others, not above tampering with the truth.

But it would be an error to let Monty's numerous personal and social failings obscure the fact that he was an incisive and clear-headed officer, who understood the nature of command and was a soldier to his fingertips. His problems lay in his character, with his peers, with the Americans, and with his superiors – other than superiors like General Alan Brooke, the Chief of the Imperial General Staff, of whom Montgomery was always wary.

Why the Americans are so antipathetic towards Montgomery is curious. Montgomery commanded American troops for only 90 days in Normandy – three months in the entire war – and then at one remove, for General Omar Bradley was their direct commander, but for some reason most American historians regard Montgomery as an unpleasant human being and a poor general – though evidence supporting the latter conclusion is not easy to find.

With the private soldiers and his immediate subordinates Monty was patient, understanding, even genial. He took care of his troops, and they repaid him with a devotion that has not changed over the years in spite of a constant stream of denigration from his numerous critics. What has to be remembered is not how posterity and historians have viewed Montgomery in the decades since Alamein, but how his men viewed him at the time.

'General Montgomery was my commander at Alamein,' writes John Statham of the 11th RHA. 'He was a dedicated, clear-thinking, experienced, meticulous soldier whom we valued because of his leadership, ability, and the care he took of his soldiers' lives. He was certainly the outstanding Allied commander and we loved him, but we also had respect for the generals who led us through the hard times.'[1]

'Monty's biggest problem was vanity,' says Major-General

'Shan' Hackett, who served under Montgomery in the Western Desert and at Arnhem. 'He had his own way of doing things, thought he always knew best, and was not open to criticism. On the other hand, with Monty at least you knew what was going on – which is not always the case in military matters.'[2]

'Monty was very highly regarded by us Australians,' writes Paul Edwards, an officer with the 9th Division artillery at Alamein:

> His first message to Eighth Army, made only a couple of days after his arrival in the desert, was more or less 'No retreat. This is where we fight it out, and we remain here dead or alive.' This was well received by the Australians, as a breath of fresh air. Monty lived close to the front, was highly visible to the men, let them know what was expected of them, and let them know as much as possible about operations.
>
> The high regard Monty was held in by Australians was shown when he visited Hobart, Tasmania, soon after the war. A gathering was held in the City Hall – I was there – and it was packed tight with ex-servicemen, many wearing the Africa Star with the Eighth Army clasp. They gave Monty a rousing reception, and Australians do not, as a rule, show their affections outwardly or wear their hearts on their sleeve.[3]

Another Australian soldier, Jack Wilkinson, of the 9th Division Cavalry (Mechanized), confirms this point: 'Monty wasted no time in getting down to business. He called parades and made it clear that from now on there would be no backward steps. He said, 'We have to get rid of this fellow Rommel' – and from then on it was build up, build up, all the time.'[4]

Ted Butler from Queensland agrees: 'Monty hated losing good men for no good reason, and as a result was denigrated for being overcautious. As one of those men I don't agree, and when he was around we felt all would be well.'[5]

Charles Butt found a lot about Montgomery in his father's papers: 'My father said that the first and most favourable impression of Montgomery was a vast improvement in supplies and that the mail from home got through – a great morale-raiser. Montgomery fought his army within its capabilities and very sensibly did not try to outrun his supply lines as had happened before.'[6]

Major Eric Schmidt of the Royal Engineers: 'Monty was only unpopular with incompetents, those who were unwilling or unable to carry out his orders.'[7]

Another Australian, Sir William Vines, once of the 2/23rd Battalion, 2nd AIF: 'Within a few weeks of Monty taking command morale everywhere in Eighth Army had risen perceptibly. Our battalion had one visit from him, and afterwards everyone down to the newest private felt they knew him personally.'[8]

Bill O'Neill was in the 1st Gordons with 51st (Highland) Division: 'Yes, we did think Monty was the best, and when he took over things changed for the better – but let us not forget Alexander.'[9]

Many veterans' accounts contain similar comments about Montgomery: he knew what he was doing; he exuded confidence; he gave clear orders which he expected to be obeyed; he was seen everywhere. Above all, Montgomery had that vital quality – grip. Monty made it very clear to his subordinates that his orders were to be obeyed and were not the basis for negotiation.

'When he wanted something to happen, it happened. Until Montgomery's time there was little thought of co-ordination with the armour – or little result of whatever thought there was. After he arrived, morale soared,' wrote Brigadier Howard Kippenberger.[10] Those who disparage Monty today should consult the soldiers he commanded in the Western Desert.

When war broke out in September 1939 Montgomery was a major-general commanding the 8th Division in Palestine, where a terrorist campaign was being waged by the Arabs against British rule and Jewish settlement. Monty was invalided back to the UK and commanded the 3rd Infantry Division in the Dunkirk campaign, where his performance attracted the attention of General Alan Brooke, later the CIGS. Monty was given command of II Corps, where he made a notable success in training and motivating the troops. But his big chance came in 1942, when he was sent to command Eighth Army after the fall of Tobruk.

Montgomery took Eighth Army by the scruff of the neck and shook it hard. There were a considerable number of sackings, at corps to battalion level. His first decision was to form a strong armoured corps – a *corps de chasse* – of two divisions, the veteran 1st Armoured and the newly arrived 10th Armoured, to exploit his anticipated success in the coming offensive – the one demanded by Winston Churchill. Montgomery also acquired one of his greatest assets: Brigadier – later Major-General – Freddie de Guingand, an intelligent and conciliatory officer who became his chief of staff, smoothed Monty's path in many ways, stayed until the end of the war, and then received scant thanks from Monty in return for his numerous services and constant loyalty.

Monty insisted on some tactical changes. From now on there were to be no more 'swanning about in the Blue', no more Jock Columns, no more ad-hoc formations – though such units as the SAS, the LRDG, and even the bizarrely named Popski's Private Army continued to flourish. Otherwise, as in Panzerarmee Afrika, the divisions of Eighth Army would fight as divisions, the various corps would co-operate, the artillery would be grouped to provide the maximum firepower, and the tanks, artillery and infantry would fight an integrated war.

None of this was revolutionary, and many of the changes – the grouping of artillery and the need to fight divisions as divisions – had been put in hand by Auchinleck. Even so, Monty's orders – and the way they were delivered: brusquely, and to groups where smoking and coughing were forbidden – inevitably caused some talk. 'Here were we, the desert veterans, and here was this new general, without even getting his knees brown, telling us what to do, and getting us up in the morning for PT,' recalls Lieutenant Neville Gillman of the 4th County of London Yeomanry.[11]

Montgomery's reputation, founded on these initial impressions, was consolidated by his first action at Alam Halfa. Montgomery fought this battle as *he* intended; Rommel was outguessed and outfought, and forced to halt and then retreat. However much Monty's victory was due to Auchinleck's prior arrangements and an abundance of supplies, he himself got the credit – not least with the troops of Eighth Army. He now enjoyed the confidence of his men, and the stage was set for a much bigger encounter: a major attack on the Axis forces just west of Alamein.

The two-month period between the end of Alam Halfa and the start of the Second Battle of Alamein – Operation LIGHTFOOT – was spent in training the troops and reinforcing the Alamein Line. By the middle of September this had become a true defensive line – one arranged in depth – the 'box' positions held by full divisions, and the whole front thickly wired and mined. If Rommel put in yet another of his pre-emptive spoiling attacks, this line would slow him down, and for his coming offensive Monty brought into this line some of the great fighting divisions of the Second World War.

These divisions were deployed as follows. In the north lay the tough and experienced 9th Australian Division, the splendid shock troops of the Desert Army. Then came the newly arrived 51st (Highland) Division, the famous Jocks, Scottish soldiers for the most part, men who had a score to settle with General Rommel dating back to the capture of the original 51st (Highland) Division at Saint-Valéry in 1940. The Highland Division had a strong spirit, uniquely embodied in its regimental pipers who would lead the battalions in the coming attack. On the first night of Alamein, Piper Duncan McIntyre of the 5th Black Watch, aged just nineteen, would pipe his battalion through the minefields and into the enemy lines; though wounded three times, he kept playing until he died.

The Jocks had character. A story going the rounds of Eighth Army before Alamein concerned a visit to the Black Watch by Admiral Sir James Somerville. When the guard failed to turn out and present arms – a normal compliment for senior officers – the Admiral approached the sentry and, showing him the thick gold rings on his sleeve, gently suggested that a full guard turn-out might be appropriate. The sentry was unconvinced. 'You may be a sergeant,' the Jock allowed doubtfully, 'but you're no' a sergeant in the Black Watch.'

South of the Highlanders came the doughty soldiers of the 2nd New Zealand Division, men regarded by most of Eighth Army – and by most of the Afrika Korps – as the finest infantry in the desert. 'The British are using New Zealanders, so they must mean business,' wrote Rommel in a dispatch. The New Zealand Division was the cutting edge of the New Zealand Expeditionary Force, which came complete with all its services – medical, ordnance, signals, supply, welfare. 'New Zealanders never served with other units', writes Fred Majdalany:

A man would rather be a sergeant in the New Zealand Division than be commissioned into an English regiment. New Zealand is a small nation. The population at the beginning of the war was barely 2 million, a country where the cliché, 'Everyone knows everyone else,' is nearer the truth than usual. So when the New Zealand Expeditionary Force went to war, it was a small, hand-picked, national army, with a nation watching its every move, a national press reporting on every detail of its performance, a Government watching over its welfare.[12]

The Division was led by another fighting soldier: Major-General Sir Bernard Freyberg, VC. Freyberg was the father figure of the Division, and its regard was reciprocated. Nothing was too good for Freyberg's soldiers. He was also more than a mere divisional commander: he was the representative of the New Zealand government in the Middle East; if any British commanders wanted to use the New Zealanders – and they always did – they had to sell their plan to Freyberg first. His splendid New Zealand infantry were always willing, but they were *not* expendable.

South of the New Zealanders came the sorely tried 1st South African Division, stubborn in defence and attack, currently somewhat subdued after their comrades of the 2nd South African Division had surrendered at Tobruk; these were men with something to prove. Then, from the Indian Army, the last division in the XXX Corps part of the Alamein Line, came the 4th Indian Division. Many of these Indian soldiers were regulars; others were wartime, 'hostilities only' soldiers, who had flocked into the army of the Raj on the outbreak of war. All of them were volunteers; there was no conscription in India, but 1.7 million Indian soldiers were to serve the Empire in the Second World War. The men of the 4th Indian Division were drawn from the warrior nations of the subcontinent – Sikhs, Rajputs, Jats, Dogras, together with sturdy Gurkha soldiers from the Himalayas. Each brigade in the 4th Indian Division contained a battalion of British infantry, drawn from the regiments of the line, regular battalions from solid county regiments like the Royal Sussex or the Essex Regiment. This division had served with the Western Desert Force in the Beda Fomm campaign of 1940 and had then gone to Eritrea, where it had achieved a notable victory against the Italians at Keren; now it was back to face Eighth Army's latest challenge.

The commander of this fine, highly professional division, was an equally professional officer, Major-General Francis Tuker, CB, DSO, OBE, whom Majdalany describes, accurately, as 'one of the star divisional generals'.[13] Tuker was a thinking soldier as well as a fighting man, the author of several books on military matters, a man who did not tolerate fools at all – never mind gladly. It is therefore hardly surprising that his career in the pre-war Army, if marked with awards, had been somewhat slow on the promotion front. By now Tuker, like Freyberg and Morshead, should have had a corps, but Tuker was not ambitious. He had raised the 4th Indian Division to the peak of efficiency; he had no doubt that it would distinguish itself in the battles that lay ahead.

These last two divisions – 2nd New Zealand and 4th Indian – should be noted, for they had been with the Desert Army from the early days and – though diverted to other fronts and other formations from time to time – would serve with Eighth Army until the end in Italy.

South of the Indian positions, on Ruweisat Ridge, lay a Greek Brigade – Eighth Army was always cosmopolitan – and the divisions of XIII Corps. This had three British divisions: 7th Armoured; the 50th (Northumbrian) Division, part of which had stoutly defended the 150th Infantry Brigade box at Gazala; and the newly arrived 44th (Home Counties) Division, which had held the ridge at Alam Halfa. Carver comments that the 44th Division had been 'royally mucked about' in recent weeks, two of its brigades, the 131st and 132nd, being launched into attacks that failed at Alam Halfa.[14] Even so, the 44th Division was ready for whatever was to come.

The southern end of the main Alamein Line was held by the famous Desert Rats, the 7th Armoured Division, a unit which had been up and down the desert since 1940. And finally, in the Qaret el Himeimat position, just above the Qattara Depression, lay General Koenig's 1st Free French Brigade, the heroes of Gazala. In the rear, behind Alam Halfa and astride the railway, lay the 10th and 1st Armoured Divisions of X Corps, Monty's designated *corps de chasse*.

Given the many previous failures in tank and infantry co-operation, much time was devoted, certainly by the wiser commanders, to integrating the armour with the infantry they were tasked to support. This went beyond mere exercises, though there were plenty of those; it was also necessary to create comradeship. General Freyberg gave a dinner for the officers of the New Zealand Division and Brigadier John Currie's 9th Armoured Brigade, so that they could get to know each other personally and become friends as well as colleagues. The New Zealand soldiers were encouraged to clamber about on the British tanks and have a go at driving them, and, as visible evidence of a common commitment, the 9th Brigade painted the New Zealanders' fern-leaf emblem on their tank turrets. Other units also strove to eliminate the errors of the past – and everyone whistled a tune that the soldiers had picked up on the tank radios, a melody from across the wire: *Lili Marlene*.

Lili Marlene became the anthem of the desert armies – British, German and Italian – a song they could all sing, in the desert and at post-war reunions. The words, from a poem written in 1917 by a German soldier, Hans Leip, were set to music in 1937 by a Berliner, Norbert Schultze. This German version – which is far sadder than the later English lyrics: the German soldier knows he will both lose his girl, Lili Marlene, and die in battle – was not an immediate success, and the song was turned down by many performers until Lale Andersen, a popular singer of the day, recorded it in 1939 – when it sold just 700 copies.

In 1941 the song surfaced again, by accident, in Belgrade, when Andersen's recording of *Lili Marlene* was one of only a handful of records available to the local radio station. Radio Belgrade played it incessantly, and it caught on with the German soldiers, who took it to the Western Desert. There it was heard and taken up by the British soldiers. As a song, *Lili Marlene* had everything: a heavily loaded infantry soldier could march to it; the 'tankies' could hear it on their radios; and it was the perfect song to sing when there was some beer about or the soldiers felt homesick. The tune was also used for a number of scurrilous army parodies.

In 1942 the British authorities thought it wise to have some British lyrics for this song and – written by Tommie Connor, whose many other hits included *I Saw Mommy Kissing Santa Claus* and *Under the Spreading Chestnut Tree* – the English version enjoyed great success and was quickly recorded by Vera Lynn and Anne Shelton. The Anne Shelton recording alone sold over 1 million copies, and *Lili Marlene* remained a popular song until well after the war.[15]

Eighth Army was growing powerful. By the time of the Second Battle of Alamein, in October 1942, Montgomery had 1,351 tanks, including 246 Grants and 285 of the new American Sherman with its powerful 75-mm gun. The Sherman was the great Allied tank of the Second World War; over 50,000 were manufactured, and they served in every theatre. But when compared with most of the German tanks it was an inferior machine. The 75-mm was an inadequate gun, and the Sherman had a dangerous tendency to catch fire when hit: the Germans called it a 'Tommy-cooker', while the Americans dubbed it the 'Zippo' and the British the 'Ronson' – after their cigarette lighters. On the other hand the Shermans were mechanically reliable and easy to service – and there were plenty of them. There were also 223 of the virtually obsolescent Valentines, and no less than 421 of the unreliable Crusaders – though the new and equally unreliable Crusader tank with a 6-pounder gun was also beginning to appear. Some of these tanks would be kept in reserve, but 1,021 tanks of various types would roll forward at the start of the battle.

The anti-tank regiments were getting the new 6-pounder anti-tank gun, and the infantry battalions the 2-pounder or where possible the 6-pounder; by the time the battle began, Eighth Army's anti-tank gunners had 850 of the 6-pounder anti-tank guns, with each motorized battalion now having 16 of them to hold off the panzers – no longer would the British gunners see their shells bouncing off the enemy tanks. The medium artillery had doubled its guns to 52, the field artillery increased from 616 guns to 832.[16] Eighth Army was putting on muscle and feeling its strength. But the old spirit of the Desert Army endured, as this letter, sent to every sapper by Brigadier F. H. Kisch in September 1942, clearly demonstrates:

Engineers in the Assault
Unlike the German Army, the British Army has no special assault engineer units. The reason for this is that every sapper is an Assault Engineer. This is our privilege and our pride.

The Eighth Army is confronted at the moment by fairly strong defensive positions of considerable length and some depth. It falls on the Sappers to open up the way for the Army to advance and whatever gaps have to be cleared there must be no failure. An immense amount depends on the resolution and skill with which this task is tackled.

The Army Commander is confident that his sappers will do all
that is required of them in this first step to the coming Victory.
Signed, F. H. Kisch
Brigadier, Chief Engineer, Eighth Army

Brigadier Kisch's units had a difficult task, for the German
defence line at Alamein was getting thicker and stronger all the
time, and filling up with troops. Across those thick belts of wire
and mines, Rommel's Panzerarmee Afrika had the original
Afrika Korps – 15th and 21st Panzer Divisions – plus the 90th
Light Division, the 164th Light Africa Division and, a new addition, General Bernard Ramcke's brigade of parachute infantry,
plus the tank and infantry divisions of the Italian Army. These
consisted of XX Corps, containing the Ariete Armoured Division
and the Trieste Motor Division, plus the Littorio armoured division and three infantry divisions: the Trento, Bologna and
Brescia. These Italian infantry divisions would be bolstered by
Ramcke's parachutists and an Italian parachute division, the
Folgore, which had arrived without transport and was virtually
immobile. This force mustered a total of 104,000 men.

In armour, Panzerarmee was much less well endowed than
Eighth Army. It had only 200 tanks, mostly Panzer Mark IIIs, and
only 30 of the Mark IVs had the long 75-mm gun; the rest of the
panzers had the 50-mm gun and the Italian armoured divisions
still had the obsolete M13 tank. In anti-tank guns Rommel had
only 24 of the fearsome 88-mms, and the previously useful Pak-
50s were less effective against the Sherman and Grant tanks.

Rommel was also short of fuel and ammunition, and repeated
requests to the Comando Supremo in Italy failed to produce
enough of these essentials, putting his entire position at risk. In
addition, he was suffering from jaundice complicated by stomach ailments and circulation problems which led to periodic
fainting fits. Many of his senior officers were also worn down by
more than a year of constant strain, and his units were under
strength and tired; nevertheless, these were experienced soldiers
and, German or Italian, they would hold their positions. By
fighting on the defensive, Rommel could also hope to reduce the
advantages in men and *matériel* held by Montgomery.

In the five weeks between Alam Halfa and the opening of the
Battle of Alamein, Eighth Army trained relentlessly by day and

night, developed an elaborate deception plan in the south involving dummy tanks and laying a dummy water pipeline to the south to conceal the real point of assault in the north – and greatly increased its strength in men and tanks.

Montgomery's insistence on the need to train the troops and build up adequate reserves of fuel and ammunition meant that Eighth Army could not attack during the September moon period. The full moon in October did not shine until the third week of October, and Montgomery opted to attack on the night of the 23rd/24th. Alan Brooke persuaded the ever-impatient Churchill to accept this delay, not least because an attack at the end of October would divert enemy attention away from the western Mediterranean, where the Anglo-American landings – Operation TORCH – were due to begin on 8 November.

Montgomery's first plan, which he revealed to the divisional commanders on 15 September, was to confuse the enemy with two attacks, one at each end of the line. The strongest attack would be in the north, where the 9th Australian, 51st (Highland), 2nd New Zealand and 1st South African Divisions of Leese's XXX Corps were to attack on a 4-mile front, pushing forward for a depth of up to 4 miles and forcing two gaps in the enemy mine-fields through which the tank divisions of X Corps could pass. Once through, the X Corps tanks were to take up defensive positions 'on ground of their own choosing' – that which offered some tactical advantage and decent cover – and destroy the enemy armour as it came up. That done, Eighth Army would turn on the Axis infantry manning the Alamein Line and destroy them, now unsupported by armour, in their turn.

Meanwhile, to divert enemy attention and hold the other Axis divisions in the south, Horrocks's XIII Corps, specifically the 7th Armoured Division and the 44th Division, would mount an attack north of Himeimat, which would be seized by the French. Monty made it clear that these attacks were not to be pressed too far: he anticipated needing 7th Armoured later in the battle. Major-General John Harding, GOC of the 7th Armoured Division at Alamein, confirms this point: 'The general plan of campaign called for a major attack in the north and a holding attack by 7th Armoured Division with the 1st Free French Brigade under command in the south, designed to retain the German armour on that flank. I was given the most explicit instructions by General Montgomery personally that I must keep my division in being as an effective fighting formation.'

The crux of the main attack was for Lumsden's X Corps to get though the enemy minefields and establish itself on that 'ground of its own choosing'[17] on the far side of the minefields; the armour was to press on to that place and not become involved in any of the fighting inside the Alamein position. Once through, X Corps was to pivot north, turning on Miteiriya Ridge, which lay in front of the New Zealand position and which the New Zealanders were to seize and hold and so get across the enemy supply lines. Monty calculated that this would provoke Rommel into committing his armour; once his armour had been destroyed, the rest would be easy.

This view did not attract much support from Morshead and Freyberg, who were still vastly disillusioned with the perform-ance of the armoured units. When Monty declared at his com-manders' briefing that if the infantry divisions were unable to clear the minefields the armoured brigades must fight their way through, both generals called out loudly, 'They won't!' As we shall see, these two officers were almost correct in this assump-tion – but not entirely.

Nor is it entirely clear that the infantry divisions could clear corridors through the minefields for the tanks; they would have enough to do in quelling enemy opposition. In his book on the battle, Field Marshal Carver states that 'XXX Corps had no responsibility for clearing gaps for the armour and each armoured division had therefore to form a minefield task force of its own.'[18] On the other hand the Official History states plainly that 'The XXXth Corps was responsible for clearing all the ne-cessary lanes though the British minefields',[19] which could hardly be more definite, but leaves open the question of who would clear the lanes through the enemy minefields. These would be covered by fire, and could be cleared only by the infantry sap-pers – after the enemy positions putting down that fire had been suppressed by artillery fire, or so one hoped.

The important point was that the attack must not be held up. If necessary the tanks must press forward, regardless of loss, to break the enemy line. This would be costly. Lumsden warned his troops that they must on no account 'rush blindly on to the enemy's anti-tank guns or try to pass through a bottleneck which is covered by a concentration of enemy tanks'. In such cases 'a proper, co-ordinated plan must be made'.

He did not say who would make that plan, and there was clearly a difference of views between the tank-corps commander and his infantry colleagues before the battle even began – and surely such a plan should be made before the battle began. All agreed that a tank breakthrough would be difficult in the face of anti-tank gun screens and minefields. The infantry commanders also suspected that, as so often before, the tank men might lack the ability – or the will – to force a breakthrough or provide them with support. When difficulties arose, it was this factor – the matter of will and not the more concrete ones of guns and mines – that surfaced in the arguments.

Just how easy this attack would be was hard to say. Montgomery was certainly not as confident of rapid success as he appeared to be, noting in his diary that 'a battle of more than a week was more than possible', and the notes for his final briefing to senior officers on 19/20 October read, 'Organise for a dogfight of a week. Whole affair about twelve days' – a calculation that turned out to be extremely accurate.

The German dispositions had 15th Panzer Division in the north, facing the Australians and 51st Highland; further south were the Littorio, facing the New Zealanders, Trento and Bologna facing the South Africans, Ramcke's Parachute Brigade well forward, then 21st Panzer and the Ariete, Folgore and Brescia Divisions, with the newly arrived Pavia Division at the extreme south. Other forces were held in the rear, and all the Axis positions had been dug-in, wired and covered by machine guns, mortars, anti-tank guns and artillery.

Montgomery was perfectly well aware that the German and Italian positions on the Alamein Line would not be easily overcome. Mines – both anti-tank and personnel – were one major problem and led to the setting up of the Eighth Army Mine Clearing School, which trained infantry soldiers to clear mines, since it was becoming clear that there would not be enough sappers to go round. Steps were also taken to develop the mineclearing Scorpion flail tanks, but these tanks were to prove less than successful in the battle.

On 6 October, realizing that his plan was too ambitious, Montgomery issued a fresh set of orders, revising those issued earlier and scaling down his hopes for the first night. In this new plan, after the breakthrough, X Corps would cover the infantry divisions and hold off Rommel's counter-attack while the enemy infantry in the line was 'crumbled' or eliminated. This 'crumbling' phase might last several days before the enemy strength was eroded, and only then would there be a 'breakthrough'. In the event it took several assaults to achieve the second phase, and another all-out attack – SUPERCHARGE – to effect a final breach. Eighth Army did not finally break through the German and Italian line until 7 November, two weeks after the start of the battle, just one day before the start of Operation TORCH.

During these weeks of preparation Panzerarmee suffered the loss of Erwin Rommel: on 19 September he handed over command to General Georg Stumme of Panzerarmee and went to an Austrian spa for a prolonged rest, though declaring that he would return to the command when the British attacked. General Wilhelm Ritter von Thoma, a veteran of the Spanish Civil War, took over command of the Afrika Korps, while many other officers, ill with jaundice or amoebic dysentery, also went home on sick leave. On the way to Austria, Rommel stopped in Rome to harry the Comando Supremo over the question of reinforcements and supplies, and he was still in Austria when the Alamein battle started on the night of 23/24 October 1942.

Alf Curtis of the 9th Australian Division remembers the waiting:

> 23 October dawned no differently from other days – sporadic firing along the front, movement of vehicles, and the odd aircraft. The skies were blue and enhanced by vapour trails from the circling fighters. Then, as dusk approached, two searchlights – ours – reached up into the sky, which was unusual but conveyed nothing to us. Then about ten, the beam of roving light came to rest over the stationary one and at that the whole Allied front erupted into flame. Over 1,000 guns opened up, and the intensity of the firepower was beyond what we had experienced, the whole night sky lit up by flashes and explosions ... the battle of Alamein had started.[20]

Allan Austin remembers the opening barrage:

> The main barrage at El Alamein began at 2140 hours on 23 October. The relative quiet was suddenly torn apart as a thunder-

ing, crushing barrage of shells from over 1,000 guns rained down on the enemy positions. This was the first major artillery barrage of the war, the first since the massive artillery bombardments of the Western Front during the First World War, and shattering.[21]

Peter Smythe was a signals officer in the 25th New Zealand Battalion, 6th New Zealand Brigade, and sent me extracts from letters written home in 1942. The first letter is dated 24 October:

Again I am lying in a slit trench in comfort, having been on my feet for ten hours. At the moment tanks, the number of which I cannot calculate, are pouring a hail of steel at Jerry over the Miteiriya Ridge. All around me shells are flying, but it is quiet after the four hours of shelling last night. This scene is a nightmare, no one can really believe it.

After a four hour march the night before I rested up yesterday, 23 October. We marched about 3 miles last night behind a monstrous barrage, and I looked like a Christmas tree – webbing, binoculars, maps, revolver, ammo, compass, pack with rations and toilet gear, a pick and telephone and later a rifle and, I nearly forgot, a Mills bomb – a 36 grenade. In the battalion attack I was with the signallers all the way, and they are putting up a great show.

It is daylight now and warmth is in the air. A piece of shrapnel from one of our own shells – we are lying close to the barrage – kicked sand into my face, and two more just landed 50 yards away, so I am keeping the old head down. Dick Webb, an officer from Christchurch just came by – the 25th are mostly Wellingtonians. Now about 20 fighter planes are marching up above and a parachute is coming down. 4.45 p.m. We are all heads down, for we are being shelled quite heavily. All home comforts! I just poked my head up and, presto, a cup of coffee comes along from our signals storeman – we have started another bombardment. No rum so far.

Tuesday 27 October
I've gone through the worst 24 hours of my life since I started writing on Saturday. Sunday was quiet and we went down 2 feet in our holes and lay low. A Yankee newspaper correspondent turned up in the evening and asked where was the front line – his answer was a mortar bomb landing about 12 yards away from him. He cheered us up a bit, and was extraordinarily oblivious to damage, going right forward to the real front line. I hope to meet him again some day.

Yesterday was the worst day. I awoke dog tired but had to keep on the go – lines, stores, getting men replaced, God knows what. Then my dispatch rider was sent to hospital and I took over the jeep went out and salvaged wireless sets and gear from wrecked trucks close by. Orders for another attack – the prisoners were coming back in droves, 200–300 at a time. One of my men captured about 50 single handed, with a jammed rifle last night. The forward companies went in behind another barrage before the moon came up.

I was a bit late and found the moon coming up as we set off. Then the barrage stopped and in the next three hours I added three years to my age. I lost my marking tape and then on to a stony ridge which the tanks had been holding. Then I lost my way and found myself and party pinned down by mortar fire, a sniper and a machine-gun. We went forward in rushes – paused by one wounded fellow and gave him some chewing gum. Then had to lie flat to join some cables. I prayed then, for I really was afraid as the machine-gun shot odd ones over us. This morning for an hour we had our heaviest mortar shelling.[22]

Close behind the opening barrage at Alamein came the infantry, deploying steadily into their attack formations, the sappers moving ahead to clear the mines, the skirl of bagpipes being heard far across the battlefield whenever the guns paused – somewhere in the darkness of that shell-torn night the pipers of the Highland battalions were leading the companies into the attack.

W. J. O'Neill fought at Alamein with the 1st Battalion the Gordon Highlanders:

We did not wear kilts in this battle. As we stood ready the barrage began, and when it stopped we moved forward, bayonets fixed and a solitary piper playing us in and leading the way. The barrage had lit up the night, but now it was terribly dark, but we just kept walking forward. Then a peculiar thing happened to me. I don't know how far we had gone when I suddenly fell in a slit trench. It was quite deep, and I panicked a bit because I could not get out. I sat for a while, praying to God, and the next thing was that someone fell in on top of me. Luckily for him he did not fall on my bayonet.

When we finally sorted ourselves out it was the padre of the regiment, and he asked me if I was all right. I said, 'Yes, I think so,' and he gave me some words of comfort and said that Jesus would look after me, and whether that was true or not I went though that battle and the rest of the campaign without a scratch. I saw some of my mates shot and wounded and others killed. When I was demobbed in 1946 I had six campaign medals and got a gratuity of £73.[23]

William Vines was with the 2/23rd Infantry Battalion AIF:

The barrage opened at 2140 hours on 23 October. We were in reserve for the next five days but under fire for much of the time, and we took casualties. Several times we were ordered into action only to have the order countermanded at the last minute as the situation changed. Five days after the attack started good progress was made and the enemy lines were penetrated along an irregular front, although no breakthrough had been achieved. The 2/24th and 2/48th had had much fighting and sustained heavy losses, and early on the morning of 28 October I laid white tape out as the start line for our attack that night, riding on the backs of Valentine tanks. We were to pass through the 2/13th and the 2/15th after they had reached their objectives.

Our move began at 2300 hours in bright moonlight, and with the bursting shells as well our tanks were sitting ducks, sharply illuminated. Armed with anti-tank and heavy machine-guns, the Germans knocked out a lot of our tanks, while others were lost in the imperfectly cleared minefield through which we attacked. Within a couple of hours those of us left were on foot, pressing the attack with support fire from the few remaining tanks.

At one point I was talking with my friend Colin Riggs when a burst of machine-gun fire cut him across both legs. I helped him bind his wounds, using his and my field dressing, and gave him a small flask of whisky which I had carried for weeks for just such an emergency. We next met in the Heidelberg hospital in Melbourne some months later.

By 0300 hours we had not made much progress and had lost most of our tanks and troops. Bernie Evans, the CO, was furious about our heavy losses in what I think he felt, as we all did, was a very ill-conceived attack. We would have done much better on foot, as we had done before, dealing with the anti-tank gunners and then using our tanks in the supporting role rather than as troop carriers in the forefront of the attack.

All that remained of the battalion at this time were about 60 all ranks, including six officers, Bernie Evans lined us up in the dark and we headed for our objective into machine-gun and mortar fire. We had got quite a long way before we were brought to a halt, where we scraped shallow holes in the rocky sand, determined to hang on to what we had. Come the dawn we were delighted to see the Germans running away from the entrenchments that had barred our progress, and we moved forward without any opposing fire to a position 900 yards from where we had started. During the night we had taken 4 officers and 158 enemy prisoners and captured a large quantity of enemy equipment.[24]

The great barrage that struck the German positions at 2140 hours on 23 October seems to have come as a complete surprise to the Axis forces. It certainly surprised General Stumme, who died of a heart attack on the way to Panzerarmee Headquarters, leaving his force temporarily without a commander. Even so, in spite of this deluge of shells, the Germans and Italians held their ground and prevented the New Zealanders and 51st (Highland) Division clearing a path through their minefields for the tanks of the 1st and 10th Armoured Divisions.

John Statham of the 11th Regiment RHA:

In September we were the first unit to be equipped with the US 105-mm howitzer mounted on Grant tanks. We moved up the coast road on 19 October, and for three nights we kept moving, hiding under canvas covers during the day. We were then in front of the guns and took no part in the barrage, as our job in the 1st Armoured Division was, as usual, to support our tank regiment, the 9th Lancers. I was a sergeant on one of our tank-mounted guns.

The barrage opened and we started advancing in the moonlight, crossing the first minefield, through which a lane about 15 feet wide was being cleared by sappers supporting the Highland Division. There were many dead Jocks and sappers about, mostly killed by booby traps, and I will never forget the wail of bagpipes mingled with the roar of the guns. Our main fear was of being trapped behind our tanks in the third minefield when dawn broke – then we would be a fine target for Jerry. Well, we were, but somehow we managed to spread out a little and we were then too busy to care much as we started to winkle out the 88-mms so that our tanks could advance.

The fighting was very tough, as the Germans held their ground. At one point our tanks were held up by a well-sited

88-mm. The Lancers sent up a tank to sort it out, but it was brewed up. They then sent another, which suffered the same fate, then another and another. The fifth tank managed to do the job.[25]

While this battle went on in the minefields, in the far north the attack of the 9th Australian Division went well. On the first night the Australians had two objectives: the first was the enemy's forward defences, about a mile ahead; the second was the main enemy position, perhaps 2 miles ahead. The forward defences were overrun by midnight, but when daylight arrived the Australians were still some distance from their final objective, the Blue Line. The Highlanders of 51st Division had a somewhat more difficult task, with many of the strongest and deepest defences on their front. Their attack was strongly contested, and by dawn one brigade was still embedded in the forward enemy defences and some of the enemy positions were still untaken. The Highlanders' supporting tanks had come up but had run into minefields – and casualties had been heavy.

The New Zealanders faced similar difficulties on their way to Miteiriya Ridge. Freyberg only had two brigades, one having been detached to X Corps, and his plan called for the infantry advance to be swiftly followed up by the Grants, Shermans and Crusaders of Currie's 9th Armoured Brigade. This attack went well, and by dawn Kippenberger's 5th Brigade was west of the Ridge and Brigadier Gentry's 6th Brigade was on top of it. The tanks supporting the infantry had come up, had been held briefly in the minefields, but were now on hand. The 1st South African Division took most of its objectives – except on the right flank, close to the New Zealanders, where it was held up by machine-gun fire and minefields – and the 4th Indian Division, which had been charged with making diversions and holding the enemy on its front, could report success as well. All in all, XXX Corps had done well, pushing deep into the enemy defences in the face of tough resistance and minefields.

The same cannot be said of the *corps de chasse*, Lumsden's X Corps which, says Michael Carver, 'had spent a most trying and frustrating night'.[26] As related above, the two divisions of this corps were tasked to pass though corridors cut in the enemy defences: Major-General Raymond Briggs's 1st Armoured Division through a corridor cleared between the Australians and the Highland Division, Major-General Alec Gatehouse's 10th Armoured Division through a corridor cleared on the New Zealand front. These corridors now existed, so where were the tanks?

The tanks were stuck in or before the enemy minefields, which were more extensive than expected and had yet to be fully cleared. The root of this problem seems to have lain in the fact that XXX Corps and X Corps, while advancing in the same area, had not co-ordinated their advance. This failure suggests a clear flaw in the higher command, which should have studied their proposals, spotted this flaw, and done something about it. These enemy minefields were an obvious problem, but XXX Corps had no direct responsibility for clearing gaps in the minefields for the X Corps tanks. Nor was this a corps task in Lumsden's force; each tank division had to form its own teams and clear mines on its own front, creating and marking three gaps for the tanks to pass through, while working in close co-operation with the infantry division clearing enemy positions on that front at the same time. This division of tasks was not successful; the mine clearing became disjointed, and the forward movement of the tank divisions varied – and slowed.

Briggs's 1st Armoured Division had to give up one of its cleared paths to the New Zealanders and did not get through the final minefield until dawn, and then on only one path. The Division then ran into anti-tank guns and more scattered mines beyond the enemy's first-line defences. By 0800 hours on 24 October it was clear that only some tank regiments had got through, while others were still stuck before the enemy line or in the minefields. All were taking losses. Gatehouse's 10th Armoured Division believed that there were only two enemy minefields on its front and by 0430 hours its sappers had cleared a path through to Miteiriya Ridge. By dawn there were four cleared paths on to the ridge but for some reason only one – code-named Boat – was being used.

As a result there was considerable congestion on the XXX Corps front, all visibility being obscured by clouds of dust. And then another minefield was discovered and the advance stopped. German anti-tank guns, including 88-mms, were pouring fire into the 10th Division as it milled about before the ridge, where elements of the New Zealand and South African divisions were also trying to get forward. Carver describes the scene here as 'like a badly organized car park at an immense race meeting held in a dustbowl'.[27] None of this was of much help in getting the armour forward for the next phase.

Further south, in the XIII Corps area, the only units actively engaged on the first night were 7th Armoured Division and the Free French. The 7th Armoured Division was tasked with forcing a way – if possible without incurring heavy losses – through two deep minefields – 'January' and 'February' – north of the Himeimat feature, which would be attacked by Koenig's Foreign Legionnaires. Those tasks completed, 50th Division and 44th Division were to advance and straighten out the front and, that done, the entire Corps was to press forward.

By dawn, 7th Armoured's attack had stalled in front of the February minefield in the face of anti-tank guns, and also before January after the loss of many of the mine-clearing parties. The Free French attack on Himeimat began well, but then the Germans counter-attacked and drove the Legionnaires back. Shortly after dawn a German force, supported by captured Stuart tanks, attacked Group A, commanded by Colonel Amilakvari; Group A was without anti-tank guns, and during the withdrawal the Colonel was killed and many of his men were lost. This left the Himeimat feature, with its excellent visibility, firmly in German hands. The Official History comments that 'On the XIII Corps front daylight on the 24th October saw a somewhat unsatisfactory situation.'[28]

Neville Gillman was a tank commander with the 4th CLY in 7th Armoured Division:

We spent the 24th. sitting in our tanks in the enemy minefield, being shelled fairly frequently. On the next night we were ordered to push on through the February minefield, but it gets a bit dim after that. When we got through, everything opened up on us from front and flank. My searchlight and periscope were shot away inches from my head as we went through the gap. There were lots of mines and a screen of anti-tank guns waiting for us – and one by one my squadron went off the air. Then the Colonel came on and said, 'Any tank which is still a runner, pull out and come back.' We had been lying doggo, between two knocked-out tanks, but we started up. I said, 'Driver reverse', and as we started to move the shell came in that ended my career with 7th Armoured.

The shell, an 88-mm I think, came in one side and blew the other side of the turret wide open, killing all the crew except the driver and myself. Being small, I was not sitting on the commander's seat but squatting on it, and that was what saved me. I felt a blow on my leg and fell into the bottom of the fighting compartment, where all the ammunition was already on fire. But I hauled myself out of the turret – I don't know how – and rolled off on to the sand. My leg was broken in two places, but the driver, Corporal Kennedy, hauled me to a slit trench and went off to get help and I sat there in the dark, feeling pretty isolated. I was taken back to an aid post, but the leg got gas gangrene and eventually they had to take it off.[29]

As early as daylight on 24 October, less than 12 hours into the battle, it was clear that Montgomery's first attempt to breach the Axis defences had stalled. Neither Lumsden in the north or Harding in the south had broken through, and no further advance was possible until the mines were lifted – a task that could hardly be done in daylight.

Casualties in the first 24 hours were high. The Highland Division had lost around 1,000 men, the New Zealanders 800, the South Africans and Australians about 350 each. About 1,000 prisoners had been taken – most of them Italian – and the ground around and before XXX Corps was littered with Axis dead and wounded, mostly from shellfire. The units dug in, removed their dead, tended their wounded, cleaned their weapons, and prepared to attack again that night.

There were growing doubts about the commitment of the armour. Brigadier Currie's 9th Armoured Brigade, supporting the New Zealanders, had done all that could be hoped for and was dickering with German armour across Miteiriya Ridge. Freyberg wanted Currie to push on, but Currie's tank strength was much reduced – the Wiltshire Yeomanry had only four tanks left – and any further exploitation needed support from X Corps, which Lumsden seemed reluctant to provide, declaring that a further advance here was 'just not on'.

This point was arguable, but not all the arguments favoured the infantry. To send armour against an unbroken anti-tank screen was to invite its destruction – that was one lesson that Eighth Army had absorbed at Sidi Rezegh – and the 'crumbling' of the enemy infantry must also ensure the destruction of the anti-tank screen. That was probably a job for the artillery, but the lifting of mines was clearly an infantry task – or one for the divisional sappers.

The basic rule for any battle is as follows: tanks, infantry and artillery had to work together and in the correct combination. The infantry, sappers and artillery had to deal with the enemy anti-tank guns, clearing a path for the tanks which would then support the advancing infantry against any counter-attack by enemy tanks. Tanks were to be used against infantry and soft-skinned transport, not against anti-tank guns. They might be used against enemy tanks, but the outcome then would depend on the quality of their guns and armour and the tactical position they were able to adopt.

The essential point is that an anti-tank screen had to be reduced by artillery firing high-explosive shells to kill the crews and dismount the guns, or by infantry with mortars and machine-guns – or by infiltrating close enough to use rifle fire and the bayonet. Reducing an anti-tank screen was *not* a task for a frontal assault by tanks; when tanks took on an anti-tank screen, as the panzers did at Snipe (see below), considerable losses would follow. If the tank commanders were cautious, they had good reason – as Neville Gillman's account given above clearly illustrates.

Nevertheless, the attack must be pressed. At a meeting that day between Montgomery, Leese, Freyberg and Lumsden, it was decided that Gatehouse's 10th Armoured Division would move forward through the New Zealand lines to support Currie's 9th Armoured Brigade thrust, supported in turn by much of the XXX Corps artillery. Montgomery made it clear that, if this did not happen, heads would roll.

There seems to have been a certain amount of confusion at this time, especially between the HQs of 51st (Highland) and 1st Armoured Divisions, with no one very certain where the infantry and armoured units had got to – a situation that was hardly surprising after a massive night attack. In fact the tank brigades supporting the infantry were pressing forward in spite of loss. The Bays, supporting the Highlanders lost 11 Shermans in the first push for Kidney Ridge – a position at the north-western end of Miteiriya Ridge – and most of the other tank regiments had taken similar losses, either in the minefields or from anti-tank guns. The reluctance of the tank commanders to commit their tanks before these enemy positions had been reduced by infantry or artillery is understandable. One notable feat that night was an attack by the Seaforth Highlanders on the enemy positions to their front; the attack was successful but costly – in one company the soldiers were rallied on the objective by the company clerk, all the officers and the company sergeant major having been killed or wounded.

The first night's fighting had achieved mixed results, and heavy fighting among the enemy defence lines would continue for the next few days, also with mixed results. On the night of 25/26 October the Australians put in the first of three set-piece attacks in the north, aiming to take the high ground south of the coastal railway – a salient called Thompson's Post. The first attack was partially successful, but not without loss; in this engagement Private P. E. Gatwick won a posthumous Victoria Cross for attacking a mortar position and then a machine-gun nest.

The overall situation on 26 October was that the infantry divisions had taken some part of their objectives, supported in most cases by their attached armoured brigades, which had sustained heavy losses. The problems lay with the *corps de chasse*, X Corps, which had not got forward and – at least according to General Freyberg – was making no great efforts to do so. When Lumsden told de Guingand that part of the 10th Armoured Division's attack should be abandoned, Lumsden and Leese were summoned to Montgomery's caravan in the middle of the night of 26/27 October and told firmly that no part of the attack was to be abandoned. When Leese was dismissed, Lumsden was held back and told that, if he and his divisional commanders were not willing or able to break through the German line, Montgomery would find others to do so.

This blunt warning was needed, but came a little late. By the time Lumsden returned to his headquarters, his tank regiments and brigades were moving forward, breaching the minefields and crossing Miteiriya Ridge in the face of fierce opposition, while in the north the 9th Australian Division had made good progress. With battle raging right down the Alamein Line, Montgomery switched his main effort to the northern area, where the 9th Australian Division would continue to do well – the relentless vigour of the Australian attack was the outstanding feature of the Battle of Alamein.

Elsewhere, said Montgomery, the New Zealanders were to hold Miteiriya Ridge, X Corps was to push west from the 1st Armoured Division's shallow bridgehead beyond the mine-fields, and pressure was to be maintained everywhere along the line to keep the enemy from interfering with the Australian attack. To keep the enemy dispersed, 7th Armoured was to con-tinue its attacks in the south – an order that ran counter to Harding's original instructions that, whatever happened, his division was to be kept in being for use after the breakthrough.

In the end, 7th Armoured, supported by the 50th (Northum-brian) Division, put in a strong attack which gained very little ground and resulted in a 'costly failure',[30] after which 7th Armoured withdrew east of the minefields. In the north, the Australian attack was successful, though met by strong German counter-attacks organized in person by Field Marshal Rommel, who returned that day from Austria and resumed command.

It was becoming clear to Montgomery – and to Alan Brooke and Churchill in London – that all was not going well at Alamein, and Churchill at once began to fret. Brooke records in his diary that Montgomery suddenly became 'Your Mont-gomery', as the Prime Minister braced himself for another fail-ure. Casualties were mounting, gains had been limited, none of the essential objectives had been achieved on time – and without them no further progress was possible. Losses continued to mount over the following days: by 26 October the Highland Division had lost over 2,000 men, the New Zealanders a third of their strength, the Australians over 1,000 of their peerless infan-try. Intelligence estimates of heavy enemy losses were not borne out by the constant Axis resistance along the front, and with Rommel back on the scene the possibility of a strong armoured counter-attack could not be discounted. What to do? While Montgomery was considering his options at his Advanced HQ, one of the great encounters of the Alamein battle was taking shape: the struggle for Snipe.

Snipe was the code name for a low ridge about a mile west of Kidney Ridge; there was another position nearby, code-named Woodcock. The 2nd Rifle Brigade – which is not a brigade but a battalion of light infantry – commanded by Lieutenant-Colonel Victor Turner, was tasked with advancing to Snipe, while another light infantry battalion from the KRRC (60th Rifles) advanced on Woodcock. These battalions were to lift mines and create an anti-tank screen to protect the advance of Briggs's 1st Armoured Division against any counter-attack by German armour. The KRRC got lost and eventually took up a position 1,000 yards short of Woodcock, but Turner's men duly advanced to Snipe on the night of 26/27 October. They were accompanied by the battalion's 'S' Company with 6-pounder anti-tank guns, plus some from 239th Battery 76th Anti-Tank Regiment, Royal Artillery – 19 guns in all. The battalion dug in or built rocky sangars, taking up a semi-circular defensive position facing towards the west; then it began to get light.

The tanks of the 24th Armoured Brigade were supposed to come forward at dawn, but their advance was delayed because the Woodcock position appeared to be in enemy hands. This left Turner's battalion on its own, and even Turner was uncertain whether he was in the right position; 'God knows where we are,' he said to one of his officers, 'but here we are and here we'll stay.'

As it grew light, the Riflemen became aware of an Italian tank leaguer to their front in the west and a German one to the north. As these leaguers broke up and their vehicles started to move west, the Riflemen and gunners opened up with their anti-tank guns, knocking out 14 enemy tanks before their own positions were located, though the first fire directed at Snipe came from the tanks of the 47th RTR, the leading element in the 24th Armoured Brigade. The 24th Brigade arrived at Snipe around 0830 hours, and six of its tanks were at once hit and set ablaze. The Brigade attempted to get forward, lost more tanks, and withdrew to the east behind the Rifle Brigade. This was good practice, but it left the men at Snipe on their own, confronted with a growing quantity of enemy armour and under heavy artillery fire.

During this time, Sergeant R. W. Binks of the 239th Battery knocked out a Panzer Mark IV over a mile away, but artillery fire was now falling on the Snipe position, knocking out several guns and killing or wounding a number of men – the Germans knew how to quell the fire of anti-tank guns. The Riflemen needed artillery support to silence these enemy batteries, but the gunner officer who should have been with them to direct supporting fire had got lost – and now a considerable amount of *British* artillery fire was falling on the Snipe position.

Snipe was then attacked by a force of 15 Italian tanks followed by a group of 25 German tanks; these were engaged as they came on, the range falling until the Riflemen were firing over open sights, and eight German tanks were knocked out, though the Snipe position was still being heavily shelled and mortared and losses among the gun crews were mounting. By 1300 hours, when yet another tank attack came in, only one gun could still bear. This was manned by Colonel Turner, the battalion commander, Lieutenant Jack Toms, the platoon commander, and Sergeant Charles Calistan – no one else was left.

They held their fire until the tanks were 600 yards away and then knocked out six in rapid succession before running out of ammunition. Lieutenant Toms then drove off under machine-gun fire and came back with more shells, his jeep being hit and set on fire as he reached the gun pit. The Colonel and Lieutenant Toms unloaded the ammunition, Colonel Turner being wounded by a shell splinter that penetrated his steel helmet. Toms was hit a few minutes later, but in spite of this they reloaded the gun and knocked out three more of the advancing enemy tanks – 'Well done . . . a hat trick,' declared Colonel Turner.

The defenders of Snipe continued to hold the position for the rest of the day, under mortar and shell fire and constant attacks by enemy armour. Low on ammunition and encumbered with wounded, Turner refused to fall back. 'How he inspired us,' recalled Sergeant Calistan. 'The enemy tried to shift us with an infantry attack but we soon sent them on their way with our Bren-gun carriers and our infantry, who were in position before us . . . the Colonel got a nasty wound and we wanted to bind it up but he would not hear of it. Keep firing – that was all he wanted.'

The 2nd Battalion the Rifle Brigade was finally relieved just before midnight. Of the 19 guns that had moved up the previous night only one could still be used but before the Battalion's lines lay 32 German or Italian tanks and 5 self-propelled German guns – and this was not the entire total, for a number of knocked-out enemy tanks had been removed before this count could take place. Enemy losses are not known, but greatly exceeded the 72 men killed and wounded of the 2nd Rifle Brigade. The story of the stand at Snipe soon became known in Eighth Army, and the awards duly arrived: a Victoria Cross for Lieutenant-Colonel

Turner and the Distinguished Conduct Medal for Sergeant Calistan (who was killed in Italy in 1944).

The Kidney Ridge position remained in enemy hands, and Montgomery therefore decided to go over to the defensive here, while opting for a further advance on the flank of the Australians in the north. Their attack went in that night – an attempt to force a way north, over the road and railway, and get behind the enemy holding Thompson's Post. The attack began at 2200 hours, supported by Valentine tanks of the 46th RTR. Minefields and dust, plus strong resistance, took their usual toll – 307 Australians killed and wounded and the loss of 15 tanks – but this attack, while failing to take the Thompson's Post position, did reap some solid gains, not least in attracting Rommel's attention to the coast.

The British Official History pays tribute to the three Australian set-piece attacks around Thompson's Post, 'which contributed so markedly to the successful outcome of the battle'. These concluded with yet another attack on the night of 30/31 October, which put the Australians astride the road and railway. During this engagement Sergeant W. H. Kibby won a posthumous Victoria Cross by making a lone attack on a machine-gun post – the last of three heroic attacks made during the Alamein battle by this Australian soldier.

Fighting in the north and south of the Alamein Line went on until the end of October, with heavy losses to the Allied tanks and infantry and no apparent reduction in the Axis resistance. Resistance was also building in London, where Churchill was still awaiting the rapid victory he believed Montgomery had promised. The Prime Minister was smelling stalemate and becoming increasingly critical of Alan Brooke, taunting him about the failure of his two chosen commanders, Alexander and Montgomery, to crack Rommel's front when Ultra seemed to indicate that Rommel had little with which to oppose them.

In fact, the constant pressure exerted by Eighth Army and the Desert Air Force was steadily wearing Rommel's forces down and the time was right for another major effort – Operation SUPERCHARGE – a drive by the 2nd New Zealand Division along the coast road. But this axis of attack worried Alexander and de Guingand, for it appeared to be an attack on the enemy at his strongest point.

The Official History comments that 'SUPERCHARGE was in many respects a repetition of LIGHTFOOT', a night attack by infantry followed with a rapid advance by the armour, but the emphasis this time was on the word 'rapid'.[31] The infantry was to consist of the 2nd New Zealand Division backed up by two brigades of British infantry, the 151st from the 51st (Highland) Division, the 152nd from the 50th (Northumbrian) Division, each with a regiment of Valentines in support. This attack would be supported by all the available artillery, and would have the reliable 9th Armoured Brigade in immediate reserve.

Freyburg was directed to attack just north of Kidney Ridge, push forward for 2,000 yards, and establish a strong front along the Rahman Track. That done, 1st Armoured Division, which had moved forward during this assault, would *immediately* come forward, cross the Rahman Track, and reach the open desert. Zero Hour for SUPERCHARGE was 0105 hrs on the night of 1/2 November.

The attack went well. Only one minefield was encountered, and the attacking British and New Zealand troops were on their objectives, well behind the enemy minefields, on time and in good order. The advance was then taken up by Currie's 9th Armoured Brigade, which went forward for another 2,000 yards before coming under heavy anti-tank fire near the Rahman Track and sustaining heavy losses – 70 out of 94 tanks were knocked out, and 230 officers and men were killed or wounded. But the 9th Brigade knocked out 40 enemy tanks and a number of guns, and broke a way through for the 1st Armoured Division.

Writing of this day later, Montgomery stated:

If the British armour owed any debt to the infantry of Eighth Army, the debt was paid on November 2 by the 9th Armoured Brigade, in heroism and in blood. During the rest of the Desert War there was no further discord between the two arms, armour and infantry, as far as I am aware. Brigadier Currie, when told of his task, said he expected 75 per cent casualties and Freyberg said that the Army Commander would accept 100 per cent tank casualties in return for success – and the 9th Brigade suffered very nearly that percentage.[32]

Brigadier John Currie, commander of the 9th Armoured Brigade, was killed in Normandy in 1944.

The 2nd and 8th Armoured Brigades of the 1st Armoured Division came up, but also ran into the anti-tank screen; another 54 tanks were lost here, and no further ground was gained. General Freyberg, who had been pleased with the progress of his forces so far, began to feel that, yet again, the armour was dragging its feet, and he urged Leese to order Lumsden's men to get a move on.

Given the losses sustained against the anti-tank guns, this view now seems mistaken, but this was clearly the crux of the battle and in that context Freyberg was right to demand more effort – though some artillery fire on that German anti-tank screen would have been useful. Leese of XXX Corps was fairly content with the way things were going. Rommel had not counter-attacked, and Leese felt that XXX Corps and X Corps would be well placed to beat him off if he did. However, Freyberg won the argument and Briggs was ordered to move on. The advance continued, with the Australians and 51st (Highland) also moving on the enemy positions to their front.

Rommel was actually in no position to counter-attack. On 2 November he had just 35 tanks left and only about one-third of the anti-tank guns and artillery with which he had started the battle. He was also very short of fuel, and no further supplies were in the offing. There were no German reserves, and the Italians – apart from their gunners – had been stunned by more than a week of shelling, bombing and ground attacks and were no longer reliable. The time had come for Panzerarmee to fall back to Fuka, a position that Rommel had already marked out for his next stand. On the way he could hope to pick up more tanks and German soldiers to enable him to hold the British off when they eventually came up.

Rommel was relying on the assumption, based on previous experience, that the British follow-up would be slow. The problem now was a lack of transport: Panzerarmee was using a great number of captured British vehicles, but these were breaking down through a lack of maintenance and a shortage of spares. The only option was for the Germans to take the transport held by the Italians – leaving their allies to retreat as best they could.

The German retreat from Alamein began on the evening of 2 November. By mid-afternoon on 3 November the retreat was well under way and was going to plan when an order arrived from Hitler: Panzerarmee was not to retreat. It was to hold its ground and fight to the last man and the last round. A similar instruction arrived a few minutes later from the Comando Supremo in Rome.

Rommel showed these orders to von Thoma, who told him bluntly that the remnants of Panzerarmee could not possibly hold their positions and would be totally destroyed if they tried to do so. In this dilemma, Rommel was able to exploit the fact that, without transport, his Italian units could not get away in any case. He ordered the Italian 10th and 21st Corps were to stand fast in accordance with Hitler's directive, while the German withdrawal continued and Rommel applied to OKW for permission to withdraw to Fuka – which he was doing anyway. It was at this moment, with that order to hold fast from OKW, that Rommel's long-held admiration for the Führer began to fade.

Cyril Brian of No. 6 STC again: 'By first light on 2 November we had broken the German lines and they were in full retreat. We had the tanks in front of us, with rollers and chains to sweep the mines as we passed though the minefields, and as we arrived they were just putting up white tape to mark the corridors as a sign it was safe to pass and that night we slept in the German dugouts.'[33]

This was the time for Montgomery to commit the *corps de chasse*, reinforced by the 7th Armoured Division from the south. Montgomery's plan for this stage of the battle called for Lumsden's corps to drive the Axis forces back against the coast while Freyberg took the New Zealanders cutting west through the desert to Fuka to cut off Rommel's retreat – a repeat of the Beda Fomm tactic. The 12-day battle of Alamein – a period exactly in line with Monty's most pessimistic estimate before it began – was over. The pursuit of the enemy could now begin.

Estimates vary on the full extent of German losses at Alamein. One account allows Rommel just half his original force – some 50,000 surviving soldiers and 20 tanks[34] – while another claims that some German divisions had just 10 tanks left and the total troop strength across all Axis divisions came to just 7,500 men.[35] This seems far too low, but Eighth Army certainly took 30,000 prisoners – 10,000 of them German – and official estimates of enemy killed and wounded vary from 10,000 to 20,000. The Axis also lost 320 tanks and 84 aircraft, and 1,000 enemy guns were abandoned on the battlefield. On 4 November a bulletin from Cairo announced that the Panzerarmee Afrika was in full retreat.

Eighth Army losses came to 13,500 men, of whom 2,500 were killed; the Army also lost 500 of its 1,350 tanks – of which 350 were soon repaired – 111 guns and 95 aircraft. A high cost, but a victory at last as Eighth Army – men, tanks and guns – flowed though the Alamein Line and set off after their retreating enemy. If it could catch him and beat him again, its triumph would be complete.

The final word on this battle rests with General Montgomery. Writing in 1967, on the twenty-fifth anniversary of Operation LIGHTFOOT, he stated, 'When all did so well it would hardly seem right to single out any for special praise. But I must say this – we would not have won the battle in ten days without that magnificent 9th Australian Division.'

51 (Highland) Div.

8

Alamein to Tripoli
October 1942–January 1943

Montgomery advanced with circumspection, making sure he was always well balanced, operationally and logistically, so that he would not suffer the fate of the other British commanders who had reached El Agheila before him.

William Jackson, *The North African Campaign, 1940–43*, p. 303

Even his severest critics concede that Bernard Law Montgomery was the victor of Alamein. There are numerous arguments over the conduct of the battle – some say that it lasted too long or was too costly in lives, and many comment that the battle did not go exactly as originally planned, though it is hard to find a battle that ever does go as originally planned – but the victory, if a narrow one, goes to Montgomery's credit.

War does not lend itself to exactitude and generalship can never be a precise science. Apart from the fact that war is an unnatural activity, in which all sensible participants are frightened and the scope for error is almost unlimited, there is also the existence of the enemy, whose immediate purpose is to upset any pre-arranged plan. Nor need much time be wasted on the other popular argument: that the landing of Anglo-American forces in Tunisia – Operation TORCH – made Alamein an unnecessary battle as, taken front and rear, Rommel's defeat was now inevitable.

There are a number of problems with this theory. First, Tunisia is almost 2,000 miles from Alamein, and it seems unlikely that the Anglo-American landings so far away would seriously disturb Rommel at this time. By that argument, the D-Day operation in France in June 1944 should have made the Russian summer offensive in Poland unnecessary. Rommel had to be pushed out of Egypt and Libya in 1942, not least to drive the enemy from those North African airfields from which the Axis air forces were still punishing Malta. Second, the Tunisian campaign did not go as planned. The terrain was mountainous, the weather vile, the Allied troops inexperienced, the enemy tenacious and swiftly reinforced. The notion that Eighth Army could have sat tight at Alamein until TORCH finished enemy resistance in North Africa is not sustainable. Alamein was a victory, and a necessary one.

Victory excuses many mistakes, but Montgomery's multiplying critics, if thwarted somewhat over Alamein, swiftly found easier ground for complaint in his conduct of the subsequent pursuit, which, it is alleged, allowed the enemy to escape to fight another day. This pursuit began on 4 November, and on that day Montgomery issued a message to his troops, part of which reads:

> The enemy has just reached the breaking point and is trying to get his Army away. The Royal Air Force is taking a heavy toll of his columns moving west on the main coast road. The enemy is in our power and he is just about to crack. I call on all the troops to keep up the pressure and not relax for one moment. We have the chance of putting the whole Panzer Army in the bag and we will do so . . .

Clearly, Montgomery was well aware of the state of Panzerarmee – Ultra was helpful here – and very determined to complete its destruction. That order is full of energy, and its intent is clear in his direct command to his subordinates to 'keep up the pressure and not relax for one moment'. And yet, in spite of this firm directive, much of the surviving Panzerarmee – admittedly a very small force – did get away to fight another day. So what went wrong, and why did it happen?

Panzerarmee was certainly much reduced. On 5 November – the first full day of the pursuit – Panzerarmee Afrika reported that its unit strengths were as follows. 15th Panzer Division: 8 tanks,

200 infantry, 4 anti-tank guns, 12 field guns, no 88-mms. 21st Panzer Division: 30 tanks, 400 infantry, 16 anti-tank guns, 25 field guns, no 88-mms. 164th Light Africa Division: about 600 officers and men of three panzergrenadier battalions, no 88-mms. There was no return from the 90th Light Division but it is unlikely that its units or the Italian formations were in any better shape. This being so, Montgomery had a chance to finish off these remnants and deal a shattering blow to German military prestige – a prospect increased by the capture of General von Thoma, commander of the Afrika Korps, who fell into British hands on 4 November. Montgomery certainly tried to catch and crush Panzerarmee, but a number of factors combined to help the enemy, or some of the enemy, get away – a point that Montgomery's enemies have never ceased to labour in the decades since Alamein.

The first of these factors was the severe traffic congestion west of Alamein. The minefields were extensive and many had not been cleared or not completely cleared. The swept corridors were crowded with hundreds of tanks and armoured cars and detachments from the various divisions, all competing for space and creating a terrible traffic jam. The British front was also congested by hosts of Italian soldiers, abandoned by the Germans and anxious to surrender. There was similar congestion among German units retreating on the coast road and RAF patrols reported nose-to-tail traffic between El Daba and Fuka – traffic which they proceeded to bomb.

Another argument holds that these problems were equally inhibiting to the Germans and are therefore no excuse for delay. Not so. Eighth Army could not simply follow the enemy directly down the coast road; its task was to outflank him and get ahead of him, and that meant swings south, across the open but heavily mined desert. Nor could the pursuers keep up with the pursued along the coast road, which had been mined, booby-trapped and much damaged by retreating Axis sappers. It is much easier to blow a gap than fill it in again, much quicker to destroy a bridge than build a new one: comparing the speed of the German retreat with the speed of the British advance is not comparing like with like.

As Eighth Army attempted to outflank the enemy columns, its tanks and armoured cars soon began to run out of petrol. Moving across the desert in low gear uses up a great deal of fuel.

However, the fuel trucks were also caught in the traffic congestion astride the former front line – and these petrol trucks were
all two-wheel-drive, and very prone to getting stuck in the tank-
churned sand west of Alamein.

There was also the problem of the enemy as Major Eric
Schmidt explains:

> During the Battle of Alamein the sappers were on minefield tasks
> by day and on tank-busting by night, to prevent the German tank
> recovery teams from evacuating tanks capable of repair on the
> field. We achieved that by placing a large charge against the turret
> ring under the gun and so rupturing the turret from its mounting
> and making it impossible to move in any direction – the tank was
> a write-off, and we destroyed over 20 in this way.
>
> There were then reports that the enemy were using aerial bombs,
> booby-trapped, in their defences and minefields, and we had to
> train every sapper on the various types of German bomb fuse –
> which the Germans, most obligingly, listed by number on all their
> bombs. When the Germans began their retreat they even booby-
> trapped corpses, so we made grappling hooks from lengths of re-
> inforcing bar and cables, so that we could pull the bodies aside and
> again many lives were saved – although to our great sorrow our
> Brigadier Kisch was killed by a booby-trapped mine in the final
> week of the war in North Africa; he knew every sapper officer by
> name, even humble second lieutenants such as I was at the start.
>
> The offensive spirit in the Western Desert Force and later in
> Eighth Army never wavered. We were always certain that sooner
> or later we would win a decisive victory.[1]

Jim Sewell of 7th Armoured Division also took part in the
Alamein pursuit, and his account confirms that of Major
Schmidt:

> Several days later we passed through the now quiet battlefields
> at Alamein, still strewn with smashed and burnt-out equipment.
> The following day, as our convoy stopped for lunch on the coast
> near Buq-Buq, one of the guardsmen took a kick at an innocent-
> looking can. There was a terrific bang, and when the dust had set-
> tled one soldier lay minus a leg. The enemy left many booby traps
> behind them, and sometimes they booby-trapped their own dead
> comrades. The next 12 days or so proved very interesting,
> moving through the battlefields of El Adem and Tobruk with

hundreds of burnt out lorries or tanks, then negotiating a blown bridge or bouncing across a partially filled bomb crater.[2]

Nevertheless, in spite of all these difficulties there *was* hot pursuit. The 2nd New Zealand Division was at El Agramiya, well west of the Rahman track, by the night of 4/5 November, and was coming up to the coast road by Sidi Hameish, west of Fuka, by the morning of 7 November. The 22nd Armoured Brigade tracked 21st Panzer to the landing grounds south-east of Mersa Matruh by 6 November before running out of fuel. The 2nd Armoured Brigade, moving south of Minqar Qa'im, ran out of fuel on the evening of 6 November and did not receive fresh supplies until the following day.

German traffic on the coast road or retreating over the desert was constantly harassed by the Desert Air Force, which now contained some American fighter squadrons, and by the armoured cars of the 1st Royals, the 10th Hussars and the 1st South African Armoured Car Regiment, who harried Axis columns as far west as Acroma, well beyond Tobruk. The story that Montgomery's 'caution' let the enemy escape unscathed from Alamein is a total myth.

John Black of the 27th New Zealand Machine Gun Battalion, took part in this pursuit:

Lieutenant Gardiner set out the gun line and gave me instruction to search the ground ahead for targets while he borrowed a rifle from one of the boys and set out to see whom our support was. He found nobody there, but English tanks arrived a little later and covered the gap between our infantry and us.

Lieutenant Gardiner arrived back with five German prisoners, and he and I then took up position in one of the knocked out tanks and relayed ranges to our gunners, who promptly opened fire on the enemy, who seemed to be wandering about in a dazed fashion. We found some good targets and enjoyed the shooting, and when the dust cleared there were no Germans in sight – all except the wounded were below ground. After so many setbacks and disappointments, the boys felt that this was the turning point in the war – and so it was. What a great feeling! After Alamein, Lieutenant Gardiner was awarded the DSO – an award usually reserved for colonels and brigadiers – and Sergeant Cattanach and I received the Military Medal.[3]

William Vines of the 2/23rd Australian Battalion concludes his account of this battalion:

> In the days after the battle we recovered our dead from all over the battlefield for reburial in the Alamein cemetery, and we reorganized as we were rejoined by officers and troops from LOB [left out of battle] and others recovered from wounds and illnesses sustained earlier. Major Wall became acting CO and was subsequently promoted to lieutenant-colonel and to command the battalion. We did not fight again in North Africa, and Colonel Wall was killed on the first day of our next action in New Guinea.[4]

Peter Smythe was with the 26th New Zealand Infantry Battalion and sent in extracts from his diary:

> About 1 November, or maybe the next night, I'm not sure, I stripped off and had the first 'wash all over' for about a week, with half a kerosene can of water and a sponge. Our next move at night saw a rather hectic episode. We were miles from anywhere, in the middle of a lot of sand, and my wireless truck got stuck. I went back in my jeep to find it, but not only couldn't find it, I could not find my way back to the convoy. So I circled around, and by a mere fluke ran into our quartermaster, who had the route marked on his map. So off again, one eye on the speedo, and – ah – found the convoy. The wireless truck turned up next day – they usually do. Later on two of my trucks loaded with stores were lost for three days and one for a week, but it turned up in the end so we don't worry.
>
> The first night we moved on to take over from some Scotties of the 51st (Highland) Division. The track was 18 inches to 2 feet deep in dust, and riding in an open truck you can imagine what it was like – twice we bumped the truck in front of us. But we found the position and settled in as a reserve battalion with two battalions in front of us. This part of the line was quiet for us – a few shells and one day some bombs, but generally the area was quiet.
>
> During the chase we just ploughed along, huge 60-pounder guns on one side, trucks, vans, ammo wagons, tanks, armoured cars, jeeps, God knows what, in one mad chase after Rommel. Next day we expected to attack a town on the coast, but that fell through and we moved forward for more miles and then the fun started.
>
> First, we were short of petrol. On one day we moved only 200 yards, yet according to the BBC we were 'racing across the desert

in pursuit'. On another morning a German column passed quite close and opened up on us with machine-guns. Our Bren-gun carriers raced out and rounded them up, coming back loaded with loot – revolvers, binoculars, telephones, wireless sets, etc.

Then the rains came, and for two whole days it rained and we were bogged in 2 feet of mud. That was the night I slept in the jeep with my feet poking out in the rain. Then the sun came out and we dried out. Each day we expected to have to attack some strongpoint; each day Jerry ran so fast we could not catch him. And so it was.

On the last day of this strange chase, as we came on to the main road, burnt-out trucks, smashed tanks and littered junk lay on all sides. At one aerodrome we passed, at least a dozen planes were wrecked all around it. And that brings me to 12 November. Never were we in such high spirits. On the night that German general was captured – von Thoma – the news went down the column like wildfire and all the BBC news bulletins were listened to with keenest interest.

The latest *2nd NZEF Times*, which came today, brought horrid news. In the casualty lists appeared the name of Lieutenant Doug Sutherland, whom I knew well – his mother lives only 150 yards away from Mum in Fendalton, in Christchurch, and his death will be a terrible blow to his widowed mother and two sisters.[5]

Actions between the advancing British and the retreating German units continued until 6 November. And then, as the above account relates, the rains came on 7 November, turning the desert into a swamp and creating a great deal of fog. Major-General John Harding, then commanding the 7th Armoured Division, had no doubt that the rains and steady German resistance slowed down Eighth Army's advance:

I think it was on 6 November that we passed through the New Zealand Division who were engaged with the enemy rearguards at Fuka. After some delay, caused by minefields, we climbed the Fuka escarpment and then made contact with a strong force of German armour – the remains of 15th and 21st Panzer – barring our way. That night came rain.

The rain was torrential. It certainly delayed us and caused us great difficulty, but it seemed to us that there were too many divisions trying to cut off the enemy and competing for fuel and the limited amount of transport available to get it forward. Better results would have been achieved if the pursuit had been conducted by one division – ours – and all available transport put at its – our – disposal to keep it – us – going. But General Montgomery was determined to avoid the mistake, common on previous campaigns, of outrunning his supplies.

Correlli Barnett has pointed out that 'The rains fell impartially on the Briton and German and the Rommel Papers make clear that the Axis retreat was as greatly hampered by it as the British pursuit.'[6] No doubt Rommel's retreat was hampered by the weather, but not to the same extent. Rommel's axis of retreat was down the coast road, an all-weather surface. The British were attempting to get ahead of his forces by hooking forward across the open desert, which rapidly became a bog – and it should be remembered that even in the much better weather of the previous summer Rommel's forces had not succeeded in overtaking and outflanking the retreating British.

Rommel's supply lines were growing steadily shorter, and his ability to refuel and rearm his forces grew by the hour. The advancing British forces were – as described – outrunning their fuel trucks, which were somewhere behind the minefields or caught in the traffic jams, struggling to get forward. Many of those fuel trucks that did get forward were quickly bogged down as the desert turned into a swamp.

Then there was German opposition, active in rearguard actions by retreating units, or passive in the delaying tactics of the German sappers. It takes only a few minutes to lay a demolition charge in a culvert or place a booby trap in an abandoned vehicle, but to repair the one and to find the other can take hours or days. The rain also grounded the Desert Air Force, removing one major source of harassment from Rommel's forces.

It can be argued that had better arrangements been made for the pursuit, there would have been no traffic congestion and no delays in bringing up fuel, but there is no case for saying that the enemy were simply allowed to get away. Many did not get away. On 5 November XIII Corps alone took 6,000 prisoners, and between 4 and 17 November 17,000 German and Italian prisoners entered the British POW camps as Rommel's retreat continued. Rommel was falling back, and he intended to go on falling back until the British outran their supply lines and were forced to give him a breathing space. According to Rommel, that breathing space would lie somewhere south of the Gulf of Sirte.

Meanwhile there were dramatic happenings elsewhere in North Africa. On 7 November 1942, an Anglo-American force commanded by Lieutenant-General Dwight D. Eisenhower landed in North Africa. The First Army, commanded by a British officer, Lieutenant-General Kenneth Anderson, and consisting of American and British units, landed astride Algiers. Three more US divisions – later the US II Corps – landed at Casablanca and Oran. All these landings were met initially by strong Vichy French resistance, though this quickly petered out, a general French ceasefire coming on the morning of 10 November. This Allied landing – Operation TORCH – was the first commitment of American ground troops against the Axis powers. When it was fully developed it would place the German and Italian forces in North Africa between the jaws of an Allied vice.

To co-ordinate the actions of the Allied forces in the west with Eighth Army in the east, a new Allied Headquarters was established in Algiers, with the US general Eisenhower appointed Supreme Allied Commander in the Mediterranean. After Alamein and TORCH the eventual outcome of the war in North Africa was never in doubt, but a lot of hard fighting still lay ahead – not least in the mountainous terrain of Tunisia. Before it could get to Tunisia, however, Eighth Army had to drive Rommel out of Libya.

In spite of the information coming in from Ultra, which described the desperate state of Panzerarmee Afrika, Montgomery followed Rommel's forces cautiously, declining – largely because of the current bad weather – to try the short cut across the Jebel Akhdar to cut the coast road again at Beda Fomm. Given the history of previous advances, a certain caution was understandable: Montgomery was not going to split his forces for a wide-ranging pursuit and so give Rommel any chance of a counter-attack. Panzerarmee was a resilient force under a commander noted for dash, and Montgomery was not going to play to Rommel's strengths. Monty had the numbers, and he intended to use them, pressing forward in force, gradually grinding the enemy down. This was sound policy, for, as he fell back – and in spite of those desperate pleas for aid sent to Rome and picked up by Ultra – Rommel's strength was increasing.

On 10 November, German unit returns were as follows. 15th Panzer Division: 1,177 all ranks, 5 anti-tank guns, 11 field guns, no tanks. 21st Panzer Division: 1,009 all ranks, 5 anti-tank guns, 6 field guns, 11 tanks. 90th Light Division: 1,000 all ranks, 10 anti-tank guns, 2 troops field artillery. Ramcke Parachute Brigade: 700 all ranks, 5 anti-tank guns, 2 field guns. 19th Flak Division: 24 88-mm and 40 light anti-aircraft guns. 164th Light Africa Division: 2 battalions and 2 troops of field artillery. Rommel had done much with smaller forces in the past, but the significant point that November was a shortage of tanks.

In the first seven days of the pursuit, from 4 to 11 November – the 11th being the day on which Montgomery was promoted to full general and awarded the KCB – Eighth Army had driven Rommel back 250 miles, taken thousands of prisoners, and forced the enemy to abandon a great deal of equipment, including many tanks, which had been left in the desert, out of fuel and beyond the reach of the Panzerarmee's recovery teams. Rommel's forces had withdrawn out of Egypt, through the frontier wire, and streamed past Fort Capuzzo and the port of Bardia, where the leading tanks of the 22nd Armoured Brigade arrived just too late to stop the last train out. The British supply problems had been eased slightly by the capture of the small ports of Matruh, Sollum and now Bardia, but the British advance was delayed here by a lack of fuel and two days passed before, on 13 November, the 11th Hussars led the 7th Armoured Division into Tobruk. This was a useful propaganda coup but Tobruk was in ruins.

There were 101 wrecked ships cluttering Tobruk's harbour – some sunk by bombing, others scuttled by the enemy – and it was a week before the first supply ship could unload, but after that 800 tons of fuel and dry stores were being put ashore here every day. This amount would be vastly exceeded after the capture of the much larger port of Benghazi – which fell on 20 November – and the clearance of the 86 sunken ships cluttering its harbour. Once ashore, these supplies had to be lifted forward to the advancing units, which meant a rapid clearance of mines and major repair work on the roads and tracks.

One further, chronic problem – small in itself, but major in impact – was the continuing uselessness of the British 4-gallon petrol container, accurately known as the 'flimsy'. After an hour's bouncing on a desert track, these tins would split at the seams and allow their contents to cascade over the desert. Apart from the obvious fire hazard to trucks and crews, it is estimated that over 30 per cent of the fuel painfully delivered to Tobruk or Benghazi was lost in this way – and would continue to be lost until the Allies captured or manufactured more of that most useful piece of kit the German petrol container, still known as the jerrycan.

After the recapture of Tobruk, the advance – or pursuit – paused for two weeks. This not inconsiderable delay was due to the need to reorganize the Army and pull it together. Eighth Army was now scattered over several hundred miles – back to beyond the Alamein Line – and some changes were about to be made.

The first was that the Army was to lose the last of its splendid Australian divisions. With the Japanese rampaging through the Pacific and South-East Asia, the Australian government wanted all its troops back; the 9th Australian Division was duly taken out of the line and returned to Australia. The 1st South African Division also left, returning to South Africa to reform as an armoured division. The 44th Division was disbanded, its units being used to reinforce other divisions of the Army.

The Australians were not allowed to leave without a final word from Alexander:

Officers, warrant officers, non-commissioned officers and men of the Australian Imperial Force; these great days we are living in are a time for deeds rather than words, but when great deeds have been done there is not harm in speaking of them. And great deeds have been done.

The battle of Alamein has made history and you are in the proud position of having taken a major part in that great victory. Your reputation as fighters has always been famous but I do not believe you have ever fought with greater bravery or distinction than you did during that battle . . .

There is a hard and bitter struggle ahead before we come to final victory and much hard fighting to be done. In the flux and change of war individuals will change. Some will come; others will go. Formations will move from one theatre to another and where you will be when the next battles are fought I do not know. But wherever you may be my thoughts will always go with you and I shall follow your fortunes with interest and your successes with admiration. There is one thought I shall cherish above all others – under my command fought the 9th Australian Division.[7]

Apart from those units departing, there were some internal changes. The 50th (Northumbrian) Division and the 4th Indian Division were redeployed to XXX Corps, and General Horrocks was given X Corps in place of General Lumsden, who had failed to satisfy Montgomery and left Eighth Army. (Lumsden was killed in 1945 during a kamikaze attack in the Pacific, when serving as a liaison officer with the American fleet.) With XIII Corps much reduced by these moves, XXX Corps became the main element in the Army – containing the New Zealanders, 51st (Highland) and the veteran 7th Armoured Division.

These moves reduced the strength of Eighth Army, and all took time. In that time Rommel was able to review his situation and lay fresh plans, taking into account the presence of the Anglo-American forces in the west and the constant badgering from Hitler and OKW.

Meeting his principal subordinates at El Agheila on 24 November, Rommel announced his decision. Panzerarmee would abandon Tripolitania and concentrate its forces in Tunisia, joining with the Axis forces there and striking first against the raw troops in Anderson's First Army or the US II Corps. That done he would turn again to smite the advancing Eighth Army, which would by then be some 1,500 miles from its base in Egypt and at the end of a long and tenuous supply line. This decision to abandon Libya was promptly blocked by the Comando Supremo, and Rommel therefore flew to Germany to obtain the consent of the Führer.

This consent was not forthcoming. Hitler detested giving up ground, and Rommel records that 'There was a noticeable chill in the atmosphere from the outset.'[8] The atmosphere became extremely frosty when Rommel suggested that since Malta was still in Allied hands and the difficulties in shipping supplies to Africa were therefore not likely to ease, it might be as well to face facts and consider abandoning North Africa entirely.

At this 'The Führer flew into a fury', ordering Rommel to hold the Mersa Brega (El Agheila) line at all costs while more supplies, troops and tanks were sent to join him – though at this time any troops or supplies that the Führer could spare from Russia were being sent to the German forces in Tunisia. Frustrated by Kesselring and the Comando Supremo in Rome and now by Hitler, Rommel returned gloomily to North Africa, assembling his forces at El Agheila. There they dug in behind deep mine-fields to await the arrival of Eighth Army.

The El Agheila position was extremely strong. A mixture of marshes and minefields, with plenty of soft sand and a wide anti-tank ditch, it had the sea at the northern end of the line and a salt marsh to the south. All in all, it was a good place to make a stand, but Rommel did not want to stand here or anywhere in Tripolitania. He therefore informed the Comando Supremo that he could only hold the position for a few days if the British put in a determined attack as he lacked either the troops to defend it in depth or the fuel to fight a tank battle. The reply from Comando Supremo was that he was to hold as long as possible, and might then fall back to the port of Buerat, 200 miles east of Tripoli.

Montgomery's forces arrived at Mersa Brega on 15 December, Monty having sent Freyberg's New Zealanders south on a 200-mile desert march around Rommel's position. They were to block the coast road while 51st (Highland) attacked at Mersa Brega and 7th Armoured struck at Bir el Suera, south of the Mersa Brega salt marsh. Both divisions were tasked to hold Panzerarmee in position until the New Zealanders got behind it. Rommel quickly grew aware of this intention and, had his tanks had sufficient fuel, would have fallen back and struck at Freyberg's troops, who were a long way from any possibility of assistance by the rest of Eighth Army.

Lacking fuel and to avoid being trapped, Rommel abandoned the Mersa Brega position on 16 December, brushed aside the leading elements of the 2nd New Zealand Division on the coast road and headed west for Buerat. This withdrawal was made before the New Zealanders could cut the road, but it still cost Rommel 450 men and 18 of his precious tanks. On arrival at Buerat, Rommel received another order from the Führer: he was to fortify the port and defend it to the last man and the last round of ammunition.

Rommel had little patience with such histrionics and for once the Italian Comando Supremo supported him. On 2 January 1943 Mussolini agreed that Rommel could withdraw into Tunisia, or at least to the old Mareth Line fortifications along the

Tunisian–Libyan frontier – if Rommel would first hold up the Eighth Army advance for a further two months. With Eighth Army still rolling on, his troops worn out, very little fuel for his remaining tanks, and scant reinforcement, Rommel considered that there was little chance of such an extended delay.

In addition, Rommel was not convinced that the Mareth Line defences that the Comando Supremo was so keen on were even defensible. Built in the 1930s by the French to protect Tunisia from the Italians, they were both dilapidated and easily out-flanked. 'A line of antiquated French blockhouses which in no way measured up to the standards required by modern warfare' was how he described them in a dispatch to OKW. Rommel therefore began moving his forces back into Tunisia, placing them behind the Mareth Line. This move started with 21st Panzer, which went back on 14 January, leaving all its remaining tanks and most of its artillery behind with 15th Panzer.

Having been forced out of Tripolitania, Rommel decided to make his stand at the Gabes Gap, a little east of the Mareth Line. This position was not unlike the one the British had found at Alamein: a short and defensible position along the Wadi Akarit, between the Chott el Fejaj salt marshes and the sea. While his troops were moving into that position, Rommel would do what he could to hold the port of Buerat while General Jürgen von Arnim, now commanding the German forces in Tunisia, kept the First Army and the Americans away from Gabes. The details of operations carried out by the Anglo-American forces in Tunisia in November and December 1942 lie outside the scope of this book, but, as these armies were to work together later for the final destruction of the Axis forces in Tunisia, a brief account of First Army's exploits since the start of TORCH has to be included here and will be expanded in later chapters.

The task given to the British First Army by General Eisenhower was to 'build up rapidly a striking force through Algeria and the adjacent ports' and 'occupy Tunisia at the earli-est possible date'.[9] This was easier to order than achieve. At this time First Army contained only an incomplete infantry division, part of an armoured division, a parachute brigade, some anti-aircraft units, and Nos. 1 and 6 Army Commandos. This rag-tag collection of forces was the nucleus of what, on 6 December, became Lieutenant-General C. W. Allfrey's V Corps, but for the moment they were barely capable of carrying out their assigned task.

General Anderson's attempt to move on Tunis from Algiers – a distance of some 500 miles, mostly over mountains – began as a *coup de main* on 14 November. This thrust, supported by parachute landings, soon came to a halt and was completely over by 30 November, defeated by solid German resistance and terrible weather. More units – the British 6th Armoured Division and the British 78th Infantry Division – arrived by mid-December, the start of the rainy season in the Tunisian mountains. The US forces also took time to build up their strength, and this Allied delay – and the winter weather – greatly helped the Germans to strengthen their hold in Tunisia.

Following the Vichy French armistice in North Africa on 10 November, Hitler initiated a contingency plan, Plan ANTON, for the immediate occupation of all Vichy French territory in Metropolitan France – the Unoccupied Zone – and in North Africa. The South of France was quickly occupied by ten German divisions, the French fleet at Toulon being scuttled by the crews before it could fall into German hands, the warships sinking even as German troops were beating down the dockyard gates. OKW then took steps to reinforce the Axis forces in North Africa with the immediate dispatch of more Luftwaffe squadrons to the Tunisian airfields – some equipped with the new Focke-Wulf fighter – and an airlift of troops and supplies to von Arnim via Sicily. These initial moves would shortly be followed by the arrival of the 10th Panzer Division. The Germans were clearly going to make a fight of it.

Vichy French resistance to the Anglo-American landings in Algeria and Morocco, though brief, gave the Germans time to concentrate their forces in Tunisia, where they quickly formed a wide bridgehead around the ports of Tunis and Bizerta. Through these ports German reinforcements – including a number of the new Tiger tanks, armed with the fearsome 88-mm gun – quickly arrived, and by the end of November this bridgehead contained some 15,000 German troops with 50 Panzer Mark IVs and about 40 Tigers confronting First Army. This new force, XC Corps, was placed under the command of an Afrika Korps veteran, General Walther Nehring. In the south-east, along the Mareth Line, German forces confronting Eighth Army included the leading elements of the 10th Panzer Division from Italy and 21st Panzer from Panzerarmee Afrika.

Small resources in men, guns and tanks obliged the Axis forces in Tunisia to fight a defensive battle, but here they were fortunate, for the terrain of Tunisia is very suited to defence – and would come as a great shock to the Western Desert soldiers. Tunisia is not the North Africa of popular imagination. Tunisia is green and mountainous, with large towns and cultivated valleys. In spite of its location on the supposedly sun-kissed North African shore, its winter weather is frequently vile, marked by heavy and prolonged rainstorms which turn the ground into swamps and the numerous river valleys (wadis) into dangerous torrents. Given the timing of TORCH, it is not surprising that the Anglo-American campaign in Tunisia got off to a very slow start.

A particular feature of the Tunisian terrain is two mountain ranges running north to south from the Cape Bon peninsula – the Western Dorsal and the Eastern Dorsal. These rocky ranges are crossed by a number of narrow passes, but they were to provide the dividing line between the two Allied forces. The First Army and the US II Corps operated to the west of the Dorsals, aiming for Tunis and Bizerta, the Eighth Army came in from the east, to thrust north between these ranges and the coast, though Sfax and Sousse, heading towards Cape Bon (see the map on p. xvii).

During November and December, First Army, such as it was, was moving east along the coast road from Algiers, 500 miles west of Tunis, through Bone and Tabarka, where it was joined by British and US parachute units which had leapfrogged ahead. A smaller force, Blade Force, covered the inland flank. On 19 November German forces were encountered by Blade Force at Medjez el Bab, 50 miles west of Tunis, and after three days of fighting the result was a German victory. This first Allied thrust on Tunis came to a halt on 30 November, largely because of German air superiority, but heavy fighting on this front continued into December. Even so, Eisenhower's attempt to grab Tunis before the Germans could reinforce it had failed.

Hitler ordered a rapid increase of forces in Tunisia, intending to raise them to six or seven divisions – though only four actually arrived – replacing General Nehring with General von Arnim and renaming XC Corps the Fifth Panzer Army. On 6 December von Armin struck again at Medjez el Bab and inflicted heavy losses on the 1st US Armored Division. The weather continued to deteriorate, constant rain turning the ground into deep mud, and Eisenhower decided to withdraw the Allied forces to the Jebel el Almara, a ridge north-east of Medjez el Bab that soon became better known as Longstop Hill. Longstop overlooked the Medjerda valley and the road to Tebourba and Tunis and had to be taken. The Coldstream Guards therefore took it on 22 December and handed the position over to the 1st Battalion of the US 18th Infantry Regiment, which was promptly driven off the hill by a German counter-attack.

An American counter-attack failed to retake Longstop. This failure delayed the advance on Tunis by V Corps for two days, until the Guards came back to retake the hill. Unfortunately, by this time the Germans had dug in on another position slightly further north, and General Allfrey, with the rain teeming down and the valley flooded, called off the attack. The rain continued to fall for the next six weeks, and the Allied advance on Tunis foundered in the mud.

The story of First Army and the US II Corps during the early weeks and months in Tunisia, and of how they learned the harsh lessons of this war, is much the same as the story of the Western Desert Force and Eighth Army in previous years. The American and British forces in Tunisia were being taught all the lessons that the Eighth Army had learned so painfully in the desert campaign: the need for close tactical air support, the necessity of fighting divisions as divisions and avoiding a dispersion of force, the need to avoid sending tanks against anti-tank gun screens, the need to cope with the terrain and the weather and the endless problems of supply.

The essential point in the context of this history is that the Anglo-American forces in Tunisia had not defeated the Axis powers in Tunisia or taken the city of Tunis by the end of 1942. Nor would they do so before Eighth Army crossed the Mareth Line and forced a way though the Gabes Gap. The conquest of Tunisia would require the presence of Eighth Army. With that much established, we can now return to the Montgomery's forces closing up on Buerat.

Montgomery's plan, issued on 7 January 1943, stated that, on arriving at Buerat XXX Corps should attack on two widely separated lines: the 50th (Northumbrian) and 51st (Highland)

Divisions along the coast road, the New Zealanders and 7th Armoured Division hooking inland via Tarhuna.[10] X Corps would be in reserve, and the attack would be supported by the fighter and bomber aircraft of the Desert Air Force. The main problem was, as ever, one of supply: Eighth Army now depended entirely on the RASC and Royal New Zealand Service Corps transport companies for logistical support. If the battle went on for any length of time, essential supplies of fuel, ammunition and food might well run short – though at least the constant rain provided plenty of water. During this stage of the advance, the 7th Armoured Division lost its popular commander, Major-General John Harding:

> By this time it was clear that there was no room for two divisions to move on Tripoli so the Army Commander halted the New Zealanders and ordered us to continue the advance alone. I knew from the Long Range Desert Group that the Beni Ulid–Tarhuna track offered better going, so I planned to advance on that axis, with 8th Armoured Brigade leading, keeping to the open desert as the track itself would be mined. After discussing matters with Brigadier Custance while sitting on the top of his tank, I was about to return to my own tank when a salvo of 105-mm shells landed on the ridge just in front of us and I received numerous wounds. That was the end of the hunt for me and the most bitter disappointment. For over two years my target had been Tripoli, and it was to my great joy that I heard later that the crews of the two turretless Honey tanks that formed my headquarters brewed up tea in the main square of the town on the day it was captured; how I wish I could have been with them.

Bombing of the Axis positions at Buerat began on 12 January, and XXX Corps moved forward on 15 January, moving slowly, coping with minefields, demolitions and booby traps along the coast road and with bad going in the open desert south of Buerat. There was only slow progress until the night of 17/18 January, when Montgomery summoned Major-General Douglas Wimberley of the 51st (Highland) Division and told him to get a move on. After that the advance towards Tripoli continued by day and night.

With XXX Corps rolling forward across the Wadi Zemzem and across the desert towards Beni Ulid, the Buerat position was soon outflanked. Rommel was anxious to abandon it, and he pulled out on 15 January – the day Eighth Army advanced directly on Buerat. On 19 January Panzerarmee left Tripoli – comprehensively wrecking the port before departure – and fell back another 200 miles to the Mareth Line, crossing the Tunisian frontier on 23 January. Rommel's rearguard, the 90th Light Division, fought a brisk action with the Highlanders on the coast road, where mines and cratering held up the British advance – there were 109 major craters on the road between Buerat and Homs alone – but on the night of 22/23 January British patrols entered Tripoli and the first armoured units rolled in soon after dawn.

The leading unit was 'B' Squadron of the 11th Hussars from the 7th Armoured Division – the famous Desert Rats. The Division had earned this distinction. It had fought its way up and down this desert, in victory and defeat, for almost three years. In that time Tripoli had become a tantalizing goal, always out of reach and seemingly unattainable. As the Desert Rats' dusty tanks and armoured cars rolled into it that morning, they marked the end of the desert campaign and a significant milestone on Eighth Army's long road to victory.

Eighth Army entered Tripoli three months after the opening of the Battle of Alamein, and Alexander recorded this event in a dispatch to Winston Churchill:

> Sir. The orders you gave me on August 10, 1942, have been fulfilled. His Majesty's enemies, together with their impedimenta, have been completely eliminated from Egypt, Cyrenaica, Libya and Tripolitania. I now await your further instructions.

To celebrate this achievement, Eighth Army held a parade through Tripoli – an event witnessed by Winston Churchill, for years the stoutest supporter of the soldiers, and the severest critic of their generals, but now their guest of honour. 'The enemy had been pushed forty or fifty miles west of the city,' he wrote. 'I spent two days in Tripoli and witnessed the entry of the Eighth Army through its stately streets. At the head were the pipers of the 51st (Highland) Division, spick and span after all their marching and fighting . . .'[11]

This parade was also watched by Ray Cooper of the 22nd Armoured Brigade:

We entered the city on 23 January, with the 11th Hussars in the lead as usual. I do not remember exactly when it took place, but shortly afterwards there was then a Victory Parade with our tanks lined up side by side on the main street and 50 pipers of the 51st (Highland) Division, those wonderful fighting Jocks, leading the parade. The sound of the pipes was quite wonderful and moved me greatly.[12]

Later that day, in an old Roman amphitheatre, Winston Churchill addressed about 2,000 officers and men from a variety of Eighth Army units, praising their efforts in words they would remember: 'When this war it over it will be enough for a man to say – "I marched, and fought, with the Desert Army."'

That day, 23 January 1943, was a great day for the troops of the Desert Army. The parade, held on the day that Eighth Army passed out of the Western Desert and into history, was some recompense for all the hardships they had endured – a brief hint of glory before the hard times began again.

Others should have been there that day, to hear Churchill's words, march in that parade, and share that brief moment of glory: those Highland pipers who fell leading their battalions into the fury of Alamein, the doughty soldiers of the 9th Australian Division now on their way home, the South African soldiers now heading for the Union to retrain and return to Eighth Army in Italy, the Royal Navy men who had sailed in the Spud Run up to Tobruk, the pilots and ground crews of the Desert Air Force – and many thousands of fighting men, soldiers from Britain and many nations of the Empire, who remained and still remain east of Tripoli, in the silent war cemeteries of the Western Desert.

XXX Corps.

9

Tripoli to Tunis
January–May 1943

Due to continual rain there will be no hope of an immediate attack on Tunis. Am attempting to organize and maintain a force to operate aggressively on the southern flank.

General Eisenhower to the Combined Chiefs of Staff,
24 December 1942

From January 1943 until the end of the war, the story of Eighth Army becomes increasingly involved with that of other armies: the Anglo-American First Army in Tunisia, the US Seventh Army in Sicily, and finally the US Fifth Army in Italy. Even though this book concentrates on the exploits of the British Eighth Army and will therefore only touch on the actions of these other armies as they affect the fortunes of the Eighth, the actions of these other armies had to be borne in mind. The most critical of these actions came in matters of command and strategy, and since these matters were to become very critical indeed they should be looked at now.

The basic difference between the Allied commanders – American and British, political and military – from the time the USA entered the war in 1941 lay in a dispute over the best and speediest way to defeat Nazi Germany. The Americans had a simple doctrine for defeating an enemy, one dating back to the American Civil War of 1861–5: gather a massive amount of strength and head directly and as soon as possible for the enemy heartland.

This doctrine might cost lives in the short run, but the Americans believed it would end the war more quickly and there-fore cost the victor fewer casualties in the long run. The way to apply that doctrine in the present circumstances was by a cross-Channel invasion from Britain to France and thence to Germany – an invasion that the American leaders wanted to launch as soon as possible, preferably in the summer of 1942, six months after the USA entered the war. When that proved impossible, the invasion date went back to 1943, but the same doctrine applied.

The problem with this doctrine was that it had not been tried out in the field since Ulysses S. Grant's Wilderness campaign in 1864 – a campaign which had indeed proved very expensive in lives. The US contribution to the First World War, though vital, had not lasted long: the US First Army went into battle in France on 1 August 1918 – 14 weeks before the war ended. The USA had been in the present war for just over a year, and had been fight-ing the Germans on the ground for around two months. Nevertheless, the US Chiefs of Staff arrived for the Allied con-ference at Casablanca in January 1943 quite certain that theirs was the right strategy, that any diversion from a cross-Channel attack and a direct advance on Germany across France to the Rhine was a mistake and any Mediterranean 'adventure' at best a sideshow.

The British did not see it that way. They had been fighting the Germans for more than three years already in this war, and many of their commanders had fought the Germans for four long years in the First World War. They knew they were up against a powerful military-industrial machine which was as yet undamaged, and they did not have the resources, the manpower or the appetite for what was basically a strategy of stark attrition. At this time, the British Official History says drily, the Americans, 'had not the same experience in weighing what was desirable against what was practicable'.[1]

This is not to say that the British were against a cross-Channel invasion. Far from it: they had been planning such an invasion since the evacuation from Dunkirk in 1940, had set up the

Combined Operations Headquarters to develop the necessary equipment, shipping and operational techniques, and had had commando soldiers probing the coast of German-occupied France for the past two years. British reservations were not over the invasion of France but over when this invasion should take place. The British wanted to wear the Germans down first by attacking on the widest possible front, drive Italy out of the war by opening a 'Second Front' in Italy that would consume German strength and aid the Red Army by drawing off divisions from the Russian front. When that had been done, and when the Allied bomber forces had greatly reduced Germany's industrial capacity and the Allies had built up their forces in men, *matériel* and landing craft in the UK, then would be the time for a cross-Channel invasion – and that time was not yet.

From these basic disagreements on fundamental strategy two misconceptions arose among the American commanders in Europe and in Washington. First, that the British were reluctant to undertake a cross-Channel invasion at all; second, that the unre-constructed arch-imperialist Winston Churchill aimed to establish British spheres of influence in the Balkans and the Mediterranean and was attempting to use American blood and treasure to ensure Britain's post-war position as an imperial power.

Both of these suspicions were unfounded – and American sus-picion of Britain's post-war 'imperial' ambitions ignores one of President Franklin D. Roosevelt's bluntly-admitted personal post-war aims: the abolition of the colonial empires of Britain, France, Holland and Belgium – all of which vanished shortly after 1945. We shall return to these strategic and political matters as the war in the Mediterranean develops, for they were to affect the operations of Eighth Army and the conduct of the entire Italian campaign.

There was another point, rarely mentioned but always pres-ent. The US commanders might be new to this war, but they did not see what they had to learn from British commanders who had suffered defeat after defeat at German hands since 1939. The first Duke of Wellington's sage remark after his participation in the Duke of York's disastrous Flanders expedition in 1794, 'Well at least I learned what not to do, which is always something', was either not known or not mentioned in US military circles, and inter-Allied relations were not always easy.

Evidence for this appears in various parts of the US official histories and in the memoirs of some American commanders, and the cause may have been due partly to the long history of Anglo-American antagonism, dating back to the American Revolution of 1776, and to some basic misunderstandings over national attitudes. Some US commanders seem to have been gripped with Anglophobia or to have had a massive inferiority complex towards their more experienced British allies, while the British officers' seemingly casual laid-back approach to the war often came across as condescension. These tensions were not helped by differences in humour.[2]

The Casablanca Conference in January 1943 – a meeting called both to discuss Allied strategy for winning the war and to firm up plans for the immediate future – did not begin with any meeting of minds, but it did decide that a cross-Channel invasion was impossible in 1943, largely owing to the need to defeat the U-boat menace in the North Atlantic, write down the strength of the Luftwaffe, and curtail Germany's industrial capacity. From this it followed that in 1943 the Allies should complete the conquest of North Africa and them move on to the invasion of Sicily – an operation which must therefore be planned while the North African campaign was still in progress. From February 1943, therefore, Alexander's 18th Army Group was charged with the overall command and conduct of the Tunisian campaign, which would involve both armies in the final defeat of the Axis powers in North Africa, and with the initial planning for HUSKY, the Allied invasion of Sicily.

After the fall of Tripoli in January 1943, Eighth Army advanced to the Mareth Line, moving into Tunisia to play a part in the last stage of the North African campaign. With the failure of the First Army advance on Bizerta and Tunis in December 1942, Eisenhower decided to hold his front as far east as possible. By mid-February 1943 Eisenhower's forces in Tunisia held a line which began in the south at Sidi bou Zid, just west of the Eastern Dorsal, and ran north, straddling the Western Dorsal and touching Medjez el Bab, with isolated detachments cutting the roads towards Tunis from Gabes, Mahares and, in the north, Mateur. This line was held – from the south – by the US II Corps, the French XIX Corps and Allfrey's British V Corps. This deployment meant that Patton's II Corps – as it soon became – would be the one to link up with Eighth Army when Montgomery forced his way through the Mareth Line and the Gabes Gap.

By the end of January there had been some changes in the Axis command. Field Marshal Kesselring, the Commander-in-Chief, South, was to take over command of the German forces in Tunisia; von Arnim and Rommel would be his field commanders and he would act as their intermediary with the Comando Supremo. There would be two German–Italian armies fighting in Tunisia, and some overall commander was clearly needed, to co-ordinate strategy and arbitrate during disputes. A further problem was that Rommel was again ill, and Hitler directed that von Arnim should command all the German forces in Tunisia until Rommel was fit for duty.

Rommel then decided that he would stay in Tunisia, and this arrangement was dismantled. Then Rommel became ill yet again, and General von Arnim assumed command of the Army Group Africa, comprising Panzerarmee Afrika, facing Eighth Army and the US II Corps in the south, with von Arnim's original command, the Pz AOK 5, or Fifth Panzer Army, and a new Italian First Army – or German–Italian Panzer Army – under General Giovanni Messe, together confronting First Army in the north.

On 19 February von Arnim sent an armoured force, formed around the 10th Panzer Division, through the Kasserine Pass, a narrow valley through the Western Dorsal east of Tebessa. The scanty US forces defending the pass held up the German advance for a while, but their commander appears to have lost control of the battle, chaos duly reigned, and the II Corps commander, Lieutenant-General Lloyd R. Fredendall, was quickly sacked. (When Eisenhower asked Alexander for his advice on this matter, Alexander, always conscious of the need to maintain Allied unity, replied tactfully that 'He was sure the American Army had better generals'.)

Fredendall was replaced by Lieutenant-General George Patton Jr, with Major-General Omar Bradley as his deputy. Alexander was also less than happy with the current performance of the First Army commander, Lieutenant-General Kenneth Anderson, recording, 'Am doubtful if Anderson is big enough for the job, although he has some good qualities.'[3] He even asked Montgomery if Leese could be spared from commanding XXX Corps to take over First Army. Alexander also warned Churchill and Alan Brooke that 'final victory in North Africa is not around the corner'. Monty declined to part with Leese, Anderson remained in command of First Army, and Alexander received his orders for the spring offensive from General Eisenhower:

> You are appointed Commander of the Group of Armies operating in Tunisia. This appointment takes effect from 20 February, 1943 . . . these forces consist of the British 1st Army, which exercises command over United States and French Forces in Tunisia, the British Eighth Army and such reserve forces as may be placed under your command. Your mission is the early destruction of the Axis forces in Tunisia.[4]

Alexander found First Army's affairs in a mess – which was not entirely Anderson's fault – and decided to reorganize and regroup his forces. When this process was complete, on 26 February 1943, the First Army consisted of the British V Corps (three British divisions under General Allfrey), the US II Corps (one US armoured and three US infantry divisions under Patton) and XIX Corps (two French divisions under General L. M. Koeltz). This force was ordered to move through the Dorsals from the west and push the enemy back to Bizerta and Tunis.

While all this was going on, Eighth Army was moving up to the Mareth Line. This line, which ran from the Matmata Hills to the sea, had been much neglected since its construction by the French between the wars, but it was still the most formidable defence line encountered by the Eighth Army since Alamein. Even getting close to it would be a problem, for the Mareth fortifications were screened by deep wadis (now flooded by the winter rains) and a thick belt of minefields. Since Alamein, mines had become an increasing problem which the Allied armies were ill-equipped to deal with. Clearing with Scorpion flail tanks had not proved effective and sweeping with mine-detectors was very slow. The sappers were often forced to use more direct and dangerous methods. The 4th Field Squadron of the Royal Engineers, when ordered to clear one of the Medenine minefields 'as quickly as possible', simply lined out across the minefield at 6-foot intervals and 'beat it like a field of roots'.

Jim Sewell, who served in one of 7th Armoured's transport companies, recalls this time:

I was blessed with an abundance of mail, which I answered as promptly as possible and recorded in my diary. Receiving mail and parcels could be a joyous event, but it could also bring sad or tragic news – the death of a child in the Blitz or the loss of a parent could be devastating. I remember one of our corporals – a stocky, jovial chap from the West Country who acted as postman – delivering mail to a small knot of us drivers. On this occasion he was both shattered and livid. He had just received a letter from his wife telling him that she was expecting a child by a Canadian serviceman back home. But, as I pointed out – and was not too popular at the time – this corporal was among the brothels' best customers back in Cairo.

We left Tripoli and moved forward to the Mareth Line, making our way forward cautiously until about 0300 hours this night, and dispersed to dig our slit trenches. We were in a series of hills, strongly defended by the enemy. After a short settling-in period, Laurie and I took our load of anti-tank mines up to the Scotties while a terrific artillery bombardment was taking place. We backed right into the gun line, which was under a line of trees, and looked out across the dusty arena where the gladiators were to clash.

As expected, three days later the Germans attacked at 0600 hours, their armour sallying forth to meet a devastating fire – losing more than 40 tanks in the first onslaught, with one of our gunners claiming five tanks with six shots. The following weeks were exciting but dangerous, working long hours with little sleep and poor food, grabbed at any time of the day.[5]

For reasons apart from the enemy minefields, Montgomery was not over-keen on making a frontal assault on a well-prepared enemy position; he knew from personal experience how costly and ineffective such assaults could be. He had been brooding over how to breach the Mareth Line since January, even before the fall of Tripoli. Believing that there must be a way to outflank this position, he had sent the Long Range Desert Group to explore the country south of the Matmata Hills, seeking a way round the enemy flank. All the maps and common report said that any outflanking route was impassable to tanks and vehicles, but the LRDG was able to confirm that there was a way – difficult but possible – past the Mareth Line via the Tebaga Gap, a valley that ran between the Chott el Fejaj salt marsh and the Matmata Hills. That LRDG information was the basis for Montgomery's Mareth plan.

While the LRDG was on its exploratory patrol, the 7th Armoured Division had moved west towards Mareth while the 51st (Highland) and 2nd New Zealand Divisions rested and reorganized at Tripoli. The weather continued foul, and the advance towards Mareth was hampered by torrential downpours which quickly turned the ground into a swamp. These storms ended for a while on 15 February, and 7th Armoured – now supported by 51st (Highland) – took the Medenine airfields on 17 February. On the following day, Eighth Army received a useful and surprise reinforcement: General Philippe LeClerc's Fighting French units came into Eighth Army's lines after an epic march north across the Sand Sea from Lake Chad.

On 26 February von Arnim launched a spoiling attack, Operation OCHSENKOPF, east of Bizerta, and this, plus the aftermath of the Kasserine debacle, made it ever more urgent for Eighth Army to move into Tunisia and take some of the weight off the Anglo-American forces north of Gabes. Before that could happen, Rommel counter-attacked at Medenine, using his desert veterans – 90th Light, 21st Panzer, 15th Panzer, 164th Light – and some Italian divisions, both infantry and armoured, plus 10th Panzer. This attack began on 3 March with probing attacks against the lines of 51st (Highland). By 5 March the enemy's intentions were clear, and the main attack came in on 6 March.

Fortunately, Eighth Army had learned a lot about fighting defensive battles in the last year. No longer would tanks fight tanks – that was a job for the anti-tanks guns, especially the powerful 6-pounders. Rommel's tanks moved up during the night – a technique that the Allied armies were only just starting to employ – and promptly ran into the British anti-tank screen, well-prepared defences based on minefields and backed with plenty of artillery. Rommel lost many of his precious tanks at Medenine – two to the 6-pounder gun of Sergeant Andrews of the 1/7th Battalion the Queen's Regiment, part of the 131st Brigade, the infantry component of 7th Armoured. Sergeant Andrews's battalion accounted for 27 German tanks that day.

By the time this attack came in at Medenine, Montgomery's forward element – XXX Corps – had been joined by the 2nd New Zealand Division, which had the 8th Armoured Brigade and the 201st Guards Brigade under command. The battle at Medenine went very badly for the Axis units, who seem to have lacked any central command and control: observers in the 201st Guards Brigade reported the enemy tanks on their front 'wandering about vaguely'. One unit of 10th Panzer rumbled up to the tank screen put out by the 73rd Anti-Tank Regiment, RA, and promptly lost five tanks, while 15th Panzer got a bloody nose from the guns of the 131st Infantry Brigade and the 2nd Scots Guards – an action which attracted warm praise from the New Zealanders: 'a truly grand victory for the Tommy [anti-tank] gunners . . . the way in which they held their fire was an example to us all.'

The German attack at Medenine went on all day, but by 1730 hours the panzers had ground to a halt. That evening Rommel gave the order to break off the attack – an order that marked the end of his last battle in North Africa. Losses on the British side at Medenine are described in the Official History as 'trifling', but the Axis forces lost over 600 men and around 50 tanks, and on 7 March Rommel ordered them to pull back. 'The operation had lost all point the moment it became clear that the British were prepared for us; we had suffered tremendous losses, including 40 tanks totally destroyed. But the cruellest blow was the knowledge that we had been unable to interfere with Montgomery's preparations.'[6]

Montgomery's account of this time makes great play with the need for 'balance' – a word that also appears regularly in his later memoirs. The need for 'balance' is paramount, said Monty, 'for balance on the battlefield implies the disposal of available forces in such a way that it is never necessary to react to the enemy's thrusts and moves; a balanced army proceeds relentlessly with its plans in spite of what the enemy may do'.[7]

According to Montgomery, 'a balanced force cannot be defeated, for its armour, infantry, artillery – and logistical services – are always in the right place and proportion'. The striving for 'balance', a total determination not to be wrong-footed or caught off-balance by Rommel or anyone else, was the basis of Montgomery's strategy and success. It may also account for the many allegations of 'caution' and 'slowness' which his critics, both at the time and since, have so often – and so successfully – deployed against him.

These allegations have to be weighed against the circumstances of the time and cannot always be dismissed, but in early

March 1943 caution seems to have been advisable, for Eighth Army was not balanced. Only three divisions were currently available for action – 2nd New Zealand, 7th Armoured and 51st (Highland) – plus some infantry and armoured brigades. Monty had moved two of these divisions up to Medenine partly to take the airfields and prepare for his forthcoming Mareth battle, partly in response to an order from Alexander to move forward, threaten Mareth, and take some of the pressure off First Army, but he was not able to do much more until he was reinforced.

The German Supreme Commander in the Mediterranean (Commander-in-Chief, South) was Field Marshal Albert Kesselring, a Luftwaffe officer and a very competent general, who would continue to contest the advance of the Allied armies throughout the Italian campaign. Kesselring had served in the First World War as an artillery officer, and he stayed in the Army after the war, resigning in 1933 to take up a post in the then secret Luftwaffe. Kesselring had commanded the 1st Air Fleet in the Polish campaign, taking over the 2nd Air Fleet for the Low Countries campaign and during the Battle of Britain, and again in Russia during the early stages of BARBAROSSA. He was then sent to Italy, where he was based at the Comando Supremo in Rome with responsibility for all German forces in the Mediterranean. Rommel and Kesselring did not always agree but they managed to work together with an acceptable degree of harmony.

However, relations between Rommel, commanding Panzerarmee Afrika, and General Jürgen von Arnim of Fifth Panzer Army were strained. Von Arnim was an aristocrat who had joined the Kaiser's Prussian Foot Guards in 1909 and served throughout the First World War as an infantry officer. Staying in the Army after the Armistice, he rose steadily in rank and was a major-general in September 1939. In December 1939 he was promoted lieutenant-general, and in November 1941, during the Russian campaign, he was given command of a panzer corps. On 2 December 1942 he was transferred to North Africa and given command of Fifth Panzer Army in Tunisia. He therefore considered that his experience matched that of Rommel, and saw no need to defer to Rommel's rank or proposals.

Rommel was tired and ill. This was not the kind of tiredness that could be reduced by a weekend off or a few nights' rest: this was physical, mental and emotional exhaustion – the result of prolonged strain and heavy responsibility. Even before Alamein he had been far from well and had become increasingly abrasive with his peers and superiors.

Von Arnim was jealous of Rommel's reputation, and believed that the Field Marshal was attempting to overshadow him and to impose his own strategy on Fifth Panzer Army. Von Arnim also despised their Italian colleague, General Giovanni Messe, the commander of the Italian First Army – of which General Cramer's Afrika Korps was the most potent part. The reputations of the Italian generals have not come well out of the North African war, but General Messe was a competent commander and Rommel for one respected his abilities.

Von Arnim's feelings can be at least partly understood, for he had an unenviable task. New to Africa – where Rommel was the star – he was confronted in Tunisia with a powerful enemy that could only get stronger. He never received the forces he had been promised by Hitler; only four fresh divisions had arrived from Italy, and only one of these, 10th Panzer, was a tank unit – though the Hermann Goering Division, if not yet up to strength, was well equipped and fully trained. Facing enemies on two fronts in Tunisia, Kesselring disposed Fifth Panzer Army to confront First Army; the Italian First Army – largely the former Panzerarmee Afrika – would face Eighth Army. Alexander's task was to bring both Allied armies against these Axis forces and drive them into the sea. To do that he had first to bring Eighth Army through the Mareth Line and the Gabes Gap and fight a co-ordinated Allied campaign, beginning with an attack by both armies.

On 17 March General Patton led the US II Corps forward to open First Army's attack – Operation WOP, a thrust towards Gafsa. Three days later Eighth Army attacked the Mareth Line. Montgomery's plan for Mareth called for Leese's XXX Corps to thrust directly at the Line, while a strong force, designated the New Zealand Corps and commanded by Freyberg, made its way round the Matmata Hills and emerged in the enemy's rear at El Hamma, west of Gabes. The final corps, X Corps, would remain in reserve until the battle developed. Before this attack went in there would be some preliminary attacks – code-named WALK and CANTER – by XXX Corps, timed to coincide with the opening of WOP and to clear the way across the Wadi Zeuss.

Operation WALK, mounted by the 201st Guards Brigade at the commanding 'Horseshoe' feature on the Wadi Zeuss, was an expensive disaster. The Horseshoe feature, just south of the Medenine-to-Mareth road, was an obvious target, and the Germans had established a strong defensive position there – well dug in, surrounded by mines and wire, and garrisoned by two panzergrenadier battalions of the 90th Light Division. The strength of this position was not known to British intelligence, so only two battalions, the 6th Grenadiers and the 3rd Coldstream, were sent in on the night of 16/17 March – and were promptly decimated. British losses ran to over 40 per cent of the troops committed – the 6th Grenadiers lost all but three of the battalion's officers – and the Germans held their ground. Some days after the battle, over 700 anti-personnel mines had to be lifted to retrieve the bodies of 69 Grenadier Guardsmen.

The CANTER attack by the 69th Infantry Brigade of 50th (Northumbrian) Division was more successful and less costly, the advance breaching the Wadi Zeuss position and forcing the defenders back to the Wadi Zigzaou, a shallow valley which formed part of the main Mareth Line defences. This valley was found to be full of water, and the far side was backed by a deep anti-tank ditch and minefields. The sappers built a tank track across the Wadi Zeuss, but this was promptly washed away by more heavy rain and this attack too came to a halt.

Two days later, on 19 March, Freyberg started his New Zealand Corps on the march round the Matmata Hills. This 'Corps' contained the full 2nd New Zealand Division, two brigades and supporting arms, plus the armoured cars of the King's Dragoon Guards, the 8th Armoured Brigade and the 111th Field Regiment, RA – a force amounting to 25,000 men, 151 tanks, 112 field guns (25-pounders) and 172 anti-tank guns (mostly 6-pounders).

It had been hoped that this flanking move would not be noticed, with all enemy eyes fixed on the Mareth Line, but Rommel was always anxious to know where the New Zealanders were, and Luftwaffe patrols soon picked up Freyberg's advancing columns. Even so, the New Zealand advance continued rapidly, and by 20 March Freyburg was approaching the northern end of the Matmata Hills and preparing to thrust on El Hamma, only 10 miles south of the Gabes

Gap. With Freyberg poised to strike, the time had come for XXX Corps to put in its assault on the main Mareth Line.

The assault across the Wadi Zigzaou would be made by the 50th Division. Its attack on 20 March did not go well: the valley was still full of water over deep mud, and impassable to tanks. The infantry got across and after the sappers built a causeway of brushwood fascines, four tanks got over in support – but then one tank broke though the causeway and blocked it completely. Had there been German forces opposing the attack at this point the British infantry would have been in serious trouble but this part of the Mareth Line was held by Italian troops, who proved very willing to surrender. In these first attacks, Lieutenant-Colonel D. A. Sergrim of the 7th Green Howards won the Victoria Cross.

A narrow bridgehead was established beyond the wadi and more infantry and tanks were ferried across, but it would have been better, bearing in mind previous experience and the inevitability of German counter-attacks, to send over more anti-tank guns. By dawn on 21 March the attack at Mareth had stalled and the Germans were bringing up more troops – a battalion of the 200th Panzergrenadier Regiment, a troop of anti-tank guns, and 15th Panzer's artillery – to reinforce the Afrika Korps.

Montgomery then sent a signal to Alexander, reporting the current situation and advising the Army Group commander that 'I am preparing a dog fight in the Mareth area which may last several days.' He requested that Patton's attack be pushed towards Maknassy, to bring pressure on the German rear and prevent a further build-up of resistance at Mareth. Freyberg's New Zealand Corps was now some 15 miles south-west of El Hamma, and a critical moment was clearly approaching.

Patton was very willing to help but his attack had stalled in the Eastern Dorsal and General Messe was sending in more troops to help 15th Panzer stem Leese at Mareth while 21st Panzer and the 164th Division blocked Freyberg at the Tebaga Gap. Meanwhile, inside Tunisia, von Arnim sent 10th Panzer to check Patton at El Guettar and Maknassy. The Germans were reacting with their customary speed and skill, and the Mareth attack would indeed become 'a dog fight'. By dawn on 22 March the Germans had blocked Freyberg at Tebaga and 15th Panzer had managed to eliminate the XXX Corps bridgehead over the

Wadi Zigzaou, where the 50th RTR was virtually wiped out fighting off the Panzer Mark IVs and some of the new and powerful Tiger tanks, equipped with the 88-mm gun.

Leese ordered his men to dig in and hang on along the Wadi Zigzaou while Montgomery switched the weight of his attack to Freyberg's corps, sending the 1st Armoured Division to their immediate assistance while the 4th Indian Division cut across the hills for Tachine and Toujane, taking another road towards Gabes. Neither the difficulties confronting 50th Division nor the move by 4th Indian Division were communicated to Freyburg, who formed the understandable if mistaken impression that his New Zealanders were being asked to tackle the Mareth Line on their own.

Nor was Freyberg best pleased when Montgomery told him that, when 1st Armoured arrived at his position, the command of the flanking thrust would pass to General Horrocks. 'For maintenance and other reasons essential to have Corps HQ on your flank,' said Montgomery, 'and am sending Horrocks to take charge. Am sure you will understand. You and he will work well together and should achieve decisive results.'

This note was extremely optimistic. Freyberg was both older and senior to Horrocks and a very able general. He was also quite determined that 'No newcomer should intrude on the handling of the New Zealand Division'. Montgomery's bland message therefore cut no ice at Freyberg's HQ, where an embarrassed Horrocks met a hostile reception. Horrocks was unable to take total charge: the Official History refers to their joint set up as a 'dyarchy', and it says much for the common sense of both generals that this unfortunate arrangement worked at all.

This move up by the 1st Armoured and 4th Indian Divisions would take some time – three days was the best estimate, not helped by another of those great traffic tangles, this time at Medenine – so Montgomery again asked Alexander to send Patton forward towards Gabes, while the Desert Air Force flew constant sorties against German and Italian units in the Matmata Hills and along the Mareth Line.

Alexander, with a better knowledge of what Patton's men were up against – namely 10th Panzer – declined to do as Montgomery requested. Instead he asked Patton (Allied generals were always reluctant to give *orders* to another ally's generals) to 'demonstrate' towards the Axis supply dumps on the coast, posing a threat the Germans would not welcome. Unfortunately for Patton, the German response to his threat was a strong attack by 10th Panzer on the US 1st Infantry Division at El Guettar on the Gafsa–Gabes road. This attack was initially successful, but then 10th Panzer ran into minefields, lost 38 tanks, and was obliged to pull back. Thus encouraged, Alexander detached two more US divisions to Patton's II Corps and called for an all-out attack towards Gabes on 28 March – an attack timed to coincide with that of Horrocks's X Corps attack through Tebaga.

This method of attack was concocted between Horrocks, Freyberg and the Desert Air Force commander, Air Marshal Sir Harry Broadhurst, who suggested that the Air Force could blast a way down the Tebaga defile for the tanks. This offer was accepted, and the attack was laid on for 26 March and led by the New Zealanders, whose infantry would punch a hole in the enemy line through which the British armour would exploit. Freyberg was still unconvinced about the armour's resolve and worried about what would happen if the 1st Armoured tanks did not arrive on time. He therefore asked Horrocks for some assurance: 'If we punch a hole in the enemy line, will the tanks really go through?' Horrocks replied that they would – 'And I am going with them.' This reply did much to restore good relations between the generals.

Their combined attack went exactly as planned. The RAF bombers pounded the Tebaga defile, dropping 400 tons of bombs, and the tanks of the 8th Armoured Brigade went forward to support the New Zealanders, who were well inside the enemy lines, lined up waiting to advance along the line of an old Roman wall. The 1st Armoured Division, led by the 2nd Armoured Brigade, duly went forward, Brigadier Fisher declaring, 'Speed up, straight through, no halting', and the British tanks and New Zealand infantry advanced together. This offensive rolled over all opposition until dawn on 27 March, when a number of 88-mms drawn up across the far end of the defile forced a halt. Messe had time to withdraw his forces though the Gap, but by 28 March the New Zealand Corps and X Corps occupied a front from El Hamma to Gabes, and by the evening of 29 March the Battle of Mareth was over. Montgomery was already sending his troops on to the next obstacle north of Gabes, the Gabes Gap and the Wadi Akarit.

Patton was meanwhile pushing his forces forward at El Guettar, which he attacked on the night of 28/29 March. This attack was not successful, and Messe's army – which might have been trapped between Horrocks's and Patton's forces – was able to get away to the Wadi Akarit position. Both generals tried to hustle Messe out of this position, but Messe was a sound general and would not be moved. Horrocks told Montgomery that a frontal assault on the position might dislodge the enemy but would be costly, and, since he was anxious to conserve his armour for the coming advance on Tunis, Montgomery ordered Leese to move on Wadi Akarit with XXX Corps, attacking on 6 April.

On 30 March Patton tried again with another thrust down the Gafsa–Gabes road. This proved no more successful than the previous attacks, but had one advantage for Eighth Army in keeping two panzer divisions – 10th Panzer and 21st Panzer – away from the Wadi Akarit position. Even so, Patton was disappointed with the lack of progress of his corps and sacked Major-General Orlando Ward, commander of the 1st (US) Armored Division. Alexander told Patton not to attempt any more of these costly offensives but to concentrate on holding the Axis forces on his front and writing them down with a series of limited attacks. Limited they may have been, but they proved very costly to the American infantry in the five days before Eighth Army attacked at Wadi Akarit.

The defences on this section of front depended not so much on the wadi itself as on a range of hills on its western edge – steep slopes rising to the 1,000 feet of the Ras Zouai. This hill feature offered wide observation over the coastal plain and buttressed the inward end of the enemy line, and from there a series of deep minefields, covered by artillery, led across the 15-mile gap to the coast. All of this made the Wadi Akarit a difficult position to attack.

Leese decided to use Major-General Francis Tuker's 4th Indian Division to attack the Ras Zouai position; Tuker's troops included Indian and Gurkha soldiers who were well acquainted with mountain warfare on the North-West Frontier of India – men happy to work at night, ready to use the bayonet and the kukri. This proved a wise decision: Tuker's men went into the hills on the night of 5/6 April and had cleared the position entirely by daylight.

This success was followed by an all-out attack across the plain by infantry of the 51st (Highland) and the 50th (Northumbrian) Divisions, supported by plenty of artillery and accompanied by the 8th Armoured Brigade. This attack was successful, but the fighting was costly. Here Private E. Anderson of the 5th Battalion East Yorkshire Regiment won a posthumous VC: Anderson was a stretcher-bearer, and had carried three men to safety before being killed while bringing in a fourth. The Yorkshiremen fought on, in spite of heavy casualties and the loss of their commanding officer, and by mid-morning the Italians of the Spezia and Trieste Divisions, holding the Wadi Akarit position, were surrendering in large numbers.

This collapse called for remedial action, and at midday on 6 April von Arnim released 80 tanks of 21st Panzer from El Guettar – where they were facing Patton – and ordered them to confront Leese at the Wadi Akarit. The battle there was going well for the British, but an attack by the New Zealanders and X Corps did not start until the early afternoon on 6 April and ran into 88-mm fire and the Tiger tanks of 15th Panzer as it emerged round the end of the Jebel Roumana.

Messe's forces battled on throughout the day, but knew that they could not hold out much longer against increasing Allied pressure. An immediate withdrawal was advisable, and by the morning of 7 April there were no German or Italian forces still in contact on the Eighth Army or the US II Corps fronts. Pushing forward though the minefields, the British and American forces, coming from the west and east, finally made contact that evening and took a good look at each other.

Most of the Eighth Army soldiers had never met an American before and were not over-impressed with First Army. Lieutenant Roy Farran of the 3rd Hussars in Eighth Army describes the British soldiers of First Army as follows: 'The First Army painted their trucks a dark green, dressed a little more smartly and filled the gutters with drunken soldiers . . . the men drank the local wine like beer and suffered in consequence'.[8] This mild hostility seems to have been mutual: the men of First Army regarded the men of Eighth Army as scruffy, untidy, barely disciplined and in sore need of a little close-order drill. In time they would know each other better.

The men of Eighth Army had not fully understood why the men of First Army – British and American – were making such heavy weather of the fighting in Tunisia. Once they had reached the Tunisian frontier in January, they realized that the terrain in Tunisia was very different from the open desert and began to appreciate – and share – the problems First Army had encountered in recent months, some of which were explained by Winston Churchill in a letter to Marshal Stalin in March 1943:

> Since we entered Tunisia, we have taken some forty thousand prisoners and killed or wounded some thirty-five thousand German or Italian troops. First Army have lost about twenty-three thousand men, Eighth Army about ten thousand. Two-thirds of these casualties have been British. The difficulties are compounded by the terrain, which is mountainous, with flat plains surrounded by rugged peaks, every one of which is a fortress which aids the enemy's defence and slows our attack.

Now there were two Allied armies in Tunisia and the end of the North African campaign could not be long delayed. In the weeks which followed their junction at the Wadi Akarit, First and Eighth Armies subjected the German and Italian forces to a series of alternate blows, First Army advancing north-east towards Bizerta, Eighth Army heading up the coast from Gabes, making for Sfax and Sousse and Enfidaville, the two armies aiming to link up south of Tunis and push the remaining Axis forces into the sea at Cape Bon.

The situation on 8 April was that the US II Corps was moving on Gafsa, IX Corps of First Army was attacking at the Fondouk Gap, and XXX Corps of Eighth Army was pressing towards Sfax on the coast of the Gulf of Tunis. Sfax fell on the morning of 10 April – and one result of this success proved unfortunate.

General Montgomery had bet General Eisenhower that he would get to Sfax by 15 April; if he succeeded, Eisenhower would give Monty an aircraft for his personal use. Having taken Sfax five days early, Monty now demanded his prize – a B-17 Flying Fortress and crew. This demand caused a certain amount of angst in Allied circles. Eisenhower had imagined this bet was a joke, but Monty insisted that a bet was a bet and that the aircraft be handed over. Eisenhower reluctantly obliged, but this glimpse of Montgomery's adamantine character was not forgotten. The incident did nothing to improve Monty's already fragile relationship with his American allies.

Jim Sewell of the RASC, serving with 7th Armoured, took part in this move to Sfax:

> During one advance we were completely lost and somehow got too far ahead and mixed up with our forward infantry. We took the chance that the verges were not mined, and pulled off and stopped by an Italian corpse, minus the head. While we were contemplating this grisly sight, some high-ranking officer stopped, gave us a telling-off, and told us to dig a grave. He then departed hurriedly, and so did we – in the other direction.
>
> Verges were dangerous. On another occasion we lost touch with the company just as darkness descended. In such a situation you drove forward cautiously, peering into the night for sight of the company number, carved out of an empty petrol tin with a candle inside, and Laurie spotted this just about midnight. When daylight came we were having breakfast and there was an almighty explosion by the roadside. Where we left the road there was a well, and a jeep with three men in it had gone to investigate and hit a very powerful mine. It was incredible that upwards of 150 heavily ladened vehicles had passed within inches of that mine in the dark.
>
> My diary for 13 April 1943 – a Tuesday – reads, 'Surprise move at 5 p.m., up to 10 miles from Sfax, a pleasant run, much like England, masses of red poppies in the fields.'
>
> The following day we moved up another 70 miles and pitched the bivvy in a field – the first bit of real grass I had seen since leaving England. It was a wonderful feeling and that night I heard the cuckoo, the nightingale and an owl.[9]

Montgomery now ordered the sappers to get the port of Sfax operating, and sent X Corps forward to capture Sousse and link up with First Army at Kairouan. Sousse fell on 12 April, and the forward elements of X Corps then moved up against the enemy's lines at Enfidaville, the south-eastern end of the Axis line that now ran north-west from Enfidaville, to Pont du Fahs, Medjez el Bab and Sedjenine.

On 12 April Alexander told Montgomery that the last push on Tunis would be made by First Army while Eighth Army pushed against the Enfidaville position, tasked to hold as many Axis units there as possible and give Anderson and the Americans a clear run. Montgomery was also ordered to send an armoured division and an armoured-car regiment to First Army to assist in its final assault. The 1st Armoured Division and the King's Dragoon Guards from X Corps were duly attached to Lieutenant-General J. T. Crocker's IX (British) Corps of First Army.

It is interesting that Montgomery, normally anxious for his full share of glory, made no objection to these orders, perhaps because they were clearly sensible. Writing in his memoirs of this campaign, he notes that the Enfidaville position was strong and 'a very difficult undertaking to break through', while the country was 'generally unsuitable for tanks except in the very narrow coastal strip and even there water channels and other obstacles existed. In the circumstances the decision that the main effort should now be transferred to the Plain of Tunis was a logical one.'[10]

Cracking the Enfidaville position required a major attack, and Montgomery chose the 2nd New Zealand and 4th Indian Divisions for the main assault, with 50th (Northumbrian) Division making a subsidiary attack on the coast and 7th Armoured Division covering the western flank. A great weight of artillery was mustered, and the attack began on the night of 19/20 April.

As anticipated, the Enfidaville position was strongly held and stoutly defended. Fortunately, the New Zealanders got forward and took their objectives: Enfidaville fell on 20 April, and heavy counter-attacks on the next two days were beaten off, Eighth Army forward units advancing 6 miles beyond Enfidaville by dusk on the 21st. With this much achieved, Montgomery called off his attack and elected to hold the ground already won.

This again was a sensible decision. Pressing on would prove costly to veteran divisions that had already been tasked for the invasion of Sicily. This invasion was now in the advanced stages of planning, and was an operation in which Patton and Montgomery were to have the leading roles. Indeed, Patton had now handed over the US II Corps to Bradley and departed to take up his new command: the Seventh (US) Army.

There was no room to deploy the Eighth Army's superiority in armour north of Enfidaville for the final push on Tunis, so on 30 April Alexander visited Montgomery and a further regrouping of forces took place. Still more Eighth Army units were transferred to First Army for this final phase, including the 7th Armoured Division, Tuker's 4th Indian Division, the 201st Guards Brigade and much of the medium artillery. With them went General Horrocks, sent to command IX Corps in First Army, Lieutenant-General Crocker having been wounded. This left Eighth Army with just four divisions – 2nd New Zealand Division, 50th (Northumbrian) Division, 51st (Highland) Division and a French division – and two tank brigades.

On 6 May 1943, First Army launched Operation STRIKE, a thrust on Tunis from Medjez el Bab. Bizerta and Tunis fell on the following day, with 7th Armoured Division – the veteran unit of Eighth Army, which had been in North Africa throughout this war – leading the Allied soldiers into Tunis. Although sporadic enemy resistance continued until 12 May, after three years of fighting the North African campaign was effectively over. On that day General von Arnim surrendered to Major-General Tuker and more than 250,000 German and Italian soldiers laid down those arms that they had not previously destroyed. They had fought until they could fight no more, until they had nothing left to fight with, and their opponents treated them with kindness and respect as they came into captivity.

Douglas Brunton was at the finish with the 1st Derbyshire Yeomanry:

> One morning we were out in the scrub observing when our troop officer came over and said he had heard over the wireless that our regiment had just entered Tunis. In two or three days the firing had died down – no more shelling or sniping, and a great feeling of relief. All this time we had been pushing on to Cape Bon, and at one crossroads we saw a column of the once proud troops in field grey, four deep and as far as the eye could see, marching towards a wire POW camp and guarded by 100 or so of our soldiers. I think most of them, like us, were happy it was over and glad they had survived.[11]

Douglas Brunton went on to Italy and we shall meet him again.

On the night of the surrender, General Alexander sent a signal to the Prime Minister, Winston Churchill: 'Sir, It is my duty to report that the Tunisian campaign is over. All enemy resistance has ceased. We are masters of the North African shore.'[12]

After three years of fighting – up and down the desert and over the mountains, sometimes defeated and sometimes dismayed, always brave if frequently baffled, but always willing to come on again with a certain dogged persistence – Eighth Army had finally achieved its reward. Two thousand miles and seven months on from Alamein, the Axis armies had finally been destroyed. The war in North Africa was over and Eighth Army now made ready to fight in the very different terrain of Sicily and Italy.

78 Div.

10

Sicily

July–August 1943

*Sicily should have been invaded immediately after the occupation of Tunis
. . . but a two-month delay occurred.*

Major-General J. F. C. Fuller, *The Second World War*

Even before the Axis surrender in North Africa, the question
arose, Where next? From the purely military point of view – and
putting aside the logistical difficulties – General Fuller is right.
Having crushed the Axis armies in North Africa, it seemed only
sensible to follow this victory with a lunge across the sea at Sicily.
But there were, unfortunately, some naval and military problems
inhibiting such rapid action. The Allied armies needed to rest
and reorganize, and not enough landing craft were available for
a major amphibious operation. The real problem, however, was
not men or ships but arguments over strategy. The very question
'Where next?' caused dissension among the Allies.

The nub of the issue was time – and the Normandy landings.
Was the time right to carry out Operation OVERLORD, the invasion
of France, with any hope of success? The final decision, taken at
the Casablanca Conference in January 1943, was that OVERLORD
could not be mounted until May 1944. That being so, what was
to be done in the meantime? Again, at Casablanca the decision

was made to press forward across the Mediterranean and drive Italy out of the war. This process would begin with the invasion of Sicily – Operation HUSKY.

This decision was not made without a great deal of argument. Some authorities – mainly American – favoured attacking Sardinia and Corsica as stepping stones to a landing in the South of France. Other pundits – mainly British – were for a major landing in Greece or the Balkans. These views were strongly held, but it appears likely that the postponement of OVERLORD made the attack on Italy inevitable. Having taken Tunis, Sicily was the next obvious objective – a short sail across the Mediterranean. The Axis had retreated in that direction on evacuating Africa, and it was logical to pursue the defeated enemy there – and defeat him again.

There were also some political considerations. It was clear from the comments of tens of thousands of Italian prisoners of war that the Italian population had no real interest in this conflict. Another good shove by the Allied armies might topple Mussolini from power, encourage defections elsewhere, and bring about a government in Rome that would be anxious to abandon the Pact of Steel and come to terms with the Allies. This would deprive Hitler of his closest ally and force the German armies either to abandon the Italian peninsula or to commit more forces to its retention.

That, of course, was the optimistic scenario. There was another one, in which the Italian soldiers, though less than forceful in the desert and Tunisia, might fight tenaciously in the defence of their homeland and, supported by the Germans, give the Allies a bloody nose on the Italian mainland. A glance at the map will – or certainly should – also have revealed to the Allied commanders that any advance up Italy, from Calabria to the Alps, would involve a continuous offensive campaign in a country designed by nature for defence. Churchill's assertion that Italy represented the 'soft underbelly of Europe' was wildly out of touch with the topographical facts.

Added to this was the fact, much stressed by the Americans, that a campaign in Italy, while undoubtedly useful in dispersing and engaging enemy forces that might otherwise be deployed in France, would achieve precisely the same effect of dispersing and engaging the Allied forces. The question of who was containing whom in Italy was debatable. It is at least arguable that it might have been better to husband all available forces in Britain for a massive cross-Channel attack in early 1944. Unfortunately, there was a snag with that argument too: if there was to be no land offensive in the West for another year, where would the Western Allies prosecute the war until then – and how would Stalin react if they stood idle for a full year?

Then there were difficulties over the long-term strategy and post-war aims of the two Western Allies, some of which were mentioned in the previous chapter. The Americans were anxious to end the war quickly and bring the boys back home, leaving European affairs in the hand of re-established democratic governments and the United Nations. The fact that US troops and aircraft are still deployed in western Europe at the start of the twenty-first century shows how little foresight lay behind that understandable anxiety.

At this time the three US Joint Chiefs on the Combined Chiefs of Staff Committee – General George C. Marshall of the US Army, General 'Hap' Arnold of the US Army Air Force and Admiral Ernest King of the US Navy – were very wary of Churchill's pre-occupation with affairs in the Balkans and did not share his growing suspicion about Soviet Russia's long-term aims in Eastern Europe. The Americans tended to see Churchill's doubts over Russian integrity as an example of his entrenched imperialism, and a threat to Allied unity. As the Allied armies advanced painfully up the Italian mainland and the Russians overran the Balkans in 1944 and moved towards Austria in 1945, Churchill's suspicions increased, but even in early 1943 the Americans were resistant to further operations in the Mediterranean theatre.

So, when the decision to invade Sicily was taken at Casablanca, General Marshall went on the record as saying that 'He was most anxious not to be committed to interminable operations in the Mediterranean' and wished northern France to be the scene of the main operations against Germany.[1] Marshall also told the Combined Chiefs of Staff in Washington that 'The Mediterranean is a vacuum into which America's great military might could be drawn off until there is nothing left with which to deal the decisive blow on the Continent' – a comment that jars somewhat with his previous eagerness to attack the Germans in France in 1943 or even the summer of 1942, when America's military might was only starting to gather.

The proposed Italian campaign was also a step back from the 'Germany First' principle with which America entered the war. This principle was based on the sound strategic doctrine that, when faced with an array of enemies, the strongest should be defeated first. The notion that defeating lesser powers – 'knocking away the props' – will hasten victory is generally unfounded: the major power supports the lesser ones, not the other way round. If the Allies in Europe did not proceed in accordance with that principle by attacking Germany directly and without delay, there were those in the United States – most notably Admiral King, the US Navy member on the Combined Chiefs of Staff Committee, and a committed Anglophobe – who urged that US power should be promptly diverted to the campaign against Japan in the Pacific.

Speaking in the House of Commons in the summer of 1943, Churchill remarked that 'We have got to fight them [the Germans] somewhere unless we are just to sit back and watch the Russians', but this – while undoubtedly true – cut little ice with the Americans if 'somewhere' meant the Balkans. However, the Anglo-American armies clearly had to do something in 1943 if only to support the Red Armies of Marshal Stalin, the only land forces engaging the Germans anywhere in the late spring and early summer of that year. Hence the decision to invade Sicily and open a 'second front' in Italy. The Italian campaign might be an Allied operation, but it remained very much Churchill's baby. His reputation would suffer if it went awry.

There is another point, emerging at this time, which would have a greater effect later. Churchill was very anxious to bring Turkey into the war. Churchill's papers until well into 1944 are full of comments on the need to enlist Turkey on the Allied side, and he persisted in this view in spite of all opposition and plenty of evidence that Turkey had no intention *whatsoever* of entering the war on anyone's side. Turkey had learned one lesson between 1914 and 1918: that wars were best avoided. In continuing to press the issues of Turkey, the eastern Mediterranean and the southern Balkans, Churchill used up a lot of his political capital in a fruitless cause.

The decision to invade Italy having been taken, the operation had to be planned. This proved difficult, because the commanders who would be directly concerned with the landing –

Eisenhower, Alexander, Patton and Montgomery – were then engaged in Tunisia and had little time to spare for what happened after that. The initial invasion plan was therefore prepared by the staff in Room 141 at the Allied HQ in Algiers, where matters did not run smoothly.

The American representative on this Allied Staff Committee – code-named Force 141 – Major-General Clarence Huebner, did not get on with General Alexander. The sulphurous atmosphere at Allied Forces HQ (AFHQ) improved only when Huebner was sent to command the US 1st Infantry Division and was replaced by Brigadier-General Limnitzer. After that the planning proceeded apace, but the details only came to the attention of the field commanders in April. By that time Eisenhower was having doubts about the Sicily operation, warning the politicians and the Combined Chiefs that the presence of two German divisions on the island made the prospects of success much less likely – and adding that Alexander and Montgomery shared this view, which was not exactly the case. This argument did not play well with Churchill. 'If the presence of two German divisions is held to be decisive against any operations of an offensive or amphibious character open to the million men now in French North Africa, it is difficult to see how the war can be carried on,' the Prime Minister commented tartly. 'Months of preparation, sea and air power in abundance, and yet two German divisions are sufficient to knock it all on the head. I do not think we can rest content with such doctrines. What Stalin will think of this, when he has 185 German divisions on his front, I cannot imagine,' he added later.[2]

General Montgomery's opposition was to the strategic plan, not the presence of two German divisions – Montgomery states that he first saw the plan on 23 April, and promptly declared that, in making the plan, 'the system of absentee landlords led to all the obvious disadvantages'.[3]

Montgomery's objections were based on two factors. First, the two assault armies – the American Seventh under Patton and Montgomery's Eighth – were to land too far apart: the Americans in the north-west, the British in the south-east. The whole island would lie between them. The armies would not be able to support each other in case of need, and the plan would provide the enemy with the chance to split the Allied forces, attack their inward flanks, and destroy them in detail.

Second, the Force 141 planners had made various assumptions which Monty felt were both unfounded and dangerous: that there would only be Italian forces in Sicily, that these would put up only a token resistance – and that few, if any, German forces would be deployed to support them. Montgomery felt that the Italians would fight better when their homes were threatened, and that the Germans would certainly support them – and the presence of those two German divisions seemed to substantiate this view.

While Montgomery understood the object of dispersing the landings – in order to seize the widely dispersed Sicilian airfields – he felt that this requirement was a secondary consideration when compared with the needs of the assault forces. This latter view, forcefully, even tactlessly, expressed, may have marked the start of the long decline in good relations between Montgomery and Air Chief Marshal Sir Arthur Tedder, who was in command of air operations for Sicily and – as in Normandy a year later – regarded the rapid capture of local airfields as essential for the provision of air cover.

Montgomery proved adamant on both these points, and at an Allied conference in Algiers on 3 May his views prevailed with Eisenhower – though the British Official History comments that 'General Montgomery continued to behave in his least-tactful manner' by suggesting to Eisenhower that Eighth Army – i.e. Montgomery – 'should command and control the entire operation with the US II Corps coming directly under Eighth Army command'.[4] Alan Brooke, the CIGS, was right to tell Alexander that Monty had to be 'gripped' – or put in his place. Montgomery's suggestion was not adopted, but Monty was not 'gripped' either.

The HUSKY plan was revised to take heed of likely Italian and German resistance, and the landing beaches were brought closer together. Both Allied assault forces would land in the south of the island, between the town of Licata, in the centre of the southern coast, and the Gulf of Noto, just north of the Pachino peninsula, the south-eastern tip of the island. XXX Corps and XIII Corps of Eighth Army would go ashore astride the Pachino peninsula, and the US II Corps of Patton's Seventh Army – the US 1st, 3rd and 45th Divisions, with the 2nd (US) Armored Division in floating reserve – would land on their left, along the Gulf of Gela.

Once ashore, Eighth Army would thrust north along the east coast for the ferry ports of Catania and Messina, while Seventh Army protected its western flank. Air support would be provided from Malta, 55 miles to the south, from which even short-range Spitfire fighters could cover the landing beaches and the southern parts of Sicily. What was not clarified at this time was how the campaign would be conducted after the troops were established ashore, other than the flank-protection task of Seventh Army mentioned above.

At this point a close study of the map on page xviii will be helpful. Sicily is a large, triangular island, covering some 10,000 square miles – about as big as Wales or the state of Vermont. Understanding the topography is vital to any appreciation of the campaign and any understanding of the subsequent disputes about how that campaign was conducted. Three points should be noticed. First, Sicily is extremely mountainous – especially in the north, where the Madonie, Nebrodi and Peloritani mountain ranges lie inland from the coast. The second main feature is the Catania plain – flat, but seamed with rivers and dry valleys. Third, the main physical feature of the island is Mount Etna, an active volcano 10,000 feet high and 20 miles in diameter at the base.

Etna lies close to the east coast, just to the north of the Catania plain, and any army attempting to drive from Syracuse to Messina must either (i) force a way through the narrow gap between Etna and the sea or (ii) find a way across the Catania plain and around Etna to the west. There was no easy way to Messina.

Only one road, Route 114, runs through the narrow gap between Etna and the east coast, and there was no road close to Etna on the landward side. A major assault west of Etna must either go inland as far as Leonforte to find a good route or force a passage up the roadless Simeto valley to the east–west Route 120. Getting up to Messina from Syracuse was sure to be a difficult task, and Alexander's plan laid this task on Eighth Army.

The other main feature of Sicily in 1943 was a shortage of roads. The main roads – with the exception of Route 124, which runs from Syracuse to Leonforte – run along the coasts. The coastal roads link the main towns – Palermo, Catania, Syracuse and Messina – the roads in the north and north-east running along a narrow plateau between the mountains and the sea. The inland roads were largely unmetalled tracks, suited for donkey and cart traffic but less than ideal for tanks and supply trucks. They linked a scattered collection of highly defensible hill towns and mountain villages, many of them offering perfect artillery observation over the surrounding countryside. To these physical features can be added the summer sun and an abundance of malarial mosquitoes whose existence and industry had not been anticipated by the Allied command.

Malaria was a notable feature of the Catania plain and the British troops in this area were soon ordered to take a mepacrine tablet every day and to have their sleeves down and long trousers on after dusk. Mosquito-repellent cream was also issued, but, according to the troops, attracted mosquitoes in squadrons. The sum total of all this is that Sicily would be a hard nut to crack, especially if well defended.

The Axis forces deployed to defend Sicily consisted of the Italian Sixth Army under General Alfredo Guzzoni, who had his headquarters at Enna, in the centre of the island. Sixth Army had two corps (four field divisions) – one in the north-west corner of the island and the other positioned to oppose any landing on the Pachino peninsula in the south-east. To these field divisions could be added four or five Italian coastal divisions, occupying defensive positions and concrete shore battery fortifications. As already related, two German divisions had also arrived, and these were under the command of a first-class German officer, Lieutenant-General Fridolin von Senger und Etterlin. Like Pastor Bach, the heroic defender of the Halfaya Pass, von Senger und Etterlin was a fighting cleric who would later confront the Allies at Cassino. By the time the Allies landed there would be 200,000 Italian soldiers on the island, 32,000 German troops, and around 30,000 Luftwaffe ground and air crews. (With its task of bombing Malta and the Allied convoys, Sicily had long been a major base for the Luftwaffe.)

Ultra revealed that the two German divisions – 15th Panzer, with 16,000 men, and the Hermann Goering Division, with 15,500 – had been divided into brigade-sized battle groups (*Kampfgruppen*). With the 29th Panzergrenadier Division (which was then in transit) and two regiments of the 1st Parachute Division, these units would comprise XIV Panzer Corps. These divisions, Italian or German, could be swiftly reinforced by air or by tanks and troops ferried across the 3-mile-wide strait between Messina and the Italian mainland at Reggio Calabria. Although most of the available ferries were destroyed by Allied air attacks in the weeks before the landing, German troops were soon arriving – one unit, the doughty 1st Parachute Division, landing by parachute.

Eighth Army's assault astride the Pachino peninsula would begin with an airborne landing. Just before midnight, at 2359 hours on 9 July, the 1st Air Landing Brigade of the British 1st Airborne Division would come in, its gliders towed by the USAAF 51st Troop Carrier Wing, which would supply most of the Waco gliders and C-47 (Dakota) parachute aircraft or glider tugs. The airborne soldiers were tasked to capture and hold the Ponte Grande bridge, which spanned the Anapo river on the road from the landing beaches to Syracuse. This would be followed with a landing by troops of No. 3 Commando, tasked to take the coastal battery at Cape Murro di Porco, south of Syracuse. Two divisions of XIII Corps – the 5th and 50th – would then come ashore north of Cape Passero: the 5th to capture Cassabile, link up with the airborne troops and advance on Syracuse, the 50th to take Avola on Route 114/115 between Syracuse and Ragusa and protect this XIII Corps bridgehead from any counter-attack from the south or west. That done, the 5th Division was to secure bridgeheads over the Simeto river and push north to take Catania, while XXX Corps took over the XIII Corps bridgehead.

Landing further south, astride the tip of the Pachino peninsula, XXX Corps would put ashore the veteran 51st (Highland) Division and the newly arrived 1st Canadian Division. This latter unit would be making its debut on European soil, where the Canadians would shortly establish a fine and enduring reputation. The 51st (Highland) Division was to capture the town of Pachino near the tip of the peninsula. The Canadians would protect the left of the corps beachhead, but had the prime task of taking the Pachino airfield and landing engineers to bring that airfield quickly into commission as a fighter base. That done, 51st (Highland) would move to Avola to relieve the 50th Division for the advance on Catania, while the Canadians were to advance towards Ragusa and make contact with the US 45th Division of the US II Corps. What would happen after that depended on the outcome of this initial phase.

While the British and Canadians were landing around the Pachino peninsula, the Americans would land along the Gulf of Gela to the west. Here too the landing would be preceded by an airborne landing – by the 505th Parachute Infantry Regiment (505th PIR) of the 82nd Airborne Division. The landing force would consist of II Corps Headquarters, the 1st, 3rd and 45th Infantry Divisions, the 2nd Armored Division, and a proportion of the 9th Infantry Division, currently in army group reserve. Seventh Army also contained three US ranger units, the US equivalent of the British commandos, led by Lieutenant-Colonel William O. Darby, and a French unit of Moroccan *goums*, lightly equipped troops supplied with a mule train and skilled in mountain warfare.

II Corps would be commanded by Major-General Omar Bradley, the US Seventh Army by Lieutenant-General George Patton Jr. A man to note was Major-General Lucian K. Truscott, commanding the 3rd Infantry Division – an officer who was to become one of the finest and most respected Allied commanders in the Italian campaign. All these US divisions, with the exception of the 82nd Airborne, had served in Tunisia.

The prime strategic task of the US Seventh Army was to protect the left flank of Eighth Army. For particular tasks in the assault phase, the 45th Division was to capture the airfields at Comiso and Biscari and link up with the 1st Canadian Division. The US 1st Division was to land at Gela and take the airfields there and at Ponte Olivo, while the 3rd Division was to take the port and airfield of Licata and establish a local bridgehead. The 505th PIR Combat Team – the equivalent of a British brigade group – would land west of Gela to block approaches to the landing area from the east and west.

This plan is typical of those made for any amphibious and airborne operation, with detailed planning for the landing phase and for the first probes inland. The object is not just to get ashore but to stay ashore in the face of enemy reaction, and that requires a detailed plan for a set-piece battle. There has also to be an outline strategic plan – what the *overall aim* is and how it might be achieved, all being well. Knowledge of this strategy would be particularly useful to the logistical units, but any details of how this strategy might be implemented on the ground would have to wait until the landings had proved successful – and some landings might be more or less successful than others. The steps taken would therefore depend on the situation at the time – when the beachheads were secure and had formed a bridgehead.

Assembling the landing forces for HUSKY was one of the first problems for Montgomery, as some changes were taking place in Eighth Army. Two strong and experienced formations, the 7th Armoured and 2nd New Zealand Divisions, were not tasked for Sicily. Instead the 1st Canadian Division, commanded by Major-General Guy Simonds, would join Montgomery's force – landing directly in Sicily from the troopships bringing it to the Mediterranean – and two British units, the 50th and 5th Divisions, would complete the reinforcement. Other units were also dispersed: the 51st (Highland) and 78th Divisions, the latter formerly with First Army, were in Tunis, while the 1st Airborne Division was further inland in Tunisia, at Kairouan.

The 5th and 50th Divisions, plus the 231st Infantry Brigade – the 'Malta Brigade', commanded by Brigadier Robert Urquhart, who would command the 1st Airborne Division at Arnhem in 1944 – were in Egypt. The various HQs were also well dispersed: X Corps HQ was in Tripoli, XIII Corps HQ in Cairo, XXX Corps HQ and Task Force HQ in Tunis, while Allied Forces HQ was in Algiers. Communication was not always easy, and meeting for detailed discussions was almost impossible.

Drawing up these plans and mustering the troops and landing craft, which included a large number of the new American DUKWs (amphibious lorries – and always called 'Ducks') took some time but D-Day was set for 10 July 1943. By 3 July the Eighth Army staff were in Malta. The invasion fleet came together in the next few days and moved into Sicilian waters soon after dark on 9 July. A gale then sprang up, spreading sea-sickness among the soldiers and raising doubts about the effect of the high winds on the airborne landings, but it was too late to stop and wait for better weather. Towards midnight the transport ships began to close on the landing beaches and ears were cocked for the arrival of the airborne soldiers.

The invasion fleet for HUSKY was the largest yet mustered by the Allies, amounting to some 3,000 ships and major landing craft. The covering force for Eighth Army included Force 'H' – the battleships *Nelson*, *Rodney*, *Warspite* and *Valiant* – and a cruiser force, Force 'K', comprising HMSs *Newfoundland*, *Orion*,

Mauritius and *Uganda*, plus six destroyers. Two other naval forces – Force 'Z', comprising the battleships *Howe* and *King George V*, and Force 'Q', another cruiser force, containing HMSs *Aurora*, *Penelope*, *Cleopatra*, *Euryalus*, *Sirius* and *Dido* – were also on hand.

From the US Navy, to support the landings of Patton's force, came the cruisers *Savannah*, *Boise*, *Philadelphia*, *Brooklyn* and *Birmingham* and 36 destroyers, all deployed to support the three US landing beaches. Command in the landing phase would be exercised from various headquarters ships: HMSs *Largs*, *Bulolo*, *Hilary* and *Antwerp* for Eighth Army, and USSs *Ancon*, *Biscayne* and *Samuel Chase* for the US forces. Also present would be 2 British aircraft carriers, 23 Royal Navy submarines, 71 British destroyers and 48 American destroyers, plus a vast number of other craft from both navies and the two merchant navies.

The total came to 1,614 warships and transports from the UK and 945 ships from the USA, plus 31 vessels from various other Allied nations, and this grand total of 2,590 ships would rise as the days passed. These ships and their accompanying transports would put ashore 181,000 Allied soldiers – 66,000 American and 115,000 British and Canadian – supported by naval and ground-based aircraft from two Allied air forces and the British Fleet Air Arm. Operation HUSKY was *big*.[5]

At dusk on 9 July gliders of the 1st Air Landing Brigade of 1st Airborne Division took of from their airfields in Tunisia. This force flew in 144 Waco and Horsa gliders towed to Sicily by 109 US C-47s and 35 RAF Albemarles. Two hours later 222 C-47s took off, carrying the 505th PIR Combat Team and the 3rd Battalion 504th PIR. These airborne soldiers, British and American, were to make the first major assault on Axis-held Europe – and were flying directly into a disaster.

The British 1st Air Landing Brigade lost seven gliders when their tugs failed to clear the North African coast. The rest headed for Malta and made a good landfall, turning towards Sicily before being buffeted by strong winds that loosened the formations. Nevertheless, more than 90 per cent of the tugs and gliders made the airborne rendezvous off the Pachino peninsula and turned east for the glider release point. Four more aircraft had already turned back over the sea, and two aircraft now released their gliders, which landed in the sea off the peninsula. This was before any of the tugs had reached the glider release point south of Syracuse. By the time that point was reached, says the US Official History, 'chaos had set in'.[6]

Though estimates vary, it appears that 115 of the 144 British gliders were released in the right spot. Of those released, only 54 landed in Sicily – and of those only 12 landed in the right area. The others landed in the sea, and many of the heavily laden airborne soldiers of the 1st Air Landing Brigade were drowned. Their commander, Brigadier 'Pip' Hicks, swam ashore from his ditched glider with members of his staff. Fewer than 100 of his soldiers were in position to attack the Ponte Grande bridge at H-Hour, but they attacked anyway – 100 soldiers instead of a full brigade.[7]

The US paratroopers, arriving two hours later, were no more fortunate. Their C-47 pilots seem to have lost control of events: 'losing direction, missing check-points, the pilots approached Sicily from all points of the compass'.[8] As a result the 3,400 men who jumped were scattered all over the southern end of the island. No fewer than 33 sticks (a stick is an aircraft-load of airborne soldiers) landed in the Eighth Army area and 53 sticks in the landing area of the US 1st Infantry Division, miles east of the destined drop zone. Nearly all were well scattered: only the 2nd Battalion 505th PIR landed together – 25 miles from its proper drop zone.[9] These airborne landings served to alert the Axis commanders to the imminence of the Allied seaborne invasion, which began at 0245 hours on the morning of 10 July.

The beach landings of the Eighth Army divisions around the Pachino peninsula were successful. The landings achieved surprise, and the Italian coastal defenders put up very little resistance apart from some artillery fire that was quickly quelled by naval gunfire or the overrunning of the batteries by the assault troops. By 0800 hours the 5th Division had entered Cassabile, had consolidated its beachhead, and was pushing north to establish contact with the 8 officers and 65 men of the 1st Air Landing Brigade, mostly from the South Staffordshire and Border Regiments, who were hanging on at Ponte Grande, 10 miles to the north.

This force was under attack all morning by Italian troops of the 385th Coastal Battalion and elements of the Hermann Goering division sent out from Syracuse; by mid-afternoon all but 15 of these airborne soldiers were wounded or dead. At 1530 hours the position at Ponte Grande was overrun, only eight men escaping south to meet the 2nd Battalion the Royal Scots Fusiliers, the advance elements of the 5th Division, which came forward to retake the Ponte Grande bridge by early evening.

Following up this success quickly, the 5th Division marched past Syracuse and, having diverted troops into that city, rolled on astride the eastern coastal road, Route 114, towards Augusta. All was going well until early evening, when the leading elements ran into the German troops of Group Schmalz, one of the tank and infantry battle groups of 15th Panzer, at Priolo. Group Schmalz had been tasked to support the Italian Napoli Division in attacking any Allied landings on the east coast, but Colonel Wilhelm Schmalz had been unable to contact the Italians when news of the landings reached him. He had moved out alone, and his troops – well dug in and supported by anti-tank guns and Tiger tanks – brought the advance of 5th Division to a halt.

Further south, the landings of the Highlanders and Canadians of XXX Corps had gone well and the troops there were pushing inland against light opposition. The overall result on the first day was that Eighth Army had got ashore on a wide front, was making steady progress and was in no danger of eviction. Supplies were coming ashore slowly but steadily, over beaches still affected by the recent gale.

Eric Garner, a sapper sergeant in Eighth Army, recalls some of the problems.

Off 17th Brigade's Blue and Red beaches there was a sandbar, and it caused chaos in the initial landings. Our heavily loaded men, dumped into about 5 feet of water, had to wade to the beach some distance away. A gap was blown in this bar by means of stuffing a hosepipe with explosive and weighting it down with bricks. This did the trick, and some craft were able to get closer in. By 12 July we had constructed jetties on both beaches by means of taking stones from the vineyard walls behind the beach to form walls and bulldozing firm sand to form a jetty capable of allowing landing craft to put anyone ashore dry-shod. Meantime large numbers of vehicles had drowned in trying to get ashore, and our bulldozers were heavily engaged in towing them to dry land.

All the British beaches were under air attack during the first few days. My own unit had two killed and about ten wounded on the first day ashore. Also, one of our explosive dumps was hit and most units in the Beach Group had casualties during this period.[10]

Another sapper, Reg Wheatley, gives an account of an amphibious landing:

We sailed into the Mediterranean, and on the way to Sicily everything was checked – kit, rifles, wireless, stores – again and again. We were also broken into small groups and told how we would be called into the LCAs [landing craft, assault] when the time came. We would land in battle order, and each man had a specific task – my group of three had to take a motorbike ashore. Each man had his own apprehensions of what lay ahead, and the morning of 10 July had us anchored about 10 miles from the coast of Sicily. The 754th Army Field Engineer Company had now embarked on what was for most of us the first taste of action.

It was early morning and still dark when my group was called over the Tannoy to board an LCA. We had no problems climbing down the net into the small craft, despite the cumbersome motorbike. As we pulled away, the water was very choppy and – would you believe it? – I was seasick. I was feeling extremely uncomfortable as we sailed in, and those who were not feeling sick were standing up, giving a commentary on what they could see. The sounds of battle were everywhere, naval guns were roaring away, fires could be seen ashore, aircraft were falling from the sky, but I was oblivious to most of this through seasickness – had Adolf Hitler and the entire German Army been waiting on the beach it would not have bothered me.

Suddenly I felt the craft scraping sand. The ramp crashed down and I surged ashore with great relief, landing on Sicilian shores without even getting my feet wet, and within seconds my seasickness disappeared. We got the motorbike off the LCA and proceeded across the beach through a gap in the minefield to the assembly area. We had landed at a place called Cassabile.[11]

The Americans landing in the west had an even less easy time. Their landing craft had become disorganized on the run-in to the beaches, and the 45th Division landed an hour late; the US Official History says the 45th Division beaches presented 'a deplorable picture' throughout D-Day.[12] Surf on the beaches was a problem that would affect both the initial landings and the later supply operation but it was already clear that 'By nightfall on D-day, 10 July, the Seventh Army was firmly established in Sicily'[13] and the leading elements were pushing on against light opposition.

This lack of resistance in the US landing area was because the landings had taken the enemy by surprise and the Italians were not noted for a rapid response. Enemy aircraft were in action over the beaches by the dawn of D-Day, sinking the USS *Maddox*, a destroyer, but the first reactions of the Axis commanders in the centre of the island on 10 July was to muster their forces to stem the US advance north from Gela. This attempt to organize a resistance was disrupted by poor communications and stout action by scattered groups and companies of the 82nd Airborne Division and American rangers. Any Axis attacks were small-scale, unco-ordinated affairs, mainly by Italian forces in the beachhead area. An attempted dawn attack on the US beach-head by two *Kampfgruppen* of the Hermann Goering Division also petered out, 'the task forces [*kampfgruppen*] soon lost contact with each other . . . and 0900 hours came and went with both groups still struggling towards their assembly areas'.[14]

This enemy confusion did not last. By mid-afternoon Tiger tanks and infantry had scattered the 1st Battalion 180th Infantry Regiment near Biscari, north-east of Comiso, before being counter-attacked and repulsed by the 3rd Battalion of that regi-ment. However, as darkness fell on 10 July the Seventh Army had safely landed and only the problems caused by the failure of the parachute drop were causing any real concern.

On the Anglo-Canadian front the port of Syracuse had fallen virtually undamaged to the 5th Division and supplies were coming ashore there by dawn on 11 July. On that day Mont-gomery brought his Tactical HQ over from Malta and contact was made between the US and Canadian forces at Ragusa. According to his later account, Montgomery was 'confirmed in my view that the battle of Sicily would be primarily a matter of securing the main centres of road communication'.[15] Eighth Army was therefore pushing ahead from the Pachino beaches, the Canadians getting up to Ragusa, the 5th Division attempting to outflank resistance on Route 114 by pushing a brigade inland to Floridia and Solarino.

The main event on 11 July took place on the US front, where an attack by 60 tanks – Tigers and Panzer Mark IVs of the

Hermann Goering Division – was driven off, the Germans losing 43 tanks. This happy result was balanced by another airborne disaster. Early on 11 July, Patton ordered the 504th PIR Combat Team to be parachuted into the area held by the 1st Infantry Division. This force flew in after dark on the night of the 11th/12th – and was promptly greeted by heavy anti-aircraft fire from the Allied fleet anchored offshore.

The Allied shipping had been attacked by enemy aircraft at 2150 hours, when the USS *Boise* and her supporting destroyers were straddled by bombs. This attack ended just before the aircraft carrying the paratroopers arrived, and the naval gunners and the troops ashore, fearing a renewal of the bombing, opened up on them with every gun they had.

'Some paratroopers were killed in their planes before they had a chance to get out. Others were killed in their 'chutes while descending. A few were even shot on the ground.'[16] The US Official History's account of this tragedy goes on for pages, and makes sorry reading. Of the 144 aircraft that left Tunisia that night, 23 were shot down and 37 were badly damaged over the US beachhead; the 504th PIR suffered 229 casualties, none of them inflicted by the enemy. Indeed, so far the great majority of Allied casualties in Sicily were in the British and American airborne units – caused either by the carrier or tug aircraft failing to land the men successfully or by 'friendly fire'.

To the right of the Americans, the British XXX Corps had made some substantial gains and looked like driving a wedge between the Hermann Goering Division and the Axis forces at Catania. On the XIII Corps front, Group Schmaltz was falling back slowly before the British advance, and the 5th Division took the port of Augusta on 12 July – HMS *Exmoor* entered Augusta harbour at 1000 hours that day, but soon left again, chased by 'a considerable volume of fire from various unfriendly gents ashore'.[17] The port was in British hands by noon, but clearing out the snipers took another day and the British were then held up by German defensive positions along the Lentini river. It was becoming clear that Eighth Army's advance up the east was going to be contested every step of the way.

By this time, some dissension was becoming apparent among the Allied commanders. So far, both armies were making good progress with their respective tasks, but the American 1st and

3rd Divisions were getting well ahead in the centre and were anxious to thrust towards the north-west, where Patton had his eyes on the city of Palermo. If the British were going to have the glory – or at any rate the publicity – of taking Syracuse, Augusta, Catania and Messina, Patton wanted Palermo. So did many of his officers.

Major-General Geoffrey Keyes, the deputy commander of Seventh Army, spent 12 July with Truscott's 3rd US Infantry Division and phoned Patton for orders that evening, pointing out the lack of opposition to their front and the possibility of pushing on to Caltanisseta. Patton could not order such an advance, because the purpose of Seventh Army, as related, was to protect the flank of Eighth Army. Alexander had Ultra information that a powerful counter-attack was about to come in from the west of the island, and wanted to keep the 3rd Division on the left flank as a blocking force. This seems a misjudgement which might not have arisen had Alexander been on the spot. The Americans could have blocked any Axis thrust from the west equally well by advancing, as Truscott's 3rd Division were shortly to do, heading north-west towards Palermo at some speed and with considerable élan.

On the British XIII Corps front, matters were not going so well. The taking of Augusta on 12 July was to be the last British success for some weeks; Catania did not fall until 5 August, and those soon-to-be familiar allegations of 'slowness' and 'caution' that still dog the reputation of Montgomery and the British Army began to emanate from the Americans – and from the RAF. On 13 July Montgomery unwisely told Major Robert Henriques, the British liaison officer at Patton's HQ, that he hoped to be in Catania that night. The reason why it took another 23 days can be attributed to various factors. The difficulties of heat and terrain were common to all the armies in Sicily, but on the XIII Corps front the narrow axis of advance offered little space for deployment and few chances to outflank a determined enemy – the axis of advance was simply too narrow. To get forward, Montgomery elected to employ his airborne and commando soldiers, for the sea and sky were his 'open flanks'. This need to move around the flank drew Monty's attention to the matter of the Primasole Bridge.

Wars or campaigns often make particular demands on different arms of the service. The desert campaign of 1941–3 put the stress on the tank men and the infantry. The campaigns in Sicily and Italy were basically 'engineers' wars'. Axis sappers constantly strove to delay the Allied advance and create unbreakable defensive lines; Allied sappers were always well forward, clearing mines and building or rebuilding roads and bridges. Without the sappers the Allied armies could not advance with any speed – every narrow mountain road had been blasted into the valley, every verge and field was sown with mines, every bridge had been blown. In Sicily the bridges were to prove a particular hazard, their destruction being a reliable method of slowing the Allied advance.

The best way to ensure a rapid advance was to take the bridges by *coup de main*, before the enemy could retreat across and blow them up. That had been the task of the 1st Air Landing Brigade at Ponte Grande, and that was now the task of Brigadier G. W. Lathbury's 1st Parachute Brigade, which was dropped on to the Primasole Bridge on the Simeto river south of Catania on the night of 13/14 July. On the same night, No. 3 Commando would land from the sea and take the Ponte di Malati bridge across the Lentini river. With these two bridges and the defences around them in British hands, the advance of the 5th and 50th Divisions would surely speed up.

Brigadier Lathbury's plan was:

> To land between 2030 hours and midnight, each side of the river Simeto, to seize and hold a bridgehead until relieved by Eighth Army. It was hoped that this relief would arrive within twelve hours. The bridge was known to be defended by concrete pillboxes and Catania airfield, three or four miles to the north, could produce a lot of flak. Furthermore, we were unlikely to achieve complete surprise after the two previous airborne operations of the same nature.

There was also a problem with the aircrews of the USAAF Transport Wing tasked to fly the paratroopers in, some of whom were wary of approaching the Sicilian coast and nervous of the flak. Given the experiences of their colleagues at the hands of the naval gunners at Gela it is hard to blame them, but the effect on the British troops bound for Primasole was unfortunate. Many of the paratroopers were dropped too low from aircraft going too fast; the entire brigade suffered losses in landing accidents and, like the US airborne troops, was widely scattered and lost many of its vital weapon containers.

When Brigadier Lathbury arrived at the bridge – having been dropped 3 miles away – only 50 of the 2,000 or so men he had started with were present. All of these were from Lieutenant-Colonel John Frost's 2nd Parachute Battalion, though rifle and machine-gun fire and grenade explosions from the surrounding countryside revealed where other paratroopers were in action. 'It was obvious things had gone wrong,' wrote Lathbury, 'most of the wireless sets had gone astray . . . there were no communications with any of the battalions and no one knew what had happened.'[18] The loss of the brigade wireless sets – the only means of communication with Eighth Army – was to have far-reaching consequences as the battle for Primasole developed.

More men trickled in overnight. Frost took his 50 soldiers to high ground overlooking the bridge, and Lathbury deployed another 40 in four groups on either side of the river. The two other battalion commanders, Lieutenant-Colonel Alistair Pearson and Lieutenant-Colonel E. C. Yeldham of the 1st and 3rd Parachute Battalions, arrived with another 120 men, but the battle for the bridge had already begun and Lathbury soon discovered that the troops opposing the paratroopers were German, not the anticipated Italians.

'We climbed an embankment and began to walk towards the bridge,' writes Lathbury:

> Facing me was a lorry with an 88-mm in tow. I assumed it had been captured, but a few seconds later several grenades were tossed out and landed at our feet. Other men, of sterner stuff, carry on unmoved or even press on regardless. Personally, I always think my wounds are crippling if not mortal and take the appropriate action, which is to fall to the ground and call loudly for assistance.
>
> Matters were soon under control, and after I had been patched up and restored with a large tot of whisky I found I could get about, if somewhat slowly. While this was going on there were sounds of strife from the far end of the bridge where a lorry full of Germans had been dispatched with an anti-tank grenade. Incidentally, it was my birthday, but I have had many better ones.

By some strange coincidence, these German soldiers at Primasole came from *their* 1st Parachute Division, which had been dropped (accurately) into the same area an hour or so before Lathbury's men arrived. The German paratroopers were joined by the Italians of the 213rd Coastal Division, and as daylight arrived on 14 July the battle for Primasole really got under way.

Meanwhile No. 3 Commando had come ashore. The 50th (Northumbrian) Division was confronting a possible hold-up at another bridge, the Ponte di Malati over the Lentini river, 2 miles beyond the 50th Division position at Lentini and 12 miles from Primasole. This bridge, 5 miles from the coast, was to be captured by No. 3 Commando, which would then hold it to prevent its destruction and cut off the retreat of the Italian Napoli Division. The presence of Group Schmalz and the 1st Parachute Division in this area had either not been passed to the commandos or not been factored into their plan.

The commandos were met with opposition on the beach, and their second wave to come ashore had not yet appeared. It was, in fact, still detained on their landing ship, HMS *Prince Albert*, for the LCAs taking the first lift ashore had got lost on the way back. When they did return to the mother ship they arrived loaded with wounded, and getting the wounded off and the second lift loaded took still more time. Colonel John Durnford-Slater, the CO of No. 3 Commando, therefore had only 150 men ashore, but he elected to press on to the bridge. This gave the commandos some idea what the 'heavy' infantry of the assault divisions were up against in terms of terrain: thick undergrowth, stone walls, marshes, clumps of prickly pear, vineyards, voracious mosquitoes, and deep streams. Getting through all this in the dark took even more time.

When they reached the bridge they found it guarded by several pill-boxes and an alert enemy, but these obstacles were quickly overrun and the demolition charges on the bridge were removed. That done, the commandos dug in and settled down to await the second lift and fend off the enemy, pending the arrival, hopefully within a few hours, of the 50th Division. By daylight, Durnford-Slater had around 200 men on hand, but enemy resistance was increasing in size and scale. This culminated with the arrival of a Mark IV panzer, which trundled on to a nearby ridge and proceeded to pound the commando positions with its heavy gun, knocking the pillboxes to pieces and raking the ground with shells and heavy machine-gun fire to which the lightly equipped Commandos had no means of replying.

More tanks arrived during the morning, together with three battalions of a panzer grenadier regiment and an Italian tactical group of tanks and infantry. Vastly outnumbered – and with 25 per cent of his men killed or wounded in the last few hours – Durnford-Slater ordered his surviving men to break into small groups and make their way back to the British lines. Most of them did so, though one commando section, led by Sergeant 'Knocker' White, joined up with a wandering group of Airborne machine-gunners; together, this little force held off the enemy all day until relieved by troops of the York and Lancaster Regiment.

An equally gallant stand was taking place at Primasole where the Airborne perimeter was steadily shrinking under constant Axis pressure. Dug in at either end of the bridge the paratroopers hung on under constant shell and mortar fire, beating off infantry probes with rifle and Bren-gun fire, enduring strafing and bombing from German and Italian fighter bombers. The paratroopers' only support was occasional 6-inch-gun salvos from HMS *Mauritius*, cruising somewhere offshore. Lathbury's men were hanging on and determined to continue hanging on, but where was 50th Division? Radio communications were poor to non-existent, and only one radio contact was made all that day, before the batteries faded: it appeared that the 4th Armoured Brigade was coming forward from Augusta, but was meeting strong resistance on the way from Group Schmalz.

By nightfall the Airborne bridgehead on the north bank of the Simeto had been lost, but the surviving troopers were still hanging on south of the river, denying the enemy sappers access to the bridge. Again, all well and good – but where was 50th Division? In spite of direct orders from Montgomery and the corps commander, Lieutenant-General Miles Dempsey, to push on at all costs, the leading elements of this division – the 4th Armoured Brigade and the 6th Battalion Durham Light Infantry – had gone into leaguer at dusk a mile or so to the south and were making no great effort to push up to the Simeto. To be fair, these men had had very little sleep for the last four days, and when they finally arrived on the following morning and took over the Airborne positions on the south bank of the Simeto the battle at Primasole was by no means over.

The first task of the 8th and 9th Durhams was to retake the bridge. Their attack, supported by the guns of the 24th and 98th Field Regiments, RA, went in at 0730 hours on15 July. The first attack by the 9th Durhams was pressed with considerable resolution, but failed: shelled by tanks and raked by machine-gun fire, only a few platoons were able to cross the river where they were promptly counter-attacked and driven back, having lost over 100 men and 9 of their officers. They settled into the Airborne trenches on the south bank and continued to keep the German demolition teams away from the bridge.

Another frontal attack was ordered, this time by the 8th Durhams. This attack was prevented by the arrival of a dusty Scotsman in a parachute smock, Lieutenant-Colonel Alastair Pearson of the 1st Battalion the Parachute Regiment. Pearson told the Durham's CO that 'If you launch this attack in daylight, it's about the best way I know of destroying your battalion,' and said that he knew another way across the river.

Taking Pearson's advice, the 8th Durhams crossed the river 300 yards upstream from the bridge and took the German positions on the north side of the bridge in a flanking attack with the bayonet. The 6th Durhams then crossed, and the two battalions spent the rest of the day beating off a series of tank and infantry attacks. In the process they established a slightly wider bridgehead on the north bank. More than that they could not do.

A brief stalemate then set in on the Eighth Army front while attempts were made to find another way into the Catania plain to take the city. This stalemate was due not to any slacking in Eighth Army's resolve, but to stubborn German resistance. The German military cemeteries at Catania contain some 7,000 German soldiers killed in the fighting nearby, most of them – like the hundreds, if not thousands, who have no known grave – killed in the fighting around Primasole. The Durham Brigade lost more than 500 men, killed, wounded or missing, at Primasole. The ground around the bridge and along the banks of the Simeto was strewn for days with British and German dead and a quantity of wrecked tanks and transport.

While this battle was going on south of Catania, an intriguing inter-Allied row was brewing over the use of Route 124, west of Vizzini. This argument became quite heated and is an example of many Anglo-American arguments in this and other campaigns, and since the Americans appear to be the aggrieved party, their case will be stated first.

On the evening of 12 July, Major-General Troy Middleton, commanding the 45th Division, ordered his regimental commanders to drive on towards to Route 124, the 'Yellow Line' that marked a phase line in the II Corps advance north from the landing beaches. Unfortunately, General Montgomery had ordered Leese to send the 1st Canadian Division west to Caltagirone and then north towards Piazza Armerina and Valguarnera. His aim was to thus outflank the Catania plain and create a two-corps thrust to the north: XIII Corps up the coast road, where it was currently stalled, XXX Corps up the centre of the island, where it would turn east and move north of Mount Etna. This seems an entirely sensible plan in the current circumstances, but it required the use of at least part of Route 124 west of Vizzini, and the US II Corps Commander, General Omar Bradley, did not like this – at all.

'This will raise hell with us,' he exclaimed. 'I had counted heavily on that road. Now if we have to shift over, it'll slow up our entire advance.'[19] The US Official History goes on to state, 'To General Bradley it appeared that General Montgomery planned to take Messina alone while the Seventh Army confined its efforts to the western half of the island'.[20]

Since this is exactly what Seventh Army was supposed to do – and had always been supposed to do – it is hard to see why Bradley was so aggrieved. But the crux of the issue is which army, the Seventh or the Eighth, had control of Route 124? On the same page the US Official History comments that 'Although there had been no prepared plan after the seizure of the initial assault objectives, the assault plan itself contained *by implication* [my italics] the general scheme . . . while the Eighth Army thrust forward into Catania and then into Messina, Seventh Army was to protect the flanks and rear of the main striking force.' The US History attributes this division of tasks to Alexander's supposed belief that the US troops lacked combat experience. This allegation is common in US accounts, both personal and official, but criticism of the US soldier is hard to find in any British account.

The point that there was 'no prepared plan' after the initial assault begs the question: who allocated Route 124 to Seventh

Army? Given the paucity of good roads in the centre of Sicily, this is a very specific point indeed. Besides, there *was* a plan: the initial plan – the one described above for the 45th Division. In the initial plan, the task of this division after landing was to take the airfields at Comiso and Biscari – both of which are a good way south of Route 124 – and this road is not referred to in these orders at all, even 'by implication'.[21]

The map reveals that the 45th Division was somewhat divided in direction at this time. Some elements were heading east towards Ragusa to link up with the Canadians; others were heading north-east towards Vizzini; others directly north towards Grammichele and Caltagirone on Route 124. Meanwhile, the 1st Canadian Division was moving across their front, keeping contact with the US 1st Division, which was moving north-west, on the left from Ponte Olivo to Mazzarino and Caltanisseta.

In effect, the 45th Division was being 'pinched out' between these two formations, and some changes in direction were necessary. Either the Canadians stopped advancing and let the 45th Division through or the 45th Division would have to pull back to the coast and start again towards the centre north and west of Sicily – where Seventh Army was supposed to operate anyway, protecting Eighth Army's left flank.

In a footnote, the US Official History states that the taking of Route 124 was allocated to the Seventh Army in the original plan[22] – perhaps in the first Force 141 plan – but this footnote clashes with the other statement, that there was no plan other than for the assault phase. No evidence to support this footnote is provided. Its claim is also contradicted by the tasks laid out in the detailed initial plan given in the British Official History. And even if this claim is correct, 'taking' a road line is one thing; using the road later, in the light of the current situation, is quite another.

The most likely explanation is that the road was open to whoever needed it – or got there first. The US Official History refers to the 'confusion that may have existed',[23] a comment which suggests that the issue of who had been allocated the road was not as clear cut as its previous pages had claimed. Everyone wanted Route 124, and the map reveals why. If Monty could push up Route 124 west of Vizzini – which the 51st (Highland) Division took on 14 July – he could reach the road to Catania between Grammichele and Caltagirone and use it to come in on

Catania from the west, outflanking the resistance to XIII Corps on the coast road. Equally, Route 124 could support the US divisions as they went north-west towards Enna and Palermo, both of which were definitely in the US sector. A division on the move takes up many miles of road, so which division should have this one? The decision was Alexander's and he should have taken it sooner.

On 13 July Montgomery signalled to Alexander in Malta, 'The 45th Division is advancing between Vizzini and Caltagirone. My troops are advancing from Vizzini on Caltagirone. Unless something is done there will be intense military confusion on road Vizzini to Caltagirone. Suggest 45 Division moves to Gela and whole American effort is directed on Caltanisseta to Canicatti to Agrigento.'

Since this would mean turning the 45th Division about and sending it back to the beachhead to start again, it is hardly surprising that the American commanders took exception to this proposal. In fact Eighth Army needed Route 124 for only a short distance. A little Allied 'give and take' was called for, and some fresh guidelines from Alexander could have sorted the matter out quickly, but in the absence of such measures it appears that Montgomery had asked Alexander to give him the road and Alexander had agreed, deciding, on balance, that XXX Corps needed the road more than the 45th Division.

Alexander tidied up this vague and confusing situation in a directive issued at 2000 hours on the night of 13 July. This established a boundary between the two armies: 'Boundary between Seventh and Eighth Armies, the road Vizzini–Caltagirone–Piazza Armerina–Enna – *all inclusive to Eighth Army*' [my italics]. As we shall see, this directive was not written in stone: when the time came, Seventh Army would move east. Nevertheless, whatever the rights of the matter, Bradley felt aggrieved and another name was added to Montgomery's ever growing list of enemies.

A contributing factor in this brief affair was Patton's rooted desire for Palermo. Patton saw no reason why he should not grab some glory there, and since that city was clearly in the US area he was fully entitled to do so. Taking Palermo was not the prime task of his army, but Patton felt that the task of covering Eighth Army's flank could be performed equally well by striking out for the north coast – and taking Palermo.

This task was given, piece by piece, to a US Provisional Corps consisting of Truscott's 3rd Infantry Division, the 82nd Airborne Division and the 2nd Armored Division. Patton ordered the Provisional Corps to take Palermo some hours before Alexander authorized him to do so, and this move to the north and west went ahead from 19 July, making good progress against light opposition. On the first day alone the Americans advanced 75 miles – the only serious resistance coming from one Italian anti-tank gun at the Verdura river[24] – and Palermo fell on 22 July. The 1st and 45th Divisions were also reaching the north coast at Campofelice and Cefalu further east. Having arrived there, the old question arose: Where next?

General Bradley was anxious to turn east for Messina, and, in the words of one Seventh Army officer, his troops were not prepared to 'sit comfortably on our prats while Monty finishes the goddam war'. With the bulk of Axis power concentrated on the Eighth Army's front, a thrust east along the coast road from Palermo to Messina was an obvious task for Seventh Army, but another problem then arose. Who took Messina, instead of being an Allied issue, became a national issue: not 'Which army was now best placed to get to Messina and drive the enemy into the sea?' but 'Which army would get the glory for doing so?' The short answer is that Seventh Army was best placed to make for Messina, because the bulk of the German and Italian forces were busy stemming Eighth Army outside Catania. Had both armies come from the same nation no dispute would have arisen and this sensible strategy would have been seen for what it was – a sensible strategy *and an Allied one*.

With the establishment of the Primasole bridgehead, the way was open for XIII Corps to make a strong thrust on Catania and Messina up the east coast – had not the Germans remained determined to stand in the way. Looming ahead was the tall bulk of Mount Etna, and, as already described, the only road north to Messina ran through the narrow neck of land between that mountain and the sea. That gap the Germans were determined to hold. That they would eventually be driven out of Sicily by the ever increasing Allied pressure was obvious, but they were determined to go in their own time, after causing the Allies as much loss as possible.

Lieutenant Eric Brown was in Sicily with an anti-tank unit:

During preparations for the Sicily landings we practised with our 17-pounder Pheasants, which had been issued to replace our 6-pounder anti-tank guns. General Leese came to inspect them with mixed feelings, because he could see that the adapted 25-pounder chassis was very awkward. We appreciated this encouragement to do our best, and our increased firepower was awesome compared with the 2-pounders we had had a year ago. We reached Syracuse on 11 July, and in the advance 119th Battery followed the front but did not get involved in any tank battles. Nevertheless, the terrain around Etna proved very difficult to negotiate with the 17-pounder guns.[25]

In the face of stubborn resistance the advance of the 5th and 50th Divisions was inevitably slow. Eighth Army entered Catania on 5 August, but only after the Germans had packed up and left. The Germans had not been driven out of the city, and would be ready to fight all the way to Messina.

While the Americans were heading up towards Palermo at the end of July, XXX Corps was pushing north towards Gerbini, south-west of Catania, the Sferro Hills, and the hill town of Adrano, north-west of Catania. The fighting was hard and relentless, many positions being taken at the point of the bayonet; in the close-quarter fighting around Gerbini, the 7th Black Watch alone lost 18 officers and 160 men. Sferro Station and village west of Gerbini were taken by the Gordon Highlanders – enduring 'some of the heaviest shelling these troops ever experienced, even in North Africa'.[26]

This stubborn defence obliged Montgomery to bring forward his reserve unit, the 78th Infantry Division, which arrived from North Africa at the end of July, its trucks bearing the defiant message 'Nothing to do with Eighth Army' alongside the divisional sign; 78th Division had served with the First Army in Tunisia, and was proud of it. The 1st Canadian Division of XXX Corps had meanwhile advanced to Leonforte and turned east towards Agira. The Canadians had pushed hard against strong pockets of resistance, mostly from 15th Panzer, and had been obliged to halt from time to time, to let the 51st (Highland) Division on their right flank catch up again. They had also bypassed Enna – detailed as a XXX Corps objective by Alexander's directive of 13 July – an action that produced a snarl at General Leese from a still peeved General Bradley: 'I have just learned that you have side-slipped Enna, leaving my flank exposed. Accordingly we are proceeding to take Enna at once, even though it is in your sector. I assume we have the right to use any of your roads for this attack.'

Leese's apology was accompanied by a crate of Scotch whisky, and good relations were further cemented some days later when Bradley threw a tea party for his British opposite number – but this exchange indicates that liaison between the Allied armies, even between two corps fighting side by side, could stand some improvement.

The first unit to reach Agira was Urquhart's Malta Brigade, a British unit attached to the 1st Canadian Division, which arrived on 19 July. The men had marched over 150 miles in the last week, in full kit and summer heat, and were exhausted. Urquhart had intended an immediate attack, but decided to wait 24 hours, to give the men some rest and bring up the artillery. The Canadian Division's attack finally went in on the night of 22/23 July, and the battle for Agira against strong opposition from Hermann Goering and 15th Panzer units went on until 28 July. In one engagement of the battle the Royal Canadian Regiment lost 47 men killed or wounded, and the Hastings and Prince Edward Island Regiment a further 80, for no territorial gain.

The Canadians do not appear to have been well handled in these battles around Agira. Their attacks were made in the same fashion, infantry and artillery co-ordination was poor, and there was a tendency to reinforce failure, a process that led to further loss. The war diary of the Hastings Regiment makes this point: 'despite reports of strongly held enemy positions, three identical attacks were launched in succession'. This was not entirely Simonds's fault: the front was narrow, and Route 121 from Nissoria to Agira was the only viable axis of advance for tanks. The final Canadian attack was supported by 80 25-pounder field guns, and the town fell on the afternoon of 28 July, the defenders fighting to the last in the town centre. This action cost the 1st Canadian Division 438 casualties and the Malta Brigade a further 300. German losses, killed, wounded and captured, came to around 1,000.

During this battle, news arrived from Rome. On 25 July 1943 the Italian Fascist dictator, Benito Mussolini – the Duce – who had ruled Italy since 1922, had tendered his resignation to the

King, Victor Emmanuel, and relinquished control of affairs to
Marshal Pietro Badoglio. On emerging from the Royal Palace,
Mussolini had been arrested and taken under guard to the Gran
Sasso, a remote spot high in the Apennines.

The news of Mussolini's fall sent shock waves through Italy.
This blow radiated to Kesselring, the German commander at OB
Sud, the German headquarters in Italy, and to Hitler's headquarters, for what would the Italians do now? A change of leader indicated a change of policy, and, though Badoglio claimed that Italy
intended to stay in the war, few believed him. The Germans laid
plans to take over Italy should their ally desert them and command of the battle in Sicily was transferred to German hands; a
message from Rome instructed General Guzzoni, the area commander, to hand over to Lieutenant-General Hans Hube, and this
was done on 30 July.

The Allied troops in Sicily had other concerns, as Sapper Reg
Wheatley of the 754th Army Field Company Royal Engineers
describes:

> On 31 July we packed up and marched to the town of Noto, which
> seemed a nice enough town – though my most vivid memories
> are of hordes of starving children begging food from us, and my
> first attack of malaria. We were given a meal of meat and vege-
> table stew, which I could not eat and watched as these children
> gobbled it down. The mosquitoes had broken my malaria
> defences, and I was taken off to hospital. [27]

By 1 August, with the Americans at Palermo and other points
on the north coast, Canadians established at Agira, and the
British encircling Catania from Adrano, the scene was set for the
last phase of the Sicily campaign: the advance on Messina. For
the Americans, this began with a thrust by the 1st Infantry
Division on Troina, a hill town on Route 120 north of Agira.
Their first attack, on 1 August by the 39th Infantry Regiment,
was thrown back with loss, and further attacks on 2 and 3
August were no more successful and very costly; the Germans
were now contesting the US advance, and the days of rapid
progress were over.

Another attack on Troina on 4 August, backed by the guns of
18 artillery battalions and 3 squadrons of fighter-bombers, also
failed to quell the defenders. On 5 August Patton arrived to spur

the 'Big Red One' on, anxious that the hold-up there did not hand the glory of taking Messina to the detested Montgomery. Eighth Army entered Catania that day, the 5th and 50th Divisions moving out immediately up Route 114, the narrow road between the sea and Mount Etna.

The US attack on Troina on 5 August was somewhat marred by a US air strike falling on General Sir Oliver Leese's HQ. No damage was done, and that day the American infantry got forward, taking Troina on 6 August after 'the worst six days of fighting since Gela'. After that action the divisional commander, Major-General Terry Allan, was replaced by Major-General Clarence Huebner and the 1st Infantry Division came out of the line for a well-earned rest. The main US axis of advance was switched to the north coast road, Route 113, where the US 3rd Infantry, 2nd Armored and 82nd Airborne Divisions were slowly making ground towards Messina.

If moving slowly, they were still going somewhat faster than the British and Canadians. By 10 August the Eighth and Seventh Armies had come together, forming a curving front line across the base of the Messina peninsula on a line running from Cefalu, through Enna and Leonforte to just south of Catania – the Seventh some 75 miles from the ferry port, the Eighth about 52 miles. The two armies finally met at Randazzo on Route 120, north of Mount Etna where the 51st (Highland) Division met patrols from the US 9th Division.

The defenders of Sicily were still hanging on grimly, falling back in phased stages, evacuating such men and supplies as they could spare across to Calabria. The Allied air forces and navies were doing very little to inhibit the withdrawal of the Axis forces, the navies claiming that their ships would be vulnerable to coastal artillery if they entered the Straits of Messina, the air forces claiming that an abundance of flak guns on either coast would make any bombing mission costly.

In the next few days both Allied armies tried to outflank the German defences with a seaborne landing: the Americans at Cape Orlando, where the landing force came ashore after the beach had already been taken by the 3rd Division, and the British landing No. 2 Commando at Scaletta on 15 August. On the following day Seventh Army entered Messina, followed within a few hours by troops of Eighth Army. The campaign in Sicily was over, the Americans had beaten the British to Messina – and General Patton was jubilant.

In fact neither army had much to crow about. The main German forces had evacuated the island, almost at their leisure, on 12 August, leaving only demolitions, mines and a few scattered outposts to hold up the Allied advance that continued slowly for the next three days. Some 62,000 Italian and 40,000 German soldiers, together with 10,000 vehicles, 47 tanks, 94 guns and 17,000 tons of fuel and ammunition, had been shipped across to Calabria before Messina fell. The Germans had fought superbly, and, as Montgomery had predicted, the Italians had fought much better on their own soil than they had in North Africa. The Axis forces had not been hustled out of Sicily or totally defeated or obliged to surrender: Messina was not Tunis.

The Sicily campaign is notable for its lessons rather than its victories. Clearly the Allies still had a lot to learn: about inter-army co-operation, about the need to fight an *Allied* battle with fewer concerns about national prestige, about the handling of airborne operations, and about the need for the High Command – in this case either Alexander or Eisenhower – to exercise some grip over the Allied armies and their commanders on a day-to-day basis. This grip was needed all the time, not simply in response to disputes or the pressure of events.

While it is widely alleged that the British were too slow, the evidence suggests that this 'slowness' was related to two factors: (i) Montgomery's engrained belief that he must not outrun his supplies and (ii) German resistance – which after the first few days was mainly deployed on the Eighth Army front. When the Americans did confront strong German opposition, as at Troina, they too had difficulty getting forward. The battle for that small town took the Americans six full days, and the US Official History is critical of the way that it was handled.[28] That said, Truscott's 3rd Division and the US 82nd Airborne were the outstanding units among the Allied armies in Sicily.

The lessons of Sicily were not without cost. Eighth Army suffered 12,000 casualties in the campaign, the US Seventh Army 9,000. Further losses were sustained by the navies – the Royal Navy taking 725 casualties, the US Navy losing 1,030 sailors – and also by the Allied air forces in bombing and ground-support operations and most notably among the transport squadrons during the various airborne assaults. One unexpected feature of this campaign was the losses caused by malaria: mosquitoes cost the Allied forces more soldiers than mines, bullets and shells put together, and the malaria contracted here would break out again among the Allied divisions fighting in Italy and Normandy.

So the Sicily campaign ended with some gains in territorial and political terms but no real reason to suppose that the war in the Mediterranean was going to be quickly over or won without further cost. The next step would clearly be an invasion of the Italian mainland, where the arguments – both military and political – would continue.

50 (Northumbrian) Div.

11

Salerno to the Sangro
September–December 1943

Every 500 yards there is a new defensive position for a company, every five miles a new line for a division . . . an advance up Italy involves an interminable process of one more river to cross, one more mountain barrier to overcome.

Fred Majdalany, *Cassino: Portrait of a Battle*, p. 22

When Metternich, the nineteenth-century Austrian statesman, described Italy as 'a geographical expression', he was referring to its lack of political unity, but his remark also makes perfect sense topographically. Italy is indeed defined by its geography, and in the summer of 1943 its physical features and climate were to have a profound effect on the conduct of the coming campaign.

Italy is a boot-shaped country, running for more than 1,000 miles between the Alps and Calabria, but little more than 100 miles wide at any point. Its main physical feature is the Apennines, the mountainous spine which splits the country in two and has peaks reaching up to 6,500 feet – arid in summer, snow-capped in winter.

The Apennines are twice as far from the western coast as they are from the Adriatic, but rocky ribs and isolated outcrops reach into the coastal plains from either side of the central range, offering more obstacles to the attacker while providing perfect defensive positions and high points for artillery observers. The coastal plain on the western side averages some 25 miles in width; on the Adriatic side the plain is even narrower – some 15 to 20 miles. In the 1940s, roads across this bleak terrain were few and narrow, most of them, as in Sicily, running along the coast. Apart from mountain tracks, there were only two main lateral roads in the south of the country: one from Naples to Termoli and one, further north, from Pescara to Rome. One result of this geography was that the armies east and west of the Apennines would effectively be fighting separate wars.

To these various difficulties can be added the weather, which ranges from very hot and dry in summer to torrential rains, snowstorms and floods in winter. Peacetime tourists may visualize Italy as a sun-kissed paradise; the wartime soldiers found it little better than a hell on earth – albeit a damp and chilly one.

Ernest Smallridge, an infantry man, gives a soldier's eye view of Italy:

> Observing the terrain, it was easy to see that the infantry were going to have a very tough time. Having dug in at the top of all the hills, the Germans had the advantage in every engagement, and when necessary could withdraw on to the next hill. Because of this situation, there were times when a complete stalemate existed, and only when times were less frantic could we get more civilized and wash our filthy bodies. But the journey to the north was a slow and painful business.[1]

When, after Sicily, the Allies decided to press on with an invasion of the Italian mainland, the old question arose yet again: Where to go? General Eisenhower, the Allied Supreme Commander in the Mediterranean, had his headquarters in Algiers, but the conduct of military operations in Italy was vested in General Sir Harold Alexander's 15th Army Group, which consisted of Montgomery's Eighth Army and the US Fifth Army under Lieutenant-General Mark W. Clark. General Patton was in temporary disgrace, after an incident involving shell-shocked soldiers in a hospital, and the Seventh Army had been broken up to provide units to Fifth Army, which was also receiving units from Eighth Army. Eighth Army was entirely British or Commonwealth, and currently consisted of just XXX Corps and

XIII Corps. The US Fifth Army was 50 per cent British, consisting of three American divisions of VI Corps under Major-General Ernest J. Dawley and three British divisions of X Corps, currently under Lieutenant-General Brian Horrocks. Both armies were supported by strong tactical air forces – Eighth Army by the Desert Air Force – and by units of the Allied fleets.

Lieutenant-General Mark W. Clark would become the controversial figure of the Italian campaign. Clark had served in France during the First World War – where he was wounded in action – and had acted as Eisenhower's deputy during the recent campaign in North Africa. Clark was a competent general, but, like his British opposite number, Bernard Montgomery, he had certain character flaws. The US Official History introduces Clark with the comment that he was 'aggressive, hard working, with a flair for public relations'.[2] This is curious, because comments on a general's experience and command capabilities are surely more usual and more relevant to his appointment than 'a flair for public relations'. Nor is this comment entirely accurate: General Clark actually had an *obsession* with public relations.

Fred Majdalany – admittedly no Clarkophile – comments that Clark was 'a rangy, handsome American . . . suggesting the kind of film star who would have looked good in a ten-gallon hat', and Clark did indeed bear a resemblance to Randolph Scott, the cowboy star of the 1940s and 1950s. No man is entirely responsible for his appearance, but Clark's concern for his image went beyond mere looks. All dispatches sent out from Fifth Army HQ by war correspondents had to bear the full title 'With Lieutenant-General Mark W. Clark's Fifth Army' – any marked simply 'With the Fifth Army' would be returned to sender for correction. Clark was also concerned that photographers took only the 'good side' of his face. In words or pictures, General Clark intended to attract only favourable notices.

All this is harmless enough, perhaps, but Clark's craving for recognition went deeper and did considerable harm – not least to Clark himself. Major-General Lucian K. Truscott, an officer who became the star Allied commander in Italy, comments in his memoirs that Clark 'usually arrived at my command post with an entourage including correspondents and photographers. His concern for personal publicity was his greatest weakness. I have sometimes thought that it may have prevented him from acquiring that "feel of battle" that marks all top-flight commanders, though extensive publicity did not seem to have that effect on Patton and Montgomery.'

Vanity was not Clark's only fault: he was also autocratic and chippy, not simply towards the British – that goes without saying – but also with his American colleagues and subordinates, many of them officers with greater battle or command experience, whose advice he should have taken or at least listened to.

To balance the picture, Mark Clark was no raving Anglophobe like Admiral King and George Patton. With British generals taking his orders and British troops dying under his command, that was not possible and Clark was a big enough man to realize that, while arguments were inevitable, by and large the Anglo-American alliance functioned well. Clark grew to know the quality of his British and Commonwealth soldiers, and his memoirs give frequent and generous praise to at least some of his British subordinates, at least some of the time. That said, the chippiness remains. Clark's desire that Fifth Army – or rather Lieutenant-General Mark W. Clark's Fifth Army – should hog the spotlight and get any available credit was to be a constant factor in the Italian campaign, and would lead to several unfortunate events.

Plans for the invasion of the Italian mainland had been considered and reconsidered even before the Sicilian campaign ended, and the final decision came down to just three amphibious operations. The first, Operation BAYTOWN, called for two infantry divisions of Eighth Army to cross the Straits of Messina to Calabria, take the town of Reggio Calabria, and advance north up the toe of Italy. The second, Operation AVALANCHE, required the Fifth Army landing force, consisting of the US VI Corps – the 36th (Texas) Division and the 3rd, 34th and 45th Divisions – and the British X Corps – consisting of the 46th and 56th Infantry Divisions, with the 7th Armoured Division in reserve – to land on the 20 miles of beaches at Salerno, 50 miles south of Naples, and take that port.

It should be noted, in view of what follows, that BAYTOWN and AVALANCHE meant that Eighth Army would land some 200 miles south of Fifth Army, with a great deal of rugged country in between – and this after the argument over the wide dispersion of the Allied forces initially planned for the much less difficult landing in Sicily. The decision to land troops in Calabria was taken on 16 August, the day after the Sicilian campaign ended, and Eighth Army crossed the Straits of Messina on 3 September. AVALANCHE would follow on 9 September.

The final operation, drawn up later but implemented at the same time as AVALANCHE was Operation SLAPSTICK, a landing by the British 1st Airborne Division at the port of Taranto to establish a bridgehead on the heel of the peninsula as a base for subsequent Eighth Army operations on the Adriatic coast. This last operation was organized hurriedly after Italy surrendered on 8 September – the day before Fifth Army landed at Salerno – and 3,500 men of the 1st Airborne Division duly went ashore at Taranto on 9 September.

The Fifth Army landings at Salerno were to provide one of the epic battles of the Italian campaign – and yet another Anglo-American argument – so, before returning to Eighth Army in Calabria and on the Adriatic front, the actions of Fifth Army must be sketched in. The brunt of the early fighting in Italy fell on this Anglo-American army, and its tenacity in hanging on to the slender Salerno bridgehead during days of heavy fighting made later developments possible. This tenacity was even more of a feat because the German commanders in Italy had been expecting a landing in the south and were fairly sure where it would come.

Following their withdrawal from Sicily, and anticipating the defection of the Italian government, the German forces reorganized. The basic decision the Germans had to take after the fall of Sicily and Mussolini – and the subsequent surrender of Italy to the Allies on 8 September – was where the German Army should stand, or indeed if it should stand in Italy at all. One option was a rapid evacuation to the line of the Alps, but this was quickly discarded – not least because Hitler had a deep aversion to giving up ground. The Italian Army was never a major factor in these German decisions; those Italian soldiers who did not throw away their uniforms and weapons and go home after 8 September were quickly disarmed, though Italian partisan activity, largely inspired by the Communist Party, was to become a major factor in the 1944–5 campaign north of Rome.

With a total evacuation of the peninsula out of the question the next decision was, where to make a stand? Italy is ideal for defence, but the two long coastlines provided obvious targets for outflanking amphibious landings – provided the Allies could muster enough landing craft. It might therefore be as well to withdraw all German forces to the north and defend only the Po valley and the passes of the Alps. Rommel was certainly in favour of such a move but Hitler was eventually persuaded by the views put forward by Field Marshal Kesselring.

Kesselring was an optimist. He believed that all of Italy could be held and that even if the German Army was forced to withdraw, it could do so in its own time, falling back to a series of pre-arranged positions, charging the Allies a heavy price for every yard of ground given up. This view prevailed with Hitler: the German Army would take on the Allied armies in Italy from the moment the first Allied soldier stepped ashore.

It also seems likely that Hitler was influenced in this decision by strategic factors. The US Official History notes that 'To Hitler an Allied campaign in Italy as an end in itself made little sense',[3] but the long-term consequences of losing Italy could be significant. If the Allies had the main Italian airfields, their heavy bombers could range at will over the Reich and destroy the vital Romanian oilfields that supplied around half of Germany's oil supplies. From Italy, major amphibious operations, supported by air power, could be launched into the Balkans to support the Russian advance and the Yugoslav partisans of Marshal Tito. Should Italy fall, a thrust east through Trieste and the Ljubljana Gap on to the Hungarian plains could carry the Western Allies into central Europe, Austria, even to Vienna. From the Allied point of view, much of the Italian campaign was seen as a sideshow; to Hitler it was a dagger, pointing directly at the Reich.

It will be seen later that what Hitler feared, Churchill wanted – though for rather different reasons. Hitler feared that a junction between the Russian and Western Allies would unite large forces for a final invasion of the Reich. Churchill, apprehensive about Soviet Russia's long-term intentions in eastern Europe once the war was over, wanted the Western Allies to meet the Russians as far east as possible and have troops from the Western armies in Austria well before the end of the war. Churchill feared that if the Red Armies took over eastern Europe it would take a very long time to get them out again; in the event it took about 50 years.

OKW supported Kesselring's plan, and to help carry it out a new German army, Tenth Army, was created on 8 August. This army became operational on 23 August, a week after the ending of the campaign in Sicily. Tenth Army was commanded by Colonel-General Heinrich von Vietinghoff, who had previously commanded an army corps in Russia and then forces in France. After taking up his new post, von Vietinghoff reviewed the Allied options and declared that 'Allied landings in the Naples–Salerno area represent the main danger to the whole of the German forces in Southern Italy.'

German forces in the south of Italy had expanded considerably since the fall of Sicily in August, to a ration strength of 125,000 men. About 30,000 men of the 26th Panzer and 29th Panzergrenadier Divisions were in Calabria, facing the prospect of a thrust across the Straits of Messina by Eighth Army. The Hermann Goering Division, 15th Panzergrenadier Division and 16th Panzer Division, much written down but still totalling some 45,000 men, were deployed on the west coast of Italy, between Gaeta and Salerno. The crack 1st Parachute Division, with around 17,000 men, was stationed around the airfields of Foggia on the Adriatic front. Finally, in army reserve close to Rome were the 3rd Panzergrenadier Division and the 2nd Parachute Division, totally some 43,000 men. These units were resting, training and re-equipping when Montgomery's Eighth Army made an amphibious assault across the Straits of Messina on 3 September.

This BAYTOWN operation was put in hand quickly. The fighting in Sicily ended on 15 August. XIII Corps, tasked for BAYTOWN, had already made some preliminary plans, but was not advised of its landing-craft allocation until 23 August. Some training was called for: the 3rd Canadian Brigade had never made an assault landing, and had time for only one day's training before this assault began. Loading schedules were completed on 27 August, and loading began on 31 August. Two days later all was ready and the landings began at 0345 hours on 3 September.

Montgomery's assault was massive – even excessive – and the Calabria landing can be described in Second World War parlance as 'a piece of cake' – if not quite as easy as envisaged by General Eisenhower, who declared that the Straits of Messina could be 'crossed in rowing boats'. The crossing, by leading elements of the Canadian 1st and British 5th Divisions of XIII Corps, plus an armoured and an infantry brigade and some commando units, was covered by RAF bombing, a barrage from 600 guns on the Sicilian shore and the 16-inch guns of the battleships *Nelson*, *Rodney*, *Warspite* and *Valiant*. Freddie de Guingand, Monty's Chief of Staff, described this support, correctly, as 'a sledgehammer to crack a nut'.[4]

The main opposition came from mines, booby traps and demolitions. The 29th Panzergrenadier Division had already withdrawn from Reggio, and the town fell without fighting. From there XIII Corps moved north along the coasts of the toe, the British on the north side, the Canadians on the south, their immediate objective the neck of land at Catanzaro, 80 miles to the north. Getting there would not be easy and, in view of later US complaints, it should be noted, that Montgomery had been allocated only enough supplies to take his forces to the Catanzaro neck. The advance was also plagued by German demolitions and booby traps – and the narrow, winding Calabrian roads, which alone reduced progress to a crawl. For the moment this hardly mattered. The Anglo-American assault at Salerno – Operation AVALANCHE – would not go in for another week, and no great opposition was expected when it did.

There appears to have been a certain lack of co-ordination between these two operations, BAYTOWN and AVALANCHE. Since the landings were made 200 miles apart, the two operations were clearly not designed to be mutually supporting – and the country between was not open to rapid advances: the Allies should have learned that lesson in Sicily. It also appears that the orders given to General Montgomery for his moves following the landings were not clear, and the fault here lies with the commanders at AFHQ and 15th Army Group. According to the US Official History, 'AFHQ expected Eighth Army to push up the Calabrian peninsula and along the west coast of Italy to Naples.'[5] If so that was not in the orders given to Montgomery by Alexander at 15th Army Group HQ.

Montgomery's orders stated, 'Your task is to secure a bridgehead on the toe of Italy to enable our naval forces to operate through the Straits of Messina. In the event of the enemy withdrawing from the toe you will follow him up with such force as you can make available, bearing in mind that the greater the extent to which you can engage enemy forces in the toe of Italy, the more assistance you will be giving to AVALANCHE.'

The second part of this order was somewhat short on specifics, lacking any sense of urgency and depending on what the enemy would do. The physical evidence – notably the 200-plus miles of mountain road between Reggio and Salerno – suggests that the BAYTOWN and AVALANCHE operations were designed as two separate events by two separate armies; the need for a rapid link-up appeared only later, when AVALANCHE got into trouble. Engaging enemy forces that were determined to withdraw, leaving a trail of wrecked roads and bridges behind them to delay pursuit, would not be easy. And then there was the problem of supply: how could the trucks and tanks of XIII Corps be kept supplied with fuel over this distance? The more they were pursued, the quicker these German forces would end up at Salerno, leaving their pursuers some distance to their rear, hacking a path over wrecked roads and bridges and seriously short of fuel.

However, again according to the US Official History, 'never having received a directive outlining the long-range course of BAYTOWN, Eighth Army planners had no clear idea of what was expected of Eighth Army'.[6] If this is so, one wonders why the Eighth Army 'planners' did not ask for such direction, but the US account goes on:

> The trouble was that Eighth Army was under 15th Army Group control and AFHQ never received the Army's detailed plans. As a result of this lack of co-ordination, no one was entirely sure whether the (Eighth) Army was simply to land in Calabria to open up the Straits of Messina, whether after landing it was to prepare for a major advance, or whether it was to make an effort to contain the enemy in order to assist the Salerno invasion.

Presumably this means that no one at AFHQ – Eisenhower's headquarters – knew what Eighth Army was doing, and again did not ask for the plans. But Alexander's orders to Montgomery make it clear that Eighth Army was to open up the Straits of Messina and then, in the event of a German withdrawal, follow up with such force as was available and attempt to contain the enemy in Calabria. There is no suggestion that Eighth Army should 'prepare for a major advance' – indeed, with only two divisions of XIII Corps ashore in Calabria and limited supplies, it is hard to see how a 'major advance' would have been possible.

The allegation that BAYTOWN had no clear aim is extremely unlikely. The first part of any operational order defines the *aim* of the operation – why it is being carried out and what it has to achieve. The chain of command is quite clear – AFHQ to 15th Army Group to Eighth and Fifth Armies. So 15th Army Group, having been ordered to invade Italy by AFHQ, tasked Eighth Army with BAYTOWN, told Montgomery what supplies, support and shipping he would get – and asked for his plan. This plan, once accepted, would be implemented, and it would certainly have an aim. The implication that Monty – of course – failed to present his plans to his superiors is unlikely: without their support, shipping and supplies there would have been no plan. Yet here we are expected to believe that there were three possible aims for BAYTOWN and that the commanders responsible for the entire operation – Eisenhower, Alexander and Montgomery – were not aware which of them applied to the task in hand.

One thing can be said with some certainty: Montgomery was not aware that his army might have to advance quickly to the aid of the Anglo-American forces landing at Salerno. Monty's strongly expressed views on the close support necessary between landing forces during the recent invasion of Sicily is proof of that. Had such assistance been foreseen or part of the plan, he would have had plenty to say about it. Besides, nobody expected Fifth Army to get into trouble at Salerno.

XIII Corps of Eighth Army went ashore in the toe of Italy on 3 September. The Italians surrendered on 8 September, Fifth Army landed at Salerno on 9 September, and on 11 September Admiral Sir Andrew Cunningham could signal the Admiralty, 'Be pleased to advise their Lordships that the Italian battlefleet now lies at anchor under the guns of the fortress of Malta.'

While these dramatic events were taking place, Eighth Army was pushing up from Reggio. On the night of 3 September a commando force drawn from Major Paddy Mayne's 1st Special Raiding Squadron landed near Bagnara, bumped into the German rearguard from the 15th Panzergrenadiers, and drove them into the town. The fighting in Bagnara went on until the 15th Infantry Brigade of the 5th Division arrived on the following day, wiped out the remaining Germans, and pressed forward towards Rosarno, some 40 miles north of Messina. Here the 15th Brigade was joined by the 13th Brigade, which had made a sea-borne landing at Gioia Tauro, 20 miles north of Messina. It there-fore appears that Eighth Army – having landed and advanced 40 miles in 24 hours – was pressing ahead quickly and using amphibious landings to help its troops forward. This rapid progress came to a stop when the bridges over the river Messina north of Rosarno were found destroyed.

Eighth Army had already evolved the basic tactic of the Italian campaign: advance until held, then hook round the enemy front with an amphibious landing. On 8 September No. 40 (Royal Marine) Commando landed at San Venere near Pizzo, north of the river Messina, where they were greeted with heavy mortar and machine-gun fire. The marines held on all day until Urquhart's Malta Brigade was able to force a way across the river and join them, the two units pressing on again on 9 September. This brisk little engagement cost the 231st Brigade some 200 casualties. On that day General Mark W. Clark's Fifth Army went ashore at Salerno and the British 1st Airborne Division landed at the port of Taranto in the heel of Italy.

On 10 September, in spite of more blown bridges and opposition from German artillery and rearguards, the 231st Brigade reached Tiriolo, north-west of Catanzaro. On the 11th, the 17th Infantry Brigade of the 5th Division reached Nicastro, west of Tiriolo. The 15th Infantry Brigade then took over the advance and went for-ward to Cosenza, and then up to Scalea on the Gulf of Policastro, arriving there, now 150 miles from Messina, on 14 September.

Meanwhile, the 1st Canadian Division, moving along the east-ern shore of the toe, was doing equally well along Route 106 in spite of demolitions 'going off practically in our faces'.[7] Leading elements of this division reached the Catanzaro neck on 10 September, and the rest of the division closed up next day – after advancing 100 miles in a week. By 16 September this division had moved around the 5,500–6,000 foot Sila Grande and Sila Piccola massif to the next narrow neck, between Spezzano and Belvedere, where these two divisions – 5th British and 1st Canadian – must either link up or go their separate ways, north to Salerno, east around the gulf to Taranto. In spite of rough roads, blown bridges, demolitions, booby traps, mines and enemy opposition, Eighth Army, with its tanks, guns and trucks, was averaging 15 miles a day – which, given the constant wind-ing of these back-country roads, was very good going.

XIII Corps was now fully extended, however, and resistance was stiffening. Eighth Army had taken most of the toe and was preparing to advance around the instep to join the 1st Airborne Division north of Taranto, but from 11 September this move came second to a more pressing requirement: the need to move north and take some of the pressure off Clark's embattled forces at Salerno, where the Anglo-American landings had been con-tested from the moment the troops stepped ashore.

Hoping to achieve surprise, the US VI Corps had decided to land without naval gunfire support, while the British X Corps – now commanded by General Sir Richard McCreery after General Horrocks had been wounded in an air attack shortly before embarking – elected for the full range of gunfire support and was very glad to have it.

The Germans now had 16 divisions in Italy. Eight were in the north under Field Marshal Erwin Rommel's Army Group B, and eight were in the south – OB Sud, later Army Group F – under Field Marshal Kesselring, with Kesselring nominally subject to Rommel's orders. Kesselring was not remotely convinced that the landing of two divisions of Eighth Army in Calabria was the full extent of the Allied intentions. It was more than probable that further landings would follow, and a simple calculation of the basic requirements necessary for an amphibious operation – an adequate beach within reach of Allied fighter cover and close to a major port – led him to pick Salerno as the most likely spot. He therefore sent the fully equipped 16th Panzer Division, 17,000 men, 100 tanks and 36 assault guns from Hube's 14th Panzer Corps – to Salerno, and they were firmly established and waiting in the hills behind the beach when the Allied troops splashed ashore.

The violent German reaction to the landings took the Allies by surprise, and they found themselves fighting for a foothold before they got far off the beach or had time to dig in. Heavy fighting in the Salerno beachhead went on for ten days, but the crux came on the evening of 13 September, four days into the operation, when, says the US Official History, 'the Fifth Army found itself at the edge of defeat'. Plans were being laid by Fifth Army staff officers to evacuate the beachhead or move troops from the VI Corps area to the X Corps area. Constant German pressure, heavy losses and an inability to expand the beachhead into the surrounding hills had brought Clark's advance to a halt, and von Vietinghoff was mustering his forces to push the Anglo-Americans into the sea.

The US Official History attributes this dire scenario to one basic reason: 'an inability to build-up the beachhead by water transport as fast as the Germans could reinforce the defenders by land'. This in turn is attributed to 'a lack of lift for the initial landings, a factor that had been recognized well before the event'.[8] These comments reinforce the impression that the Allies had a lot to learn about amphibious operations in 1943 – getting enough troops ashore and supplying them thereafter is the fundamental problem with all amphibious operations; if those basic requirements cannot be met, the landings must be called off.

This problem may be related to a lack of experience of amphibious operations among the US Army commanders. Such operations are a specialized field of the military art, and one that the Americans had entrusted to that splendid formation, the United States Marine Corps, which was then fully employed in the Pacific. Some idea of the US Army's attitude to amphibious operations in the summer of 1943 can be gauged from Eisenhower's comment that 'The Straits of Messina could be crossed in rowing boats', and the view expressed by George Patton to General John P. Lucas, commander of the landing forces at Anzio in 1944, that 'A landing operation requires little training. The troops only had to move straight ahead on being put ashore.'[9]

It is fair to add that even by 6 June 1944 the US Army had still to reconsider this opinion, but Churchill had some harsh things to say about this attitude to amphibious warfare in a speech to the House of Commons on 21 September 1943: 'When I hear people talking in an airy way of throwing modern armies ashore here and there, as if they were bales of goods to be dumped on the beach and forgotten, I really marvel at the lack of knowledge which still prevails of the conditions of modern war.'

The British had realized the need to study amphibious warfare after Dunkirk and had set up the Combined Operations Headquarters (COHQ) to raise commando units and carry out amphibious training. This revealed the need for rapid reinforcement after the landing, and strong support in the invasion phase.

Once Kesselring realized that Salerno was a major assault, more German divisions were rushed to the beachhead area and, sitting on the hills around the beach, they subjected Clark's forces to a merciless pounding and constant attacks. After the first day, when the British Official History refers to the fighting as 'scrappy',[10] German resistance mounted steadily, and before long the Fifth Army bridgehead was in serious trouble. One solution to this dire situation was the rapid arrival of Eighth Army in von Vietinghoff's rear, and urgent calls went out for Montgomery to get a move on and prevent a costly and humiliating evacuation from Salerno.

The problem for Montgomery was one of supply. He now had the equivalent of two and a half divisions ashore in Calabria – some 58,000 men – with all their trucks and tanks. An infantry division alone had some 3,000 vehicles, and the roads they had to travel over were as described above: poor and narrow at the best of times, very slow indeed in the summer of 1944. Many roads had been blasted into the adjacent valley by the retreating enemy, and any plans to get ahead by sea were thwarted by a shortage of landing craft – everything that could float was carrying supplies to Salerno. Getting up to Salerno overland was not a matter of motoring. Every truck and tank needed fuel; every soldier had to be fed. Every mouthful of food and pint of petrol that Eighth Army consumed had to be shifted forward 200 miles or more from Reggio in the toe, since the little ports along the shore were not able to handle much traffic – and, again, most of the shipping that might have used them had been sent to supply Salerno. The commanders at AFHQ and 15th Army Group could not have it both ways: two armies needed supply, and the decision – the right decision in the circumstances – was to supply Fifth Army. This meant that Eighth Army must make do with what it had, and as a result it moved slowly; Alexander did not allocate more shipping to Eighth Army until 15 September, when the crisis at Salerno was over.

In the end, the Salerno beachhead held. The arrival of a paratrooper force from the 82nd Airborne Division and shells from the powerful 16-inch guns of the battleships *Warspite* and *Valiant* tilted the balance by 15 September, and finally the imminent arrival of Eighth Army from the south obliged von Vietinghoff to break off and pull back to the Volturno. 'The arrival of Eighth

Army had no particular significance,' says the US Official History. 'The Fifth Army had fought it out alone and they had won.'[11]

This dismissive statement might have pointed out that Montgomery never claimed to have 'significantly' helped Fifth Army – and might also have mentioned that half of the 'US' Fifth Army soldiers at Salerno were British: the final casualty total for Salerno shows that 4,007 British soldiers and 1,667 American soldiers became casualties in the eight days' battle for the beachhead. German losses totalled 3,472 before Kesselring called off the battle on 17 September.

The harsh fact remains that the Salerno battle had not been well handled. It had rapidly become a 'soldier's battle' – one in which the outcome depended on the officers, NCOs and men in the front line, rather than their commanders in the rear. On 20 September General Dawley was relieved of command of VI Corps and replaced by General Lucas, but there were criticisms of those somewhat higher up the command chain. The US Official History points out that General Clark was 'sensitive of his prerogatives and understandably anxious to make good in his first command . . . he rarely if ever requested advice from his subordinate commanders or talked things over with them. His habit was to stride into command posts, receive reports and issue instructions . . . those who may have expected him to seek their guidance were disappointed that he did not do so.'[12]

In a history of Eighth Army, none of this would matter but for the attempt to shift some of the blame for the travails of Fifth Army at Salerno to the slowness of the Eighth Army coming up from Calabria. The US Official History devotes six pages to this matter,[13] and, as an example of what Eighth Army might have done, quotes the experiences of three war correspondents who left Nicastro on 13 September in a jeep and met patrols of VI Corps at Ogliastro, south of Salerno, 48 hours later, on 15 September, having met no opposition on the way. Quite what this feat by three non-combatants, weighed down only by notebooks, pencils and perhaps a typewriter, has to do with the advance of an entire Army Corps is not clear.

The US account concedes this point, stating that 'the movement of small groups of men is, of course, quite different from the advance of an army or even a battalion'.[14] But in that case why raise the point and devote six pages of text to this particular example? A better one might be the later advance of 7th Armoured Division – then of the Fifth Army – north from Salerno, about which the divisional historian comments that, 'unable to disperse laterally on this stone-walled countryside, the Division deployed from front to rear and at one time was spread out *over 55 miles of narrow road*'(my italics). To compare the advance of a full army corps in such conditions with the progress of a few jeeps is ludicrous. If it took two full days for these journalists to drive 200 miles, the problems of advancing with two divisions can only be wondered at.

Another example of progress in Calabria can be found in the Canadian Official History. A rifle platoon of the Loyal Edmonton Regiment, with a section of sappers and some 6-pounder anti-tank guns, set out on 9 September to reconnoitre an inland route from Cittanova to Catanzaro, arriving there on 13 September. Covering just 100 miles took this party of just 50 men four full days because of 'blocked turns, cratered roadbeds and blown bridges'.[15] There is no real evidence that Eighth Army was dragging its feet on the road to Salerno.

The point being made in the US Official History is that the rapid arrival of Eighth Army on the German flank would have made a difference at Salerno. This is true. Also, that Eighth Army might have moved quicker, which is probably true: all armies can move quicker. They can also move a lot slower – it depends on the circumstances. In the event, Eighth Army probably moved as fast as it could in the circumstances, and attempts to prove otherwise founder on an absence of facts.

While the Anglo-American Fifth Army was slogging it out at Salerno, Eighth Army was coming up from the toe towards it and making its way round the instep towards Taranto. Patrols of the 5th Division met units of the US VI Corps at Vallo della Lucania, almost 200 miles from Reggio, on 16 September. On the same day, patrols of the 1st Canadian Division met troops of the 1st Airborne Division near Metaponto on the Gulf of Taranto, hundreds of miles north-east of Reggio. The accusations that Eighth Army was not pressing on at best speed at this time is not entirely accurate.

By 20 September the situation had stabilized. Eighth Army's forward units had advanced 300 miles in 17 days – an average of 17 miles a day – and the main problem now was to repair the roads and bridges and bring up supplies for a further advance towards Bari and Foggia. This was when the bulldozer again made its contribution to the Allied advance – a contribution that would continue and grow throughout the Italian campaign, matched only by that of the prefabricated Bailey bridge. The Allied armies in Italy would have got nowhere without the engineers, the 'sappers'.

Eighth Army now had to move its main strength over to the Adriatic side of the Apennines and concentrate at Taranto. Taranto was a naval base, and its capture by the 1st Airborne Division on 9 September had been a bold move, since the Division was entirely unsupported and strong German forces were thought to be in the area. The Division arrived at Taranto in time to see the Italian battlefleet sail south to surrender at Malta, but found the harbour mined. The fast minelayer HMS *Abdiel* struck a mine when anchoring, and sank in minutes, taking with her 48 naval ratings and 120 paratroopers.

Once ashore at Taranto, 1st Airborne took over the airfield at Grottaglie and sent out patrols to the north. The enemy was first encountered on 11 September, when the divisional commander, Major-General G. F. Hopkinson, was mortally wounded while visiting the 10th Parachute Battalion. The Division entered Brindisi and Bari and pushed on towards the airfield complex at Foggia; by now it was meeting rearguards from the German 1st Parachute Division, but its advance continued.

Eighth Army was now concentrating on the Adriatic front, aiming to take Foggia and the port of Termoli. Before that could happen, its centre of supply had to be shifted from Reggio Calabria to Taranto, and this move could not be completed before 1 October. Meantime, XIII Corps would continued to press north across the mountains inland, protecting the right flank of Fifth Army as it moved along the coast to Naples – which fell to units of the British 7th Armoured Division of X Corps on 1 October – and up to the Volturno river.

By 20 September strong Allied bridgeheads had been secured at Salerno and Taranto and XIII Corps was linking the two Allied armies in the Potenza–Auletta area, in the centre of the country. The Germans had now taken over Italy, and Benito Mussolini – rescued from the Gran Sasso by SS officer Otto Skorzeny and some airborne troops – was free again and about to found a puppet Fascist republic – the so-called Republic of Salo – in the north of the country. On 24 September Montgomery regrouped his forces for the drive north, planning to advance on Foggia with XIII Corps, which would now consist of the Canadian 1st and the British 78th Divisions, plus 4th Armoured Brigade and the Canadian 1st Tank Brigade. These units would concentrate first in the Bari area. The 5th Division would remain in the Potenza area as the link between Fifth and Eighth Armies, reverting later to the command of Lieutenant-General Allfrey's V Corps, which then consisted of the 8th Indian and 1st Airborne Divisions, which would remain initially in the Taranto area. Eighth Army also contained the 2nd SS (Commando) Brigade consisting of No. 3 Commando, No. 40 (Royal Marine) Commando and the Special Raiding Squadron.

It will be seen from this Eighth Army Order of Battle that not much remained of the old Desert Army. The 7th Armoured Division was now serving with X Corps in the US Fifth Army and – like other desert veterans, the 51st (Highland) Division and the 50th (Northumbrian) Division – would soon be on its way home to take part in the Normandy landings on D-Day 1944. The New Zealanders would soon be coming back to Eighth Army, as would Tuker's 4th Indian Division, but Eighth Army was fighting a new war now: the old, free-wheeling desert days had gone for ever.

General Montgomery was now experiencing some problems with the commander of the Italian Seventh Army, General Rizzio. The Italian Army had surrendered unconditionally in September, and the Italians were now considered 'co-belligerents'. Montgomery did not know exactly what this term meant, and neither did Rizzio. However, since Rizzio was the senior officer in the south of Italy – and a 'co-belligerent' – it seemed to him that he should be the commander of the Allied armies, and that Eighth Army – and General Montgomery – should come under his orders. Monty therefore decided to meet Rizzio, 'to see him quickly and get the matter cleared up before trouble arose'. Montgomery gave no details of the actual meeting, but nothing more was heard of Rizzio's plan to take over Eighth Army.

Between 20 September and the end of the month, Eighth Army pushed north on the Adriatic coast, past Bari and over the Ofanto river to Foggia, heading for the lateral road between

Termoli and Vinchiaturo. The first task was to secure the Plain of
Foggia and those airfields that the RAF and USAAF bomber
commanders were so anxious to use. Foggia was taken on 27
September, the engineers moved in to repair the nearby airfields,
and the advance continued. Ever careful of his supply lines,
which were fully extended and leaving him short of reserves,
Montgomery intended to stop at Termoli to build up stocks of
fuel and ammunition before pushing on to the main east–west
lateral road at Pescara. Once there the intention was to swing
west, follow the road over the Apennines, and so outflank Rome.
'The capture of Rome,' says Montgomery, 'though of little military importance, was stated to be of great political importance
and the city now became the next main Allied objective.'[16]

The advance on Termoli was on a two-division front: 78th
Division on the coast road, Route 16; 1st Canadian Division
through the mountains to Vinchiaturo astride Route 17, ready to
join the Americans in the capture of Naples if that city had not
yet fallen. Troops opposing this move on Termoli came from
strong elements of the 1st Parachute, 29th Panzergrenadier and
26th Panzer Divisions. This move began on the night of 2/3
October with a commando landing by men of the 2nd SS
(Commando) Brigade on the port of Termoli, to secure the crossings over the Biferno river. The commandos got ashore without
difficulty, and a brigade of the 78th Division then landed in support, but then the Germans reacted, sending 16th Panzer over
from the Fifth Army front to retake the town.

The two commandos units, No. 3 (Army) Commando and No.
40 (Royal Marine) Commando with Major Paddy Mayne's
Special Raiding Squadron (SRS) – a total of around 600 men –
were in position inside the town, with the leading elements of
78th Division already across the Biferno, when the German
attack came in – and the Bailey bridge across the river was
quickly destroyed.

Roy Farran of the SRS sent an officer over to the 78th Division
asking for help, and then encountered an infantry brigadier who
assured him, '"Everything is under control, old boy." At that
moment a Spandau started to rake brigade headquarters with a
storm of fire and sent the brigadier diving for cover under an
armoured car. Personally, I did not think matters were at all
under control.'

The enemy pushed hard against the Termoli perimeter, artillery and mortar fire being interspersed with bombing, and by dusk on 3 October German tanks had moved into the town and were within a hundred yards of the commando positions. The next day was taken up with street fighting until the bridge was repaired and the 38th Irish Brigade entered the town. 'I saw them march in,' says Peter Young, then a major in No. 3 Commando, 'and I can recall a young sergeant in one of the rifle companies, leading his section along, the light of battle in his eye. He looked a good type, and I would have had him in 3 Commando given half the chance, but I expect he bought it. Most of the good ones get killed in the end, you know.'[17]

'The battle at Termoli was the only time when I thought we might be defeated,' said Colonel Durnford-Slater of No. 3 Commando, 'and after the operation General Montgomery told me to take the unit back to Bari where, he said, there was plenty of wine and plenty of girls.'[18]

German tanks and panzergrenadiers entered Termoli again on 5 October. British reinforcements could not get forward over the flooded Biferno, bridging proved difficult, and a fierce battle raged at Termoli until 7 October, when another brigade of 78th Division was landed in the British bridgehead. The enemy then fell back to the next river line, the Trigno, 15 miles to the north, and the British prepared to follow up and repeat the process over every other river on the way to Pescara.

This was not to be. Autumn was arriving in southern Italy, the weather was deteriorating, and the Allied advance – so far fairly rapid – was turning into a steady slog over the mountains from one river line to the next; the British Official History states that 'Eighth Army now faced some tactically ugly country.'[19] Nor were matters going any better for the Canadians advancing through the high ground inland, on the axis of Route 17. The Germans were taking full advantage of the ground and making a stand in every mountain village; taking the tiny hamlet of Motta took a full day, taking Vinchiaturo took three full days. Since the Canadians of XIII Corps in the mountains and the 78th Division of V Corps on the coast were steadily drawing apart, the 8th Indian Division of V Corps was sent into the line to clear the heights beyond the Biferno. Eighth Army pressure continued on the Trigno line, and on the night of 27/28 October the

38th Irish Brigade of the 78th Division – the 1st Royal Irish Fusiliers, 6th Inniskilling Fusiliers and 2nd London Irish Rifles – advanced to the river to force a crossing.

The Trigno was a wide river, flowing below high banks and overlooked by German positions on the north bank. A heavy fire was brought down on the Irish battalions, two of the battalion colonels were killed – as well as all the company and platoon commanders in the Royal Irish Fusiliers – the advance was halted with loss, and the troops dug in to hold what little they had gained: a narrow bridgehead on the north bank. Fighting here went on for the next few days, until the sappers made a crossing with bulldozers and tanks of the 46th RTR got across the river on 3 November.

Thus supported, the Irish Brigade advanced again. By mid-morning it was in the railway station at San Stefano, where a German tank attack was driven off, the anti-tank guns of The Buffs knocking out three Mark IVs while the Inniskillings cleared the town. Opposition was provided by the 16th Panzer and 1st Parachute Divisions, and they fought hard for every yard of ground, putting in a constant series of counter-attacks, many with tank support. Nor was it simply that the enemy fought tenaciously for every position: when forced to withdraw, they strewed the countryside with mines and booby traps and left behind small parties of German infantry armed with a new weapon, the tank-busting infantry panzerfaust.

'I don't recall much trouble with the panzerfaust here – that came later, in Normandy,' says Field Marshal Lord Carver, who was then commanding the 1st RTR in 7th Armoured Division, 'but they did have a quantity of small, mobile, anti-tank guns. Italian vines are not arranged like they are in France. In Italy, vines are braced up 10 or 12 feet above the ground on high wires, and from a tank turret you can't see down through them. German gunners or men with a panzerfaust could duck under the vines, deploy their weapons, and still have good cover.'[20]

Fighting on the Trigno line went on until 8 November, and continued steadily after the line had been forced and the 8th Indian Division had driven 16th Panzer back across the Sangro. While this battle was going on, the autumn rain fell steadily, turning the rivers into torrents and the countryside into a sea of mud. Then, on 10 November, the first snows fell on the peaks of the Apennines.

The onset of the Italian winter – a season about which, says Major Fred Majdalany, the Italian Tourist Board tends to be reticent – compensated the Germans for the Allies' current superiority in manpower. The Allies now had 14 divisions in Italy while the Germans had just 9 manning these successive defence lines in the south. On the other hand, the Germans had another 14 divisions above Rome, and some of these could come south if the situation grew critical. Besides, a 14-to-9 divisional ratio between attacker and defender was by no means adequate when fighting in terrain where tanks could be employed only with difficulty and air support declined with the arrival of winter weather. Alexander would not get more troops: the growing American concerns about OVERLORD, now six months away, would oblige the Allied commanders in Italy to manage with what troops they had – and not even all those would be allowed to remain.

Expectations of rapid advances up the Italian peninsula were still high. Commenting on a forecast by General Alexander in October 1943, Churchill wondered, 'Is he really not contemplating being in Rome until January or February?' The Chiefs of Staff replied that it might be possible to take Rome before Christmas without an amphibious landing, but should such a landing prove necessary, the city might not be taken until January. Rome did not actually fall until June 1944, and the Official History's comment that 'It seems doubtful whether anyone in high places fully understood what a winter campaign in Italy implied' seems all too accurate – if blessed with hindsight.

Nor were the weather and manpower the only problems. The shortage of landing craft which had inhibited the Salerno operation had worsened, and those outflanking seaborne landings that had helped the Allied armies forward so often in the past – most recently at Termoli – were now only a remote possibility. The only way forward was by battering a path up both coasts, over the rivers, and through the mountains – and the enemy – a method that was sure to be slow and most costly in lives. This battering was duly undertaken, and carried Eighth Army forward to the next river line on the Sangro, which the 78th Division had pushed patrols across by 22 November. Here the 2nd New Zealand Division arrived from Egypt at the end of November and went into the line on the left flank, close to the mountains.

The Sangro, swollen with rain, was now 4 to 6 feet deep, fast flowing below banks 12 feet high and about 100 yards wide. These features alone made it a formidable position, but something worse lay beyond the river, where open country stretched for 2 miles to a high escarpment. This gave total observation over the river plain, and the top was crowned by the village of Fossacesia near the coast and by the villages of Santa Maria and Mozzagrogna 4 miles inland. All three were German strongpoints, and the plain was thickly sown with mines and covered by guns and mortars. Even so, it was here, close to the coast, that General Montgomery elected to cross the river and play his part in breaching the German 'Winter Line' – that series of defensive positions that straddled Italy from along the Garigliano close to the town of Cassino in the west, across the central mountains to the Sangro and the Adriatic.

This Winter Line, parts of which were also called the Gustav or Helene Line, had been created by German engineers and thousands of Italian forced workers, who had laboured with picks, shovels and explosives to create a defensive belt across the peninsula, miles deep in places, well wired, studded with pillboxes, dug-in tanks and guns, and strewn with anti-tank and anti-personnel mines – the latter including thousands of the wooden-cased, hard-to-sweep schu mine, which could blow off a man's foot. 'This line', says Eric Linklater, 'was no mere check line but the inner doors of the fortress of Italy, locked and barred.'[21] Fortunately, on the Sangro front this line was not yet complete, but four German divisions – 16th and 26th Panzer, 29th Panzergrenadier and 1st Parachute Divisions – grouped into LXXVI Panzer Corps, stood ready here to stem Eighth Army's advance.

Montgomery ordered XIII Corps to press hard on the left flank while the main attack would be made by V Corps, which was to close up on the Sangro and send in the 8th Indian and 78th British Divisions, supported by the 4th Armoured Brigade while the New Zealanders and the Canadians pushed on to the towns of Orsogna and Ortona respectively.

Eric Garner again:

To my mind, and that of most people in Eighth Army, the Sangro was a 78th Division battle with great support from 8th Indian

Division or the 2nd New Zealand Division. The critical point was to secure and bridge the passage of Route 16, the only road in the region capable of handling a full division. About 1,000 feet of bridge and abutments had been blown, and the whole area was mined and under artillery observation. On 21 November five battalions of 78th Division crossed the river and we got a 140 foot Bailey across the main stream.

On the next day 4th Armoured Brigade and 11th Infantry Brigade got over, and then the river rose and the Bailey bridge submerged. By 30 November 78th Division had captured the La Colli ridge and was halfway to San Vito, which it captured on 3 December and moved on to the Moro. The brunt of this Sangro battle was taken by 78th Division – the best British division in Italy. The New Zealand Division was new to Italy at this time and had still to adapt to the conditions – which it did very quickly.[22]

Brigadier Howard Kippenberger of the 5th Brigade 2nd New Zealand Division writes about the situation on his front:

There were high hopes of a quick success, a rapid advance to Pescara and thence a move on Rome through the Apennines. The actual Sangro crossing would be done by companies in single file, the men hanging on to ropes fastened to posts driven in on either bank. Supporting arms would not be able to cross until the Bailey bridge to be thrown across in 6 Brigade's sector was completed and as it was improbable that 19 Regiment's tanks would find a way over there might be a difficult period.

The New Zealanders crossed the Sangro with very little trouble. 'All went smoothly enough', writes Kippenberger:

Both battalions waded across, some of the companies shoulder deep in the icy water. The 23rd Battalion got established with only ten casualties and the 21st had some trouble getting up the bluffs but was well handled and before long was on its objective with only 21 casualties. We also had 80 prisoners of the 65th Division . . . generally it was a satisfactory and surprisingly-easy little affair.

The experience and professionalism of the 2nd New Zealand Division contributed to this outcome on the Sangro, but this happy experience did not last. The 8th Indian Division, which had attacked at Mozzagrogna, was soon held up, the enemy counter-attacking with tanks and flame-throwers. As related, the 78th Division forced a crossing over the river, but it was unable to establish a Bailey bridge for tanks, as the banks of the river were so wet the earth would not take the weight. As Linklater remarks, Eighth Army's plan to get up to Pescara and turn west 'did not fructify. On the Adriatic side the villainous weather broke and released the full spate and malignity of winter before the Indians could move, and that was the first mishap.'[23]

Winter had arrived in Italy, and the weather would dominate events for the next few months. But the Sangro was crossed, and the Winter Line was breached on the Adriatic front by 30 November. Eighth Army's advance continued, slowly and painfully, to the strongpoints of Orsogna and Ortona – the first in the mountains, the second on the coast – while the rain and sleet beat steadily down, the rivers rose in spate, the countryside became a swamp, and the condition of the front-line soldiers was pitiable.

The advancing British, Canadians and New Zealanders were facing considerable opposition. To add to the increasing problems caused by rain, mud and mines, panzer troops from two divisions, 16th and 26th Panzer, and soldiers of the redoubtable 1st Parachute Division – allegedly the finest division in the German Army – were now manning the Adriatic front with 88-mms, self-propelled guns, and plenty of mortars and machine-gun fire.

The New Zealand attack on Orsogna, spearheaded by the Maori battalions and supported by Kittybombers of the Desert Air Force and tanks, went well at first and the New Zealanders soon had two battalions in the town. That night the Germans counter-attacked with tanks and flame-throwers, and pushed them out again. Then the New Zealanders' difficulties really began: it proved impossible for their supporting tanks to get forward, and equally impossible to manhandle 6-pounder anti-tank guns up to help the Maoris who had occupied a spur north of the town but were in urgent need of supply and support. The Maoris beat off several attacks, but their position became untenable and they were ordered to withdraw – and found it very difficult to evacuate their wounded down the slopes.

The attack on Orsogna was renewed next day, when the divisional engineers bridged the next river, the Moro, and got behind the Orsogna position: Then more heavy rain fell and the ground became a quagmire, hopeless for tanks. The New Zealanders battled for Orsogna for over a month, from the end of November until the beginning of January 1944, fighting in terrible conditions, the men soaked to the skin and plastered with mud, and casualties mounting steadily. Then they heard they were to move west across the Apennines to Fifth Army. 'We heard welcome talk of a move,' writes Kippenberger. 'We had lost interest in the Adriatic coast and after all we had failed to take Orsogna, our first failure and we were tired of looking at it all day.'[24]

While the New Zealanders were fighting in and around Orsogna, the 1st Canadian Division was engaged in the fight for Ortona – a battle that was to become *the* street-fighting epic of the Second World War. Before it arrived at Ortona, a coastal town with 10,000 inhabitants, 15 miles north of the Sangro, the Canadian Division, now commanded by Major-General Vokes, had already endured plenty of fighting. It crossed the Moro, just south of Ortona, to the sound of heavy demolitions; while the Canadians were battering their way up the coast, the Germans were turning Ortona into a strongpoint.

Even getting up to Ortona proved difficult. The Moro had to be crossed and various ridges captured, all against opposition from the 90th Panzergrenadiers and elements of 26th Panzer and 1st Parachute Divisions. The Division finally arrived before Ortona on 20 December – the 19th Indian Brigade moving on to attack Tollo further north – and the task of reducing Ortona was handed to the 2nd Canadian Infantry Brigade.

The advance into Ortona was led by the Loyal Edmonton Regiment and the Seaforth Highlanders of Canada – and they ran into opposition within a few yards of their start line. Piles of rubble blocked the streets, impeding the progress of tanks, and houses demolished by German sappers provided perfect cover for snipers and panzerfaust teams. The Germans had devoted a great deal of effort and ingenuity to the defences of Ortona. The piles of rubble exposed the bellies of tanks to anti-tank guns or panzerfausts as the tanks climbed over them. Booby traps abounded – some of them massive: an entire platoon of

Canadians was lost when the house it was in blew up. Apparent
paths through the rubble-strewn streets were snares, leading the
advancing Canadians into ambushes, and from every house and
cellar machine-guns and mortars took their toll.

Victor Bulger of the 1st Regiment Royal Canadian Horse
Artillery (RCHA) supplies an account of Ortona:

> The Royal 22nd Regiment – the 'Van Doos' – had first to capture
> Casa Berardi, a farm, and then move on to the crossroads on the
> Ortona–Orsogna road. Unknown to General Vokes, this area had
> been reinforced by 1st Parachute, the cream of the German Army.
> The battle started on 14 December with a tremendous artillery
> barrage, and 'C' Company – 81 all ranks plus 7 tanks – moved off.
> They were met after a few hundred yards by four Jerry tanks and
> a company of infantry. In the subsequent fighting 'C' Company
> was reduced to 50 men and they were now outnumbered ten to
> one, but they stayed in position until by noon that day only 30
> men were left.
>
> Captain Trinquet of 'C' Company reported that 'We're sur-
> rounded, the enemy is in front of us, behind us and on our
> flanks – the safest place is on the objective.' Heavy fighting went
> on all that day as more troops came up and joined the battle – a
> house-to-house struggle with the Jerry 1st Parachute Division.
> From 12 to 18 December, the RCHA guns fired over 20,000
> rounds, and on the 18th over 9,000 rounds – a record for the
> regiment. The total expenditure of artillery ammunition from 20
> November until 20 December was over 80,000 rounds, most of
> it after 6 December.
>
> The 1st Canadian Division advanced 3 miles from the Moro to
> beyond Ortona at staggering cost. The terrain along the route was
> a wasteland of shell-torn trees, wrecked houses, dead animals,
> and the bodies of troops, both Canadian and German, waiting for
> burial. Our RCHA had 34 killed, wounded or captured – includ-
> ing seven battery captains – in the fight for Ortona.[25]

The Canadians took Ortona the only way it could be taken:
street by street, house by house, room by room. It took them a full
week, right over Christmas, without a pause in the fighting. It
was not until 28 December that a patrol of the Princess Patricia's
Canadian Light Infantry broke out of the town and moved north
to make contact with the 48th Highlanders of Canada, who had
been battering their way north, west of the town.

'After Ortona,' says Fred Majdalany, 'the Canadians became the acknowledged experts in street fighting. For the rest of the war officers who had fought at Ortona toured the Allied military schools, lecturing on this subject. Ortona is a small piece of Canadian history. But it was the end of Eighth Army's efforts to break through on the Adriatic front.'

Montgomery's drive for Pescara had been prepared and mounted with all his usual skill and attention to detail, and Eighth Army deployed all its power in the attempt to get forward. But it was stopped – defeated even – not by the enemy but by the climate and, most of all, by the terrain. The front was narrow, and the physical obstacles continuous. As the war correspondent Christopher Buckley wrote, 'Our men battled across the Sangro, but behind the Sangro was the Moro and behind the Moro was the Foro and behind the Foro was the Pescara . . . and that was without the problems of Orsogna and Ortona.'

Nor was this all. At the end of 1943 Montgomery was ordered to hand over command of Eighth Army to Lieutenant-General Sir Oliver Leese. Montgomery was to return to England and take command of the Allied ground forces for Operation OVERLORD. As a rule, troops are not too worried about who occupies the remote post of Army Commander. Many private soldiers do not even know the name of their brigade commander. But Montgomery was different. Eighth Army was very much Monty's Army; he had done well by the soldiers since he took command in the summer of 1942, and they repaid his care and attention with a devotion that the decades since the Second World War – and constant attempts to denigrate him, both as an officer and as a gentleman – have done little to change.

Nor was this a one-sided affection, as this passage from Monty's final message makes clear:

It is difficult to express to you adequately what this parting means to me. I am leaving officers and men who have been my comrades during months of hard and victorious fighting and whose courage and devotion to duty have filled me with admiration. I feel I have many friends among the soldiery of this great Army. I do not know if you will miss me, but I will miss you more than I can say and especially will I miss the personal contacts and cheerful greetings we exchanged when we passed each other on the road.

What can I say to you as I go away? When the heart is full, it is not easy to speak. But I would say this to you. You have made Eighth Army what it is. You have made its name a household word all over the world. You must uphold its good name and traditions. And I would ask you to give my successor the same loyal and devoted service you have never failed to give to me.

1 *Free French Div.*

12

Cassino

January–March 1944

Before the war there were posters on all British railway stations, every winter: 'Come to Sunny Italy.' You don't want to know what the sappers said about that in the Italian winter of 1943–4.

Sergeant Eric Garner, 754th Field Squadron, Royal Engineers,
Eighth Army

Lieutenant-General Sir Oliver Leese, the new commander of Eighth Army, was a guardsman. Commissioned into the Coldstream Guards at the outbreak of the First World War, he was a platoon commander during the 1916 Battle of the Somme and ended the war with the MC and a DSO, having been wounded three times. The inter-war years were spent in the usual British Army pattern, rotating between regimental service and various staff appointments with a slow but steady rise in rank. Leese took part in the campaign which ended at Dunkirk in 1940, and a year later was promoted to major-general and charged with raising and commanding the Guards Armoured Division.

During this time he met General Montgomery. Monty must have seen Leese's potential for Leese was one of the officers summoned to take over senior commands in Eighth Army in 1942. Promoted to lieutenant-general in command of XXX Corps

before Alamein, Leese remained in command of XXX Corps
throughout the North African and Sicily campaigns. He
returned to Britain in August 1943, but Montgomery never
forgot a friend (or an enemy), and, when the time came for
Monty to leave Eighth Army, Leese was sent out to replace him.

Leese therefore came to the command of Eighth Army with a
useful blend of experience. Having fought as an infantryman
throughout one hard war, raised an armoured division in the
next one – though he never led it in action – and seen useful service as a senior commander in some of the hardest campaigns
from 1940 to 1943, he had all the necessary qualifications. As a
bonus, he knew Eighth Army, in which he was a popular and
well-respected figure. If the troops had to lose Monty, Oliver
Leese would do them very well.

Whether Leese was entirely successful as an army commander
is another matter, and there is some evidence that he reached his
peak commanding a corps. And, in spite of many attempts,
Leese does not seem to have captured the hearts of his soldiers,
as Donald Featherstone of the 51st RTR relates:

> It is difficult to tell you anything about the ethos of Eighth Army
> at this time – early 1944. We just carried on like the other units did
> in those days – same jokes, same background, etc. Monty had
> gone and General Leese was now commanding Eighth Army,
> who I don't think impressed us very much. Monty was an
> extremely good commander in my opinion, although he had
> many personality quirks that have been remembered more than
> his deeds.[1]

Montgomery was a hard act to follow. Although Alexander
remained satisfied with Leese's performance, Alan Brooke, the
CIGS, was less certain and came to feel that Leese lacked grip
and failed to push Eighth Army in the later stages of the battle
for Rome. The general feeling that arises from reports of his time
in command of Eighth Army is that Leese had been promoted
above his level of ability and was never likely to give Eighth
Army the leadership it required. When he left he was not missed,
and his later tenure of high command in the Far East was short
and unsuccessful. For the moment, however, Leese had Eighth
Army; it remained to be seen what he would do with it.

Taking up his command on New Year's Day 1944, he arrived

at a difficult time. Eighth Army had always been a cosmopolitan force, but previously the majority of the units had come from the UK or the Empire; now it became ever more diverse. Eighth Army now included Lieutenant-General C. W. Allfrey's V Corps, Lieutenant-General S. C. Kirkman's veteran XIII Corps, a Polish Corps – actually two light divisions, each of two brigades – the Canadian Corps, and a mixture of divisions that included the splendid 2nd New Zealand Division, the veteran 4th Indian Division, and the 5th and 78th British Divisions, formerly of First Army – plus units of South African troops.

These were all fine units – the Polish Corps was especially noted among the new arrivals – but the chronic problems of command, communication and training, which had always plagued Eighth Army, were not eased by the need to control such a varied force in the very middle of a hard campaign. Nor was this all: already stalled on the moribund Adriatic front, Leese was soon to see large parts of his army sent across the Apennines to help Fifth Army in the six-month long struggle for Cassino.

The Italian campaign was not going well in the early months of 1944. Kesselring now had 21 divisions opposing the Allied 18. Most of these German divisions were either deployed along the deep defences of the Gustav Line, concentrating at Cassino, or constructing more defence lines in the north of Italy and before Rome. Therefore, before we can follow the Eighth Army units and Eighth Army itself into the various battles at Cassino, it is necessary yet again to go back a little and take a brief look at the progress of Clark's Fifth Army since the fall of Naples.

After breaking off the battle at Salerno, General von Vietinghoff withdrew by stages to the Volturno, ordering the Allied advance to be delayed with demolitions and various defence lines in order to give his troops time to develop a major defensive line north of the Volturno, running from the Garigliano river in the west to the Sangro in the east – the Winter Line. For the next few weeks the Germans fell back steadily from river to river, from one defensive line to the next, delaying pursuit while taking a steady toll of their Anglo-American pursuers. The aim of this delaying action was to give the defenders of the Gustav Line – the main part of the Winter Line – time to thicken their defences at Cassino.

During the autumn and early winter of 1943–4 Fifth Army

endured all the travails then being inflicted on Eighth Army on the Adriatic front. The advance continued, but slowly. It took Clark's men three weeks to cover the 30 miles from Salerno to the Volturno, where Fifth Army arrived on 5 October. It then took another nine days to get across the river, the actual crossing taking two days, from 12 to 14 October. Once across the Volturno, while every attempt was made to broaden the front, the axis of advance narrowed to one road, Route 6, once the Roman Via Casilina, the main road between Naples and Rome, on which every bridge was broken, every river flooded, every verge and field mined.

Captain D. H Deane of the 3rd Battalion Scots Guards provides some diary accounts of this time:

18 January 1944
Early reveille. Moving off in trucks with our hearts in our mouths. Along dreary roads of destruction, with blood wagons coming the other way. Turn off to debussing area and wait – wait interminably it seems, as no one knows what for. At last move off and march for equally long time, troops absolutely whacked. Cross the Garigliano in sinister silence. A very pretty American girl is dishing up coffee to the ambulance drivers. I wonder if we look heroic, filing away into the darkness. More marching for about 10 miles, and arrive in a field with damn all to shelter us from the cold.

11 February
The nastiest day of my life – perhaps. Moved off in pelting rain, knowing we would have to move out of the shelter of the trench once we had crossed the river. The rain was torrential, and we were soaked to the skin before we started to climb the white 'safe line' tape, waiting here and looking at the ominous graves all around. No one knows where we were when we arrived to take over from the Northants, who fled, leaving us with dugouts caving in, four dead Germans, all trenches filled with water, and a 'Good Luck' from the one leading them – a sergeant. Last night was horrible. We had to dig the trenches to suit our size, and as we dug the water poured in and the dead Germans smelled ever more evil. George then arrived and insisted that one section dig in on the skyline. The moon had risen in all its glory and, when we started digging, down came the stonk, wounding Guardsman Kelly in the chest quite badly. I gave him morphia and Corporal

Above Egos collide: General Montgomery and General George Patton confer over their maps in Sicily, 1943

Right Charismatic and popular, but not always decisive: General Sir Harold Alexander in Italy, 1943

General Bernard Montgomery, Commander of Eighth Army, and American Lieutenant-General Mark Clark, Commander of the Anglo-American-French Fifth Army, make an inspection tour of the forward positions on the Italian front, 1943

German Field Marshal Albert Kesselring, commander of Nazi forces in Italy, with an officer and a camouflaged soldier on the Cassino front

The Italian winter and the enemy unite against the Allies: British infantry pass a bogged-down Sherman tank on the Sangro river front, 1943

The Cassino front, February 1944. The rocky terrain and the dominant position of the abbey are clear

The devastation of Monte Cassino begins: bombs fall on Cassino town,
February 1944

Heavy bombing and shelling create fresh obstacles for the infantry: New Zealand
soldiers in Cassino, 1944

After the fall of Cassino the cost is clear: Polish dead on the Cassino battlefield, May 1944

Above left Il Duce is not always right: Scottish infantry and Canadian armour meet in Italy, 1943

Below left Eighth Army was an Empire Army: Indian Troops at Cassino, March 1944

On their way to the Po Valley and the distant Alps, the 6th Iniskilling Fusiliers advance to the attack, Italy 1944

Watson took charge very competently. Shelled continuously until Left Flank Company brought down a colossal barrage on themselves, wounding eight.[2]

Out of the line, on the Adriatic front, matters were more relaxed, as Sergeant Victor Bulger of the Royal Canadian Horse Artillery relates:

> I was a gun sergeant in B Battery, RCHA, with the 1st Canadian Division. We had fired several shoots using supercharge cartridges, and the recoil system of our 25-pounders needed repacking and I was told to take the gun back to the RCEME workshops for repair but to be back as soon as possible as a big attack was pending. We located the workshop south of San Vito, and they got working on the gun until the RSM laid on a parade for the men and told them they would be working on their saluting drill. One of their sergeants said, 'Tell the RSM that if we stay off parade we can finish this gun today and you can get back to your unit.' We could hear heavy firing and I knew that our gun would be needed, so I went to the RSM and passed on the message. The RSM looked down at me and said, 'Sonny Boy, this war has been going on for more than three years, and the way I figure it, one gun won't make any bloody difference. Tell those honkers to get on parade.'
>
> In my case it meant that we would have another night's sleep in safety without going into the line with the gun, but I mention this to show that the army in the rear worked nine to five with an hour and a half for lunch, while the men in the front line worked 24 hours a day and caught their meals and sleep when they could. The repairs were finished next day, and we went back to our battery.[3]

The rain fell relentlessly day after day, the weather was bitterly cold, the ground was sown with mines, every house was booby-trapped. The enemy had to be levered out of every position but on both sides of the Apennines the biggest obstacle to progress was now the weather. The various battles fought by Fifth Army at this time – from Salerno to Naples, over the Volturno, and through the Mignano Gap to the Garigliano and Rapido – fall outside the scope of this book, but the aim of all this fighting on the Fifth Army front was to reach the entrance to the Liri valley which led north to Rome. The snag was that the door to the Liri valley had a lock on it – Cassino. To break that lock would require the full efforts of both Allied armies.

Cassino – town, mountain and monastery – had been a bastion against any attack on the Eternal City from the south since the time of the Byzantines. To the natural defences of the Cassino position – steep rocky hillsides covered with prickly pear and scrub and seamed with crevices; the linking of the Liri with the Rapido to form the Garigliano, all three rivers sending flood waters across the valley floor – the enemy had added all that ingenuity and experience could provide in the way of fortification.

The trees and undergrowth had been cleared to make fields of fire, millions of mines had been sown; every gully had been laced with wire; trenches and strongpoints had been blasted out of solid rock; machine-guns, artillery and mortars – including the multi-barrelled nebelwerfers – had been brought up and concealed; and tanks and tank turrets had been buried in the ground and in the houses of the town to create steel pillboxes. This combination created what was arguably the strongest defensive position confronting any army anywhere during the Second World War – and certainly the strongest defensive position in western Europe.

The centre of this position was the town of Cassino and the hills immediately around it. One of these hills was crowned with the ruins of a medieval fort – and therefore known as Castle Hill – another with that marvellous Renaissance gem the great monastery of Monte Cassino, built on a site chosen by St Benedict in AD 529 as the mother house of the Benedictine order. The monastery of Monte Cassino was occupied by a community of Benedictines who were still going about their religious duties in the winter of 1943–4 as German troops began to fortify the surrounding terrain and the sound of gunfire announced the gradual approach of the Allied armies.

This was not a new experience for Monte Cassino; dominating the road to Rome, the monastery had been at the centre of wars before. Monte Cassino had been totally destroyed by invading armies in AD 581 and again in AD 883. In 1349 the abbey was destroyed in an earthquake, and in 1503 the Spanish Grand Captain Gonzalo de Cordoba was prevented from destroying it again only when St Benedict appeared to him in a dream and talked him out of it. No such intervention was likely to happen this time. When the Allied armies came up to the Rapido valley and met the German forces of the XIV Panzer Corps under

General von Senger und Etterlin, the new defenders of the road to Rome, Monte Cassino – historic, beautiful and symbolic – would find itself at the epicentre of modern war, with all its destructive power.

By January 1944 the Allied strategic position was clear but complicated. All eyes in Washington and London were now fixed on OVERLORD, the Allied invasion of France, which was now just six months away. Eisenhower and Montgomery, who were to play a leading part in that operation, had already left to take up their new appointments and would shortly be followed by the US 82nd Airborne and the British 7th Armoured, 51st (Highland) and 50th (Northumbrian) Divisions, all destined to make their next appearance on the battlefields of France. The surrender of Italy in September had also inspired Churchill to urge yet more ventures in the eastern Mediterranean – in the Dodecanese at Rhodes, Leros and Cos: Italian-held islands close to the Turkish shore – but rapid German intervention had disarmed the Italian garrisons, often with loss, and then defeated the British attempts to obtain a lodgement.

The command structure in the Mediterranean had also changed. General Sir Henry Maitland Wilson had taken over the post of Supreme Allied Commander from Eisenhower, though Alexander remained in charge of 15th Army Group – or, as it soon became, the Allied Armies in Italy (AAI). The major problem facing Maitland Wilson at AFHQ was what to do about the winter stalemate on the Italian front. Clearly any solution to that problem on the Gustav Line at Cassino depended on some form of amphibious landing, to outflank the German defences and get the war in Italy moving again. That solution was in turn inhibited by the chronic problem of the Mediterranean campaign: a shortage of landing craft, especially LSTs (landing ships, tank).

A shortage of landing craft – or the unwillingness of Admiral King to supply them to the European theatre – and arguments over the employment of those landing craft currently in that theatre still continued. It is one of the great ironies of the Second World War that the conduct of the main Allied campaign in 1943 and early 1944, before the launching of OVERLORD, was seriously inhibited by the lack of fewer than 100 LSTs.

The Mediterranean campaign needed a permanent fleet of landing craft. It was not simply a question of putting troops, tanks and trucks ashore in the initial invasion: once ashore, these had to be supplied and supported, and the amount of amphibious lift available, certainly in January 1944, was not enough to guarantee the success of the proposed plan for outflanking the Gustav Line, Operation SHINGLE, a landing behind the Gustav Line at a point close to Rome – Anzio.

Since landing in Sicily the Allies had often used amphibious landings to outflank the enemy defences and move the land front forward. Given the nature of the ground and the absence of strong naval and air opposition – though there was opposition, in as much strength as the enemy could muster – such landings made good strategic sense. With regular training and growing experience, the Allied armies and navies were getting good at amphibious operations, but these could not be mounted without the craft.

The aim of Operation SHINGLE was simple. Clark would send VI Corps – half US, half British – ashore at Anzio to create a bridgehead behind the Gustav Line, threaten Rome, and inhibit the movement of supplies to the German troops around Cassino. This growing force would quickly compel a German withdrawal from the Gustav Line, leading to a rapid link up of the two Allied forces and the fall of the Italian capital – with all the political benefits that would then accrue. There was absolutely nothing wrong with the Allied strategy.

The SHINGLE plan called for a phased operation. In the first phase, to be mounted on 17 January, the British X Corps of Fifth Army would force a crossing of the Garigliano and turn east to threaten the left side of the Liri valley. Three days later the US II Corps would cross the Rapido 5 miles south of Cassino and head directly towards the Liri valley. At the same time General A. P. Juin's Free French Expeditionary Corps – which was trained in mountain warfare and equipped with mules for mountain supply, and was now part of Clark's Fifth Army – would strike into the hills north of Cassino and turn left towards the right side of the Liri valley, cutting behind the monastery. Attacked frontally and on both flanks, Cassino – hills, town and monastery – would quickly fall.

This would not be achieved without some days of heavy fighting, but during this time the second phase would begin at Anzio. Two days after II Corps attacked at Cassino, the US VI Corps, consisting of the British 1st Division and the US 3rd Division, under Lieutenant-General John P. Lucas, would land at Anzio and move inland towards Route 7 and Route 6, cutting the two main roads to Rome. Under such a double blow, the Germans must retreat and Cassino must fall. If Cassino fell, the road to Rome up the Liri valley would be wide open for an advance by Fifth Army.

It was not to work out like that. The Anzio landings on 22 January 1944, went well at first, the troops getting ashore in the face of negligible opposition and advancing towards the Alban Hills. Then, for some still disputed reason, their advance stalled. The most likely explanation is that, after VI Corps's experience of encountering strong and rapid German resistance on the beach at Salerno, Lucas elected to build up his position close to the shore before advancing inland; Lucas might have done this anyway, but he was also advised to do so by Clark, who thereby contradicted Alexander's specific orders to push inland. As a result, instead of gaining ground towards the Alban Hills and threatening enemy communications with the Gustav Line – which was the very purpose of SHINGLE – the Allied troops at Anzio dug in to await a counter-attack.

This was not long in coming. Realizing what was happening, Kesselring did not panic. Although the Anzio landing was a complete surprise, he mustered troops, sealed off the Anzio bridgehead, brought up heavy artillery, and subjected the Allied troops in the bridgehead to a pounding siege that would last until the first days of June. Within a week of the landing, three and a half Allied divisions in the beachhead were being contained by five German divisions. The result was another stalemate.

Churchill, heavily committed to a successful Italian campaign, complained bitterly that he had 'hoped to fling a wildcat ashore and had ended up with a stranded whale', but that was only half the problem. SHINGLE had been intended to unlock the door to Rome at Cassino. Now that door must be forced open, so that troops from Cassino could get up and relieve the troops penned in the Anzio bridgehead.

Matters did not go much better in the first phase of the operation at Cassino. What later came to be called the First Battle of Cassino began well when the British X Corps made a successful night crossing of the Garigliano on 17 January, five days before the Anzio landing, and established a small but firm bridgehead beyond the river. Juin's French Expeditionary Corps also did fairly well, though neither force was able to penetrate the enemy positions in depth and get as far as the mountainous walls of the Liri valley. Disaster came on 20 January, when the US II Corps launched the 36th Division in an assault across the Rapido.

The attempted Rapido crossing was an expensive failure. The river was high, the banks were mined, the enemy was alert, and the American assault never stood a chance of success. The attack was pressed home with great resolution and much courage, but with a total lack of progress. After two days the US 36th Division – a National Guard (Territorial) formation from Texas – was back on the south side of the river, having lost 1,681 men, of whom over half were missing. For a while the 36th Division was reduced to just one infantry regiment – three battalions – and the remnants of six other battalions of the 141st and 143rd Infantry Regiments, both of which had been chewed to pieces in the German defences.

The soldiers of this battered division were not in a good humour after the Rapido battle. They felt the attack had been badly handled, and their ire did not decline with the passage of time. After the war, the 36th Division Association demanded an official inquiry into this attack and the plans and actions of General Clark. The inquiry completely vindicated Clark, who can hardly be blamed for a whole catalogue of disasters in an operation that had been mounted far too quickly in order to help the landings at Anzio – which in turn had gone ahead too rapidly because the landing craft which took the troops ashore were already tasked for OVERLORD and were due to be sent to the UK.

On 24 January, two days after the Rapido disaster, Clark ordered the remaining division of II Corps, the 34th Infantry Division, to attack to the north of Cassino and force its way into the mountains above and behind the town. Since the Rapido could be forded north of Cassino, the 34th Division was at least spared some of the agonies that had ravaged the 36th Division, but otherwise there was little to choose between the two assault areas. The 34th Division got across the river successfully, and, although its left-flank assault was repulsed at the old Italian barracks just north of Cassino town, the right-flank elements got up into the hills above the town and in six days of terrible fighting – some of it in snow flurries – took the mountain village of Cairo, 5 miles north of the monastery.

This battering on the Cassino front by the British X Corps, the US II Corps and the Free French Expeditionary Corps, all of Fifth Army, went on for several weeks in the most terrible winter weather. As it continued, it gradually became apparent to the army commanders that the key to the entire Cassino position was not the town but Monastery Hill. The hill, which dominated the entire area – and was crowned by the monastery – was the objective that had to be taken.

Monastery Hill is surrounded by various other hills – including the Colle San Angelo, Point 445 and Point 569 (the last two named from their height in metres) – but the most obvious way to the monastery lay along a narrow steep-sided ridge known as Snakeshead Ridge, which is shaped rather like a boomerang and dominated at the elbow by Point 593. From 24 January to 11 February the US 34th Division tore itself to pieces trying to take Cassino town and Point 593, and was unable to do so. This was in spite of displaying a courage and tenacity that excited the admiration of the Allied armies, not least that of Major-General Howard Kippenberger, now commanding the 2nd New Zealand Division – a unit that knew all there was to know about infantry warfare, and that was now about to take up the struggle at Cassino.

'The Americans had battled since January with a stubbornness and gallantry that was beyond all praise but they were fought out,' wrote Kippenberger. 'Some of the 18 battalions in the line had lost 80 per cent of their effectives and they were utterly exhausted.'[4] This was especially true of the units in the mountains; when the troops of the 4th Indian Division, the second unit in Freyberg's newly formed New Zealand Corps, took over the US positions on Snakeshead Ridge, they had to evacuate many half-frozen American soldiers on stretchers.

The first month of fighting for this mountain bridgehead cost the 34th Infantry Division more than 2,000 men. In return, the Americans had gained a bridgehead in the hills above the Rapido, but there were two snags with it. First, this bridgehead was difficult to supply: everything had to be taken up by mule or porters, under shell and machine-gun fire all the way there and back – a distance of some 7 miles. Second, the Germans at Cassino were strengthening their defences all the time as these early Allied attacks revealed weaknesses or suggested improvements. As winter gripped the mountains and the Allied troops grew weary, the German defences at Cassino grew stronger rather than weaker.

By early February the soldiers of the US II Corps had fought themselves to a standstill and the time had come for someone else to have a go. With VI Corps locked up at Anzio, reinforcements could only come from Eighth Army. Therefore, on 3 February 1944 two divisions of Eighth Army – the 2nd New Zealand and 4th Indian – were formed into the New Zealand Corps under Freyberg and brought over from the moribund Adriatic front to take up the battle for Cassino. The war east of the Apennines would be left to Allfrey's V Corps and the rest of General Leese's much reduced force, while the New Zealand Corps was attached to Fifth Army for what came to be called the Second and Third Battles of Cassino.

The account which follows is a diversion from the original aim of restricting this story to the exploits of Eighth Army as an army. I believe this is justified on two grounds. First, these units would return to Eighth Army when their work at Cassino was done; their shift to the Fifth Army was a temporary attachment. Second, two of these divisions – the 2nd New Zealand and the 4th Indian Divisions – were old desert formations, units which had marched with Eighth Army since before Alamein. To leave these divisions now, as they go into their last great fight, is beyond me. A final point is that the British Official History (Vol 5) also devotes considerable space to the operations of British units in the Fifth Army, and it would distort this history to concentrate on the moribund Adriatic front while these famous Eighth Army units were involved in the bitter fighting at Cassino. Of the four battles at Cassino, the second and third were fought by Eighth Army divisions attached to Fifth Army, and Eighth Army, transferred in full from the Adriatic front, played the major role in the fourth and final battle.

The New Zealand Corps took over from the US II Corps at Cassino on 12 February, and began preparations for the next attack by taking over the positions of the 34th Division. Among the troops arriving was Sergeant D. L. Garven of 'C' Squadron, 19th Battalion Armoured Regiment:

The New Zealand Division started arriving at Cassino on 4 February. This was the first time we had had our own armour, and the 4th Brigade was equipped with Sherman tanks. The weather was very bleak and it rained continually, which deferred our attack for a week or so, and when the Maoris attacked our unit was not able to support them, because it was impossible to get forward over the sodden ground. We still went forward to contact the Americans, in our case the 756th US Tank Battalion, and the relief was completed. In the next three weeks we remained in full view of the monastery and Monte Cairo, and the regiment received a lot of attention from German guns and aircraft, causing several casualties – though fortunately a lot of German shells turned out to be duds or did not explode in the soft ground. The monastery was bombed on 15 February.[5]

Freyberg's plan for his assault on 15 February was simple. The New Zealanders would take Cassino town. The Indians would first take over the positions occupied by the 34th Division in the mountains above the town and would then press on down Snakeshead Ridge to take the monastery. That done, they would press on down Monastery Hill to Route 6 and the Liri valley, opening the door for the advance of an American armoured division. As a first step in this plan, General Freyberg wanted the destruction – the obliteration – of the monastery of Monte Cassino.

The bombing of the monastery of Monte Cassino on 15 February 1944 was one of the most controversial actions of the Italian campaign. It was seen by many, at the time and since, as an act of wanton destruction that had no military purpose whatsoever and may even have improved the enemy's defensive capability. Since accounts of how this bombing was ordered vary, it is necessary to trace the progress of this controversial decision step by step.

The story begins with Major-General Francis Tuker of the 4th Indian Division. Having observed the monastery and heard from the US troops he was relieving that Monastery Hill was the key to the position, Tuker went into Naples and found a book which described the monastery's construction in some detail. This book stressed that, whatever its religious purposes, the monastery of Monte Cassino was also a fortress. This being so, General Tuker sent a request to his corps commander, General Freyberg: the monastery-fortress of Monte Cassino must be reduced by heavy bombers.

The crux of the argument surrounding this request hinges on

whether or not the monastery of Monte Cassino was occupied
by the Germans. Later evidence suggests that it was not, though
this evidence also suggests that the German defences were very
close to the monastery buildings – within a few yards – and that
the buildings were an integral part of the defences, screening
enemy activity from view though not actually containing any
troops. A report from the commander of the German 1st
Parachute Division to XV Panzer Corps states that 'No troops or
weapons have entered the monastery. On divisional instructions
military police have been on 24-hour guard to ensure no troops
enter monastery.' It is hard to see how the hilltop could have
been bombed and the monastery spared, but that is not the argument. The argument is over who was directly responsible for
ordering the bombing of Monte Cassino.

Freyberg had no authority to order the bombing, and therefore
passed the request on to his current superior, General Mark W.
Clark. Clark was not at his headquarters and was apparently out
of radio contact, so this request was handed to Clark's chief of
staff, Major-General Alfred Gruenther. Unable to contact Clark,
Gruenther called 15th Army Group (or AAI) HQ where, unable
to contact Alexander, he laid Freyberg's request before
Alexander's chief of staff, Major-General John Harding. In passing this request along, Gruenther added that, whatever Freyberg
said, Clark did not consider the bombing necessary.

There was then considerable toing and froing between Clark
and Gruenther and Gruenther and Harding, culminating in a
call to Gruenther from Harding to the effect that, if General
Freyberg considered the destruction of the monastery a 'military
necessity', then Alexander felt it should be destroyed. There was
then more toing and froing. Clark declared that, were Freyberg
an American officer, his request would be refused, but 'in view
of General Freyberg's position in the British Empire Forces . . .
the situation was a delicate one and General Clark hesitated to
give him such an order – to attack without bomber support –
without first referring the matter to General Alexander'.[6]

General Clark's eagerness to pass the buck over this decision –
either up the chain of command to Alexander or down the line
to Freyberg – is very understandable, if not very edifying. Clark
rightly suspected that there would be an outcry over the destruction of the monastery, but he also knew that this position had

already torn the heart out of two American divisions and that there would be another outcry if the New Zealanders and Indians were sent to attack it and suffered similar losses after he had denied their request for air support. The fact remains that Clark was the Army commander at Cassino. It was his decision, and – in the end – repeating Freyberg's opinion that the bombing of the monastery was 'a military necessity', he ordered the bombing to go ahead.

The bombing of Monte Cassino then contributed yet another inter-Allied controversy to the Cassino story. This involves the 1st Battalion the Royal Sussex Regiment – the British battalion in the 7th Indian Brigade of the 4th Indian Division, the battalion now holding the positions on Snakeshead Ridge previously held by the 2nd Battalion of the US 141st Infantry Regiment.

A study of the map on page xx will be helpful at this point. From this it will be seen that, as already described, Snakeshead Ridge is shaped like a boomerang, with the lower arm stretching down towards the monastery and a small hill, Point 593, in the bend. When the 1st Royal Sussex took over the American positions on 12 February, their understanding, and that of their divisional and corps commanders, was that the American soldiers already held Point 593. Point 593 would therefore be the jumping-off point – the start line – for the 4th Indian Division's attack on the monastery, an attack which the Sussex battalion would lead.

However, when they got on to Snakeshead, the Sussex soldiers of the 7th Indian Brigade discovered that Point 593 was still firmly in German hands. The top of the ridge and the slopes below it were littered with the bodies of German and American soldiers killed in the fighting for this vital feature, but the Germans held 593. This discovery confronted the commanding officer of the 1st Royal Sussex, Lieutenant-Colonel J. B. A. Glennie, with a problem; before he could start his attack on the monastery, he would first have to capture the start line on Point 593, 70 yards from his current front-line position. This could be done only with a night attack, for Snakeshead was observed from German positions on the surrounding heights, including Point 593, and any movement in daylight was impossible. Nor was it possible to move off the ridge and move along the flanks, for these were precipitous, cut about with deep gullies, and sown with mines and trip wires. The only way to the monastery was over Point 593. No 593, no monastery.

Colonel Glennie's next problem was that 2nd New Zealand Corps HQ thought that Point 593 was in Allied hands, and he was unable to convince them otherwise. Corps HQ therefore anticipated that immediately after the bombing of the monastery, 1st Royal Sussex would lead the 7th Indian Brigade down Snakeshead Ridge and occupy the monastery and the rest of Monastery Hill.[7] There is some doubt on this point, however, as the New Zealand Corps's Operational Instruction No. 4, sent to 4th Indian Division on 9 February, orders the Division to 'attack and capture Monastery Hill *and Point 593*' (my italics).

There was a further problem. No one had told Glennie about the bombing, and certainly not that it would take place on the morning of 15 February. There is argument on this point too, but from the war diaries of the Royal Sussex and the Official History of the 4th Indian Division – and what actually happened on the morning of 15 February – it seems to be true. A leaflet drop by shellfire on the previous day told the monks that the abbey would shortly be bombed and warned them to take cover or evacuate the monastery, but no one told Glennie *when* it would be bombed. This is a typical 'fog of war' error, and no one should be too surprised about it. Regrettable though it is, such things happen.

At 0945 hours on 15 February a wave of 250 bombers came over Cassino and 'reduced the top of Monte Cassino to a smoking mass of rubble'.[8] As the first bombs fell – some straddling his battalion positions on Snakeshead Ridge – Glennie picked up the field telephone and called brigade headquarters. Before he could say a word, a voice on the line cried, 'We didn't know either.' 'They told the monks and they told the enemy,' wrote Colonel Glennie later, 'but they didn't tell us.' Nor was that all. The bomb casualties among the Royal Sussex and the resulting confusion were followed up by an order from Corps; whatever had happened, whatever the situation, the Royal Sussex must push forward that night and clear Point 593.

Now comes the controversy. The US Official History, commenting on this event, states that 'Despite the withdrawal of Indian troops from positions close to the abbey, the bombardment inflicted twenty-four casualties among the Indian troops. More important, their pulling back permitted the Germans to regain without effort key positions that the American troops had fought bitterly to win.'[9]

This statement requires investigation. The US historian may not have been aware that Indian Army brigades had two Indian battalions and one British battalion – in this case the 1st Battalion the Royal Sussex – and it is clear that these British soldiers must be the 'Indian troops . . . close to the abbey', for none were closer. However, Glennie's soldiers had not 'pulled back' before the bombing: as related, the bombing was a complete surprise. Moreover, a German report from 1st Parachute Division to XIV Panzer Corps and Tenth Army records that a regiment from the 34th Division of the US II Corps made its final attack on the night of 10/11 February 'and was totally defeated'.[10] There was therefore no opportunity for the German troops to 'regain without effort' their positions on Point 593 – the Germans had never lost those positions in the first place.

The purpose of that statement in the US Official History is therefore hard to understand. If the men of the 34th Division had not taken Point 593 it was not for want of trying; no one was criticizing their efforts or their courage. The fact that corps command did not know that Point 593 was still in German hands is not surprising either: in war, such errors happen all the time. This comment in the US account is therefore a slur on the soldiers of a fine battalion that suffered serious losses in an attempt to take a position that the US History maintains they were first responsible for losing. In fact the fight of the 1st Royal Sussex in its attempts to take Point 593 on Snakeshead Ridge is a military epic.

On the night of 15/16 February, as ordered, the Royal Sussex sent a company – three officers and 63 men – out along the stony ridge towards Point 593. They had gone 50 yards before they were detected, and fire was then brought down on them. For the rest of the night, supported by other companies ferrying up grenades – the only weapon of any use in that tumbled ground – the Royal Sussex fought to get forward. By daylight on 16 February 2 officers and 32 men of that company – more than 50 per cent of the force committed – had been killed or wounded. No one got more than 50 yards from the start line.

On the following night, 16/17 February, Colonel Glennie was ordered to try again, using his entire battalion – a much reduced battalion – to force a way forward. More grenades were sent for, and the attack went in at 2359 hours after fresh mule-loads of grenades arrived. As they moved out, the soldiers were hit by shells from their own artillery but the attack went in and was pressed hard all night. By dawn, out of 25 officers and 250 men of four companies in the 1st Royal Sussex, 10 officers and 130 men had been killed or wounded – and Point 593 was still in German hands. In two nights this fine battalion had lost 12 out of 15 officers and 162 out of 313 men in an attempt to take a position that – allegedly – was not in enemy hands to begin with.

If a battalion attack had failed, perhaps a brigade attack might succeed – though space to deploy so many troops was hard to come by on the mountain. The 4th/6th Rajaputana Rifles came up to pass through the Royal Sussex and storm along the ridge to Point 593 while two battalions of Gurkhas, the 1st/2nd and 1st/9th Gurkha Rifles, would pick their way directly across the steep slopes below the ridge to the left of the Sussex position and attempt a direct assault on the monastery. Meanwhile, just below in the valley, the 28th Battalion of the 2nd New Zealand Division would advance across the Rapido river and attack towards Cassino station along the axis of the railway embankment above the Rapido floods.

The men of the 28th Battalion were Maoris. They made their way along the causeway in the dark, each man clinging on to the bayonet scabbard of the man in front, and once in the outskirts of the town they formed up and charged into the ruins. This assault on Cassino was a soldier's battle, the men running through wire and mines to take the station, losing over 100 of their number in the process, but holding there while sappers worked to widen the causeway and bring up some tanks. Below, success – at least for a while. Above, the same sad story.

The Rajputs went out on to Snakeshead Ridge – rocky ground thickly covered with the bodies of American and British soldiers – and were promptly greeted with grenades and machine-gun fire. Moving from rock to rock, they edged forward in the dark, through a blizzard of bullets and grenade fragments. One Rajput platoon did get briefly on to Point 593, but otherwise it was the same story as on the previous nights. By dawn the Rajputs had lost 196 officers and men, including all the company commanders. Nor did the Gurkhas do any better, though their attacks across the slope below the ridge were pressed home with similar resolution.

A roll-call after first light revealed that one Gurkha battalion had lost its commanding officer, 11 other officers and 139 men, and the other Gurkha battalion had lost almost 100 men. Four crack battalions of the 4th Indian Division had been shattered in three nights – and Point 593 was still not taken.

After first light on 17 February attention switched to the Maoris at Cassino station, waiting, weapons cocked, for either tank support or an enemy counter-attack. The tanks had not arrived by dawn, for in spite of tremendous efforts the sappers could not complete the route along the narrow causeway. This was a setback, for, as the map on page xx shows, if the station could be held and the troops there reinforced, a low-level approach to the Liri valley along the base of the hills might be possible – the station is only half a mile from the entrance to the valley and very little more to the town centre. From the station a further attack, supported by tanks, might well succeed in breaching the Gustav Line defences at their strongest point.

But this was Cassino, and at Cassino there was always another problem. The problem now was Monastery Hill, looming above the station and just a few hundred yards away. From Monastery Hill – where, following the bombing, the enemy had now occupied the ruined monastery – everything below could be seen and a great weight of accurate artillery and mortar fire could be brought down on the valley floor. To conceal the defenders of the station from direct observed fire, Kippenberger ordered the artillery to maintain a smokescreen, sending trucks back to Naples, 70 miles away, to get more smoke shells.

Screened by this choking smoke, the Maoris waited all morning for the anticipated attack. This did not come until 1500 hours, when German tanks and infantry moved against the Maori position in strength. The Maoris had rifles and Bren guns, anti-tank PIATs and mortars, but no tanks or anti-tank guns. They held on and took their toll of the German infantry but in the end they had to pull back across the Rapido. So, on 18 February the Second Battle of Cassino ended. Losses had been considerable, little had been gained.

The only extra advantage was a single bridge across the Rapido and the possibility that the attack had diverted some German strength from the latest attack on the Anzio bridgehead. This German counter-attack on the bridgehead was called off on

18 February, after a stubborn defence by the US 179th Infantry Regiment and the 1st Battalion the Loyal Regiment, backed by artillery and naval gunfire.

Back at Cassino the fighting went on, as Ernest Smallridge relates:

> We had seen the bombing of the abbey, but it became apparent that the blitz on the monastery had not impaired their ability to pinpoint a truck with one shell and knock it out with the next one, so obviously the monastery was not only an excellent bomb-proof shelter but also an efficient observation post. From up there the enemy could shell everything in the valley – not a recipe for a speedy advance.[11]

There was therefore a brief pause at Cassino while Freyberg considered his options. Another crossing of the Rapido could be ruled out – at least until the relentless rain stopped and the banks dried out somewhat. Nor did another assault through the mountains exert much appeal. That left the third option: a frontal assault on Cassino town and the monastery.

Difficult though this would be, an attack here offered some advantages. Just to begin with there were three roads into the town – much damaged and mined, but offering at least the possibility of tank deployment. By packing two divisions into a narrow front and having the fresh 78th Division in corps reserve – the British 78th Division came over from the Adriatic on 18 February – Freyberg might hope to overwhelm the defenders by force of numbers. Finally, he could rely on more air support and plenty of artillery.

That was the good news. On the other hand, this would be a direct assault on a very narrow front between the town and Monastery Hill, up which the assault troops must scramble towards their objective. The town itself was a mass of rubble, sure to impede the passage of tanks, so the call went out for bulldozers. It was recognized, even at the start of the planning stage, that this attack – Operation DICKENS, the Third Battle of Cassino – would be a high-risk affair, and Mark Clark estimated the chances of success at no better than 50–50.

The detailed plan called for the smashing of the town by heavy bombers and artillery, after which the 6th New Zealand Brigade would fight its way through the town and take Castle

Hill, the knoll at the foot of Monastery Hill. The 5th Indian Brigade would then pass through the New Zealanders and attack the monastery. That taken, 78th Division would come up and storm the entrance to the Liri valley, supported by a combat command – a brigade group – of US tanks. Given the circumstances this was a reasonable plan, relying on the application of brute force. But, as before, the attack was rushed to help the beleaguered troops at Anzio. The Second Battle of Cassino ended on 18 February. Detailed orders for the Third Battle were issued on 22 February, and the battle was due to start on 24 February – weather permitting.

The weather was not permissive. Clear skies were needed for the bombers, but the skies over Cassino did not clear for the next three weeks. It rained all day and every day at Cassino from 20 February until 14 March. The sufferings of the troops in the front-line positions at Cassino during that time – sitting in flooded trenches, soaked by day and freezing at night, constantly shelled and mortared – are perhaps better imagined than described. An officer of the 2nd Gurkhas describes this time: 'For weeks on end we have sat on a draughty mountain top in heavy snow and rain, with one's clothing and blankets soaked through. Behind the line one can always make a hole in the ground and rainproof it with a tent or bivouac. But in forward positions one's hole or sangar can either be anti-German attack proof or rainproof, but not both.'[12]

So, in this winter misery the British, Indians and New Zealanders hung on, waiting for H-Hour, losing men every day. Among those lost at this time was the stout-hearted commander of the 2nd New Zealand Division, Major-General Howard Kippenberger, who stepped on a schu mine when visiting artillery positions on Monte Trocchio. The mine blew off one foot and so damaged the other one that it had to be amputated. Kippenberger had started this war as a battalion commander, had risen through merit, and was well known and respected by all ranks in the New Zealand Division; his loss at this time was a particular blow. Nor was this the only loss; Major-General Tuker was ill and was temporarily replaced as commander of the 4th Indian Division by Brigadier H. K. Dimoline.

The rain stopped on 14 March. The Germans had just made what turned out to be their last attack at Anzio, but it seemed

necessary to start the Cassino assault as soon as possible before
the rains came again. This attack therefore began at 0830 hours
on 15 March, when groups of B-17 Flying Fortresses dropped a
concentration of bombs on Cassino town. The bombing, by successive waves of heavy and medium bombers, went on for the
next three and a half hours and was followed by a concentrated
barrage from more than 600 Allied guns. Then, at noon precisely,
the New Zealand infantry went forward, supported by tanks.
Among the tank crews was Sergeant D. L. Garven of the 19th
New Zealand Armoured Regiment:

> On 15 March the bombers arrived to bomb the town. When the
> bombing stopped, at around 1200 hours, the barrage from 600
> guns began, and when that ceased 'B' Squadron of the 19th
> Regiment went forward in support of the 25th Battalion. Their
> object was to capture Castle Hill, and the advance was made
> along two roads leading from the barracks area outside the town
> into Cassino. Two troops of tanks moved on each road, but within
> a few minutes it was found that all the reconnoitring by the sap-
> pers had been of no use. The heavy bombing had wrecked all
> roads to the objective and, because of the huge craters and demol-
> ished buildings, progress was impossible. So huge were the
> craters that the sappers did not have the equipment to bridge
> them, and the tank crews had to get out and do what they could
> with picks and shovels – covered by smoke while the gunners
> gave covering fire to the infantry. The infantry met little resis-
> tance at first, but in a short while the Germans appeared among
> the rubble and from then on it was a see-saw battle. It was impos-
> sible to maintain communications with the companies, because
> there was no set line of battle. Everything was a shambles, and
> the tanks could not move through the rubble.

'A' Company of the 25th Battalion was put in to clear the way to
the objectives, Castle Hill and Point 165, and by 1630 hours that day
'B' Squadron of the 19th Regiment had ten tanks in close support
of the infantry. Prior to this there had been some chaos when
Sherman tanks were encountered firing back at them; it was
learned later that the Americans had sent five tanks into Cassino
earlier, and these were the tanks the Germans used against the New
Zealanders. One heroic feat that day was when Corporal Fair of the
19th went forward on foot with a tommy gun and grenades and
silenced a German machine-gun. In another episode Lieutenant
Furness, a tank commander, went forward with grenades and

tossed them into a building before returning to his tank and blasting the building, taking many German prisoners.

'C' Squadron, in which I served, took part in this battle, and we had plenty of targets to deal with, but it was almost impossible to enter the town on account of the havoc the bombing did to the buildings. I spent four days and five nights in this area without any sleep before I was relieved, but next day my CO advised me that he wanted me to go back in as I knew the area. I got a fresh tank and crew and was about to set off when we were told that 'C' Squadron was about to be relieved by the 20th Armoured Regiment, and much to my relief I was ordered back to base.[13]

Cassino lay in ruins when the New Zealanders went in. But in those ruins stood men of the German 1st Parachute Division – good soldiers, tenacious in defence, not afraid to die. As the New Zealanders and their supporting tanks clawed their way over the rubble and craters, the paratroopers rose from shelter and began to fight back. The fight to get into the town went on all day, and through some oversight the leading New Zealand battalion, the 25th, was not supported by the follow-up battalion, the 26th. Nor, as Sergeant Garven's account makes clear, could the supporting tanks get forward: the streets were full of rubble, and the tank crews were sniped at as they tried to clear a path with pick and shovel. Then at dusk the rains came again, turning the shell craters into deep pools.

During the night, in pitch dark and streaming rain, the New Zealanders edged deeper into the town and the 1st/4th Battalion the Essex Regiment – the British battalion of the 5th Indian Brigade – arrived to take over Castle Hill from the New Zealanders. It was followed by the 1st/6th Rajputs and the 1st/9th Gurkha Rifles, tasked to take another position, known as Hangman's Hill, further up the slopes towards the monastery and south of Castle Hill. In short, the 4th Indian Division was proceeding in bounds up the bends in the road towards the monastery, and these attacks went ahead in spite of the difficulties of weather and terrain. The Essex established a firm base on Castle Hill, the Rajputs advanced to take the next bend, and two companies of the 9th Gurkhas went forward towards Hangman's Hill. One company was promptly held up by heavy fire and driven to ground; the second went on into the dark – and vanished.

The second day of the Third Battle was devoted to more fighting and to attempts to get the units organized and sort out the
growing problems of supply. In the town, the heart of the
German resistance was found around the ruins of the former
Continental Hotel, which, among other defensive features, had
a German tank dug in in the reception area. From the
Continental, German machine-gun nests and strongpoints
fanned out towards the Hotel des Roses and the palazzo,
between the foot of Monastery Hill and Route 6.

Up above, the battle for Monastery Hill went on with one
piece of good news; that Gurkha company which had vanished
the previous night reappeared at daylight, hanging on to the
1/9th battalion's objective, Hangman's Hill. The problem was to
get more troops and supplies up to support it, but by the third
day the situation was looking promising. From positions already
established, the New Zealand Corps could complete its capture
of the town and take Monastery Hill. The key to both was Castle
Hill, which was in New Zealand hands.

On the night of 17/18 February the New Zealanders put in a
company-strong attack on the Continental Hotel, coming down
on it from positions on one of the lower road bends on
Monastery Hill. This attack got as far as the hotel entrance before
the assault platoon commander was killed and the rest were
driven off by machine-gun fire. Meanwhile, the Rajputs were
attempting to advance to support and supply the Gurkhas on
Hangman's Hill. Their two-company attempt cost almost 30
men in getting up to the Gurkhas, and those who managed to
arrive on Hangman's Hill were unable to withdraw. They piled
up rocks into sangars and stayed there to help defend the position, with dwindling stocks of ammunition and food. The failure of both these attacks convinced Freyberg that he must pile
on the pressure to prevent this battle descending into stalemate.
On 19 February, therefore, another battalion, the 28th (Maori),
would assault the Continental Hotel while the Gurkhas and the
Essex would storm up Monastery Hill from Hangman's Hill. To
quote Fred Majdalany, 'The New Zealand Corps was going in
for the kill.'[14]

Freyberg had served on the Western Front in the First World
War and was not wedded to head-on, frontal, infantry assaults.
He had a trick up his sleeve – tanks. While the preparations for

this battle had been under way, New Zealand sappers had been hacking a track across the hills above the town from Cairo village towards Albaneta Farm. This track – named Cavendish Road – was now ready and capable of supporting a squadron of tanks; their appearance behind the German lines during this new assault was calculated to help the Gurkhas and the Essex – and dismay the enemy.

One snag for the Allied troops was the constant smokescreen put down by their artillery. This was supposed to screen their daytime movements and conceal the activities of the sappers who were attempting to clear the rubble, fill in the craters, and get tanks forward into the town. The snag was that the smoke also concealed the movement of German patrols probing or attacking the Allied positions and the empty smoke-shell canisters cascading to earth created another hazard for the troops making their way to Hangman's Hill. Even so, the move went on, and by 0500 hours on Sunday 19 March two companies of the 1/4th Essex were in position close to the summit of Hangman's Hill ready to begin their attack on the monastery and two more were on their way forward from Castle Hill.

By 0530 hours everything seemed to be ready. The Maoris were ready to attack the Continental Hotel; the tanks were ready to move around the hills towards the monastery and the Essex and Rajputs. This was the moment which the Germans on Monastery Hill chose to put in a counter-attack on Castle Hill, cutting off those troops higher up towards Hangman's Hill.

This assault began with ten minutes of drenching fire from heavy machine-guns and mortars. Then a full battalion of German paratroopers came leaping over the rocks from positions on Monastery Hill, spraying the ground ahead with fire, driving into the waiting ranks of the rear two Essex companies and the Rajputs. These swiftly scattered and went to ground, and some German soldiers reached the walls of the Castle, where a mixed garrison of British, Indian and Gurkha troops, perhaps 150 strong, mustered hastily to repel them. This first attack was beaten off with grenades and bayonets, even rifle butts. Then the British and Indian troops outside the walls got over their surprise and joined in the fighting. Hand-to-hand fighting took place all over the hill as scattered groups fought it out among the gullies. The Germans pulled back, reorganized,

and came forward again and again until this German battalion
was reduced to little more than a platoon.

Nevertheless, their attack succeeded in breaking up
Freyberg's assault on the monastery. Even the position on
Hangman's Hill was no longer secure. Of the two Essex companies that had gone up there that morning, totalling perhaps
170 men, only 70 remained – and 30 of these were wounded. The
Germans had beaten the Indian Division to the punch on the hill,
and matters were no better in the town or with the tank force
coming from Cairo. The Maoris had started their attack at first
light but had made little progress, and by nightfall their attack
had stalled. The tanks coming up from Cairo had got to within
800 yards of the monastery when they ran into a minefield. The
mine explosions alerted the Germans to the developing threat,
and paratroopers armed with panzerfausts promptly appeared
and knocked out several tanks. Nine tanks were lost, and the rest
were forced to withdraw. By dusk on Sunday 19 March the Third
Battle of Cassino was over.

The crux of this Third Battle was the fight for Castle Hill. Both
sides had seen that Castle Hill had to be taken and held or
Hangman's Hill – the best start line for a final assault on the monastery – could not be retained. Hence those various attempts to
feed troops forward, Essex and Gurkhas and Rajputs; hence that
violent German counter-attack. Hangman's Hill was still – just –
in Allied hands when the battle ended, and Freyberg sent a battalion of the Royal West Kents from the 78th Division to reinforce the
remnants of the Essex and Rajputs. This battalion arrived just in
time to beat off yet another German attack.

But that was all; for the next few days, until 19 March, when
the Third Battle was broken off, the New Zealand Corps concentrated on hanging on to what gains it had, rather than attempting to make more. The main gains were two bridges over the
Rapido: one over Route 6, the other carrying the railway. The
4th Indian Division troops were withdrawn from Hangman's
Hill and replaced by soldiers from the 78th Division, with the
1st Guards Brigade taking over New Zealand positions in the
town.

The conduct of these first three battles at Cassino has attracted
a certain amount of critical comment – not least at the time from
Winston Churchill. On 20 March, Churchill wrote to Alexander:

I wish you would explain to me why this passage by Cassino, Monastery Hill etc., all the fighting on a front of two or three miles, is the only place you must keep butting at? About five or six divisions have been worn out butting into these jaws. I have the greatest confidence in you but do try to explain to me why no flanking movements can be made?

Alexander explained that, along the whole Italian front, the Liri valley was the only spot with terrain suitable for the development of Allied superiority in tanks and artillery. He described the difficulties of terrain and weather – and therefore of supply – and went into great detail over the reasons for the tactics employed in the battles so far. He also paid tribute to the skill and courage of the German defenders:

The tenacity of these German paratroops is quite remarkable, considering they were subjected to the whole of the Mediterranean Air Force plus the better part of 800 guns under the greatest concentration of fire power which has ever been put down and lasting for six hours. I doubt if any other troops in the world could have stood up to it and then gone on fighting with the ferocity they have.

Alexander then hinted that he was planning a renewal of the battle, and would employ Eighth Army for his next offensive:

The Eighth Army's plan for entering the Liri Valley in force will be undertaken when grouping is completed. This plan must envisage an attack on a wider front and with greater forces than Freyberg has been able to have for this operation. A little later, when the snow goes off the mountains, the rivers drop and the ground hardens, movement will be possible over terrain which is at present impassable.

The effort put into this Third Battle should not be under-rated. The air attack on 15 March used 2,192 *tons* of bombs. In the next ten days, 558,000 shells were poured into the enemy positions at Cassino, turning the town into what the Official History describes as 'a lunatic giant's rubbish-heap'.[15] None of this provided the expected benefits: the terrain, the weather and the enemy still held sway at Cassino. The next attack must wait for the better weather of late spring, and until fresh forces could arrive to renew the struggle.

Losses in this last battle had been severe: the 2nd New Zealand Division had lost 1,600 men, the 4th Indian Division almost twice as many. Having taken over 3,000 casualties in recent weeks, most of them among the infantry companies, the 4th Indian Division was for the moment almost non-existent as a fighting force. Not a great deal had been gained in return for such sacrifice, and the monastery of St Benedict, shattered but defiant, stood unconquered over Cassino town.

3 Carpathian Div (Polish)

13

Cassino and Rome
April–June 1944

The fourth and last battle of Cassino was General Alexander's masterpiece; an operation in C Major with full orchestra.

Fred Majdalany, *Cassino: Portrait of a Battle*, p. 221

Before moving on to the final battle for Cassino and the subsequent fall of Rome, it is interesting to speculate on what might have happened if, in January 1944, General Alexander had gone back to Britain as Commander, 21st Army Group, and Ground Force Commander for OVERLORD and Montgomery had stayed in Italy as GOC, 15th Army Group. Had this happened, there would certainly have been far less subsequent controversy over the conduct of the Normandy battle,[1] and it is arguable that Sir Bernard Montgomery would have found a way through the Cassino impasse rather sooner than Sir Harold Alexander. This can only be speculation, but Alexander was less abrasive then Montgomery and got on well with the Americans, while Montgomery was generally regarded as master of the 'set-piece battle', the pre-planned, orchestrated type of battle that the campaign in Italy constantly required – not least at Cassino in the early months of 1944.

A certain sameness was evident in the first three assaults on Cassino. The first common feature was that the attacks were made in insufficient strength. There were good reasons for this – not least the constraints imposed by the ground and the weather – but it should have been apparent that a major attack, in numbers as well as firepower, would be needed to crack the Cassino position. Then there is the question raised by Churchill; was it entirely necessary for the Allies to go on beating their heads against the German positions here, the strongest point in the line? Could not something be done with the Garigliano bridgehead, or greater use be made of Juin's exploitation into the mountains behind Cassino? When they heard gunfire from their rear, would the defenders of Cassino have continued to hold their positions?

Some battles – the Somme, Verdun, Alamein – create their own dynamics. Three elements emerge – the attacker, the defender and the battle itself – and each has an agenda. As the fighting proceeds it gradually becomes clear, if only in hindsight, that the battle can be won only if it is fought in a particular way, that victory will go to the commander who can 'read' the battle and understand what it has to say. Cassino could not be won by simply hurling more troops over the Rapido or up the sides of the overhanging mountains – that had been tried. The battle itself was now dictating events. Some new method was needed – one that grasped the realities of terrain and enemy and weather, and managed to bend them to some workable plan.

Granted, there were many cogent reasons for the chronic problems affecting the progress of the Allied armies in Italy. A lack of troops, the terrain, the weather, a shortage of landing craft, the pressure of other events elsewhere – there was always something to prevent fast progress. But so it had been since the Western Desert Force first took the field in 1940, and it is just possible that Montgomery's style – careful, methodical and sound – would have brought greater progress on the Cassino front. As it was, the entire Italian front was at stalemate as spring drifted into summer in 1944 – and OVERLORD drew nigh.

For his next attack, the Fourth Battle of Cassino, Alexander had at last got a balance of advantages. To begin with, this time there was no great pressure over time. The Third Battle ended on 19 March, and the start of the Fourth Battle would not come until mid-May. Anzio at last seemed secure, OVERLORD was not due until mid-May at the earliest: there was no need to rush the attack, and waiting would pay dividends. Better weather in the warmer days of spring was drying out the ground and offering clear skies for the air forces, and the troops were more comfortable. Moreover, Alexander now had a sound objective: not the taking of ground but a requirement to engage the greatest possible number of enemy divisions and hold them in Italy up to and beyond the launch of OVERLORD.

Added to these was the experience of the last few months. This had revealed that piecemeal attacks at Cassino would not succeed. It would be necessary to deploy all the Allied force and to commit it on a 25-mile front between the sea and Cassino, over ground that, once dry, could carry tanks and a great quantity of transport – a force that could smash the German Tenth Army at Cassino and then, aided by a six-division-strong VI Corps, break out from the Anzio bridgehead, smash the German Fourteenth Army and thrust for Rome. The Tenth Army had three divisions straddling the Apennines, 1st Parachute at Cassino and four divisions from there to the west coast, while the bulk of the Fourteenth Army – five divisions, with a panzer division in reserve – was around Anzio.

The plan for an attack, involving the Eighth as well as the Fifth Army, would be supported by deception, a two-part cover plan to conceal the arrival of Eighth Army on the Cassino front and to suggest that a further amphibious operation was pending north of Anzio – one aimed at Civitavecchia, a beach resort north of Rome.

To this latter end the 36th Division, now resting close to Naples, was sent to carry out amphibious training, and the roads around Naples and Salerno were soon plastered with the maple leaf emblem of the Canadian Corps. This gave the impression that two Canadian divisions and the 36th Division were tasked for an amphibious assault and Kesselring, duly warned, kept part of his forces, including two armoured divisions, north of Rome, ready to repel them.

The second part of the deception plan required the Allies to conceal the fact that the bulk of the remaining Eighth Army divisions east of the Apennines was being switched to the Cassino front, with General Wladyslaw Anders's Polish Corps replacing the 78th Division in the hills above Cassino. This was not a massive increase in Allied striking power, for the two divisions of the

Polish Corps – the Carpathian and Kresowa Divisions – had only two brigades apiece. But these were Polish soldiers, and they had something to prove.

The very presence of II Polish Corps in Italy was the result of a triumph of fortitude over adversity by every Polish soldier. After the joint invasion of Poland by the Germans and their Soviet allies in 1939 – a Soviet–Nazi alliance about which Russia's history of the Great Patriotic War is strangely silent – the Polish troops captured by the Wehrmacht were taken into a brutal captivity in labour camps. Many did not survive this experience. Those Polish soldiers captured by the Russians were no more fortunate: their officers were taken away and murdered by the Soviets in the Katyn forest, and the men were either starved in prison camps or used for slave labour – until June 1941.

Operation BARBAROSSA and the subsequent retreat of the Soviet armies towards Moscow led Marshal Josef Stalin, the Soviet leader, to look more fondly on his Polish prisoners. Perhaps, if released from captivity, fed a little food, and supplied with weapons, these formidable Polish soldiers would be willing to fight on Russia's side. This offer the Poles declined; they would not fight for the state that fully intended to keep their own country in subjection. The Soviet response was to cease feeding the Poles entirely and cast them loose to wander where they would. So it was that from autumn 1941 a trickle and then a flood of gaunt, ragged Polish soldiers began to arrive in Persia, making their way to the British lines in the Middle East and so back to the war.

These survivors of the Polish Army were not the first Poles to reach the Allied lines. Polish airmen had fought in the Battle of Britain and there were Polish squadrons in RAF Bomber Command. But II Polish Corps was something different. These men had endured terrible times and great privation to get to Italy, and they approached their coming commitment to the Cassino battle with an almost frightening intensity. Nothing could stop them. Nothing would stop them. The monastery on Monte Cassino, which they were charged with taking in this coming battle, was only a step on their road back to Poland.

Alexander's plan called for the two armies to thrust north, up and astride the Liri valley. On the left would be Fifth Army, with two fresh American divisions, the 85th and 88th, tasked to cut north past Terracina on the coast. The vital element in this coming battle, the four French divisions of General Juin's Free French Expeditionary Corps would attack in the mountains on the right. Juin's 100,000-strong corps of four divisions included 12,000 Moroccan *goums* – mountain troops, lightly equipped, supplied by mules and tasked to move through the Aurunci Mountains west of the Liri valley, cutting the throats of anyone who got in the way. Their skills in mountain warfare were to prove decisive in the coming battle.

In the centre would come Eighth Army's six Commonwealth or British divisions – two of them armoured – the 8th Indian and the 2nd New Zealand Divisions, then two divisions of the Canadian Corps, then the veteran British 78th and 4th Divisions. Finally, on the right flank of this massive thrust, would come the Poles, whose attack at Cassino would be supported by fire from 1,500 guns – half of them 25-pounders – and by 2,000 tanks. While this force was thrusting up the Liri valley, any German forces east of the Apennines would be contained by the units of V Corps – 4th Indian Division and an Italian division, plus the King's Dragoon Guards, engineer units and some artillery – all operating under 15th Army Group/Allied Armies in Italy (AAI) control.[2]

The object of this new offensive was spelt out in Alexander's appreciation for the battle, drawn up in March. This declared that the object of the offensive was 'to destroy the right wing of the German Tenth Army. To drive what remains of it and the German Fourteenth Army north of Rome and pursue it to the Pisa–Rimini line, inflicting the maximum losses in the process.' The strategic aim was 'to contain and draw in German formations that might otherwise be used against OVERLORD', and Alexander added that therefore operations in Italy must 'presumably begin at least 15–21 days before OVERLORD is launched'. From this, two points arise: first, that the object of the next offensive was to contain the German armies in Italy, not to take Rome, and, second, that this attack would not be launched before mid-May. These points are spelled out here because a failure to grasp these objectives, both at Clark's Fifth Army HQ and in Washington, was to cause problems later.

By the time this next offensive – Operation DIADEM – was launched, on the night of 11 May, the German armies in Italy were organized as follows. Containing VI Corps under Truscott at Anzio was Fourteenth Army under Colonel-General Eberhardt von Mackensen – a force of eight divisions, including reserves, though part of this force was now at Civitavecchia. Facing Eighth and Fifth Armies at Cassino was Tenth Army under Colonel-General Heinrich von Vietinghoff, consisting of ten divisions including reserves. The bulk of these Tenth Army forces were in two corps: XIV Panzer Corps under General Fridolin von Senger und Etterlin and LI Mountain Corps under General Feuerstein.

The divisions of this force were greatly under-strength, with an average of 8,000 men instead of their 17–20,000 ration strength in the panzer divisions and 14,000 men in the infantry divisions. The total strength of Tenth Army was therefore around 80,000 men, but they had the advantage of fighting on the defensive in terrain ideal for defence and in well-prepared positions. With Rommel now in France, the Commander-in-Chief of the German forces in Italy was Field Marshal Kesselring. The Luftwaffe had around 340 aircraft in Italy, compared with the Allied total of some 3,000 aircraft – bombers, fighters and transports.

Kesselring's strategy in the summer of 1944 was a continuation of that which had served the Germans so well all winter; to hold their ground and give it up slowly when pressed, only to fall back to another prepared position further back. In the case of the Gustav Line across the mouth of the Liri valley, the next pre-pared position was the Adolf Hitler Line – later renamed the Dora Line – half a mile deep and 6 miles further up the valley, running between the village of Piedimonte on the eastern end and the west coast. In case that fell, Kesselring had prepared a third position, the Caesar Line, in the Alban Hills south of Rome, the long-sought objective of the Anzio forces.

Alexander tackled the complexities of the Cassino position with a plan of great simplicity. On the right flank Eighth Army would break into the Liri valley while the Polish Corps took Cassino – a double blow rather than a right and left hook. Once in the Liri valley, the Eighth would push north on the axis of Route 6. Meanwhile, on the left of the valley, Fifth Army would exploit forward from the bridgehead across the Garigliano taken by X Corps in the previous year, with II Corps moving on the axis of Route 7, heading for Anzio, the Free French Expedition-ary Corps moving into the mountains west of the Liri valley. This attack by the French corps – backed by the strong thrust of the Canadians up the axis of the Liri valley – was to be the decisive attack in the struggle to breach the German defences south of Rome once the Cassino position had fallen.

Once these Allied forces got close to Rome, and only then – and only when Alexander gave them the order to do so – the forces in the Anzio beachhead, 20 miles from Rome, would stage a breakout, heading directly east for Valmontone on Route 6, south of Rome. There they would cut the road – as at Beda Fomm – cutting off von Vietinghoff's retreating forces. Fifth Army would then move on Rome, while Eighth Army mopped up what was left of Tenth Army and the march to the north of Rome continued. Rome was the prize, but Rome was not the object of this battle: the object of Operation DIADEM was the destruction of the German Tenth Army.

Preparations for this major battle took time and began in mid-March. This caused some angst among the Combined Chiefs in Washington, who had got the idea that Alexander intended to launch the offensive in March and were taken aback when they realized that the starting date was not for another two months. More troops came forward, among them James Falck, then a sergeant in the 3rd Battalion, The Welsh Guards:

> In April my battalion was ordered to relieve an infantry battalion that had suffered many casualties at Cassino. By this time there had been three battles there, and a fourth was pending. We took over and secured a position on the reverse slope of a mountainous region, and my company was 'dug in' – it was actually impossible to dig, so we were in rocky sangars – with the ruins of the abbey above us and to the right flank. No one on either side knew exactly where the other was. We knew that there were Germans on the other side of the slope in front of us, possibly only some 100 yards ahead. In fact they were so close that our battalion signals officer decided to send messages to HQ in Welsh; as a result, next day we were showered by German propaganda leaflets written in Urdu.
>
> The forward area was covered with many decomposing bodies, both Allied and German, and there were many smelly bomb craters, full of stagnant water. The whole area gave off an almost unbearable stench. I was ordered to occupy a sangar in a forward defence line 50 yards or so ahead of the company as an attack by the enemy seemed imminent, and my orders were to fire some warning shots if they came forward. To reach this

sangar seemed to take hours as I had to crawl, but it was probably only about 15 minutes, negotiating my way past bodies. But the dreadful darkness, the night mist and the continual hail of machine-gun fire and tracer was nerve racking.

Having reached the sangar, peering over the sights of the Bren gun, my legs in 18 inches of water, my imagination was running riot. I could swear that the vague lines I could make out ahead were moving forward, and it was all I could do not to open fire on them or flee back to the comparative safety of our own lines.

Finally dawn came and I struggled out of the sangar, thankful that I could perhaps get back to the company and make my report. In my haste the bipod leg of the Bren gun caught on something in the sangar as I pulled it free. I was horrified by what I saw. There in the corner was the body of a British soldier, which I had been propping myself up against all night. He had been killed by a direct wound to the head, and had clearly been there some time, as I was the first person to occupy this sangar for a week. Someone – no doubt a German – had covered him up with a cape.[3]

So the weeks went by, the Allied troops mustered around Cassino, and the Germans waited for what spring might bring. General von Senger und Etterlin estimated that the Allies would not attack before 24 May and went home on leave and he was still in Germany on the night of 11 May 1944 when, at 2300 hours, 1,600 guns firing on the German positions on the Gustav Line opened the Fourth Battle of Cassino.

The essence of Alexander's attack was weight. On every part of the front, Alexander put more weight into the attack: more guns, more men, more tanks, more shells, more aircraft. As the bombardment opened on 11 May, the 85th and 88th Divisions of the US II Corps moved forward from the Garigliano bridgehead. Their advance was taken up 40 minutes later by the four divisions of the Free French Expeditionary Corps on their right, moving into the mountain mass west of the Liri valley, with their immediate objective the Aurunci peaks and the village of Ausonia.

Five minutes later – H plus 45 minutes in military terms – two divisions of Eighth Army, the 8th Indian and the 4th British, launched their assault boats into the rushing waters of the Rapido, paddling frantically across to the far bank, where they were greeted by a storm of machine-gun and mortar fire. By 0100 hours – H-Hour plus 2 – the Cassino front was ablaze for 20 miles, from the sea to the eastern side of the Liri valley. And then the Polish Corps went up against the defenders of Monte Cassino. Four divisions – one British, one Indian, two Polish – were now attempting to pinch out the Cassino position, but the weight of this night attack lay with the Poles. What the Americans and French, Indian, Canadian and British could do was important, but what the Poles had to do was vital: unless they could clear Monastery Hill, all the rest was virtually useless.

General Anders's plan also had the merits of simplicity and weight. Using two divisions instead of one, he intended to attack all the old obstacles – Point 593, Point 569, Colle San Angelo and the rest of those places linked by interlocking enemy fire – and eliminate them all at the same time. The Carpathian Division would take Snakeshead Ridge and Point 593, while the two bri-gades of the Kresowa Division attacked Colle San Angelo and Albaneta Farm. Soon after midnight the Poles began picking their way forward under cover of the barrage, but the Germans heard them coming and the familiar storm of machine-gun fire and grenades began to fall among them.

As had happened here so often before, the Polish attack stalled. By daylight on 12 May the Poles held a portion of Point 593 and part of the ridge to the right but they could not stay there in daylight; they had to pull back, with casualties in the forward rifle companies running up to 50 per cent. The fighting to hold Monastery Hill went on all day but on the next night the Poles came on again.

By dusk on 12 May the situation at Cassino was confused. The two US division on the left had not made much progress and there was no news at all from the French, who were somewhere in the hills above the Liri valley, from which came the sound of gunfire. In fact the French were making good progress, and General Juin was sending more troops forward to keep up the pressure. Even more usefully, the 4th British and 8th Indian Divisions were expanding their bridgehead over the Rapido, having beaten off a strong counter-attack that attempted to push them back again. If they could hold on, a major move towards the encirclement of Cassino was under way.

On the right, at Snakeshead Ridge, the Poles were almost back on their start line, licking their wounds and restocking with gren-ades. In the centre, however, matters were going well. It had been thought that the Liri valley could not fall until the two sides of the entrance were secured, but the 4th British and 8th Indian Divisions were now firmly across the Rapido and heading for the mouth of the valley. Their progress was slow, but they were grinding steadily forward in spite of minefields, mortars and constant counter-attacks.

John Williams, an artillery officer, took part in this last battle at Cassino:

> We were originally infantry, the 14th Queens, but changed later to the 99th Light Anti-Aircraft Regiment, Royal Artillery, which was to be used in shoots with Bofors AA guns against OPs and enemy infantry. We were at Salerno with Clark's Fifth Army, and returned to Eighth Army for the final battle of Cassino. My battery was No. 328, and our first job was to smoke out the Bailey bridges over the river, so that the sappers had some cover. On these jaunts German sentries had to be avoided, but one of my men, Gunner Funnel, being surprised by a German soldier, had to kick him to death, after being forced at gunpoint to march towards the German lines.
>
> A soldier's only up-to-date news is what is happening on his part of the front, or by rumour which appears to be a fact. The overall picture is really only known at Division or Corps or Army, but we knew that this operation would be under the command of General Alexander and involve both armies. H-Hour for this attack was to be 2300 hours on 11 May, and the infantry assault began at 2345 hours, by which time a dense fog had overwhelmed the battlefield like one of the old London fogs. Once again the Hun had sprung a surprise and was swamping the battlefield with smoke shells so that we could not see, causing great confusion. The creeping barrage had to be laid to protect the troops using assault boats to cross the river. The roar and crack of our guns was so thunderous that it was hard to distinguish the Jerry shells landing from our own guns firing.[4]

Tank driver Douglas Brunton of the Derbyshire Yeomanry also recalls this last battle at Cassino:

> Major Brundell stuck his head out of the hatch to get a better view and assess the situation. A German sniper shot him through the head, and he fell back into the turret, spouting blood and dying. This was not very pleasant for the other crew members, having to

deal with a dead body in a confined space. Then the Colonel arrived and took over the Squadron and they achieved the object-ive. The squadron leader's tank stopped alongside me, and there was Major Brundell lying on the engine compartment. He was an autocratic man but a good leader, and we came to regret his death.[5]

With the north bank of the Rapido clear of the enemy, Bailey bridges could be slung across and tanks could get forward on ground that was now dry enough to support them. This was the time to commit some reserves, and the two divisions of the Canadian Corps – the 1st Canadian Infantry and the 5th Canadian Armoured – plus the British 78th Division – were now coming up and would go in on 15 May. It would take another day or two of expensive fighting to be sure, but early on 13 May it seemed that the centre of the Gustav Line was caving in. To aid this process, on 14 May the French, having taken Ausonia, the back door to the Liri valley, sent in their *goums*, outflanking the German positions in the valley by moving along the heights. This advance by the French along and behind the German lines was the decisive part of the last battle of Cassino: hearing firing to their rear, and finding their supplies cut off, the Germans began to withdraw.

On 15 May the 78th Division crossed the Rapido and moved towards the entrance to the Liri valley, putting in its attack on the following day, supported by the 1st Canadian Division and the 6th Armoured Division. But the crux of this battle was still at Cassino, town and monastery. On 17 May the Poles went in again, pushing hard against the German positions on Monastery Hill, and this time nothing could stop them. They attacked in daylight, sections and platoons and companies of Polish infan-try swarming forward over the rocky hillsides with automatic weapons and grenades. Point 593 – carpeted with the bodies and bones of Allied and German dead – finally fell. Then San Angelo fell, and Albaneta Farm and there was the monastery just ahead – in ruins perhaps, but still holding out. That night, 17/18 May 1944, the Poles moved forward to snuff out any opposition inside the shattered walls and root out the last defenders from their bunkers.

Down in the valley west of Cassino, drawn up along Route 6, the British waited impatiently all night, not knowing where the

Poles were or what was happening up above. They heard the attack go in, but the firing died down somewhat as the night went on and at 0800 hours on 18 May the 78th Division decided to send a patrol across the road and make contact with the Poles. This carefully selected patrol consisted of three British NCOs, all holders of the Military Medal, and they arrived in the Polish lines at 1030 hours, just as General Anders was sending troops carrying the Polish flag across Point 593 and down the ridge to the monastery, from which the German defenders had withdrawn overnight.

The cost of taking the monastery had been high: in the fighting for the monastery and in the days that followed the Polish Corps lost 3,684 men of which over 1,000 were killed; only 102 were missing. The Poles were to fight many other battles in this war – in Italy, in Normandy and in north-west Europe – but Cassino was their greatest engagement.

Cassino remains a place of pilgrimage for Polish veterans, who later placed on Point 593 a memorial whose inscription sums up the spirit of these exiled soldiers whose country, even as they fought for it, was being taken away from them by the Soviets:

> *For our freedom and yours,*
> *We Polish soldiers*
> *Have given our souls to God,*
> *Our bodies to the soil of Italy,*
> *And our hearts to Poland.*

Cassino had fallen. Five months of terrible battle, tens of thousands of casualties, and suddenly Cassino was a backwater – a dangerous backwater, thick with mines, but the war had passed into the Liri valley. The task now was to destroy the enemy, get north, relieve Anzio, and destroy Tenth Army. With the fall of the Cassino position the entrance to the Liri valley was wide open and Eighth Army was pouring up Route 6, anxious to get to Piedimonte, 6 miles up the valley, and lever the enemy out of their Adolf Hitler Line defences – now hastily renamed the Dora Line – before the Germans could occupy them. This advance was not easy: there was considerable traffic congestion, only one road – and plenty of mines to prevent deployment off the road.

Douglas Brunton of the 1st Derbyshire Yeomanry again:

In the Liri valley the brick culverts over ditches were not built to support the weight of 20- to 30-ton tanks. After we had crushed a few it was obvious that we were never going to get anywhere, and so we were ordered to return to the road. Starting to do so we were suddenly shelled, but after some urgent radio calls the shelling stopped. It turned out that a Canadian tank regiment had seen us coming up to the road and decided we were Germans.[6]

'Does anyone realize', asks Eric Garner, 'the problems of the Eighth Army advance up the Liri valley? Four divisions attempting to move up the narrow valley: each infantry division with about 3,400 vehicles, each armoured division with about 3,000, not including the tanks, plus corps troops? Fuel, ammo, food for tens of thousands of men, maybe 20,000 vehicles in all? No wonder there were hold-ups. But we were moving the right way – north.'[7]

The main obstacle to rapid progress up the Liri valley was the Hitler/Dora Line. The Germans had been working on this for six months, and had created the usual formidable barrier. Minefields and wire had been laid in quantity, designed to force the advancing Allied infantry into killing zones. Anti-tank and machine guns were set in positions blasted from the rock, and the artillery had been pre-ranged on targets along the valley floor. All these static defences were buttressed by mobile units of tanks and infantry.

Donald Featherstone took part in this advance with the 51st RTR:

We concentrated near Caserta on 12 May and crossed the river Gari to join up with the 3rd Canadian Infantry Brigade we were to support. We went forward together, and reached a line a mile or so south of the Adolf Hitler Line on the night of 18/19 May. Intelligence reports had stated – wrongly – that the German line was only lightly held, and it was decided to rush it, with 'A' Squadron supporting the French-Canadian 22nd Regiment – the 'Van Doos'. The country was very thick and wooded, and we had a number of tanks knocked out by anti-tank guns and panzer-fausts before reaching the far end of the wood and coming in sight of the Adolf Hitler Line. More losses were sustained here, and we stayed here until 22 May, when we took part in another push to Pontecorvo where three tanks were knocked out and ten men killed or wounded in 'B' Squadron alone.

The final attack on the Adolf Hitler Line went in on 23 May, when we attacked with the Canadians on the left of the line. This attack began at 0600 hours behind a great barrage. The tanks quelled the enemy machine-guns, and the infantry reached their objectives. Unfortunately, the German defences included dug-in Panther tank turrets, and these were still intact and manned and caused many losses. During this time the tanks of 'A' and 'C' Squadrons were playing hide-and-seek in the woods with German SP [self-propelled] guns and tanks, and more losses were sustained here. But the infantry were able to press on and carry the line without further opposition, and after that we reluctantly parted company with the Canadians, who were withdrawn into Army Reserve. After this action the Canadians asked us to wear their maple-leaf emblem on our tanks and tunics, which we did from then on with considerable pride.[8]

Victor Bulger of the 1st Regiment, RCHA – the artillery unit supporting the 1st Canadian Division – took part in the advance up the Liri valley:

At 0630 hours on 19 May the Van Doos (22th Regiment) and the Carleton York Regiment attacked the Hitler Line (now renamed the Dora Line) with the 1st Division artillery in support. During the assault, part of the artillery had to be switched to support the 78th Division's attack on Aquino, a key town in the line held by German paratroopers. Captain Keith Saunders, the RCHA forward observation officer, ran forward and climbed a tree to better observe the battle and, in one narrow escape, spotted a sniper before he saw him and dropped him with a shot from his revolver; for this he was later awarded the Military Cross. The infantry brigades suffered many casualties in this attack, pressing the German withdrawal though the Hitler Line, which was studded with steel tank cupolas, pillboxes and many minefields.

The guns were kept busy for the next few days and nights, firing programmes as called for. On 20 May we fired on a 'Victor' target – using all the guns in the Corps – on an enemy HQ and saw the air force diving to bomb Pontecorvo, a few miles ahead. During all this time the men would run to the kitchen one at a time and bring back their meal and eat it when they could be spared from the gun – also wash and shave when it could be fitted in, unload ammo when the truck came round, clean the gun, finish digging the gun pits, and perhaps fit in a couple of hours' sleep, when possible.

H-Hour for the final assault on the much vaunted Hitler Line came on 23 May at 0600 hours. A thick morning haze shrouded the Liri valley when the roar of nearly 900 guns sounded the opening of the fire plan. The 3rd Brigade moved forward behind this barrage; the 2nd Brigade were pinned down on their first objective by heavy fire from the German paratroopers in Aquino. At 1300 hours a 'William' target was called for – that is, all the guns concentrated on the little town of Aquino. In a couple of minutes some 74 tons of high explosives crashed down on the town and completely demolished it. The RCHA fired over 12,000 rounds of HE that day, and the ammo trucks were kept busy bringing shells forward.

The regiment moved forward at around 0900 hours next day, and had moved a mile or so when we were stopped by heavy traffic. I noticed to the right of the road a long-barrelled anti-tank gun which was mounted on a turret and just above ground level – part of the defences of the Hitler Line and called a Panther tank turret. It had knocked out 12 or 13 of our tanks, which were in a curved line, and it looked as if they were knocked out while trying to outflank it – this was part of what was known as a *Panzerturm*, unknown to us at this time: what amazed us was the intricate defences, in great depth – acres of barbed wire, covered on the flanks by machine-guns and mortars.

A short distance up the road we stopped again while the engineers bulldozed the rubble off the road through Pontecorvo. Nearby a lorry was unloading a truckful of blanket-wrapped bodies, killed in this latest attack – a grim task. One of the gunners in our battery, Jim Brady, had heard that his brother had arrived in Italy to join the 48th Highlanders as a reinforcement. As if drawn by some secret fear, he inspected several of the new temporary graves and found his brother's 'I' tag nailed to a makeshift cross.

Pontecorvo was a complete ruin, just the odd wall or building standing, the streets full of rubble which had been pushed aside by bulldozers to clear a narrow path for the tanks and trucks.[9]

As related in these accounts, it was not until 23 May that General Leese put in a full-scale attack on the Hitler/Dora Line, but this date suited Alexander very well. The time had come for VI Corps to make its breakout from the Anzio bridgehead, and the two attacks could go ahead together. This was a timely and fortunate decision for Kesselring, alarmed at the speed and strength of the breakthrough at Cassino, had sent all his reserves south to Tenth Army, leaving Fourteenth Army at Anzio without an armoured division in support. The last available panzer unit in Italy – the 26th Panzer Division – was now north of Rome at Civitavecchia, ready to repel that expected Allied invasion. Without reserves, Fourteenth Army had just five under-strength infantry divisions to stem Lucian Truscott's six-division assault from the Anzio bridgehead.

On 23 May the 1st Canadian Division attacked the centre of the Dora Line in the Liri valley up to Pontecorvo, while the Poles – flushed with their success at Cassino – took on the Line's bastion at Piedimonte. Later that day at Anzio, the US 3rd Infantry Division, the American–Canadian 1st Special Service Force and the 1st US Armored Division attacked the bridgehead perimeter at Cisterna. The Canadians breached the Dora Line within the day, and the 5th Canadian Armoured Division was pouring north on 24 May. On 25 May the Poles completed the capture of Piedimonte, and the Dora Line then collapsed. On the same day, Cisterna on Route 7 fell to troops from the bridgehead, and II Corps units advancing from the Garigliano made contact with Truscott's forces at Anzio. After almost six months, the gap between the Allied forces at Cassino and Anzio had been closed.

The diary of Captain Deane of the Scots Guards again:

> Move off at 0500 hours, horribly dark. Keep nose to tail and drive up Route 6 to a staging area by Cassino. My God, what a place – everything covered in dirt, dust, barbed wire, mine signs. Have to dig in under sporadic shelling from a lone 75-mm and hostile aircraft. See two charming French girls. On 27 May move through Cassino; the smell and stench of death is almost unbelievable. What real destruction! Drive out on Route 6 past enemy dumps and knocked-out tanks to a small town called Roccosecco. Our task is to round up roving bands of German paratroopers and others caught in the hills. The whole situation is fantastic. 13 Platoon is taken off the hill to collect some Jerry rifles, some Spandaus and three anti-tank panzerfausts, which are new to us. The Canadian Corps is driving on fast.[10]

To say that General Alexander and the Staff at 15th Army Group (AAI) were delighted with this progress is to understate the case. After three terrible battles at Cassino and the long-drawn-out stalemate of Anzio, the Axis front had split wide open and the Allied armies were forging forward. Alexander's plan for Operation DIADEM had worked perfectly and if everyone played their part, Tenth Army would soon be in the bag and the Allied forces could move on Rome and the north, driving Fourteenth Army before them – nothing the Germans could do would stop them. Unfortunately, there was always a snag in Italy and the snag at this time was General Mark W. Clark.

Alexander's orders for the operations of Truscott's VI Corps at Anzio were quite specific. On breaking out, VI Corps was to move south of the Alban Hills and cut off the retreating German Tenth Army at Valmontone. There was nothing complicated about this. Alexander was laying the classic military trap – something similar to Beda Fomm, with VI Corps as the blocking force and the Fifth and Eighth Armies as the plunger.

The advance of Eighth Army up the Liri valley was undoubtedly slow, not because of any great enemy resistance but because of the enclosed nature of the country (which narrows sharply above Ceprano and Piccolo) and the usual abundance of German mines and demolitions. There was also the problem that far too many units were trying to use the same road, Route 6, which is a mountain road after the Liri valley ends at Arce and Piccolo. Also, the small hill towns on this road, at Frosinone, Ferentino and the rest, were all enemy defensive positions and stoutly held. The Fifth Army, heading up the coastal plain on Route 7, had no such problems and therefore made more rapid progress before linking up with Truscott's Corps at Cisterna. Truscott's task now was to head north-east from the bridgehead and cut Route 6.

Everyone knew this, and no one – including Clark – could be in any doubt about Alexander's orders to that effect. Alexander's strategy was about to reach fruition on 25 May, when Truscott's patrols were already in touch with Route 6 at Valmontone. On that day Clark sent a staff officer, Brigadier-General Donald W. Brann, to Truscott's headquarters with fresh orders.

When he read these orders, Truscott was, in his own words, 'dumbfounded'. Clark was ordering him to leave the blocking of Route 6 to the Special Service Force and the 3rd Infantry Division and send the rest of his corps north-west, directly up Route 7 for

Rome. 'This was no time to drive to the north west where the enemy was still strong,' wrote Truscott later, 'we should pour our maximum power into the Valmontone gap to ensure the destruction of the retreating German Army.'

Truscott refused to accept this order, and insisted on talking to Clark directly. When he attempted to do so, it transpired that Clark was not at his HQ – being absent from his headquarters was a habit of his when hard decisions had to be made. Nor, apparently, was Clark in contact with his staff even by radio – a curious situation for an Army Commander in the middle of a battle. Clark remained out of touch all day, and Truscott, having received a direct order he was unable to query, had no option but to carry it out. The 1st Special Service Force and the 3rd Infantry Division headed for Valmontone – where they were held off by the Hermann Goering Division while the rest of Tenth Army got past – and the rest of VI Corps moved on Rome.

The result of this diversion was the effective failure of Alexander's DIADEM offensive, whose main objective was the destruction of Tenth Army and the containment of German forces that might otherwise be diverted to Normandy. For Alexander and his soldiers this was a considerable disappointment. On the other hand, this diversion into Rome provided some wonderful publicity for General Mark W. Clark.

The US Official History produces some other reasons for this action. Clark, it is alleged, 'believed that the destruction of the enemy forces south of Rome was an impossible objective'.[11] It is strange that Clark did not mention this belief in his memoirs, or to Truscott or to Alexander at the time. Besides, what Clark believed has nothing to do with the matter. Even if he disagreed with Alexander's aims, like his unhappy subordinate Lucian Truscott he was still obliged to obey orders and attempt to carry them out. The US History seems to have forgotten about Tenth Army and maintains that the object of DIADEM was the destruction of Fourteenth Army. A look at the map and a second's thought would dispel that notion; defeated armies do not withdraw in the direction of the advancing enemy.

There is even the suggestion that '[Fourteenth Army] was more hard pressed as it withdrew beyond Rome before the US Fifth Army than was the Tenth Army which had managed to escape virtually intact across the mountains and across the

Aniene before the British Eighth Army'.[12] On the other hand, Clark states in his memoirs that 'The Germans had lost 1,500 vehicles, 110 pieces of artillery, 125 self-propelled artillery and anti-tank guns since the middle of May. Much more equipment was abandoned in flight or destroyed by our Air Force and we had taken 15,000 prisoners.'[13]

Between the start of DIADEM and the fall of Rome, the two German armies lost around 38,000 men.[14] Tenth Army alone lost over 8,000 men in the withdrawal from Cassino – about 10 per cent of its strength – in addition to those lost in the Cassino battle, plus vast quantities of equipment, so it was not 'virtually intact' when it surged past Valmontone.

If this victory was not enough and the bulk of Tenth Army escaped, the fault lies with Mark Clark, and no officially manufactured smokescreen can conceal that fact – as General Truscott's comments below make clear. Truscott's VI Corps at Anzio consisted of four US divisions, including an armoured division, plus two British divisions, Brigadier-General Robert Frederick's 1st Special Service Force and a battalion of the 509th Parachute Infantry Regiment. This corps of six divisions – virtually an army – had no difficulty brushing Fourteenth Army aside, and could, had it been allowed to do so, have shown an equal facility in blocking the pell-mell retreat of Tenth Army before the British Eighth Army.

This is not chauvinism; in his memoirs Lucian Truscott wrote, 'There has never been any doubt in my mind that had General Clark held loyally to General Alexander's instructions, had he not changed the direction of my attack to the north west on May 26, the strategic objective of Anzio would have been accomplished in full. To be first into Rome was poor compensation for this lost opportunity.'

Clark's post-war claim that the US VI Corps was not strong enough to block Route 6 is nonsense – one weak British division was enough to stop an entire Italian Army at Beda Fomm. Fourteenth Army, with a ration strength on 10 May of 76,873 men,[15] was smaller than Tenth Army by 10,000 men at the start of DIADEM and even smaller by the time of the Anzio breakout two weeks later when units had been switched south to hold the Adolf Hitler/Dora Line in the Liri valley. The allegation that Fourteenth Army was the larger and more formidable German force is not supported by the facts – and the US VI Corps had six strong divisions, infantry and armour, supported by the Allied air forces and capable of taking on any opposition.

The reasons for Clark's action are provided by Clark himself – and they make sad reading. 'I was determined that Fifth Army were going to capture Rome and was probably unduly sensitive to indications that practically everyone else was trying to get in on the act.' In an interview after the war, Clark even declared that 'he told Alexander he would, if ordered to permit the Eighth Army to participate, not only refuse but would fire on any Eighth Army soldiers who tried to do so'.

This account, given by Clark in an interview on 18 May 1948, is recorded in the US Official History.[16] If Clark would indeed have ordered his troops to fire on their British comrades in Eighth Army, one wonders if they would have done so – and what the Eighth Army soldiers would have done in reply. Speculation apart, this story tends to indicate that Clark's craving for publicity – 'a Roman triumph'[17] – had gone beyond the point of obsession into the realms of paranoia.

In fact British soldiers did enter Rome with Clark on 4 June – the US Fifth Army contained many British units. The Union Jack that the British troops hoisted in Rome that day is now on display in the study at Chartwell, Winston Churchill's former home in Kent. Among the British units passing through Rome was the 201st Guards Brigade of the 5th Division, and among their number was the amorous Captain D. H. Deane of the 2nd Battalion Scots Guards:

> Drive through Rome with the entire division, tanks and everything, and got a tremendous welcome. Patrick disgraces himself, even for an RASC driver, by giving cigarettes to the smiling civilians. Stay in Rome from 1700 to 0200 hours in a traffic block and air raid. See the loveliest girl in my life in red; I melt enough to give her a cigarette; Sergeant McCaffery gets a bit too familiar, probably tight, by enticing a vile and sexy-looking woman to climb aboard and kiss me.

So the British did play a part in the liberation of Rome. But there was another reason for Clark's eagerness to get there first – one confirmed by the following encounter on the outskirts of Rome on 4 June between Brigadier-General Robert Frederick of the 1st Special Service Force and Lieutenant-General Geoffrey Keyes of the US II Corps.

'What's holding you up here?' asked Keyes.

'The Germans, sir,' said Frederick, 'There are a couple of SP guns up there and it may take a day to get across the city. '

'That won't do,' said Keyes, 'General Clark must be across city limits by four o'clock.'

'Why?' asked Frederick.

Keyes replied, 'Because he wants to have his photograph taken.'

Frederick looked at Keyes for a long moment, and said, 'Tell the General to give me an hour.'[18]

The SP guns were duly silenced, the General and his photographer arrived, and the pictures were taken – the conqueror within his captured city. Those Allied soldiers who lost their lives on the road to Rome died without knowing that their sacrifice provided General Mark W. Clark with a photo-opportunity

This action is particularly sad because Clark is a general who grows on you. He was an American commander in the Eisenhower mode, frequently generous to his Allies, without the stark chauvinism or Anglophobia that afflicted so many of his colleagues. You begin to warm to him – and now this. The irony is twofold. First, it was always Alexander's intention that Fifth Army would take Rome; the city lay in the path of Fifth Army and Alexander had no intention of diverting Eighth Army from the pursuit of the enemy for a spot of sightseeing.

The second irony is that Clark's glory was of such brief duration. Fifth Army entered Rome on Sunday 4 June, and that feat was blazoned across the newspapers on Monday 5 June. But, alas for Clark, on the following day, 6 June 1944, Allied forces landed in Normandy and this event drove Clark's triumph completely from the headlines. *Sic transit gloria* indeed.

56 (London) Div.

14

To the Gothic Line
June–November 1944

We're the D-day Dodgers, out in Italy,
Always drinking vino, always on the spree,
Eighth Army skivers and the Yanks
We live in Rome, we laugh at tanks,
For we're the D-Day Dodgers, in sunny Italy.

Doggerel verse, sung to the tune of *Lili Marlene*,
popular in Eighth Army after 6 June 1944

After taking Rome, the commanders of the Allied Armies in Italy were confident that they could forge rapidly north to the next major obstacle, the German Gothic Line, between Pisa and Rimini, south of the river Po. Although the battle for Rome had not delivered the crushing victory that Alexander wanted, it was still considered possible to continue the offensive, keep up the pressure, and prevent the Germans switching forces from Italy to Normandy. With the fall of Cassino and the capture of Rome, the Allied armies in Italy were ready to surge forward to the Po valley and the Alps, carrying all before them.

Alexander now had 28 divisions in pursuit of 21 German divisions – not an overwhelming advantage in terms of numbers, but those German divisions were tired and much written-down, short of equipment, and without the massive support the Allied armies enjoyed from their tactical and strategic air forces. There seemed no reason why, with all the summer before them, the Allies could not drive Kesselring's beaten forces all the way back to the Alps – provided the pursuit could be maintained. That aim apart, once the Po valley was in Allied hands, various strategic possibilities would be open for further exploitation.

This advance and the benefits it would bring seemed very logical to Churchill, the British Chiefs of Staff and most of the Allied commanders in the Mediterranean – excluding the Supreme Commander, Sir Henry Maitland Wilson – but it was not to be. The Allied Armies in Italy, already reduced by sending several of their best divisions and most of their amphibious shipping back to the UK for OVERLORD, were now confronted with fresh demands for troops for Operation ANVIL, the Allied invasion of southern France. Without all their existing forces, amphibious shipping and reinforcements, Clark and Leese would find progress north of Rome an uphill struggle indeed.

Eric Garner again:

> Morale was generally very good until after the fall of Rome, and we were then too busy to care much about what was happening in France. From the autumn of 1944, though, we began to realize that Italy was really a backwater. We started losing divisions to Greece, and others, like the Canadians, were sent back to north-west Europe. The infantry was the worst affected by manpower shortages, many battalions being reduced from four to three rifle companies, and even this could only be managed by disbanding AA units and transferring their personnel to the infantry. We realized that we were the poor relations, and our strength was such that a major offensive seemed unlikely – although we had acquired several Italian groups which were equipped with British equipment.[1]

ANVIL had been planned as an operation in support of OVERLORD and was to take place in June, close to D-Day. It had the aim of diverting German divisions from Normandy, opening another front in western Europe, and providing more landing ports – Marseilles and Toulon – for the American divisions waiting in the USA for shipment to Europe. But the British had never cared for ANVIL. They believed that boosting the armies in Italy

would provide all the gains promised for ANVIL and quite a few
more besides. Among these were the opportunity for strategic
gains in the north-east of Italy with a land thrust or an amphibious landing past Trieste into Yugoslavia, followed with an
advance through the Ljubljana gap towards Austria.

Such a move not only would oblige the enemy to divert divisions for the defence of the Führer's homeland – for Adolf Hitler
was an Austrian – it would also prevent the Russians gaining all
the credit for defeating Germany in the east – and from overrunning all of eastern Europe, with all that that might mean for the
political shape of the post-war Continent. These matters have
been raised before in this book, but they must be examined again
here, because how they were resolved would have a dire effect
on the abilities and actions of the Allied Armies in Italy after the
fall of Rome.

The US Chiefs of Staff – and President Roosevelt – were not
much interested in the post-war shape of Europe. They wanted
to defeat Germany, then send their forces to defeat Japan, and
then bring the boys home for good and get on with the peace. All
this was very understandable, but lacked any long-term political
thinking. Winning the war was not the only objective: it was necessary to win it in such a way that Nazi domination of Europe
was not replaced with Communist domination and that the
ground was not laid for yet another European conflict, as after the
First World War. A difference in strategic thinking, short-term or
long-term, underlies many of the arguments over ANVIL.

This matter could be decided only by the Allies' joint military
body, the Combined Chiefs of Staff – the CCS. But the CCS was
totally split – and split on national lines. In an ideal world it
would have taken a purely objective view of military matters,
deciding what was best in the long term and how that aim could
be achieved in the short term. There should, in short, have been
an *Allied* point of view – at least among the CCS; an Allied view
among the politicians was perhaps too much to hope for.

As it was, the component parts of the CCS fought each other
with considerable enthusiasm – and not a little chauvinism – and
since the US Chiefs had control of the physical assets, in this case
control of the vital amphibious ships and the American element
in the US Fifth Army, it was their views, if not their arguments,
that usually carried the day. This difference of opinion among

the military men reached up to the highest political level, to President Franklin D. Roosevelt and Prime Minister Winston Churchill. Unless some solution could be found to this chronic dilemma, the very unity of the Western Allies was in trouble.

Each body of senior officers, American and British, had a point. There were arguments in favour of both courses of action – ANVIL and Italy – and the only way to reach a decision was to examine the merits of both cases and try to judge them fairly. One thing was certain: there could be no compromise. That old bugbear, a shortage of landing craft would see to that. Either the Allied Armies went ahead in Italy and were fully supported or Allied divisions from Italy, with all the necessary shipping, were sent on ANVIL – from which case the Italian front, starved of troops and amphibious lift, would instantly become a sideshow.

To examine the US position we must go back to December 1941, when the USA entered the war. At the Arcadia Conference in Washington, shortly after Pearl Harbor, the Allies decided on a policy of 'Germany First' – and the major step towards implementing that policy would be an invasion of France, Operation OVERLORD. Driven by American pressure, plans were laid for a landing in France in 1942 (Operation SLEDGEHAMMER) and in 1943. Fortunately these premature plans failed to come to fruition, but US pressure was always there.

In spite of agreeing to the North African landings and the subsequent invasions of Sicily and Italy, the USA never wavered from the conviction that the landing in France was one to which all other operations must be subjected. During the years before OVERLORD the Americans convinced themselves that the British, or certainly Winston Churchill, were wavering on OVERLORD and would like to wriggle out of that commitment.

There is very little evidence to support that conclusion, though there was a fundamental difference in views over the strategic conduct of the war. Fundamentally, the American philosophy was to get together the largest force, land in France, advance into Germany, and crush the enemy by numbers and superior military technology. Given the large American population and the vast industrial resources of the USA, this was a viable option for the Americans to consider, albeit a costly one in lives.

The British could not afford such an option. Apart from being a much smaller nation, in both military and industrial terms, by

1944 Britain was running out of manpower. Besides, frontal assaults were no longer the British way. Churchill and his Chiefs of Staff, though completely committed to OVERLORD, thought that it should be launched only when the Axis powers had been fully stretched and written-down by campaigns elsewhere: in North Africa, the Balkans, Russia – and Italy.

This dispute had been simmering since 1942, but in the summer of 1944 some geopolitical matters were added to the brew. The Americans were now convinced that Churchill was playing some deep political game in the Mediterranean: specifically, that he was trying to get the Allied armies involved in a costly campaign in the Balkans with the aim of establishing a British sphere of influence there after the war. There is little substance in this belief. Churchill was indeed interested in supporting partisan activity in the Balkans, specifically in Yugoslavia, but this was done with air drops of weapons and military instructors and the establishment of commando raiding forces in the Adriatic islands. No major military commitment was envisaged, and US fears of Churchill's 'Balkan adventures' were unfounded.

With the capture of Rome and the launching of OVERLORD, matters changed. Now there was indeed a political dimension. Allied victory was now inevitable, but what would be the shape of the peace? By 1944 Churchill was becoming increasingly suspicious of Russia's post-war intentions in Europe. Many of the most active resistance movements in western Europe – in France and Italy as well as in Greece and throughout the Balkans – were already under Communist control and stockpiling arms for the post-war period. These Communist movements looked to Moscow for political and military support in gaining power in their home countries after the war ended. Churchill was therefore coming round to the view that the further east the Allied armies met the Red Army the better. If the Red Army finished the war deep in Europe, the prospects for the re-establishment of democracy in the post-war world were slender indeed.

In Churchill's view, the strategic, geopolitical objective of a rapid move north towards Yugoslavia and Hungary and into Austria was not incompatible with support for OVERLORD. If the Allied Armies in Italy moved quickly towards the Po and took Venice, Trieste and Istria, they could then move through the Ljubljana gap into Slovenia, out on to the Hungarian plains, and into Vienna before the Russians. This move into the very heart of the Reich was sure to provoke some massive response from the enemy. Even if it did not fully succeed, the threat itself would force the Germans to commit divisions that would otherwise be involved in France – given Germany's chronic fear of a Soviet invasion, it was less likely that divisions would be shifted from the Eastern Front.

If such a move was backed with powerful forces, military and amphibious, Churchill's view was strategically viable and politically sensible. Military campaigns often make little sense on their own: they have to contribute to the overall strategy of the war – and to the peace that must follow the war. Churchill's plan – one supported by the British Chiefs of Staff, although with little enthusiasm from Alan Brooke – would have put pressure on the Germans during the present war and left the Western democracies in a better position to handle Soviet aggression or Communist subversion after it.

The Americans were not interested in a push towards Hungary. The Soviet leader, Marshal Josef Stalin, was currently an ally and, rather more to the point in American eyes, a republican. That he was also a tyrant and murderer was beside the point: at least he was not a wily, arch-imperialist like Churchill, trying to drag the USA into further conflict in support of British imperial ambitions. The USA intended to come out of this war as the major contributor to victory, and to leave the future of the world in the hands of the United Nations. This view, while understandable, lacked any historical depth. After the First World War, President Woodrow Wilson had left the future of Europe in the hands of the Paris treaties and the League of Nations; the result of that, eventually, was the Second World War. A similar lack of strategic vision in 1944–5 was to leave the USA and her European allies badly placed during the subsequent Cold War.

It should be mentioned that Stalin was a strong supporter of ANVIL. This fact alone should have made everyone suspicious and many people were – not all of them British. In his memoirs, Mark Clark notes that 'He [Stalin] knew exactly what he wanted in a political as well as a military way; and the thing he wanted most was to keep us out of the Balkans which he had staked out for the Red Army.' Clark added, 'I later came to understand, in Austria, the tremendous advantages we had lost by our failure to press into the Balkans . . . had we been there before the Red Army, not only would the collapse of Germany have come sooner, the influence of Soviet Russia would have been greatly reduced.'[2]

The final arguments over ANVIL went on from 7 June – D-Day plus 1 – to 8 August, and were finally resolved not by an objective weighing of the facts, but by US diktat. In his war diaries, Harold Macmillan, the British minister resident at Allied Headquarters, records that, in view of the American attitude, the British would always have to give way: 'We can fight up to a point, we can leave on record for history to judge the reasoned statement of our views and the historian will also see that the Americans never answered any argument, never attempted to discuss or debate the points, but have merely given a flat negative and a somewhat Shylock-like insistence on what they conceive to be their bargain.'

The 'pound of flesh' was this. The Americans had agreed to 'Germany First' if the British implemented that policy the American way: that meant OVERLORD *and* ANVIL. That the eventual outcome of the war in Europe and the political shape of the Continent afterwards were more important to the people who lived there than to those on the far side of the Atlantic weighed nothing in this argument.

And so to ANVIL and the fate of the Allied armies in Italy. The American Joint Chiefs of Staff, having rejected the British counter-proposal out of hand, advanced a number of reasons for pressing on with ANVIL. First of all, General Eisenhower, the Supreme Allied Commander, wanted it. Eisenhower saw the landing of Allied troops in the South of France as a means of diverting German units from the Normandy front and as a way of getting more Allied units into action against the Germans. He also wanted the port of Marseilles for the landing of men, stores and equipment to support the Allied advance into Germany.

There is some merit in Eisenhower's reasoning. An Allied landing in southern France would divert German strength – but so would the advance of Allied troops into Istria and Austria. But as for the use of Marseilles as a port, a glance at a map shows what little use it would be. By mid-August 1944 Marseilles was already 500 miles from the Allied front in Normandy – where German resistance was almost at an end – and this distance would increase with every mile the Allied forces marched towards Germany after the Normandy breakout. These miles were over 1940s-style roads, much damaged by neglect and demolition, not modern European autoroutes. The ambition of using Marseilles to support the advance in the north was therefore never realized; between the fall of the city and the end of the war, exactly three US divisions entered Europe via Marseilles, and the quantity of stores landed there still had a long way to travel.

All in all, a fair assessment of the argument over ANVIL must conclude that the best strategic option was to drop ANVIL and concentrate all Allied strength in Italy for a rapid advance towards the Po and Istria. Unfortunately, the issue of ANVIL would not get a fair assessment: the US Joint Chiefs had all the clout. They wanted ANVIL, and ANVIL there would be.

The decision to go for ANVIL – later called DRAGOON, because the British had been 'dragooned' into it – had a profound affect on the Allied armies in Italy. ANVIL required the dispatch to France of most of the US Fifth Army – all four French divisions and Truscott's VI Corps – seven divisions in all. Writing to Churchill on 18 June, Alexander stated that 'the enemy are a beaten force but not yet eliminated from the field . . . the Germans intend to hold the Apennines with the equivalent of ten to twelve divisions on a front of 150 miles. Against this, I can, *provided I have left to me intact my present force* [my italics] amass such a powerful force of fresh divisions as will split the German forces in half and eliminate the German forces in Italy.' Nothing, he added, could prevent the Allied forces marching on Vienna except the commitment of another ten of so divisions by the enemy. 'Should that be the case, I understand that it is just what is required to help OVERLORD.'

Mark Clark was also convinced that ANVIL was a mistake, writing in his war diary:

> I assume that the Combined Chiefs-of-Staff making these decisions know what they are doing and that ANVIL will contribute more to the invasion and the Second Front than our continued effort in Italy. I am convinced, however, that their decision was made long ago and without realizing the great success Fifth and Eighth Armies were to have in Italy . . . the Boche is defeated, disorganized and demoralized. Now is the time to exploit our success. Yet in the middle of this success I lose two Corps headquarters and seven divisions. It just does not make sense.[3]

The effects of the ANVIL/DRAGOON decision were soon felt. On 11 June, a week after the fall of Rome, Truscott and his VI Corps HQ were removed from Fifth Army, followed by three US divisions – the 3rd, 36th and 45th – plus the 1st Special Service Force. In July the four divisions of Juin's Free French Expeditionary Corps were also removed to form the first component in the US Seventh Army, tasked for ANVIL/DRAGOON. This, says Clark, 'stripped Fifth Army of its strength.'[4] But it did rather more than that: it deprived the Allied armies in Italy of those four divisions of crack mountain troops in the French corps who had already done so well in the advance on Rome from Cassino and whose skills would have been most useful in the coming campaign across the Apennines towards the Po.

At this point it is necessary to return to the map, for the Italian terrain was about to take a hand in strategic affairs. North of Rome, the Apennines swing east and narrow, so creating the wide Tuscan plain that runs north from Rome to the river Arno and Florence. But, as the coastal plain runs north from Pescara to Ancona and Rimini, the Adriatic front, already narrow, becomes even more slender. This would be the first bound of the next Allied advance – to the Pisa–Rimini line.

After that matters would get difficult, for the Apennines then start to swing north and west, creating a mountain barrier to any advance north from Florence towards Bologna and the Po Valley. Nor would the terrain be any more helpful on the Adriatic front. A continual series of rivers runs from the mountains to the Adriatic, and north of Rimini lies the Romagna – former marshland, low-lying and still prone to floods. Nor was it possible to make much progress in the centre, where the province of Umbria, between Tuscany and La Marche, was mountainous, well supplied with hill towns – each ideal for defence – and split in the centre by Lake Trasimeno, the largest lake in Italy.

Wherever they looked, the Allied commanders were faced with a choice of geographical difficulties – until they got over the mountains and marshes into the Po valley, where all manner of strategic opportunities awaited. From the Po they could go west into southern France, north into Austria or east into Yugoslavia to meet the Red Army and Tito's partisans. Mounting more amphibious operations would have eased this territorial dilemma considerably, but a shortage of troops and landing craft denied Alexander and his generals that helpful option. There was also a further consideration – the weather. It was now full summer, but that summer would not last long; the Allied generals needed to take advantage of every hour of good weather before the autumn rains again turned Italy into a swamp. But how could they do that when one of their armies had just been stripped of most of its troops?

The ANVIL/DRAGOON transfer left Fifth Army extremely short-handed. In early August, Clark received the 25,000-strong, US-equipped, Brazilian Corps[5] and the US 92nd Infantry Division – the first black infantry unit to go into combat. (Black Americans had previously been confined to service in the construction and labour units of the Supply Services.) These reinforcements were still not enough, so the British XIII Corps was later transferred from Eighth Army to Fifth Army. In the months that followed the fall of Rome, one feature of Eighth Army's history was a constant change in the Order of Battle as divisions were switched about, rested, transferred between corps, or removed from Italy altogether. The British V Corps took command of the 20,000-strong Italian Liberation Corps, and V Corps was replaced on the Adriatic front by II Polish Corps, which established its HQ near Ortona.

These political, strategic and geographic arguments provide a background to the last eleven months of the campaign in Italy, and with those explained it is time to return to the war.

Following the fall of Rome, the next bound north would be from Rome to Florence and the river Arno. Beyond the Arno lay the Gothic Line protecting the Po valley, the industrial heart of Italy, some 200 miles north of Rome. The Allies had to keep hard on the heels of the retreating German forces, if possible bundling them out of the Gothic Line before they had time to occupy it in any strength.

In this aim the two Allied armies would be greatly aided by the Allied air forces, which were already harrying the German retreat. The pursuit would be hampered by the terrain, a shortage of roads and the usual problems of supply, but everyone agreed – even in Washington – that the Allied armies in Italy should advance to the Pisa–Rimini line, and this advance went ahead quickly. Fifth Army, pressing on against the German Fourteenth Army, took Civitavecchia on 9 June. By 23 July Fifth

Army had reached Pisa, on the river Arno west of Florence. As Fifth Army was moving faster than Eighth Army, admittedly over the much easier ground of Tuscany, its advance gradually exposed the right flank of the German Tenth Army. However, no move was made to take advantage of this – which Alexander either did not notice or failed to exploit. Had he ordered Fifth Army to swing east into the flank of Tenth Army, much more might have been achieved.

Eighth Army was pressing north against Tenth Army on both sides of the Apennines, urged on by General Leese. 'We have the enemy on the run. He must gain time and try to delay us by stubborn rearguard actions, demolitions and minefields. We must drive him on, keep him moving day and night. Every hour gained, every German killed or captured, brings nearer the annihilation of the German Army in Italy.'

Thus encouraged, Eighth Army pressed on through the eastern Apennines into the province of Umbria. Castelnuovo, 18 miles north of Rome, fell to the South African 6th Armoured Division on 5 June. This advance continued, with XIII Corps making for the wine town of Orvieto, while X Corps, now back with Eighth Army, drove for Perugia, the capital of Umbria, their path contested by German infantry equipped with panzerfausts and the appearance of Panther and Tiger tanks. Orvieto fell to the South Africans on 14 June, Assisi on 18 June, and Perugia to the 78th Division on 20 June.

The crux of the battle here lay around the German positions north-west of Perugia. The Eighth Army arrived here as the weather broke, and sudden rain turned the countryside into a quagmire. German resistance was already stiffening, and new Axis units – the 162nd (Turkoman) Division and the 20th (Luftwaffe) Division – had moved south to form a defence line astride the great physical feature of Umbria, Lake Trasimeno.

This early rain was a great help to Field Marshal Kesselring, who was still trying to get his forces back from their pursuers and reorganize his Tenth and Fourteenth Armies – Army Group C – behind the Gothic Line. He was also aided by the slowness of the Allied advance, and by his as yet undented conviction that he could bring the Allied advance to a halt and create another stalemate.

The British Official History records that 'Eighth Army's

pursuit became a never-ending story of leading troops held up by relatively minor demolitions covered by one or two tanks or SP guns which took time to locate and destroy before the sappers could clear a way through. The most precious weapons in Eighth Army's armoury at this time was the humble bulldozer and the Sappers' simple mine probe.'[6]

Eric Garner of the Royal Engineers:

As an example of the extent of demolitions throughout Italy, a copy of a recce report from my OC dated 26 June 1944 gives some idea of the problems encountered. This report covers a 13-mile section of the road. Why anyone was interested in this particular road I know not; it was a backwater, as at the time we were working to link the lateral to the main Eighth Army at Terni. This level of demolition, 9 major demolitions in 13 miles plus lots of cratering, is about par for the course. This lot does not appear to have been very difficult, and we were attempting to get the Italians to open the route for light vehicles. Nearer the front it was a lot worse. This report indicates that every bridge was blown, and we needed a succession of Bailey bridges – one 180 foot, one 140 foot, four 100 foot – plus mine-clearing equipment and civilian labour to keep the roads open. Diverting round these demolitions was usually difficult or impossible.[7]

The Official History also makes some criticism of General Leese. 'One arm, however, lay almost unused. There were in Italy no less than three Indian divisions, 4th, 8th and 10th, all of which had experienced in and were adept at hill and mountain warfare. General Leese seemed to be unaware of their potential . . . '

This criticism is not entirely well founded. These Indian Army divisions were perhaps more suited to mountain warfare than those containing their British comrades, but, unlike the French Moroccan *goums*, their men were not mountain troops per se. They did not have the training, equipment or mule trains to sustain long, unsupported advances over the hills. And, anyway, the hills were not a problem at this time: the problems now were the weather and the enemy.

Following the tactics employed south of Rome, the Germans fell back steadily from one defensible position to another, some merely rallying points, others created for more sustained resistance. In mid-June the Germans made a determined stand at Lake

Trasimeno, where the 78th Division, the 9th Armoured Brigade and the South African 6th Armoured Division arrived on 17 June. The fighting here was concentrated on a line between the walled town of Chiusi, through Sanfatucchio to the south-western corner of Lake Trasimeno – the Albert Line to the Germans, the Trasaimene Line to the British. Here the enemy appeared in force, with three and a half divisions deployed along the Chiusi ridge – one of them the elite 1st Parachute, supported by a quantity of tanks, machine-guns and nebelwerfers manned by troops of the Hermann Goering Division. Lieutenant-General S. C. Kirkman, commanding XIII Corps, decided that a full corps attack was needed, and this went in on 21 June. The fighting here was extremely fierce, and continued until 28 June, Chiusi and the Albert Line only falling after the defenders had been outflanked by an attack mounted by the Coldstream Guards of the 24th Guards Brigade.

The Germans did not fall back far. They left plenty of booby traps and demolitions to delay their pursuers, and the fighting around Lake Trasimeno did not finally end until June 28, when the 78th Division took Sanfatucchio. The eight days of fighting for the Trasaimene Line brought the advance of Eighth Army to a brief halt for regrouping. The next tactical bound towards Florence would mean dealing with the next German defensive line at the walled town of Arrezo. Arrezo occupied a strong position on the plain, but one overlooked by the hills above the upper Arno valley.

The advance to Arezzo was slow, the troops being constantly delayed by enemy rearguards, mines and snipers; the 4th and 78th Divisions of XIII Corps were often reduced to a distance of 3 or 4 miles a day. Arrezo was held by units of the 15th Panzergrenadier and 1st Parachute Divisions, and their resistance was well up to form in a close-fought battle that lasted from 5 to 16 July, and in which the 6th New Zealand Brigade and the 1st Guards Brigade of XIII Corps distinguished themselves.

Ernest Smallridge recalls this time:

> More and more hill and mountain work. We were even seeing troops with strings of mules higher up, and I hoped we did not have to lay lines to their HQs. Perugia and Arezzo were our stopping-off places for going east or west, and we moved about

often. I remember being on the outskirts of Siena nearer to the west coast on one day and sneaking a quick swim on the east coast near Rimini on the following day. Bare footprints on the beach told me there was less chance of mines in that area. Cesena, Forli and Faenza came after Xmas, but it was a very slow advance – rivers, mines and the old problem of fighting uphill for our troops for the next few months.[8]

Nor was McCreery's X Corps moving any faster in the rocky country around Perugia and east of the Tiber. After the enemy fell back from Trasimeno on that flank, the 10th Indian Division was brought up to spearhead the Corps advance, and 'up a hill, downhill, ford a stream, up a hill, downhill, ford a stream' became the daily routine as recorded in the 10th Division history. Persistence in grinding forward eventually paid off. The Germans were not allowed to stand, and Eighth Army's advance continued, greatly aided by the fighter bombers of the Allied air forces, which were vectored on to their targets from the ground – a technique, codenamed Rover David, which identified and pinpointed enemy positions and convoys for the fighter and fighter-bomber aircraft waiting in 'cab ranks' overhead.

Arezzo fell to the 16th/5th Lancers on 16 July, and later that day the 2nd New Zealand Division crossed the Arno and turned west towards Florence. The Germans had already declared Florence an 'open city' – one which they would not defend and which, they hoped, the Allies would not attack. General Alfred Jodl, Chief of Army Operations at OKW, declared that Florence was 'the jewel of Europe and would not be destroyed'. Other Tuscan cities also benefited from this decision – Siena, the gem of Tuscany, had just fallen without destruction to the Free French Expeditionary Corps.

Eighth Army was moving steadily forward and keeping up the pressure on the enemy, but it was not costing him much in the way of casualties. XIII Corps took only 165 prisoners in the battle for Arrezo, and the various battles on the road to Florence and the Arno – though short and sharp – gave Kesselring more time to fortify the Gothic Line as the brief weeks of summer passed.

The battle for Florence was fought south of the city by the 8th Indian, 2nd New Zealand and 6th South African Divisions of XIII Corps. It lasted just three days – from 30 July to 1 August,

when the German commander in Florence, Colonel Fuch of the
10th Parachute Regiment, declared that 'his forces would not
expose themselves to defeat for the sake of the beauties of
Florence' and blew every bridge across the Arno except the
Ponte Vecchio before withdrawing to the north. Florence fell to
Indian troops of Eighth Army on 17 August. The Arno was no
longer an obstacle, and the next phase would carry the Allied
armies up to – and with any luck over – the Gothic Line and into
the Po Valley.

This withdrawal from Florence did not prevent the Germans
making good use of the ground outside the city, and there was
heavy tank and infantry fighting in the vineyards of the Chianti
country. The advancing New Zealanders grew wary of German
tanks and panzerfaust crews concealed under the high-strung
Tuscan vines and behind the thick stone walls of the farmyards.
As one New Zealand account puts it, 'Even as in the desert,
where every gun was an 88-mm, so here every tracked vehicle
heard ahead was a Tiger; as a result the New Zealand armour
grew cautious.'

While this battle for Florence was in progress McCreery's X
Corps was moving up to yet another Eighth Army objective, the
town of Bibbiena at the northern end of the upper Arno valley
west of Florence, while on the Adriatic coast the Polish Corps,
having taken Ancona, was now engaged in a deception plan,
Operation OTTRINGTON, which hoped to convince the Germans
that the main Allied push towards the Gothic Line would be on
the Adriatic via Rimini and not in the centre of the Allied line,
from Florence over the mountains towards Bologna.

Fifth Army had reached the Arno west of Florence on 23 July.
Then, like Eighth Army to the east, it was held up by a shortage
of supplies, notably petrol and artillery ammunition. The port of
Leghorn (Livorno) had been comprehensively destroyed before
the Germans left, so the supply lines were long and lengthening.
As a result of this shortage – and a need to rest units that had
been on the move continually since breaking the Gustav Line in
mid-May – after the fall of Florence and the gaining of the Arno
line in August there was a delay in launching a further advance.

This delay, however necessary and largely caused by the
needs of ANVIL, was to have serious consequences later in the
year. It deprived Alexander of several weeks of fine weather – an

asset that was never abundant during the Italian campaign, and one which should have been used while it lasted. Had Clark not lost seven divisions to ANVIL and Leese not needed to rest some of his divisions which had been fighting continually since before Cassino, there would have been no pressing need to halt. The tired or written-down divisions could have been replaced in the line by fresh or full-strength divisions and the advance could have continued. So do the actions in one time and place affect other actions later in some other place.

Meanwhile there was a small problem with morale. After the D-Day landings the Italian front disappeared from the newspapers and newsreels in the USA and Britain, where public attention was now fixed on the Allied armies in Normandy. This in itself was not a problem: the soldiers in Italy rarely saw newspapers from home or went to the cinema. The problem arose in the letters they received – and letters from home were a potent factor in morale. Back in the USA, Canada and Britain, wives, sweethearts and families started to wonder what their men were doing in Italy, a theatre of war where, if local newspapers and national newsreels were any yardstick, nothing much was happening.

To tired men, many of whom had not been home for years and were now pushing their way north against stubborn resistance, over a quantity of mines and booby traps, thinking of comrades left behind, this sort of comment was vastly irritating. In Eighth Army this irritation was exacerbated by the tactless comment of a British MP – allegedly Lady Astor, the MP for Plymouth – who said that there were a large number of Allied soldiers in Italy doing virtually nothing, but happy to stay there and so avoid fighting in Normandy; these men she referred to as the 'D-Day Dodgers'.

The natural perversity of British soldiers led them to adopt this scornful title with a certain amount of glee, but there can be little doubt that the accusation was hurtful as well as unjustified. A Jon cartoon which shows the Two Types asking each other, 'Which invasion can she mean, old man? – Sicily, Salerno, Anzio?' sets out the reaction of the Allied soldiers in Italy very well. The old anthem of Eighth Army, *Lili Marlene*, came back here as the tune of a new song, the first verse of which was given at the start of this chapter.

One unsung hero of the Allied Armies in Italy was the humble army mule. Mules were the only means of getting supplies into the mountains, and often helped in the evacuation of the wounded. Once their usefulness had been realized, mules became valuable, mule companies were formed in all the armies, and the ranks were combed for men who knew how to look after them – American cowboys, British farmhands, New Zealand shepherds. Eric Garner again:

> There were no mountain troops in Italy as such, except the French *goums*. All the Indian divisions had the usual scale of army transport, and if I remember it correctly the only division in the British Army trained in mountain warfare ended up in Holland. There were numerous mule companies formed and manned by Cypriots, Italians, Indians and I think Basutos. The mule companies were under army control and were issued out to corps as necessary. We soon got used to seeing 3-tonners passing up the line with the heads of mules sticking out the back. I think those that the British used for mule-handling came from either the RASC or the Army Veterinary Corps. The 4th Indian Division had 5 companies of porters and 800 mules at one time, so the humble mule was a significant element in our planning.[9]

At the end of July there was a change in the plan for the push towards the Po. On 28 July Leese had issued a warning order to his corps commanders, calling for XIII and X Corps to push towards Bologna in the centre of the Apennines, with the 2nd Polish Corps on the Adriatic and V Corps in Army Reserve. This plan was now to change, for Leese was now proposing a new plan – Operation OLIVE.

The origins of Operation OLIVE are obscure. Leese apparently proposed it to Alexander and Harding on 4 August at a meeting held under the shade of an aircraft wing at Orvieto airfield. No notes were taken of their discussions, but the upshot was that Alexander accepted a plan by which Leese would take Eighth Army back across the Apennines to the Adriatic front and strike up towards the Gothic Line from there, while Fifth Army took over the thrust across the mountains, on the axis Florence–Bologna.

This plan, once accepted, confronted the Allied commanders with two difficulties. One was Operation OTTRINGTON. Indications from Ultra were that this deception plan was succeeding and the Germans were now strengthening the Adriatic front. If the OLIVE attack went in there, the Allies were currently encouraging enemy efforts to oppose it.

The second difficulty was more crucial to all the forces involved: time. Summer was wasting; winter was coming on, with all the inevitable and unavoidable difficulties it would bring. Was it wise to use up any of the precious summer weeks in shifting an entire army in secret across the Apennines? Would it not be better to press on with the current plan: a full and direct thrust across the northern Apennines, at Bologna and the Po?

Leese thought not. He felt that the mountains were more of a problem than the weather – and Alexander agreed with him, also liking the idea of a 'one–two' punch. The first punch would come from Eighth Army in the east, the second from Fifth Army in the centre, and one of these should succeed in reaching the Po. Alexander also felt that there was no point forcing Leese to carry out a plan that he – Leese – did not believe in, which is a point. But there is another point, made caustically by the British Official History: that in certain circumstances it might be better to change the commander than to change the plan.

However, with Alexander willing to accept Leese's suggestion, the next hurdle was to sell this idea to Clark. This was done at an Army Group Co-ordination Conference on 10 August. At this meeting Leese made his pitch, and Clark agreed that his plan 'seemed sound'.[10] The two army commanders agreed with the concept of a double blow, but Clark felt that Fifth Army would need more men. This too was agreed, and XIII Corps – 1st (British) Infantry Division, 8th Indian Division, 6th Armoured Division and 6th South African Armoured Division – was duly transferred to Fifth Army from Eighth Army. The US Fifth Army was rapidly becoming as polyglot a force as Eighth Army, containing, among other national and ethnic groups, British, Brazilians, Italians and a regiment of Nisei, Japanese-Americans – the latter a force that was to win more combat decorations than any other US unit of comparable size.

Leese laid out his new plan to his corps commanders on 9 August. The Polish Corps was to attack the high ground west of Pesaro but not the town itself. I Canadian Corps would drive along the coastal road towards Rimini. V Corps, commanded from 5 August by Lieutenant General C. F. Keightley, would attack the Gothic Line directly on the left of the Canadian Corps and drive on west of Rimini to protect the left flank of the Army, with the 4th Indian Division moving in the hills to the west. The much-reduced X Corps would link the two armies in the Apennines.

This would be the first blow. Then, some days after Eighth Army advanced, Fifth Army would attack along the west coast and into the mountains north of Florence to deliver the second one. Task Force 45, a tank and infantry group, would move along the coast towards Viareggio and the naval base at La Spezia, the Brazilians on their right heading into the hills between the sea and the river Serchio. On their right, pushing through the spine of the Apennines, the US IV Corps and the British XIII Corps would advance as follows: the 1st British Armoured Division would thrust up the Serchio valley while the 6th South African Armoured Division headed for Pistoia on the southern slopes and pushed through the Apennines on the axis of Route 64. On the extreme right, the rest of XIII Corps would strike into the spine of the Apennines across the river Sieve and keep contact with X Corps of Eighth Army.

As a preliminary to this attack, the Allied air forces would attack all 19 bridges over the Po, right along the valley between Piacenza and the Adriatic, so cutting the Gothic Line defenders off from any possibility of rapid support. All these bridges were down by the first week of August, but the Germans kept their front line supplied by using the river ferries at night. All the Allied commanders, Alexander, Clark and Leese, held out high hopes for the coming attack. If – or rather when – the Gothic Line was breached, Fifth Army would edge north-west for Verona and Mantua, while Eighth Army would cross the rivers Po, Adige and Brenta, take Venice, and then press on to Trieste, Yugoslavia, the Ljubljana Gap – and Vienna.

Success for this thrust was made more likely by a recent thrust up the Adriatic coast by the II Polish Corps, which had taken the port of Ancona on 17 July. That done, the Poles proceeded to push along the coast and were on the start line for Operation OLIVE, the Metauro river 10 miles south of Pesaro, by 22 August. This advance had cost General Anders another 2,150 men – a heavy toll, and one that the Poles had few means of making up: finding reinforcements was always a problem for the Polish Corps.

By mid-August the rest of Eighth Army had been brought in

secret across the Apennines and stood ready to deliver a massive attack on the German lines. Three corps – the British V Corps, I Canadian Corps and II Polish Corps, mustering in all ten divisions – would advance on 25 August, attacking on a 30-mile front, supported by 1,200 tanks and fire from 1,000 guns, while, as related, X Corps protected their right flank and maintained the link with Fifth Army. All seemed possible: with the exception of the Poles, the units in these divisions had been brought up to strength, and there was an abundance of air support and artillery ammunition.

The general feeling among the members of Eighth Army at this time was that, with a modest amount of luck, Operation OLIVE might be their last offensive, carrying the Allied armies non-stop to the Po. One popular estimate suggested a timetable of 'Two days to Bologna, four days more to Venice and a week more for Vienna'. If not quite so optimistic, Leese still felt that this offensive on the Adriatic coast would be decisive.

'Now we begin the last lap,' said Leese in a message to his army. 'Swiftly and secretly, once again, we have moved right across Italy an army of immense strength and striking power to break the Gothic Line. Victory in the coming battle means the beginning of the end for the German Armies in Italy. Let every man do his utmost and again success will be ours.' This major attack on the Gothic Line began on the night of 25/26 August, ten days after the ANVIL/DRAGOON forces had landed in the South of France.

The Germans were certainly taken by surprise. Tenth Army had two corps on the Adriatic front – LXXVI Panzer Corps and LI Mountain Corps – with two divisions in Army Reserve, a total of ten divisions. However, the units in these divisions were greatly under-strength. Many of the infantry battalions mustered no more than 300–400 men, and there was a shortage of tanks, guns and ammunition – though, as with the men, what there was was of good quality. Many of the German generals, including von Vietinghoff and von Senger und Etterlin, were on leave in Germany and had to come rushing back when Eighth Army moved forward.

The opening attack went well. By dawn on 26 August the Poles were leading five British, Indian and Canadian divisions against the Gothic Line defences, which were turning out to be thicker and better defended than Leese had hoped. The defences were bolstered before the 46th Division on the V Corps front by three steep peaks rising up to 1,500 feet. This feature was attacked by the 5th Battalion the Hampshire Regiment, which took it with grenades and the bayonet, all three peaks being in British hands by 27 August. After this local success the general advance slowed, and a slogging match began. Another Gothic Line strongpoint, Green I, along the river Foglia, fell on 28 August, but these were the only gains in the opening struggle. It was rapidly becoming apparent that breaching the Gothic Line would require a grinding battle of attrition over several days.

Kenneth Riley, MM, a wireless operator in a Sherman tank of the 48th RTR, describes a day in the line during this offensive:

It was 1 September 1944, and we had been equipped with Shermans and Churchills. I had only served in Churchills, and was unfamiliar with the 75-mm gun on the Sherman. Many of my com-rades had done conversion courses, but we went back into action before my time came. I would be all right if the gun did not jam.

The tuning call for the tank radios was at 2345 hours, and at twenty to midnight I climbed into the turret and warmed up the 19 set and when all was ready we set off. We were comfortably in the middle of the column, but progress was slow – about 1 mile per hour – and the leading troops were firing at likely trouble spots, so all the haystacks along the road were on fire, set off by tracer. I soon got tired of looking through the periscope and decided to test the guns. A belt of ammo was already in the Browning, so I asked the gunner to fire a burst and test it. He squeezed his remote-control trigger and nothing happened, so I squeezed the trigger on the gun and got off a burst. We agreed that he would aim the gun and I would pull the trigger until we got the solenoid switch repaired. I then tried to doze as we jolted along, but suddenly there was an agitated voice on the headset. 3 Troop were under fire and the leading tank was 'brewing up'.

We were in a sunken road just wide enough for the tank, with 12ft-foot-high banks on either side, and while I was looking two Germans jumped out of a slit trench above me with their hands raised. We could not take them prisoner, so we relied on the infan-try to pick them up. Sunken roads felt safer than open country, but the Germans usually had their guns zeroed in on them. With a Churchill it might have been possible to plough into the bank and climb out, but a Sherman would just bury its nose into the soil.

Then we saw a figure running up the road towards us: Trooper Gale – usually called Stormy – from the leading tank. Apparently they had come to the end of this sunken road and found the village of Piave still in German hands and 100 yards away. They speeded up to take the village on the run, but were hit by a panzerfaust almost immediately. Two Liverpool lads in the driving compartment were killed instantly, the tank caught fire, and Lieutenant Hutchinson was wounded – German paratroopers who had fired the shot helped get him out. Stormy and the gunner had their pistols taken away and were taken prisoner. Then Sergeant Weekes's tank, coming up behind, saw what was happening and opened fire with his 75-mm on the group by the burning tank. Stormy said the shell grazed his thigh – how lucky can you get? – the Germans leaped for cover, and he ran the opposite way and took cover behind the hedge before coming back.

Eventually the tanks ahead began to move, and we emerged from the sunken road and went to the left, to a plateau overlooking sloping ground. The village ahead, called Gradara, had a castle on a hill and the village was enclosed by walls. To the east, our right, was Cattolica. But while we were watching there was a sudden plume of dust and masonry – the Germans had blown the bridge.

Meanwhile we were under observation. There was a sudden crash on the outside of our turret, and a cloud of brown smoke enveloped us and the tank shook, but when the dust cleared we were OK. A high-explosive shell had hit us, probably fired from 2 or 3 miles away – good shooting, as it was the start of a barrage. It left a groove along the top of the turret, and a heavy lifting ring was swept away.

It was now about midday, and I was feeling hungry. We had not eaten since the previous evening, but we missed so many meals in action that tins had accumulated. We had two-day ration packs, but we preferred compo packs, which required no cooking – though if we were stationary long enough we could try for a brew on the tank stove. We made sandwiches of bully and biscuit and passed these round, and finished the bully with Hartley's jam and were able to make a brew before the call came to move off.

The afternoon passed and the light began to fade as we were ordered back to the top of the hill and leaguered up for the night in the farmyard close to the village. The 'A' Echelon trucks were already there with petrol and ammo, and the cooks had brought up their 15-cwt truck with a hot meal for us.

The first job, though, was to clear the turret of spent cartridges and machine-gun ammo boxes. The driver and co-driver lifted the engine hatches, and we were ready to take on 50 rounds of 75-mm and 11 boxes of machine-gun ammo and 100 gallons of fuel for the engine; the petrol came in 4-gallon jerrycans. All this took about half an hour, and then we were ready to eat. The food had been waiting an hour or so and was not of the best, but it was hot and all credit to the Squadron Sergeant Major and the cooks for getting it to us. Before spreading out blankets there were sentries to post, and with only five hours of darkness we were to do 20 minutes each. I took the chance for a word with my twin brother, Stan, who was also in a 2 Troop tank. His day had been much the same as mine; they had been heavily engaged by mortars, and knocked out a battery.[11]

Eighth Army kept pressing forward, and by 1 September, after six days of heavy fighting, the Gothic Line on the Adriatic had been torn open on a 15-mile front inland from Pesaro. This breach left Kesselring with no choice; he sent three divisions of his army group reserve across to the Adriatic front from their positions north of Florence, thus weakening the forces before Fifth Army, which Alexander ordered forward on 1 September – the second blow of his double punch.

The Fifth Army history records surprise that the almost unopposed advance across the Arno plain took so long with the enemy falling back before it. Clark records that it was not until 10 September that his forces were able to get in 'a good solid blow' at the enemy to their front.[12] He therefore decided to make his main effort with II Corps at the Il Giogo Pass, slightly to the east of the more obvious and more heavily defended Futa Pass, due north of Florence. The Il Giogo was the dividing line between Tenth and Fourteenth Armies, and an attack there might sow a little confusion in the enemy camp, but either pass should carry Clark's army through the mountains and out to Bologna and the Po plain.

The II Corps attack on the Il Giogo pass began on 13 September and was soon in trouble, the advancing troops and tanks coming under heavy fire from surrounding peaks and held up by minefields. Meanwhile the Americans were also probing the Futa Pass, hoping to keep the enemy in doubt as to which was the main attack. This diversion made little difference: the Germans were able to hold off both attacks, and over the next two days the US 91st and 85th Divisions, attacking the passes, made very little progress. The Il Giogo Pass was finally breached on 17 September. Three days later the US 34th Division captured Montepiano and had breached the Gothic Line, but the cost of doing so exceeded 3,000 men, killed, wounded or missing.

Taking the Futa Pass took a full 12 days of fighting before the final breakthrough on 22 September – again at a considerable cost in lives. After that, the Fifth Army soldiers were confronted with another obstacle: the Raticosa Pass on Route 65, 12 miles north of the Futa. Before that could be tackled, more peaks had to be taken, most notably Monte Canda . . . And so it went on, week after week, battering through the mountains in the mud and rain as winter began to close in on the northern Apennines.

By 25 September, however, Alexander's strategy had apparently paid off. The Americans had breached the Gothic Line in two places north of Florence on the road to Bologna, and Eighth Army had torn a wide breach in it west of Pesaro. If all went well, there should be no major problem in reaching the valley of the Po. Unfortunately all did not go well. The Germans brought up their reserves and settled down to their usual tactic, fighting doggedly for every yard of ground – and waiting for the autumn rains.

Kesselring had rightly judged that the main danger to his position was the Eighth Army breach at Pesaro where the ground was more open. He had therefore shifted units east and placed them under von Vietinghoff, who deployed them across the Eighth Army front at Coriano and San Fortunato on a defence line south of Rimini. The task of breaking through here was given to the Canadians, while V Corps was to break across the mountains and across the Romagna plain and so into the Po valley, heading for Bologna and Ferrara. The fighting south of Coriano and along the Coriano ridge to the village of Croce went on for a full week in early September and cost Eighth Army some 8,000 men for very little territorial gain. All these divisions – 1st Armoured, 4th Indian, 46th and 56th British, 1st Canadian – were growing tired and increasingly short of manpower.

The village of Croce changed hands five times in the fighting as the 56th Division fought for a foothold. In the middle of this battle, when the ground across the front was already torn and cratered, the autumn rains arrived, plunging the troops and tanks into a quagmire. After two weeks General Leese decided that this constant daily battering was having little effect: to break the German resistance and get forward here, he must lay on yet another set-piece attack. Supported by a mass of artillery, V Corps and I Canadian Corps, backed by the 2nd New Zealand Division and the 4th Infantry Division, would take the Coriano ridge and cross the Marano river, the next obstacle to the north. With that much achieved, Eighth Army could break the Rimini Line, take Rimini, debouch at last from the mountains and the narrow coastal corridor, and get into open country of the Romagna. From there the tanks could press on up the main Via Emilia road towards Bologna, so supporting the Fifth Army assault driving north from Florence.

This attack began on 13 September and went on for a full week. The cost was considerable: 750 men were killed, wounded or went missing every day – a total of over 5,000 men in seven days of fighting, mostly from V Corps. General Sir William Jackson, who fought in this campaign, later described this attack as 'one of the most costly ever fought by the British Army in Italy', and sapper sergeant Eric Garner records that

> The little-known battles for Gemmano and the Coriano ridge were among the bloodiest of the campaign. They left 56th Division down to two weak brigades, 46th Division in no better state, and 1st Armoured so knocked about it never reformed. There was a story going about in Eighth Army at the time that 1st Armoured, which had just arrived after a year in North Africa, was inadequately trained for Italian conditions and lost a lot of tanks trying out desert tactics in the Coriano ridge attack. How true this is I do not know, but I certainly heard it some time later from some tankies in 7th Armoured Brigade. Between 25 August and 6 September casualties were nearly 8,000, and as you know we lost about 700 men every day over the next week.[13]

The Coriano battle was fought over a series of hills and ridges, across valleys already poached out by the rain, through fields which the broken banks of streams and ditches had turned into swamps. The Romagna had once been marshland, and, with the drainage ditches destroyed and the river banks breached, the land flooded swiftly. Tanks were of little use here, and the infantry advance was impeded by wide minefields full of the deadly wood-encased schu mines, which were hard to sweep. Even so, Eighth Army pressed on.

By 17 September the Eighth Army advance had reached the eastern edge of the tiny neutral Republic of San Marino, then crammed with over 120,000 Italian refugees fleeing north before the fighting. R. W. Finch was in the 11th Field Regiment, RA, with the 4th Indian Division:

> We had the Essex Regiment, the Sikhs, the Frontier Force Rifles, the Seaforth Highlanders – a mixed bag. We landed at Taranto and went north by train and truck towards the thunder of the guns and mortars. We went slowly around San Marino, which was declared neutral, but the Germans were using the roads and shelling the area. We made a quick visit to San Marino, flirting with the girls in the souvenir shops. It was my twenty-fourth birthday, and I remember meeting a well-dressed man with his wife and two daughters, both hysterical with the guns. The German Army made a formidable stand at the Gothic Line but it was really over for them.[14]

Eighth Army troops circled the Republic of San Marino and pressed on to the Rimini Line, which ran inland from the coast along the northern frontier of San Marino. This advance went more slowly now: the history of the 4th Indian Division likens progress at the end of September to that of a vehicle losing power in muddy ground – 'gradually losing speed until it finally bogs down'. But by some miracle the attack did not bog down, and on 21 September troops of Eighth Army's Greek Brigade entered Rimini.

Elsewhere the Allied advance on both fronts was slowing, partly due to a lack of manpower after the heavy casualties in recent weeks. At the end of September, Clark told Maitland Wilson that 'the infantry replacement situation is so critical that current operations may be endangered. Losses in my infantry divisions during the past five days have averaged 550 per division per day, over and above returns to units.'[15] The situation in Eighth Army was no better, and in some divisions rather worse; in recent weeks Eighth Army had lost around 14,000 men while advancing just 30 miles. These losses were worse than they appear, for they fell mainly among the front-line soldiers, particularly in the infantry companies, where losses were often in excess of 70 per cent. Manpower alone was not the problem, however: the Allied armies in Italy were used to a shortage of manpower. The other problem, though equally familiar, was not one they could cope with – the weather.

The slowing of the Allied advance during September was increasingly due to the advent of the autumn rains and the dread approach of yet another Italian winter. That long delay in August while Fifth Army regrouped after the loss of its best divisions to ANVIL was now taking effect; repercussions of wasting all that good campaigning weather while the enemy was in disarray were seen in the autumn, when the rains were tipping down and the enemy was fighting with his usual tenacity.

Matters did not change a great deal during October, as the Allied advance petered out. By the end of the month the Fifth Army advance had come to a halt in the mountains. The spearhead 91st Division was astride Route 65 just 20 miles south of Bologna, but on the right flank of Fifth Army German divisions barred any exit to the Po through Imola or Castel San Pietro. On the Eighth Army front the soldiers had reached the eastern end of the Po valley at Rimini, where the problem – apart from the enemy – was not mountains but flooded rivers. According to the British Official History, 'OLIVE can be said to have ended as Eighth Army crossed the Marrecchia on 21st September in pouring rain.'[16]

Operation OLIVE was not a success. The original concept, that an advance on the Adriatic front would provide the large Allied tank forces with good going, had proved faulty: OLIVE quickly became an infantry battle fought in the mountains, or through mountain passes, or across a flood plain quite unsuitable for tanks. The Gothic Line had been breached, but the Allied armies were not yet established at the Po river, let alone in the Po valley, and with the weather deteriorating it was not likely that any further progress could be made in the near future.

OLIVE had also been costly. Infantry losses had been high. In Eighth Army two brigades had been reduced to cadre size and all the infantry battalions, at full strength before OLIVE began, had been forced to reduce their rifle companies from four to three. V Corps lost 9,000 men, the Canadian Corps just under 4,000. Nor was it just the infantry who had suffered: the 1st Armoured Division was so reduced that it had to be broken up, its regiments and squadrons being shared out among the tank brigades or switched to other roles – the 2nd Armoured Brigade converted to using amphibious vehicles in early 1945, 18th

Brigade disappeared, and the 43rd Gurkha Lorried Infantry Brigade became 21st Independent Brigade. German losses were also high, with LXXVI Panzer Corps alone losing 16,000 men.[17] American losses in Fifth Army's mountain campaign had also been severe.

Even so, Alexander was optimistic. If Fifth Army's advance could press on and unhinge the enemy line, Eighth Army, having reached open country, could power ahead up the Via Emilia towards Bologna. To spearhead this move, the 2nd New Zealand Division was assigned to the Canadian Corps and charged with the advance up Route 16 to Ravenna. This advance began on 23 September.

Everything conspired against this New Zealand advance: demolitions, mines, booby traps, machine-gun posts, snipers, dug-in 88-mms, low cloud and gales to ground the Desert Air Force, mud, flooded streams – one New Zealand account reports that 'a stream you could normally cross in gum boots was now deep enough to drown a man'[18] – and, a major obstacle, the Fiumicino river, which was screened by flood waters deep enough to make the actual river hard to detect.

Eighth Army was now on the Romagna plain, which, says the British Official History, 'could hardly have been more unsuitable for an over-mechanized force like Eighth Army, intent on making sweeping armoured thrusts. It would not have been an easy area in summer; in winter its peculiarities turned it into superb defensive country for the tired but experienced troops of the Tenth Army.'[19] The rains that had began in mid-September fell without ceasing until the end of the month, and the rivers across the Romagna front – the Fiumicino, the Savio, the Pisciatello and a host of lesser streams – rapidly became dangerous torrents. In this wilderness of water and mud, the Eighth Army advance came to a halt.

On 1 October there was a command change in Eighth Army. General Sir Oliver Leese was sent to the Far East, and Lieutenant-General Sir Richard McCreery was promoted to command of Eighth Army. A cavalry officer and an Old Etonian, Richard McCreery had been commissioned into the 12th Lancers, with which he had served in the First World War. In the 1930s the 12th Lancers had been one of the first cavalry units to be mechanized, and McCreery had been with Eighth Army in the Western Desert. He was known to be a competent general with a sound grasp of the all-arms battle and familiarity with the various exigencies of the Italian campaign, where he had been commanding X Corps since the landings at Salerno.

McCreery was therefore able to take up the command of Eighth Army without any need to settle in, and he pressed on with the current attack, in which the Poles and New Zealanders were pushing along the coast, the Canadian Corps was in the centre, and the British V Corps was skirting the eastern edge of the Apennines. McCreery decided to shift the weight of his attack into the hills, where the going was better and drier than out on the flooded plains. The painful autumnal advance continued to the next major obstacle, the river Savio, which Eighth Army crossed on the night of 22/23 October.

That done, the New Zealand Division withdrew into Eighth Army reserve. In seven weeks of fighting the New Zealand Division had lost over 2,000 men, almost all of them in the rifle companies. Half of these – 1,108 – were battle casualties; the rest were seriously ill men afflicted with hepatitis – jaundice – which continued to ravage the Eighth Army soldiers as it had done in the desert. A similar situation prevailed in Fifth Army, where 'non-battle casualties' – respiratory ailments, psychiatric problems and, increasingly, trench foot caused by wet conditions – took as heavy a toll as death or wounds. This does not indicate any lack of German resistance: the war diary of the British 46th Division describes the opposition around Cesena as 'stiff', 'pretty tough' or 'stubborn' every day until 17 October, after which it slackened somewhat and the British advance quickened in spite of the terrible conditions. Sapper sergeant Eric Garner again:

On 24 October the Company moved north once more as far as Cesena. Most people were looking forward to getting out of the mountains and into the valley of the Po, which appeared to be flat and probably good for tanks, but we were soon disillusioned. The main routes in this area were Route 16, which ran north along the coast to Ravenna and Ferrara, and Route 9, which ran straight as an arrow north-west to Bologna and Milan. These were the only good roads. In fact this part of the Po valley was crossed by numerous rivers and streams, the majority of which were contained by flood banks some of them 40 feet high. Routes 9 and 16 actually ran across the top of embankments. The minor roads were not metalled and were suitable only for inter-village communications. Between the rivers were innumerable canals, and the whole area was subject to flooding during heavy rain. Near the coast the enemy had flooded large areas and demolished the drainage pumps. The weather was atrocious.[20]

Having crossed the Savio, and after Cesena fell to pincer attack by the 46th Division, the Canadian Corps and the 5th New Zealand Brigade, Eighth Army pushed on to the river Ronco, south-east of Forli, nearly halfway between Rimini and Bologna. This river line was reached on 25 October, but McCreery now had another problem, a familiar one to the Allied commanders in Italy – part of his army was being taken away. The Canadian Corps was now to leave Eighth Army and join the First Canadian Army in north-west Europe, where manpower shortages were increasing, and other Eighth Army units would have to leave and help tackle the problems of a Communist insurrection in Greece following the German evacuation.

All this limited McCreery's chances of following up the German retreat from the Savio, but the major problem was again the weather. Early November 1944 saw Eighth Army's front running from just south of Ravenna along the Ronco and across the Via Emilia east of Forli, then rising into the Apennines at Rocca San Casciano before swinging north across the rivers Montone, Lamone and Santerno to link up with Fifth Army.

Over the next two months, until the end of December 1944, Eighth Army's task was to push north on the eastern side of the Apennines and try to establish a new line along the river Senio, forming up there ready to push forward again when the winter weather eased.

During this time the Germans were constructing a new defence line, the Genghis Khan Line, which ran from west of Bologna to as far east as Lake Comacchio, a shallow lake on the Adriatic north of Ravenna, screening Bologna and barring Route 16 for any advance towards Ferrara and Venice. During the early winter months the Allied armies moved closer to the Genghis Khan Line and mustered their strength for what the coming year would bring. But, until the winter passed and the weather improved, further advances were impossible.

46 (North Midland) Div.

15

The Long March Ends
November 1944–May 1945

This great final battle in Italy will long stand out in history as one of the most famous episodes in this Second World War.

Winston Churchill to General Alexander, April 1945

For the soldiers of Eighth Army the winter months of 1944–5 were a saga of triumph in adversity – with the triumph element delayed until the following spring. Progress was made, but painfully; the winter campaign was reduced to a struggle for position, an attempt to prevent the withdrawal of German forces to other fronts, and to frustrate any further fortifying of their new defensive position, the Genghis Khan Line.

This line barred progress along the Eighth Army front at Argenta, in a narrow gap between the river Reno and the wide but shallow waters of Lake Comacchio, close to Ravenna. Facing the Eighth Army here were XIV Panzer Corps and LXXVI Panzer Corps, mustering no fewer than 12 divisions in the line with a further two – 26th Panzer and 98th Infantry – in reserve, all well supplied with artillery and with no apparent shortage of ammunition. They were, however, somewhat short of men: few of these German formations or their Italian Fascist counterparts were fully up to strength. When the weather eased, the prime task for Eighth Army was to cross Lake Comacchio and breach the Argenta Gap, but that must wait until the spring of 1945.

By the end of October 1944, Fifth Army's advance had stalled just 9 miles from Bologna and Eighth Army was on the river Ronco. Fifth Army spent November resting and refitting, and Eighth Army spent it in ironing out a German salient that butted into its line between Forli and the eastern end of the Fifth Army line at Monte Grande. This salient was held by five German divisions, and the weather remained vile as Eighth Army moved forward from the Ronco towards the Lamone – a task which involved taking the city of Faenza on the Via Emilia.

This advance began on 7 November, and was plagued with difficulties from the start. The front was seamed with ditches, streams and some significant rivers – the Cosino and the Montone had had their banks broken and their approaches flooded – and the ground between these rivers was covered by machine-gun and mortar fire and sown with mines. The enemy was well dug-in and had mobile battle groups equipped with Tiger tanks. Confronted by these obstacles, on 8 November the British attack stalled on the Montone, where the 46th Division and the Polish Corps were held up by stiff resistance. Even so, the 4th Division was in Forli by 9 November and the Lamone river line was reached by the Canadians, the New Zealanders and the 10th Indian Division on 28 November. Here, inching up the Po valley, Eighth Army paused for a while, building up its ammunition stocks, awaiting orders for the next advance.

Eric Garner again:

The last winter in Italy was the worst time of the whole campaign. Much of the country was under water, as the enemy had destroyed the drainage system. This is the only time I have seen a bulldozer bogged down in the mud and abandoned until the ground dried out. The weather was appalling. I believe the Po valley has the highest rainfall in Europe, and it was also foggy, freezing and bitterly cold. The front on the Senio was absolutely static, with no hope of movement until the spring, but even then it appeared unlikely that we would be strong enough to make much of an impression on the defences, since the river Santerno, 5 miles behind the Senio, was even more heavily fortified and every farmhouse between these rivers had been converted into a fortress. It was practically impossible to move off the main Route 9 – Forli to Bologna – and the minor roads were barely capable of supporting traffic and required tons of rubble every day just to keep them open.[1]

Before fresh orders for new advances came, there were some further changes in the command. The death of Field Marshal Sir John Dill on 4 November 1944 had Churchill seeking a new head for the British Military Mission in Washington. Churchill chose Maitland Wilson, proposing to Roosevelt on 17 November that Alexander replace Wilson as Supreme Commander in the Mediterranean while Clark replaced Alexander as commander of the Allied armies in Italy and Lucian Truscott returned from France to take command of Fifth Army. Roosevelt agreed, and these changes had all taken place by mid-December.

These appointments met with general approval, and Clark was clearly delighted – not least that the first news of his new appointment came in a personal message from Winston Churchill.

'I must confess', wrote Clark,

that the Prime Minister's message made Thanksgiving morning in the high Apennines look immeasurably better. In reading over the message's reference to my friendship with Alexander and my attitude to the British troops in Italy, it occurs to me that the reader might feel that Churchill's statements were overdrawn in view of the events I have related, showing my disagreements at times with the British.

If so, I would like to make it clear that our disagreements served to strengthen rather than lessen my friendship with Alexander and most of his British colleagues. Our differences of opinion were very real and very important. Perhaps for that reason they tend in an account such as this to overshadow the routine of friendly collaboration which went on day after day in the Italian campaign and which was such a paramount contribution to victory.[2]

Meanwhile, with the Allied line straightened west of Forli and Fifth Army rested, the scene was set for a major thrust by both armies: the Fifth on Bologna, the Eighth across the Lamone to the Senio and the Santerno, both tributaries of the Reno. McCreery's aim in this advance was to render 'all assistance to Fifth Army in the capture of Bologna and to take Ravenna'. The problem was that, owing to the recent changes in the Army command, Fifth Army was not able to advance when the Eighth struck out again on 3 December.

Eighth Army advanced with a phased attack. XIII Corps – which had just returned to Eighth Army control – and the Polish Corps moved south of Faenza, while V Corps and the Canadian Corps – the latter now commanded by Lieutenant-General Charles Foulkes – advanced north of the city. The advance to the Senio was a short bound of some 6 miles, and at first all went well – the 5th Canadian Armoured Division, which opened this attack on the night of 2/3 December, entered Ravenna at 1600 hours on 4 December. On that night the V Corps attack began the second phase, the New Zealanders and the 10th Indian Division pushing to the north while the 46th Division cut the defending lines at Quartolo, south of Faenza, and swung north to isolate the city by getting across the Via Emilia.

The advance was slow but steady, hampered by a chronic shortage of artillery ammunition: the 25-pounders were restricted to 70 shells per gun per day, the 105-mms to 30 shells per gun per day. The German defenders had been ordered to hold every foot of ground – an order not unconnected with the pending German offensive in the Belgian Ardennes, the Battle of the Bulge, which was due to open on 16 December – and they not only held their positions tenaciously, but put in strong counter-attacks. One such attack, on 8 December by the 90th Panzergrenadier Division, caused heavy casualties in the 46th Division, and on 10 December this division was replaced in the line by the 56th Division. The 56th Division, the 10th Indian Division and the 2nd New Zealand Division were all crammed into the shallow bridgehead astride Faenza. Faenza fell to the 43rd Gurkha Infantry Brigade on 16 December, and the advance up to the Senio line elsewhere continued until 17 December. This advance was costly, not least because of the weather, which increased the number of sick, but battlefield losses were also mounting: in the two weeks since the offensive opened, the Canadian Corps alone had lost 2,556 men, killed, wounded or missing.

There were lighter distractions, as Victor Bulger of the Royal Canadian Horse Artillery recalls:

On 3 December 1944, the RCHA moved to the area south-west of Russi. My limber gunner, Gunner Michaels, scrounged a couple of chickens and asked me if he could keep them and get the odd egg. If they did not lay, they would provide a dinner. I said OK, provided they didn't become a nuisance, and he put up a pup tent to serve as their coop. Winter conditions were setting in, and within a few days I discovered that Gunner Michael's flock had grown to 10 chickens providing 5 or 6 eggs per day. The last man on guard at night would put a lamp in the pup tent at about 0500 hours, throw a bit of feed around, and get the birds off their perches – a working hen is a laying hen.

By January our flock had grown to 17 chickens, a rooster and a duck, so we were getting between 10 and 11 eggs per day – ideal for breakfast. The only snag was when we moved, but fortunately most of our moves were at night. We had to load about three crates of chickens and a few bags of grain besides all the other stores and supplies on top of a truck. With all the comforts of home, our standard of living had greatly improved. Looking back, I am still surprised we were allowed to keep those chickens for nearly three months. But it gave us a hobby and helped us get our minds off the war – and we had fresh eggs every day for breakfast.[3]

On 19 December Clark called his first army commanders conference as Army Group Commander. He declared that he intended to send Fifth Army towards Bologna as soon as three conditions were fulfilled: if the skies cleared enough to permit the air forces to attack, if German reserves had been shifted to the Eighth Army front – in fact three German divisions had already moved across to oppose this thrust for the Senio – and if Eighth Army was able to continue its advance to the Santerno, 11 miles from the Senio. If these conditions were met, Fifth Army was to stand ready to attack at 48 hours notice from 22 December.

This plan had to be changed. On 25 December, McCreery wrote to Clark suggesting that the role of Eighth Army should be recast. McCreery pointed out that Fifth Army had originally been tasked to advance on 7 December, four days after Eighth Army went forward for the Senio. For various good reasons Fifth Army had not been able to advance, but the upshot of this delay was that Eighth Army had now been fighting the enemy alone for the last three weeks, using up men and ammunition in some quantity while three more German divisions had been moved across on to its front. Those three weeks had to be made up for, said McCreery: 'the capacity of Eighth Army to fight simultaneously with Fifth Army is automatically reduced by that length of time'.

Truscott agreed with this interpretation, and this view was reinforced on 26 December when a fierce German attack on the US 92nd Division caused that formation to fall back in some disorder to the lines of the 8th Indian Division of XIII Corps. The 92nd Division was placed under Indian Division command but with snow falling and temperatures plummeting it was clear that the enemy had used the delay on the Fifth Army front to thicken his defences around Bologna. This being so, the chances of a successful advance on the city in the present weather conditions were slight indeed. Eighth Army needed to rest and to rebuild its stocks of artillery ammunition, and the result was that both Allied armies went over to a policy of 'offensive-defence' as winter gripped the opposing lines in northern Italy. The weather and a shortage of men and artillery ammunition had enforced another delay on the Italian front.

Writing in the Divisional history, John P. Delany of the 88th Infantry Division states that 'One fresh division might have been enough to get the Fifth Army through to the Po – one fresh regiment assigned to the 88th Division might have taken the Division through Vedriano and on to Highway 9.'[4] The snag was that there were no fresh divisions. As Mark Clark put it, Fifth Army's offensive in the early winter of 1944–5 'did not stop with any definite setback or on any significant date. It merely ground to a halt because men could not fight any longer against the steadily-increasing enemy reinforcements to our front. In other words, our drive died out, slowly and painfully, and only one long stride from success like a runner who collapses reaching out for, but not quite touching, the tape at the finishing line.'

With this halting of the advance in December it became possible to rest some divisions. But then, as so often during this Italian campaign, external factors intervened. The German withdrawal from Greece in October and November had immediately plunged that country into a civil war between the ELAS Communist guerrillas, backed with weapons and supplies from Tito's Yugoslav partisans, and the Greek Royal Army, which supported the government and the King. Winston Churchill, long preoccupied with events in the eastern Mediterranean, had always feared such Communist insurrections as the war came to an end, and he promptly elected to support the Royal Army and the Greek government, first with supplies and then with troops.

The Greek Mountain Brigade was the first to go, leaving Eighth Army at the end of October, and it was followed in December by two infantry divisions: the 4th Infantry Division and the 4th Indian Division. More units were to follow if the situation in Greece continued to deteriorate. To top up McCreery's numbers, Eighth Army was joined by an Italian battle group, the Cremona Brigade, which arrived, said McCreery, 'with little equipment and less will to fight'.

There was also talk of a new strategic plan, Operation GELIG-NITE – an amphibious assault across the Adriatic by the Eighth Army, aimed at the Yugoslav coast between Split and Zara. The initial landing would be carried out by British commandos and light forces, and once ashore these would be supported by the Yugoslav partisans. But this would only be the first step: once these troops were established, the rest of Eighth Army would follow and head towards Ljubljana and Fiume, while Fifth Army entered the Po valley and swung east towards Istria.

This plan was never implemented. In his memoirs, Clark makes the interesting comment that 'his Government would have something to say before it was', and Churchill had finally to admit defeat in his long struggle to interest the American commanders in any exploitation of the Ljubljana Gap – and American politicians in the post-war political shape of Europe. After the Allied offensive into the Po valley was called off in December, Alexander laid plans for an attack by both armies as soon as the weather improved in 1945, telling his commanders that he had decided 'to go on the defensive for the present and to concentrate on making a real success of our Spring offensive'.

The Allied Armies in Italy – again officially 15th Army Group – were not idle during the winter of 1944–5. The Canadians moved forward to the south side of Lake Comacchio in early January, clearing the land between Comacchio, Ravenna and the Via Adriatica, the road to Argenta, and there was constant patrol activity in the snow of the mountains or the mud and floods of the plains. Behind the lines, fresh units were absorbed and veteran units rested; all went through an intensive retraining programme and were introduced to some new equipment, notably the Kangaroo and the Buffalo.

The Kangaroo was an early form of armoured personnel carrier, created by removing the gun and turret from a tank. The Buffalo or Fantail was similar, but had an amphibious capability and was designed for assault landings and river crossings. In January, as soon as a hard frost had made tracked movement possible, V Corps used Kangaroos in clearing the Senio front, and found these new armoured vehicles most useful. This winter pause therefore gave the armoured units and infantry the chance to try out fresh tactics using Kangaroos and tanks in the mobile role.

The Canadians, who pioneered the use of Kangaroos in Normandy, might have used these handy armoured vehicles in Italy, but the manpower situation in the British armies, if critical in Italy, was even more critical in north-west Europe. The Canadian Corps was therefore withdrawn from Italy in early February 1945 and was sent to General Harold Crerar's First Canadian Army in Holland.

These Canadian soldiers would be much missed. They had taken part in all Eighth Army's battles since Sicily and made a great name for themselves at Ortona and in the Liri valley – at some cost. Ninety-seven thousand Canadians had served in Sicily and Italy, and their total casualty list, killed, wounded or missing, comes to 25,889 men – more than a quarter of the force committed. In all their campaigns in Italy, only 1,004 Canadian soldiers had been taken prisoner by the enemy.

Eighth Army was reluctant to lose these fine soldiers and sad to see them go – two sentiments expressed in a farewell letter from General Alexander to the commander of I Canadian Corps, Lieutenant-General Foulkes:

> It is with great sorrow and regret that I see you and your famous Canadian Corps leaving my command. You have played a distinguished part in our victories in Italy where you leave behind a host of friends and admirers who will follow your future with the liveliest interest. Good luck and God-speed to you all in your coming tasks in the West, and may victory crown your new efforts as it has done in the past.

Two weeks after the departure of the Canadian Corps, General Alexander received a less happy communication from Lieutenant-General Anders of II Polish Corps, who had written to McCreery, who sent the letter on to Clark, who passed it to Alexander. Anders and his men had just heard of the outcome of the recent Allied conference at Yalta, which had resulted in tacit recognition of the Communist, Moscow-backed, 'Lublin Government' as the legitimate post-war government of Poland. The Yalta Conference had also agreed that the Russians could keep those parts of Poland they had been given by the Nazis as their reward for invading Poland in support of Hitler in 1939.

The 'Lublin Government' had been recognized at Yalta with the naive understanding that it would legitimate itself by free elections after the war. Only the most starry-eyed delegate to Yalta thought that this understanding would be adhered to by the Soviets, and it was in due course ignored. The plight of the soldiers in II Polish Corps was therefore understandable: they had escaped from their Russian captors in 1942 and then spent two years fighting the German Army on their way home to Poland – only to find that they now had no home to go to. Their loyalty was to the legitimate Polish government-in-exile in London, and they had no illusions about the fate that would await loyalists such as themselves in a Communist-dominated Poland.

Anders's letter condemned the Allied leaders – Roosevelt and Churchill – for giving in to Soviet pressure, and stated that he and his men were totally opposed to the Yalta agreement. Anders also declared that he wished to resign as commander of the Polish Corps – which could no longer fight on the Allied side. McCreery, Clark and Alexander – like all the Allied soldiers in Italy – had every sympathy with this attitude.

There was, however, a problem. The Polish Corps was a magnificent unit, full of superb soldiers, much needed for the coming campaign. Clark asked Anders to come to his headquarters, where, after expressing his full sympathy with the plight of the Polish Corps and promising to pass Anders's complaints on to Washington, he asked that the Polish Corps should stay in the line. 'If you quit now', said Clark, 'you will lose the respect of the Allied people and they are your only friends. Your men will follow where you lead.' Anders went away, promising to think things over, and returned later to assure Clark that the Poles would stand by their duty as soldiers and fight on.

So the winter passed, and on 9 April 1945 Alexander's final offensive began with a thrust by Eighth Army at Argenta. When Eighth Army's guns opened this attack, the war in Italy had less than a month to run, but this month would not be an easy one. Colonel-General von Vietinghoff, now promoted to command Army Group 'C', had two armies under command. The Tenth, under General Traugott Herr, contained four corps, including the 1st Parachute Corps – a total of 13 divisions including reserves. Fourteenth Army, under General Joachim Lemelsen, could muster four corps, one being the Italian Fascist Army of Liguria under Marshal Rodolfo Graziani. The Fourteenth Army also contained 13 divisions, plus some reserve brigades. This number of divisions – 26 in all – did not mean that von Vietinghoff had a superior force: some of his divisions were little more than brigades, and every unit was under-strength. When the last Allied offensive opened on 9 April, von Vietinghoff could muster around 500,000 troops, including 45,000 Italians. These armies also had 261 tanks – all opposing Eighth Army – 1,436 field guns of various calibres, 400 anti-tank guns, and 450 self-propelled guns. There was no air cover, and a growing shortage of artillery ammunition.

In Clark's 15th Army Group, Eighth Army could muster four corps totalling eight divisions, plus a number of infantry and armoured brigades and the 2nd Commando Brigade – a total strength of over 600,000 men including reserves. Fifth Army had two powerful corps, totalling eight divisions, including two in army reserve, plus a number of independent tank and infantry regiments – a US regiment being the equivalent of a British brigade. The total strength of Fifth Army came to over 1.3 million men, and both Allied armies were backed by the powerful Allied tactical and strategic air forces. The 15th Army Group contained some 2 million men, so von Vietinghoff's forces were outnumbered four to one.

Fifth Army's task was to renew the struggle of the previous year, take Bologna, and push across the Po. In the process it must destroy the enemy to the front, not simply push him back to a new defence line along the river Adige. This river line lay north of the Po, between Verona and the Adriatic, and another defence line, the Adige Line, had been constructed here during the winter.

The task of Eighth Army was rather more difficult, mainly because of the ground. Its front was constrained by the river Reno and the wide but shallow waters of Lake Comacchio, just inland from the Adriatic. Any way around Comacchio was barred by a series of rivers – the Senio, the Santerno and the Idice – all tributaries of the larger Reno, which flowed out of the Apennines and curved east across the Eighth Army front through Argenta and into Lake Comacchio.

These physical features presented General McCreery with a choice of difficulties. If he could cross the Reno and force a way through the gap between that river and Lake Comacchio at Argenta, he could avoid a repetition of the earlier slow and costly river assaults that would be involved in a wider advance to the north-west. The snag was that an attack at Argenta narrowed his front and presented the left flank of his advancing forces to the possibility of counter-attack. The Argenta gap was also flooded and covered by most of the remaining German armour, including Tiger tanks and self-propelled 88-mm guns. McCreery's answer to that problem was to widen the front to the east by assaulting along the west coast of Comacchio and directly across the lake, using units of the 2nd Commando Brigade carried in assault boats and Buffaloes, to outflank the Argenta position.

On 12 February Clark had directed McCreery and Truscott to prepare plans for an offensive across the Po. Having received their proposals, on 24 March he issued orders for 'an all-out attack on 10 April, 1945, to destroy the maximum number of enemy south of the Po, force crossings of the Po river and capture Verona'.

Eighth Army would attack first, crossing the Senio and Santerno rivers. Fifth Army would then advance north on Bologna, Ostiglia and Verona while Eighth Army made its amphibious crossing of Lake Comacchio, so opening a way through Argenta towards Ferrara. All being well, this would be followed with further exploitation by Eighth Army towards Venice and Trieste. Forcing the Argenta Gap would be the task of V Corps and the Poles, after they had crossed the Senio and the Santerno. The Eighth Army attack would go in one week before Fifth Army advanced, with the aim of attracting German divisions away from the American front and ensuring a speedy advance towards Bologna and Verona.

Clark's plan for 15th Army Group gave priority to the advance on Verona. With memories of the Rome fiasco, Alexander, McCreery and Truscott – the Fifth Army commander – thought that a direct thrust north would deny the Allied armies the chance of encircling and destroying the German armies on the wide plain of the Po. These objections were raised with Clark and appear to have been noted. When he issued the final orders for his Army Group on 18 March the aim had been modified. Their task now was 'to include the destruction of the maximum number of enemy forces south of the Po, and capture Verona'. D-Day for Eighth Army would be 9 April, and the Fifth Army attack would begin on the day Eighth Army crossed the Senio. This attack, the last of the war in Italy, was code-named Operation GRAPESHOT.

The critical task for Eighth Army lay at Argenta. To outflank this position, in addition to the commando attack across the lake and up the eastern shore – the Spit – to Porto Garibaldi, the 56th Division of V Corps would launch three attacks up the western shore – 'Impact Plain', 'Impact Royal' and 'Impact Slam' – which would carry the division around Bastia, Argenta and Portomaggiore.

The weather never ceased to complicate operations in Italy, and the dry spring of 1945 – normally something welcomed by the troops – proved a snag on this occasion: the warmer weather dried out Lake Comacchio until it was too shallow for the assault craft. Fortunately, the soft muddy bottom and the remaining shallows were thought to be a good place to deploy the Buffaloes and the lightly equipped troops of the 2nd Commando Brigade.

Crossing the rivers Senio and Santerno, if less complicated, was no less difficult, for here lay the bastion of the Genghis Khan Line. Set on high river banks and flood banks, this provided perfect observation over open ground and offered ideal positions for machine-guns and artillery. McCreery proposed reducing these positions by bombing and the fire from over 1,000 of Eighth Army's 1,273 guns, backing the infantry attack with the use of man-packed flame-throwers and flame-throwing Crocodile tanks, which V Corps and the Polish Corps would deploy to breach the Senio line between Fusignano and Felisio.

If the Argenta position fell quickly, V Corps was to press forward and wheel north-west to get behind the German forces south of the Po, while pressing north beyond Ferrara to seize the crossings over the river. X Corps would take command of all the forces around Comacchio and exploit to the north-east, towards Venice. This plan would be changed if there was any hold up at Argenta: in that case X Corps would move west to the Apennines, XIII Corps thrust for Budrio, west of Argenta, and V Corps take over the front east to the Adriatic.

Before the main offensive began, there were preliminary operations at Comacchio. On the night of 1/2 April the 2nd Commando Brigade attacked across the south-eastern corner of the lake, and two nights later it captured the islands in the centre. It set out in Buffaloes, but these quickly bogged down in the mud and shallow water, so the troops transferred to stormboats and swept across the lake, taking more than 1,000 prisoners and winning two VCs – both posthumous – in the process. One went to Corporal Tom Hunter of No. 43 (Royal Marine) Commando, the other to Major Anders Lassen, a Danish officer in the Special Raiding Squadron.

Major Leslie Callf, MC, of No. 9 Commando, took part in the Comacchio attack – Operation ROAST:

No. 9 Commando now amounted to just 368 all ranks, excluding attached personnel, and we moved from Ravenna at 1600 hours on 1 April, which was Easter Sunday. For this operation 9 Commando were allotted 1 Weasel and 26 stormboats, plus 6 assault boats to be used in case of breakdown. Once loaded, the Fantails broke down in the shallow water and had to be abandoned, so we attacked in stormboats and Goatley boats. My own boat travelled midway and then stuck in the mud, but information from the SBS in folboats [canoes] enabled us to push our way into deeper water where it was possible to paddle.

Time of landing was approximately 0545 hours and we advanced in extended order using a heavy mist to cover our advance. I gave the order to advance as far as Smarlacca House or such time as 9 Section in the lead were forced to stop. We proceeded at good speed until 9 Section bumped the enemy, who were dug in and facing in our direction among the sand dunes.

They opened up on us with automatic weapons, firing down the vine lanes, and threw egg and stick grenades; at the same time automatic fire was opened on the remaining boats putting in to the shore. Lieutenant Long's section swept into the enemy position and overran them, but at the cost of eight casualties, including Lieutenant Long and his batman. Then the whole troop pushed through to the enemy gun lines, with Sergeants Searle and Stephens pushing around the beach flank to engage and silence a Spandau firing up the beach; one 75-mm gun was blown up just before we reached it and another was captured intact when the German about to blow it up was killed.[5]

Lieutenant Don Long of No. 9 Commando, wounded in this attack, gives his account of the fighting:

I remember walking to the lorries with George Robinson, who said, 'The one thing I could do with before the war ends is an MC.' We were all quite sure the war would be over shortly, so I said, 'Don't be bloody silly – just hope we don't get one of those white crosses the Pioneers make.'

Well, we landed at Comacchio, but it was an awful nonsense. The Fantails wouldn't work and the stormboats got stuck, but we landed eventually and I was going over to talk to Sergeant McCreasy when it happened. We were all worried about schu mines, which could take your foot off, and as I ran over I was conscious of being blown into the air. I came down with the most awful bump, but was delighted to see that I still had both my legs, although I was by now pretty useless. It turned out later that it was not a mine; I had kicked an unexploded German grenade, and it had gone off, hurting me and taking off my batman Francis's left cheek.

I got into a hole and found a German there, looking rather glum. I pulled my Colt .45, got rid of his rifle and had him carry me piggyback up to where I found Major Callf and the battle.[6]

It took the 2nd Commando Brigade three days to fight its way up and across Lake Comacchio, and following Operation ROAST the Brigade came under command of the 56th Division for the next operation, the thrust through the Argenta Gap.

The 56th Division entered the fray on the night of 5/6 April, crossing the Reno where it enters Lake Comacchio and clearing the area west of the lake while the divisional sappers flung Bailey bridges across the river. All was now ready for Eighth Army's push through the gap and towards Bologna, which began on 9 April and was to take them across five river lines – the Senio, Santerno, Sillaro, Gaiana and Idice – and the Genghis Khan Line along the river Idice. Fortunately the dry spring weather had reduced the river levels and the extent of the surrounding floods.

The GRAPESHOT offensive began on the night of 9/10 April. Eighth Army's initial thrust, a powerful, set-piece attack of the kind that Eighth Army handled so well, began with a devastating raid on the enemy positions by 825 heavy bombers. These used fragmentation bombs to avoid heavy cratering of the opposite shore, and the bombers were followed by shelling and more attacks by medium bombers and fighter bombers. Crocodile flame-throwing tanks then moved up to scorch the nearest enemy bunkers, and there was a further burst of artillery fire on the enemy positions across the river. And then the infantry went forward.

The New Zealanders, the 19th Indian Brigade of the 8th Indian Division and the Poles waded across the Senio in the dark and began clearing the defences on the far bank with automatic weapons and grenades. They were opposed by the German 98th and 362nd Divisions, but were able to push ahead and by the following morning had crossed the Santerno river and captured Massa Lombarda. In this first attack, Sepoy Ali Haider of the 6/13th Frontier Force Rifles won the Victoria Cross, storming two enemy machine-gun nests with grenades and the bayonet to help his company get across the Senio.

The battle for the Argenta Gap began on the night of 10/11 April, when the 56th Division launched Impact Plain, exploiting its previous bridgehead. This assault was immediately opposed by the 29th Panzergrenadier Division, which von Vietinghoff had rushed up to bolster the defences of the gap. In response, McCreery committed the 78th Division, which captured a bridge over the Reno at Bastia on 14 April and joined in the fight at Argenta. This battle went on for the next four days, and while it was raging McCreery, piling on the pressure, sent in the 10th Indian Division to bolster the attack. The Poles took Imola on Route 9, inflicting heavy losses on the 26th Panzer Division in the process, and the New Zealanders were pressing up to the banks of the Sillaro.

Another officer of No. 9 Commando, Peter Bolton, takes up the tale:

After Comacchio we only had a couple of days' respite before we were off again on Impact Royal with 24th Guards Brigade. The plan was to cross the lake in Fantails and lay up, then advance by night up the west side of the lake and secure a crossing over the Fosse Marina Canal, which would open up the way north and west to the Argenta Gap.

We landed as planned with no opposition, but then came under heavy mortar fire. Luckily we had dug in on arrival, so there were no casualties, but a bomb exploded very close to the trench occupied by my batman, Private Woodcock. I stuck my head up after the bang and saw Woodcock rising like an angel from a cloud of smoke and wandering off, dazed. A ten-minute mortar stonk precluded further investigation, but he then came wandering back, asking what had happened. My rucksack, on the edge of my trench, was peppered with shrapnel and Woodcock was pretty deaf and had to be left with the MO.

We had just started to move again when there was a shout, a grenade went off, and there was a burst of fire – whose I never knew. Next, two prisoners were hustled back and it appeared that the leading scout had fallen into an enemy advance post. He thought they were asleep, but they had thrown a grenade. No casualties up to now, but our silent-approach gambit was blown. No time to wait, so I shouted to the troop to spread out across the field to our left and we charged the buildings ahead in line.

I admit it was exhilarating – a real 'over the top' bayonet charge, all of us screaming like dervishes. Someone appeared at one of the upper windows and fired several bursts at us as we ran in, and I replied with my .45 – all my shots going wide – and then I caught my foot in a hole and went down, the pistol flying from my hand; it was not on a lanyard, and I lost it. There was no time to go scrambling about looking for it, so I scuttled after my chaps as they ran into the farmyard. As I entered the yard there was what I can only describe as a God Almighty bang and I was concious of a great blast of air. As I dropped to the ground there was another great flash and bang, and to my horror I saw the barrel of a most enormous gun, just in front of me.

In the flash I saw Corporal Daniels of 4 Troop moving towards it. Then I heard the whirr of an engine turning over and immediately thought it was a tank. On the third 'flash-bang' I saw Corporal Daniels on the turret, tommy gun in hand, shouting,

'Raus, Raus Hande Hoch', and out they came. In fact it was not a tank but an 88-mm self-propelled gun. We hustled the prisoners inside the building, and I rushed out again to see if we had taken our objective.

I ran round the buildings with Gunner Riddall, and as we approached an adjacent building a figure appeared and fired at us with a Schmeisser. I felt the most terrific bang on the head and fell down, thinking, 'What a ridiculous way to die, right at the end of the war.' I felt with my fingers for the hole in my forehead, but then Riddall was shouting, 'Sir, your helmet's on fire.' The bullet had hit the rim of my helmet and deflected upward, splitting the helmet and setting the scrim and camouflage netting alight – a patch about the size of my palm was burning brightly.

Riddall had taken a shot at the guy, but we did not pursue that line; we collected a few of the chaps and assaulted that building from the opposite side, and I then ordered our Troop piper to play and I am proud to say that 4 Troop were the first to do so – though, as the night wore on, one by one the other Troop pipers were heard playing their objective tune.[7]

By 14 April, Eighth Army had crossed the Senio and Santerno rivers and driven the enemy back to the Sillaro river, which crosses the southern end of the Argenta Gap. Fifth Army duly entered the fray on 14 April, and in the next five days, until 19 April, both armies were heavily engaged. Eighth Army broke through the Argenta Gap on 19 April, when von Vietinghoff ordered his armies to begin a withdrawal to the north. But this order came too late. By 23 April the 6th South African Division of Fifth Army and the 6th (British) Armoured Division of Eighth Army had wheeled across the enemy retreat and joined forces at Finale Emilia, just south of the Po, trapping the majority of Army Group 'C' before it could escape. All resistance south of the Po ended on 23 April.

On the morning of 14 April, while Eighth Army was swarming all over the enemy between Imola and Menate, Truscott sent Fifth Army towards Bologna. Its attack was preceded by bombing from 500 aircraft, after which IV Corps advanced on the left bank of the Reno, thrusting for Ostiglia. Between 15 and 18 April the Allied strategic air forces took up the battle, sending in some 2,000 heavy bombers every day to smite the German positions east of Bologna and across the advancing front of the two Allied armies. On 15 April the US II Corps went forward east of the Reno, and now the full strength of both armies was engaged, the US 10th Mountain Division spearheading Fifth Army's breakout from the Apennines and reaching the main Via Emilia east of Bologna, Fifth Army's objective for the last six months. On 15 April General von Vietinghoff, his front stretched to breaking point, ordered a withdrawal to the line of the Po.

Von Vietinghoff had left it a little too late. A large part of his forces in the Argenta Gap positions was now trapped behind the forward elements of the US II Corps and the British V Corps. The two German divisions trapped behind the Reno were wiped out, the US 88th Division alone taking over 7,000 prisoners. II Polish Corps, pushing up the Via Emilia and crossing the Fifth Army line, entered Bologna at around 0700 hours on 21 April, followed two hours later by troops of the US 34th Division. The US 10th Mountain Division reached Ostiglia on the north bank of the Po on 23 April, and the British XIII Corps was over the river on the following day.

Von Vietinghoff was not allowed an orderly withdrawal. The Allied armies stayed close on his heels, hustling his units back to the Po, where all the bridges had been destroyed by Allied air attacks and the few remaining ferries were under constant attack by Allied fighter bombers. Allied tank and infantry units began crossing the river on 23 April, and the German situation there became a replica of that faced by German units at the Seine in Normandy the previous summer. As in Normandy, many of the enemy were able to get across the river, often by swimming, but all their stores and heavy equipment had to be abandoned.

By the evening of 25 April the Allied armies were fanning out across northern Italy and had already taken 54,000 prisoners and captured or destroyed much of the Army Group 'C' transport and artillery. The British Official History records that a survivor of the 65th Infantry Division witnessed the enemy's destruction of 31 Tiger tanks and 11 brand new self-propelled guns which could not be evacuated across the river.[8] Among the 11,000 prisoners taken by Fifth Army between 25 and 27 April was Major-General von Schellwitz, commander of the 305th Infantry Division.

After that shambles on the Po, the German collapse came quickly. German officers were already seeking surrender terms from Allied representatives in Switzerland, and von Vietinghoff made no attempt to hold a line on the north bank of the Po, which the Allied divisions crossed unopposed. On 27 April the US 10th Mountain Division took Verona and pressed on to Lake Garda, while the US II Corps headed towards the Adige Line, competing for ground with the divisions of the British V and XIII Corps, which had crossed the Po west and east of Ferrara. The Adige Line, such as it was, fell to the New Zealanders on 26 April, Allied troops rolling over the unmanned defences and those of the Venetian Line further east. By the end of April the German armies in Italy had collapsed.

So too had the short-lived Fascist Republic of Salo. On 28 April 1944 the Italian dictator Benito Mussolini, who had ruled Italy since 1922, was captured and then murdered by Italian partisans. Hearing that the German forces were on the brink of surrender, Mussolini and a few of his aides fled towards Lake Como, intending to seek shelter in Switzerland. On 27 April this convoy was stopped and searched near Dongo by Italian partisans, and Mussolini was found hiding in the back of a truck. With his mistress, Clara Petacci, the Duce was taken to a nearby house, and on the following day both of them were shot by a partisan execution squad, sent out for that purpose from Milan. This squad also shot 15 other members of the Duce's party and took the bodies of Mussolini and Petacci back to Milan, where they were openly displayed, hung up by their heels at a garage in the Piazza de Loreto.

The German retreat towards the Brenner Pass and Austria in the last days of April was harried all the way by the Allied air forces, by Italian partisans and by light units – armoured cars and lorried infantry – of the Allied armies. These armies then divided, the Fifth heading north towards the Alps, the Eighth turning east towards Venice, which fell to the troops of the 56th Division on 29 April. On that day Lieutenant-General Freyberg of the 2nd New Zealand Division was told by Lieutenant-General Sir John Harding, now commanding XIII Corps, 'The place we want to get to most is Trieste.'

Eighth Army needed to get to Trieste quickly, for some of Churchill's long-held fears over Communist ambitions in western Europe were now becoming a reality. The Yugoslav Partisan Army, equipped by the British but backed by the Russians, was now flooding across the Yugoslav–Italian frontier, intent on seizing as much Italian territory as possible – including the port and city of Trieste – and ready to defy any attempts at eviction.

Alexander decided to tackle this problem directly and unequivocally by pushing strong forces up to Trieste, making it clear that the Yugoslav advance would be resisted by force if need be. The Yugoslav reaction was further hostility and intransigence. On the evening of 1 May Freyberg invited the commander of the 4th Yugoslav Army to meet him for a discussion on boundary problems. Freyberg waited for hours at the meeting place, but no one arrived. Nor did any Yugoslav general turn up for their next appointment on the morning of 2 May – the day the war in Italy ended with the surrender of all the Axis forces to General Alexander.

Ignoring Bernard Freyberg proved unwise. On the second occasion Freyberg waited until a few minutes past the appointed hour, then sent the 9th New Zealand Infantry Brigade marching into Trieste, deployed for battle, with the 20th New Zealand Armoured Regiment in support. The New Zealanders reached Trieste on the afternoon of 2 May and were greeted in the centre by 'genuine cheering from excited crowds and equally genuine sniper fire from buildings still held by the Germans'.[9] This resistance was largely due to the Germans' being very reluctant to surrender to the Yugoslav partisans, who had a hard way with prisoners: 1,600 German troops readily surrendered to the New Zealanders. Sergeant D. L. Garven of the New Zealand 19th Armoured Regiment:

> After crossing the Po it was a mad rush in pursuit of the enemy. We eventually caught up and had a skirmish with them, which we quickly took care of, but we caught up with them again at Trieste. There we found the Germans holed up in the Palace of Justice, a five-storey building in the heart of the city. When we arrived, a lot of enemy troops were leaning out of the windows, giving us the 'thumbs-up'. We gave them ten minutes to give themselves up, after which we were ordered to blaze away for another ten minutes non-stop. That caused them a lot of casualties, and they decided to surrender.
>
> The Italians told us that the Yugoslav Army was on the outskirts of the city and intended to take over Trieste, so we sent three tanks to stop them advancing, which spoiled their plans. But from time to time they entered the city, and we allowed them

to wander around, with their rabble of patrols which included women draped with ammunition bandoliers, but we had everything under control and they caused us no trouble. The Italians welcomed us with open arms, and as we were the first Allied troops to arrive they gave us a great reception.

This was the great anticlimax – that we should end up on such a happy note after slogging all the way from the Western Desert, right through Italy, to finish our pursuit of the enemy here. But it was great to be able to relax at last.[10]

Yugoslav hostility to the Western Allies and the Allied soldiers was not new. It had been growing steadily throughout 1944 as the Russian forces swept west. Even the Red Army's raping its way through Belgrade in early 1945 had done nothing to reduce the warmth of the Yugoslav welcome to the Soviets. Towards their British and American allies, on the other hand, Yugoslav troops were increasingly insolent, offering provocation at every level, and showing an arrogance which Marshal Tito did little to discourage. In the summer of 1944 Tito made a formal visit to Alexander's HQ, arriving with a bodyguard of partisans armed with tommy guns. These stayed close to Tito throughout the meeting, fingering their weapons and gazing suspiciously at Alexander's staff. Alexander thought this behaviour 'a little bad mannered', and decided to show that suspicion was not all on one side. When he made the return visit to Tito's HQ, instead of just taking a few of his staff officers Alexander took a personal bodyguard of sixteen guardsmen – the tallest and smartest that could be found in the Guards brigades – and his aircraft was escorted – for no good operational reason – by four Mustang fighters. This display went unremarked by the partisan leader, but the point was taken. Two could play at provocation, and Tito's attitude improved somewhat thereafter.

But hostility to the Western armies continued, and Communist demands grew as the war drifted to a close. Sadly this provides the final chapter, the epilogue, to the story of Eighth Army. After that long march from Alamein, it would have been pleasant for the soldiers of Eighth Army – and their comrades of Fifth Army during the Italian campaign – to end this war in triumph, with a short series of ceremonies and parades in the welcome warmth of the Italian spring before the soldiers dispersed to their home countries and returned to civilian life. Instead, having beaten the Fascists, they now had to confront the Communists.

The 'Trieste Crisis' of April–May 1945 was the opening shot in the 50-year-long Cold War, a conflict that began even as the guns cooled. Trieste lies in Venezia Giulia, the Italian province that lies between Venice and the Italian–Yugoslav frontier. The Yugoslav Communists clearly intended to occupy and then annex Venezia Giulia, and the Western Allies were determined to prevent this, proposing to refer all territorial disputes to a post-war conference. The decision to resist Yugoslav ambitions placed General Alexander in a difficult position.

'If I am ordered by the Combined Chiefs of Staff to occupy the whole of Venezia Giulia, by force if necessary,' he wrote, 'we shall certainly be committed to a fight with the Yugoslav Army, who will have the moral backing at least of the Russians.' Alexander also expressed some doubts on the reaction of his troops if they were ordered to fight their former partisan allies.

Reg Wheatley of the 754th Army Field Company Royal Engineers recalls the day his war ended:

It was 2 May, and 754th company was lined up in convoy ready to move forward yet again when a DonR [dispatch rider] came down the road shouting, 'The Germans have all surrendered in Italy. The Italian war is over.' There was much jubilation and celebration by the whole Company, but we moved on to a place called Latisana, not far from the Austrian border. On 8 May we were building a Bailey bridge when an officer strolled over and said that the European war was over officially and that 8 May was VE Day. There was a beer ration that night, and next day we went in trucks to Venice, where I rode in a gondola. Venice seemed to be packed with troops – especially the Navy, who seemed to be riding round the canals in motor boats.

Yes, the war was over, but then another crisis loomed. Apparently Yugoslavia had laid claims to Trieste and had moved troops to a threatening position, bringing tanks down close to the border. 754th was sent up to cope with any emergency, putting up a tank trap into the side of the road close to the border. However, sanity prevailed and the trouble was averted.

In July 1945 I began my journey home, which took several days by truck, and on the fourth day we passed through Luxembourg and France. As we travelled we were greeted by waving and cheering civilians and shouts of delight by our fellow servicemen. We all wore our Eighth Army flashes with pride. The Eighth Army had won the respect of the world, and its slogan 'Alamein to Austria' was a sign that denoted troops who had been overseas for a considerable period – over four years in many cases.[11]

Charles Butt again:

On 2 May 1945 the position was that Eighth Army had 6th Armoured Division just entering Austria, the New Zealand Division in Trieste, and 56th Division in the Venice area. The Russians had advanced beyond their agreed area, and Tito was showing signs of grabbing as much of southern Austria and Trieste as he could get away with. Eventually, in June/July the Russians withdrew to their agreed boundaries and the British Zone of Austria was established, consisting of two provinces: Styria – now Steiermark – capital Graz, and Carinthia, capital Klagenfurt. Eventually, later in the year, 78th Division became responsible for Carinthia and 46th Division came back from the Middle East for Styria. Trieste was now causing further trouble – or rather Tito was – and so 56th Division went to Trieste and was joined there by the US 10th Mountain Division to present a united front. Vienna was then divided into four zones, HQ Eighth Army became HQ British Troops Austria or BTA – and so ended Eighth Army.[12]

Trieste became a test case for Western resolve in the face of Communist intransigence, provocation and hostility. Churchill for one had no doubts that these elements must be resisted, even if it came to fighting, and ordered Alexander not to give an inch in any talks and to move up more troops to underline Western resolve. British and American troops therefore moved in strength to Venezia Giulia and Trieste, where by 6 May they were confronting a Yugoslav force estimated at 60,000 men.

On 10 May the new US President, Harry S. Truman, made it clear that he regarded these Communist forces as a threat to peace and stated that his government was prepared to take a very strong line in resisting further aggression. This Allied resolve began to pay a dividend on 15 May, when the Yugoslavs began withdrawing their forces back across the Isonzo river in Venezia Giulia. But more Yugoslav forces were pressing forward into Austria, where the Fifth Army was ordered to resist further Yugoslav incursions, again by force if necessary.

During this time another problem arose – a human and moral one. Among the thousands of prisoners taken with the surrender of the German armies were large numbers of Russian Cossacks and Yugoslav Chetniks, mostly Croats. It had been agreed at the Yalta Conference that such people, if captured, would be handed over to their national forces, but there was little doubt what their fate would be after that happened.

This was not a small-scale problem but a serious moral issue. Alexander estimated that among their prisoners his armies held around 46,000 Cossacks, 25,000 Croats and 24,000 Slovenes, many accompanied by their wives and children – all 'Yugoslav Quislings', according to the commander of the Yugoslav Fourth Army. If these prisoners were handed over to the Communists, long spells in labour camps were the best they could hope for – and the Geneva Convention clearly forbade any such punishment. These people were prisoners of war, and the Allied armies had a duty to protect them.

The Geneva Convention was not invoked, and the handover of Cossack and Yugoslav prisoners duly took place among many distressing and distasteful scenes – an episode described by the men ordered to take part in it as 'a most unsavoury business'.[13] The great majority of these returned prisoners were shot, hanged, beaten, starved or otherwise done to death in a matter of days; General Helmut von Panwittz, the commander of the Russian Cossack forces – and a German officer – was publicly hanged in Moscow's Red Square. The handing over of the Croats and Cossacks to what passed for Communist justice has not been forgotten by the men who observed it, many of whom still feel that it was a shameful affair.

The Yugoslavs finally backed down over Trieste and Venezia Giulia on 19 May. It had become clear to Tito and his Soviet backers that the Western Allies were prepared to fight over this issue and were deploying troops, tanks and aircraft should this be necessary. Allied troops advanced towards the Yugoslav frontier from 22 May, and the Yugoslav armies fell back steadily before them. There was no fighting, and so it ended.

The German armies in Italy surrendered to General Alexander on 2 May. Six days later, by 8 May, the remaining German forces had surrendered to the Allies, and 8 May became Victory in Europe – VE – Day.

On that day the long march of Eighth Army was over. It had been a very long march: since leaving Alamein, this army had travelled more than 3,000 miles, from the Alamein minefields to the swamps of the Romagna and the foothills of the Alps, over desert and mountain and flooded plain, past Tripoli and Tunis, across Sicily and Italy. On their Colours, its units would eventually carry the names of a score of engagements – Beda Fomm, Tobruk, Sidi Rezegh, Gazala, Alamein, Mareth, the Sicily landings, Primasole, Catania, the Sangro, Ortona, Cassino, the Gustav Line and the Gothic Line, the valley of the Po, and finally Comacchio, Argenta and Trieste. No army had marched so far; few armies have fought so much in five hard years of war.

This was the time for farewell messages. In his message to the 2nd New Zealand Division, 2nd New Zealand Expeditionary Force, General Sir Bernard Freyberg stated:

> Nobody knows better than I do how important a part this Force played in the cause of the Allies. When the history of this war is written we shall have an impressive list of battle honours. Some of our battles have been outstandingly successful, for example those in the Western Desert from Alamein onwards, but I venture to think that we shall look back with the greatest pride to the times when we fought without adequate equipment. It was then that our star shone brightest, then that our best work was done, holding the enemy in the Middle East, until the Allies were organized on a war footing. Greece, Crete, Sidi Rezegh, Minqar Qa'im and Ruweisat Ridge are names which will be among our proudest memories.

Eighth Army's last commander, Lieutenant-General Richard McCreery, had served with it all the way from the desert to Trieste. Concluding his address on 15 July 1945, McCreery wrote:

> Today Eighth Army officially breaks up. The Eighth Army was composed of many nations; all worked together in true comradeship. This spirit of generous co-operation is a good augury for the future of the world. Eighth Army men will be playing a tremendous part if they continue in fresh fields to fight and work for right and justice with the same enthusiasm that won them great victories from El Alamein to the river Po.

Eighth Army was disbanded at the end of July 1945. It passed into history without a triumphal march past or any great parade. That seems suitable, for, though it was composed of soldiers from many nations, Eighth Army was a British Army – and the British are not very interested in military parades. Besides, the soldiers of Eighth Army had no need of public recognition. They knew what they had done: they had endured, whatever the odds against them – sometimes baffled but rarely dismayed. They kept on fighting and marching and moving on. They had done their duty as soldiers, and in the end that hard process gained the victory and the peace they so richly deserved.

Notes

CHAPTER 1: THE WESTERN DESERT FORCE

1. Throughout this book, unless a specific unit – Empire or Dominion or from any other nation – is involved (e.g. the Poles), the troops involved on the Eighth Army side will be referred to as 'British'. This is simply for reasons of space; no offence or disrespect to other Commonwealth or Allied nations is intended.
2. *The Mediterranean and Middle East*, vol. 1, appendix 1.
3. Ibid., p. 33.
4. Correlli Barnett, *The Desert Generals* (London: Allen & Unwin, 1983), p. 25.
5. Letter to the author, 2002.
6. *Other Men's Flowers* is still in print in 2003.
7. *The Mediterranean and Middle East*, vol. 1, p. 69.
8. Conversation with the author, 1990.
9. Conversation with the author, 1990.
10. The need for sand filters on tanks had still not been grasped in 1990, when another British armoured force went off to war in the Gulf.
11. This account and those that follow come from correspondence with the author, 2001–2.

CHAPTER 2: SIDI BARRANI AND BEDA FOMM

1. *The Mediterranean and Middle East*, vol. 1, p. 188.
2. Ibid., p. 200.
3. Ibid.

4. Ibid., pp. 265–6.
5. Letter to the author, 2002.
6. Gavin Long, *To Benghazi* (Australian Official History) (Canberra: Australian War Memorial, 1952), p. 38.
7. Ibid., p. 39.
8. Ibid., p. 47.
9. Ibid., p. 57.
10. Letter to the author, 2001.
11. Long, *To Benghazi*, p. 307.
12. Ibid., p. 124.
13. Letter to the author, 2002.
14. Letter to the author, 2002.
15. Letter to the author, 2002.
16. Letter to the author, 2002.
17. Letter to the author, 2002.
18. *The Mediterranean and Middle East*, vol. 1, p. 352.
19. Ibid., p. 357.
20. Ibid., p. 362.
21. Ibid., p. 364.

CHAPTER 3: TOBRUK

1. *The Mediterranean and Middle East*. vol. 1, p. 367.
2. Correlli Barnett, ed., *Hitler's Generals* (London: Weidenfeld & Nicolson, 1989), p. 297.
3. Letter to the author, 2001.
4. *Correspondence*, 2 March 1941.
5. *The Mediterranean and Middle East*, vol. 2, p. 35.
6. F. H. Hinsley et al., *British Intelligence in the Second World War, Its Influence on Strategy and Operations*, vol. 2 (London: HMSO, 1981), p. 392n.
7. Peter Calvocoressi, *Top Secret Ultra* (London: Cassell, 1980), p. 80.
8. Matthew Rogers, 'Enigma in North Africa', dissertation for the University of Reading, 2000.
9. Alan Moorehead, *African Trilogy* (London: Hamish Hamilton, 1944), p. 180.
10. Frank Harrison, *Tobruk: The Great Siege Reassessed* (London: Arms and Armour Press, 1997), p. 27.
11. Diary in translation supplied by Bill Jenkins, New South Wales, Australia.
12. Letter to the author.
13. Letter to the author.
14. Letter to the author.
15. Letter to the author.
16. Account in Rats of Tobruk fiftieth-anniversary souvenir book, with thanks to Cyril Gaylard.
17. Letter to the author.

18. Letter to the author.
19. Letter to the author.
20. Letter to the author.
21. Letter to the author.
22. Letter to the author (account supplied by Henry Tranter with permission of Ned Maxwell).
23. Correlli Barnett, *The Lost Victory: British Dreams, British Realities, 1945–1950* (London: Macmillan, 1995), p. 72.
24. Correlli Barnett, *The Audit of War* (London: Macmillan, 1986), pp. 161–2.
25. Letter to the author, 2002.
26. Letter to the author, 2001.
27. *The Mediterranean and Middle East*, vol. 2, p. 162.
28. Hans-Otto Behrendt, *Rommel's Intelligence in the Desert Campaign 1941–1943* (London: William Kimber, 1985), p. 145.
29. *The Mediterranean and Middle East*, vol. 2, p. 173.

CHAPTER 4: CRUSADER: THE BATTLE FOR SIDI REZEGH

1. *The Mediterranean and Middle East*, vol. 2, appendix 5, p. 158.
2. Ibid., p. 153.
3. Sir Arthur Wellesley, later Lord Wellington, whose Peninsular Army of 1811–13 was notoriously scruffy, remarked that 'I think it indifferent how a soldier is clothed . . .'
4. Letter to the author, 2001.
5. Barnett, *The Desert Generals*, p. 84.
6. *The Mediterranean and Middle East*, vol. 3, p. 4.
7. Major-General Sir Howard Kippenberger, *Infantry Brigadier* (London: Oxford University Press, 1949), p. 81.
8. When writing an early account of this battle, the author telephoned Field Marshal Lord Carver and explained that, after days of study, pencil-chewing, writing and rewriting, he still did not know what was going on at Sidi Rezegh. Lord Carver replied, 'Well, you have probably got it about right. None of us who were there knew what was going on either.'
9. Bernard Fergusson, *The Black Watch and the King's Enemies* (London: Collins, 1950), p. 108.
10. Letter to the author, 2001.
11. This account and many of those that follow were sent in by veterans in 2001–2.
12. *The Mediterranean and Middle East*, vol. 3, p. 69.
13. Letters supplied by Arthur Smith's daughter, Mrs Gillian Howard.
14. The diary account from which these extracts were taken was supplied by Lieutenant Eastwood's son, Russell Eastwood.
15. Letter to the author, October 2001.
16. Account sent in by Mrs B. Muir, 2002.
17. *The Mediterranean and Middle East*, vol. 3, pp. 96–102.

CHAPTER 5: GAZALA

1. Letter to the author, 2001/2.
2. Letter to the author, 2001/2.
3. Letter to the author, 2001/2.
4. Letter to the author, 2001/2.
5. Field Marshal Lord Alanbrooke, *War Diaries, 1939–1945* (London: Weidenfeld & Nicolson, 2001), entry for 21 July 1941, p. 173.
6. Major-General Julian Thompson writes, 'I agree completely that the British generals had not grasped the basics but I also contend that they were overly influenced by the Liddell Hart and Fuller teaching of the all-tank army playing ships at sea – whereas what was needed was the co-ordination of all arms, including artillery.' Letter to the author, 2002.
7. PRO WO 208261, War Office Weekly Intelligence Summaries, vol. 6.
8. Rogers, 'Enigma in North Africa'.
9. Barnett, *The Desert Generals*, p. 138.
10. *The Mediterranean and Middle East*, vol. 3, p. 204.
11. Ibid., p. 197.
12. Hinsley et al., *British Intelligence in the Second World War*, vol. 2, p. 360.
13. Rogers, 'Enigma in North Africa', p. 18.
14. *The Mediterranean and Middle East*, vol. 3, p. 223.
15. Ibid., p. 225.
16. Ibid., p. 229.
17. Ibid., p. 228.
18. Ibid., p. 233.
19. Ibid., p. 232.
20. Letter to the author, 2001/2.
21. Letter to the author, 2001/2.
22. Letter to the author, 2001/2.
23. Letter to the author, 2001/2.
24. *The Mediterranean and Middle East*, vol. 3, p. 272.
25. Letter to the author, 2001/2.
26. Letter to the author, 2001/2.
27. Winston S. Churchill *The Second World War*, vol. 1: *The Gathering Storm* (London: Minerva, 1989), p. 128.
28. *The Mediterranean and Middle East*, vol. 3, p. 274.
29. Account supplied to the author, 2002.
30. John Keegan, ed., *Churchill's Generals* (London: Warner, 1992), p. 212.
31. Letter to the author, 2001/2.
32. Letter to the author, 2001/2.

CHAPTER 6: FIRST ALAMEIN TO ALAM HALFA

1. Quoted in Barnett, *The Desert Generals*, pp. 168–9.
2. Barnett, *The Desert Generals*, p. 144.

3. Letter to the author, 2002.
4. *The Mediterranean and Middle East*, vol. 3, p. 287.
5. Ibid., p. 335.
6. Kippenberger, *Infantry Brigadier*, p. 169.
7. Letter to the author, 2002.
8. Letter to the author, 2002.
9. Barnett, *The Desert Generals*, p. 240.
10. Field Marshal Lord Carver, *El Alamein* (Ware: Wordsworth Editions, 2002), foreword.
11. Montgomery was obliged to remove this slur on his predecessor when it was published in his memoirs in 1958.
12. Kippenberger, *Infantry Brigadier*, p. 139.
13. Field Marshal Viscount Montgomery of Alamein, *The Memoirs of Field Marshal The Viscount Montgomery of Alamein, K.G.* (London: Collins, 1958), p. 97.
14. Kippenberger, *Infantry Brigadier*, p. 127.
15. Kippenberger, *Infantry Brigadier*, p. 180.
16. Letter to the author, 2002.
17. Montgomery, *Memoirs* p. 94.
18. Ibid., p. 94.
19. Ibid., p. 100.
20. Kippenberger, *Infantry Brigadier*, p. 196.
21. Letter to the author, 2002.

CHAPTER 7: ALAMEIN

1. Letter to the author, 2002.
2. Conversation with the author, 1994.
3. Letter to the author, 2002.
4. Letter to the author, 2002.
5. Letter to the author, 2002.
6. Letter to the author, 2002.
7. Letter to the author, 2002.
8. Letter to the author, 2002.
9. Letter to the author, 2002.
10. Kippenberger, *Infantry Brigadier*, p. 157.
11. Letter to the author, 2002.
12. Fred Majdalany, *Cassino: Portrait of a Battle* (London: Longmans, Green, 1957), p. 96.
13. Ibid., p. 104.
14. Carver, *El Alamein*, p. 92.
15. These details from Derek Jewell, '"Lili Marlene": A Song for All Armies', in Derek Jewell, ed., *Alamein and the Desert War* (London: Sphere, 1967).
16. Carver, *El Alamein*, pp. 78–79.

17. Ibid., p. 82.
18. Ibid., p. 113.
19. *The Mediterranean and Middle East*, vol. 4, p. 34.
20. Letter to the author, 2001. It appears that fewer than 1,000 guns were employed on the initial Alamein barrage.
21. Letter to the author, 1995.
22. Letter to the author, 2001/2.
23. Letter to the author, 2001/2.
24. Letter to the author, 2001/2.
25. Letter to the author, 2001/2.
26. Carver, *El Alamein*, p. 112.
27. Ibid., pp. 116–17.
28. *The Mediterranean and Middle East*, vol. 4, p. 43.
29. Interview with the author, 1995.
30. Carver, *El Alamein*, p. 134.
31. *The Mediterranean and Middle East*, vol. 4, p. 64.
32. Jewell, *Alamein and the Desert War*, p. 90.
33. Letter to the author, 2002.
34. David Chandler, ed., *Great Battles of the British Army* (London: Arms and Armour Press, 1991), p. 173.
35. D. A. Lande, *Rommel in North Africa* (Osceola, Wis.: MBI Publishing, 1999), p. 136.

CHAPTER 8: ALAMEIN TO TRIPOLI

1. Letter to the author, 2001/2.
2. Letter to the author, 2001/2.
3. Letter to the author, 2001/2.
4. Letter to the author, 2001/2.
5. Letter to the author, 2001/2.
6. Barnett, *The Desert Generals*, p. 240.
7. Farewell address to the 9th Australian Division, 1942.
8. Erwin Rommel, *The Rommel Papers*, ed. B. H. Liddell Hart et al., trans. Paul Findlay (London: Collins, 1953), pp. 325–6.
9. *The Mediterranean and Middle East*, vol. 4, p. 165.
10. Ibid., p. 231.
11. Winston S. Churchill, *The Second World War*, vol. 4: *The Hinge of Fate* (London: Cassell, 1951), p. 645.
12. Letter to the author, 1994.

CHAPTER 9: TRIPOLI TO TUNIS

1. *The Mediterranean and Middle East*, vol. 4, p. 111.
2. This problem may have endured. Visiting British forces in Kosovo in 2001, the author was surprised to learn that their officers had been officially

advised not to make jokes at briefings as this tended to make their allies think they were not taking matters seriously.

3. *The Mediterranean and Middle East*, vol. 4, p. 303.
4. Ibid., p. 303.
5. Letter to the author, 2001.
6. Rommel, *The Rommel Papers*, p. 415.
7. Field Marshal Viscount Montgomery of Alamein, *El Alamein to the River Sangro* (London: Hutchinson, 1948), pp. 71–3.
8. Roy Farran, *Winged Dagger: Adventures on Special Service* (London: Collins, 1948), p. 57.
9. Letter to the author, 2002.
10. Montgomery, *El Alamein to the River Sangro*, p. 96.
11. Imperial War Museum IWM G.01/4/1.
12. *The Mediterranean and Middle East*, vol. 4, p. 457.

CHAPTER 10: SICILY

1. Albert N. Garland, Howard McGaw Smyth and Martin Blumenson, *Sicily and the Surrender of Italy* (US Official History) (Washington DC: Office of the Chief of Military History, Department of the Army, 1965), p. 11.
2. Prime Minister's personal minutes, D/72/3 in Martin Gilbert, *Road to Victory: Winston S. Churchill 1941–1945* (London: Heinemann, 1986), pp. 379–80.
3. Montgomery, *El Alamein to the River Sangro*, p. 112.
4. *The Mediterranean and Middle East*, vol. 5, p. 25.
5. S. W. C. Pack, *Operation Husky: The Allied Invasion of Sicily* (New York: Hippocrene Books, 1977), pp. 48–51.
6. Garland et al., *Sicily and the Surrender of Italy*, p. 117.
7. Ibid., p. 117.
8. Ibid.
9. Ibid., p. 118.
10. Letter to the author, 2002.
11. Letter to the author, 2002.
12. Garland et al., *Sicily and the Surrender of Italy*, p. 161.
13. Ibid., p. 156.
14. Ibid., p. 149.
15. Montgomery, *El Alamein to the River Sangro*, p. 125.
16. Garland et al., *Sicily and the Surrender of Italy*, pp. 177–84.
17. Hugh Pond, *Sicily* (London: William Kimber, 1962), p. 114.
18. Hilary Aidan St George Saunders, *The Red Beret: The Story of the Parachute Regiment at War, 1940–1945* (London: Michael Joseph, 1950), p. 121.
19. Garland et al., *Sicily and the Surrender of Italy*, p. 210.
20. See also Omar Bradley, *A Soldier's Story of the Allied Campaigns from Tunis to the Elbe* (London: Eyre & Spottiswoode, 1951), p. 136.

21. *The Mediterranean and Middle East*, vol. 5, pp. 26–7.
22. Garland et al., *Sicily and the Surrender of Italy*, p. 207.
23. Ibid., p. 209.
24. Ibid., p. 251.
25. Letter to the author, 2002.
26. Pond, *Sicily*, p. 160.
27. Letter to the author, 2002.
28. Garland et al., *Sicily and the Surrender of Italy*, p. 347.

CHAPTER 11: SALERNO TO THE SANGRO

1. Letter to the author, 2002.
2. Martin Blumenson, *Salerno to Cassino* (US Official History) (Washington DC: Office of the Chief of Military History, US Army, 1969), p. 29.
3. Ibid., p. 62.
4. Francis de Guingand, *Operation Victory* (London: Hodder & Stoughton, 1947), p. 317.
5. Blumenson, *Salerno to Cassino*, p. 41.
6. Ibid., p. 41.
7. *The Mediterranean and Middle East*, vol. 5, p. 241.
8. Blumenson, *Salerno to Cassino*, p. 118.
9. Ibid., p. 315. Had this ignorance been remedied by June 1944, and had the US troops employed the specialized armour offered by the British, US casualties on Omaha Beach might well have been much reduced.
10. *The Mediterranean and Middle East*, vol. 5, p. 281.
11. Blumenson, *Salerno to Cassino*, p. 158.
12. Ibid., p. 149.
13. Ibid., pp. 138–43.
14. Ibid., p. 142.
15. Lieutenant-Colonel G. W. L. Nicholson, *Official History of the Canadian Army in the Second World War*, vol. 2: *The Canadians in Italy 1943–1945* (Ottawa: Queen's Printer, 1956), p. 221.
16. Montgomery, *El Alamein to the River Sangro*, p. 169.
17. Conversation with the author, 1987.
18. Farran, *Winged Dagger*, p. 203.
19. *The Mediterranean and Middle East*, vol. 5, p. 457.
20. Conversation with the author, 1997.
21. Eric Linklater, *The Campaign in Italy* (London: HMSO, 1951), p. 106.
22. Letter to the author, 2002.
23. Linklater, *The Campaign in Italy*, p. 108.
24. Kippenberger, *Infantry Brigadier*, pp. 346–7.
25. Letter to the author, 2002.

CHAPTER 12: CASSINO

1. Letter to the author, 2002.
2. Imperial War Museum IWM 95/33/1.
3. Letter to the author, 2002.
4. Kippenberger, *Infantry Brigadier*, p. 361.
5. Letter to the author, 2002.
6. Blumenson, *Salerno to Cassino*, pp. 402–9.
7. *The Mediterranean and Middle East*, vol. 5, p. 712.
8. Blumenson, *Salerno to Cassino*, p. 411.
9. Ibid., p. 416.
10. Helmut Wilhelmsmeyer, *Der Krieg in Italien, 1943–1945* (Graz: L. Stocker, 1995), p. 219.
11. Letter to the author, 2002.
12. *The Mediterranean and Middle East*, vol. 5, pp. 783–4.
13. Letter to the author, 2002.
14. Majdalany, *Cassino*, p. 187.
15. *The Mediterranean and Middle East*, vol. 5, p. 806.

CHAPTER 13: CASSINO AND ROME

1. See R. H. Neillands, *The Battle of Normandy: An Anglo-American Campaign, 1944* (London: Cassell 2002).
2. As already noted, the 15th Army Group was retitled the Allied Armies in Italy (AAI) in March 1944, but the term '15th Army Group' remained in use and would return officially later.
3. Letter to the author, 2002.
4. Letter to the author, 2002.
5. Letter to the author, 2002.
6. Letter to the author, 2002.
7. Letter to the author, 2002.
8. Letter to the author, 2002.
9. Letter to the author, 2002.
10. Imperial War Museum files.
11. Ernest F. Fisher Jr, *Cassino to the Alps* (US Official History) (Washington DC: Center of Military History, US Army, 1977), p. 221.
12. Ibid., p. 231.
13. Mark W. Clark, *Calculated Risk: His Personal Story of the War in North Africa and Italy* (New York: Harper & Bros., 1950), pp. 356–7.
14. *The Mediterranean and Middle East*, vol. 6, pt 1, p. 284.
15. Ibid., p. 71.
16. Fisher, *Cassino to the Alps*, p. 542.
17. Ibid., p. 242.
18. Savarid, quoted in John Ellis, *Cassino: The Hollow Victory* (London: André Deutsch, 1984), p. 458.

CHAPTER 14: TO THE GOTHIC LINE

1. Letter to the author, 2002.
2. Clark, *Calculated Risk*, pp. 350, 351.
3. Ibid., pp. 357–8.
4. Ibid., p. 349.
5. Brazil had entered the Second World War in August 1942, but had previously restricted its commitment to naval anti-U-boat patrols in the South Atlantic.
6. *The Mediterranean and Middle East*, vol. 6, pt 2, p. 13.
7. Letter to the author, 2002.
8. Letter to the author, 2002.
9. Letter to the author, 2002.
10. *The Mediterranean and Middle East*, vol. 6, pt 2, p. 125.
11. Letter to the author, 2002.
12. Clark, *Calculated Risk*, p. 370.
13. Letter to the author, 2002.
14. Letter to the author, 2002.
15. Clark, *Calculated Risk*, p. 373.
16. *The Mediterranean and Middle East*, vol. 6, pt 2, p. 299.
17. Ibid., pp. 303–4.
18. Ibid., p. 367.
19. Ibid., p. 371.
20. Letter to the author.

CHAPTER 15: THE LONG MARCH ENDS

1. Letter to the author, 2001.
2. Clark, *Calculated Risk*, p. 381.
3. Letter to the author, 2002.
4. Thomas R. Brooks, *The War North of Rome, June 1944–May 1945* (New York: Sarpedon, 1996), p. 303.
5. Letter to the author, 2002.
6. Letter to the author, 2002.
7. Letter to the author, 2002.
8. *The Mediterranean and Middle East*, vol. 6, pt 3, p. 293.
9. Ibid., pp. 327–8.
10. Letter to the author, 2001/2.
11. Letter to the author, 2001/2.
12. Letter to the author, 2001/2.
13. *The Mediterranean and Middle East*, vol. 6, pt 3, p. 348.

Bibliography

The bibliography on Eighth Army is extensive but somewhat uneven, with far more on the desert war than on the subsequent Eighth Army campaigns. The prime source here has been the various official histories – American (Blumenson; Fisher; Garland et al.), Australian (Long), British (*The Mediterranean and Middle East*), Canadian (Nicholson) and New Zealand (Walker) – together with many divisional histories and a host of letters and private memoirs. There are far more personal accounts of the desert war than of the subsequent campaigns in Tunisia, Sicily or Italy, and some of these – Cyril Joly's *Take these Men*, Keith Douglas's *Alamein to Zem Zem*, Kippenberger's *Infantry Brigadier* and Fred Majdalany's *Cassino: Portrait of a Battle* – are classics. What follows is only a small selection of the books consulted.

Alanbrooke, Field Marshal Lord, *War Diaries, 1939–1945* (London: Weidenfeld & Nicolson, 2001)

Alexander of Tunis, Field Marshal Viscount, *The Alexander Memoirs 1940–1945*, ed. J. North (London: Cassell, 1962)

—— *Official Despatch* as C.-in-C. 15th Army Group, 1947

Allan, W. L., *Anzio: Edge of Disaster* (New York: Dutton, 1978)

Anders, Wladyslaw, *Army in Exile* (London: Macmillan, 1949)

Aris, George, *Fifth British Division* (London: Fifth Division Benevolent Fund, 1959)

Barnett, Correlli, *The Audit of War* (London: Macmillan, 1986)

—— *The Desert Generals* (London: Allen & Unwin, 1983)

—— , ed., *Hitler's Generals* (London: Weidenfeld & Nicolson, 1989)

—— *The Lost Victory: British Dreams, British Realities, 1945–1950* (London: Macmillan, 1995)

Behrendt, Hans-Otto, *Rommel's Intelligence in the Desert Campaign 1941–1943* (London: William Kimber, 1985)

Bennett, Ralph, *Ultra and the Mediterranean Strategy* (New York: William Murrow, 1989)

Blaxland, Gregory, *Alexander's Generals: The Italian Campaign, 1944–1945* (London: William Kimber, 1979)

Blumenson, Martin, *Salerno to Cassino* (US Official History) (Washington DC: Office of the Chief of Military History, US Army, 1969)

Bradley, Omar, *A Soldier's Story of the Allied Campaigns from Tunis to the Elbe* (London: Eyre & Spottiswoode, 1951)

Brooks, Thomas R., *The War North of Rome, June 1944–May 1945* (New York: Sarpedon, 1996)

Buckley, Christopher, *The Road to Rome* (London: Hodder & Stoughton, 1945)

Calvocoressi, Peter, *Top Secret Ultra* (London: Cassell, 1980)

Carver, Field Marshal Lord, *El Alamein* (London: Batsford, 1962; Ware: Wordsworth Editions, 2002)

Chandler, David, ed., *Great Battles of the British Army* (London: Arms and Armour Press, 1991)

Chant, Christopher, et al., *Hitler's Generals and their Battles* (London: Salamander Books, 1977)

Churchill, Winston S., *The Second World War*, vol. 1: *The Gathering Storm* (London: Cassell, 1948; reprinted with intro. by Martin Gilbert, London: Minerva, 1989)

—— vol. 2: *Their Finest Hour* (London: Cassell, 1949)

—— vol. 3: *The Grand Alliance* (London: Cassell, 1950)

—— vol. 4: *The Hinge of Fate* (London: Cassell, 1951)

—— vol. 5: *Closing the Ring* (London: Cassell, 1952)

—— vol. 6: *Triumph and Tragedy* (London: Cassell, 1954)

Clark, Mark W., *Calculated Risk: His Personal Story of the War in North Africa and Italy* (New York: Harper & Bros., 1950)

Cowles, Virginia, *The Phantom Major: David Stirling and the SAS* (London: Collins, 1959)

Dancocks, Daniel G., *The D-Day Dodgers: The Canadians in Italy, 1943–1945* (Toronto: McClelland & Stewart, 1991)

D'Este, Carlo, *Bitter Victory: The Battle for Sicily, July–August 1943* (London: Cassell, 1999)

de Guingand, Francis, *Operation Victory* (London: Hodder & Stoughton, 1947)

Doherty, Richard, *A Noble Crusade: The History of Eighth Army, 1941–45* (Staplehurst: Spellmount, 1999)

Durnford-Slater, Brigadier John, *Commando: Memoirs of a Fighting Commando in World War Two* (London: Greenhill Books, 2002)

Ellis, John, *Cassino: The Hollow Victory* (London: André Deutsch, 1984)

Ellwood, David W., *Italy, 1943–1945* (Leicester: Leicester University Press, 1985)

Farran, Roy, *Winged Dagger: Adventures on Special Service* (London: Collins, 1948)

Fergusson, Bernard, *The Black Watch and the King's Enemies* (London: Collins, 1950)

Fisher, Ernest F., Jr, *Cassino to the Alps* (US Official History) (Washington DC: Center of Military History, US Army, 1977)

Fraser, David, *And We Shall Shock Them: The British Army in the Second World War* (London: Hodder & Stoughton, 1983)

Garland, Albert N., Smyth, Howard McGaw, and Blumenson, Martin, *Sicily and the Surrender of Italy* (US Official History) (Washington DC: Office of the Chief of Military History, Department of the Army, 1965)

Gilbert, Martin, *Road to Victory: Winston S. Churchill 1941–1945* (London: Heinemann, 1986)

Hamilton, Nigel, *Monty: Master of the Battlefield, 1942–1944* (London: Hamish Hamilton, 1982)

Harrison, Frank, *Tobruk: The Great Siege Reassessed* (London: Arms and Armour Press, 1997)

Hibbert, Christopher, *Anzio: The Bid for Rome* (London: Macdonald, 1970)

Hinsley, F. H., et al., *British Intelligence in the Second World War, Its Influence on Strategy and Operations*, vols. 1 and 2 (London: HMSO, 1979, 1981)

Howard, Sir Michael, *Mediterranean Strategy in the Second World War* (London: Weidenfeld & Nicolson, 1968)

—— *Studies in War and Peace* (London: Maurice Temple Smith, 1970)

Howarth, Patrick, *'My God, Soldiers': From Alamein to Vienna* (London: Hutchinson, 1989)

Irving, David, *The War between the Generals* (London: Allen Lane, 1981)

Jackson, General Sir William, *The North African Campaign, 1940–43* (London: Batsford, 1975)

James, Roger, *Montgomery at Alamein* (Southsea: Adart, 1990)

Jenkins, Roy, *Churchill* (London: Macmillan, 2001)

Jewell, Derek, ed., *Alamein and the Desert War* (London: Sphere, 1967)

Joly, Cyril, *Take these Men* (Harmondsworth: Penguin, 1956)

Keegan, John, ed., *Churchill's Generals* (London: Warner, 1992)

Kippenberger, Major-General Sir Howard, *Infantry Brigadier* (London: Oxford University Press, 1949)

Lande, D. A., *Rommel in North Africa* (Osceola, Wis.: MBI Publishing, 1999)

Latimer, Jon, *Alamein* (London: John Murray, 2002)

Linklater, Eric, *The Campaign in Italy* (London: HMSO, 1951)

Long, Gavin, *To Benghazi* (Australian Official History) (Canberra: Australian War Memorial, 1952)

Majdalany, Fred, *Cassino: Portrait of a Battle* (London: Longmans, Green, 1957)

Mason, David, *Salerno: Foothold in Europe* (London: Pan-Ballantine, 1971)

The Mediterranean and Middle East (British Official History), vol. 1: *The Early Successes against Italy*, by I. S. O. Playfair et. al. (London: HMSO, 1954)

—— vol. 2: *The Germans Come to the Help of their Ally*, by I. S. O. Playfair et. al. (London: HMSO, 1956)

—— vol. 3: *British Fortunes Reach their Lowest Ebb*, by I. S. O. Playfair et. al. (London: HMSO, 1960)

—— vol. 4: *The Destruction of Axis Forces in North Africa*, by I. S. O. Playfair et. al. (London: HMSO, 1966)

—— vol. 5: *The Campaign in Sicily 1943 and the Campaign in Italy 3rd September 1943 to 31st March 1944*, by C. J. C. Molony et al. (London: HMSO, 1973)

—— vol. 6: *Victory in the Mediterranean*, pt 1: *1st April to 4th June 1944*, by C. J. C. Moloney et al. (London: HMSO, 1984)

—— vol. 6: *Victory in the Mediterranean*, pt 2: *June to October 1944*, by Sir William Jackson with T. P. Gleave (London: HMSO, 1987)

—— vol. 6: *Victory in the Mediterranean*, pt 3: *November 1944 to May 1945*, by Sir William Jackson with T. P. Gleave (London: HMSO, 1988)

Ministry of Information, *The Eighth Army, September 1941 to January 1943* (London: HMSO, 1944)

Montgomery of Alamein, Field Marshal Viscount, *El Alamein to the River Sangro* (London: Hutchinson, 1948)

—— *The Memoirs of Field Marshal The Viscount Montgomery of Alamein, K.G.* (London: Collins, 1958)

Moorehead, Alan, *African Trilogy* (London: Hamish Hamilton, 1944)

—— *Montgomery* (London: Hamish Hamilton, 1946)

Neillands, R. H., *The Desert Rats: 7th Armoured Division, 1940–45* (London: Weidenfeld & Nicolson, 1994)

Nicholson, Lieutenant-Colonel G. W. L., *Official History of the Canadian Army in the Second World War*, vol. 2: *The Canadians in Italy 1943–1945* (Ottawa: Queen's Printer, 1956)

Pack, S. W. C. *Operation Husky: The Allied Invasion of Sicily* (New York: Hippocrene Books, 1977)

Peniakoff, Vladimir, *Popski's Private Army* (London: Jonathan Cape, 1953)

Pitt, Barrie, *The Crucible of War: Western Desert, 1941* (London: Jonathan Cape, 1980)

Pond, Hugh, *Sicily* (London: William Kimber, 1962)

Rommel, Erwin, *The Rommel Papers*, ed. B. H. Liddell Hart et al., trans. Paul Findlay (London: Collins, 1953)

Rosignoli, Guido, *The Allied Forces in Italy, 1943–45* (Newton Abbot: David & Charles, 1989)

Salmond, J. B., *The History of the 51st Highland Division, 1939–1945* (Edinburgh: Pentland, 1994)

Saunders, Hilary Aidan St George, *The Red Beret: The Story of the Parachute Regiment at War, 1940–1945* (London: Michael Joseph, 1950)

Schmidt, Heinz Werner, *With Rommel in the Desert* (London: Constable, 1997)

Senger und Etterlin, Frido von, *Neither Fear nor Hope: The Wartime Career of General Frido von Senger und Etterlin, Defender of Cassino*, trans. George Malcolm (Novato, Cal.: Presidio, 1989)

Share, Pat, *Mud and Blood: The 2/23rd Australian Infantry Battalion* (Frankston, Vic.: Heritage Books, 1978)

Smurthwaite, David, *D-Day Dodgers: The British Army in Italy, 1943–1945* (London: National Army Museum, 1995)

Stevens, Lieutenant-Colonel G. R., *Fourth Indian Division* (London: McClaren, 1949)

Walker, Ronald, *Alam Halfa and Alamein*, Official History of New Zealand in the Second World War, 1939–1945 (Wellington: Historical Publications Branch, Department of Internal Affairs, 1967)

Weiss, Steve, *Allies in Conflict* (London: Macmillan, 1996)

Wilhelmsmeyer, Helmut, *Der Krieg in Italien, 1943–1945* (Graz: L. Stocker, 1995)

Wilson, General Henry Maitland, *Report by the Supreme Allied Commander Mediterranean to the Combined Chiefs of Staff on the Italian Campaign, 8 January 1944 to 10 May 1944* (Washington DC, 1946)

Zuehlke, Mark, *Ortona: Canada's Epic World War II Battle* (Toronto: Stoddart, 1999)

Acknowledgements

A great many people, veteran organizations, museums and libraries helped me with this book. In Australia, thanks are due to two Royal Marine friends, Derek Lucas and Phil Herd, and in Canada to another Royal Marine comrade, Joe Cartwright, of Calgary, Alberta, who traced veteran organizations, visited Canadian museums, and hunted out information. Yet another Royal Marine, Terry Brown, drew the maps and the chapter-head illustrations, so thanks to Terry for those and for his company at Cassino and the Liri Valley. Thanks also to the princess of indexers, Sue Martin, for providing the index and checking my numerous spelling variations. Thanks also to Matthew Rogers, formerly of the University of Reading, for allowing me to quote from his excellent dissertation on the use of Enigma in North Africa.

For reading the text and pointing out errors I would like to thank Major-General Julian Thompson, CB, OBE, Group Captain Peter Bird and Eric Garner. Every book I write seems to attract at least one special helper, and Eric Garner – who served in Eighth Army with the Royal Engineers – has filled that role wonderfully in this one, not least by his mastery of the Internet. This book could not have been written without Eric, who has been a source of help, advice and inspiration throughout the entire research and writing period, and I am most grateful for all he has done – the sappers, as ever, have paved the way forward.

Thanks also to fellow writer and military historian Don Featherstone of the 51st Royal Tank Regiment for his help and advice, to Hugh Pond for permission to quote from his account of the campaign in Sicily, and very specially to Mrs Sylvia Philpin Jones for permission to reproduce two 'Two Types' cartoons drawn by her late husband, 'Jon'. Thanks also to Victor J. Bulger of Scarborough, Ontario, Canada, for permission to quote from his memoir, *The Guns of Italy*, and to Max Parsons of the 2/12th Australian Field Regiment Association for publishing my appeal for recollections in the Association's newsletter. Thanks also to Alan Rooney of Midas Tours for his help in visiting El Alamein and Tobruk. On a personal note, I would like to thank Lester, Ian and Steve of the Highworth Computer Centre, who saved me from that writer's nightmare, a breakdown in my computer, which locked in 130,000 words of the penultimate draft – without them this book would never have appeared on time; they did a great job.

Among many service organizations, I would like to thank the Middle East Forces Veterans Association (East Anglia Branch), and thanks go also to Peter Banks of the Middle East Forces Association; John Clarke, Hon. Secretary, the Monte Cassino Veterans Association; Graham Swain and Harold Tonks of the Italy Star Association; Bill Sinclair and R. C. Rowley of the 9th Australian Division Association and the Australian Returned Services League (RSL) and *RSL News* in Australia and New Zealand; John Searle of the 2/13th Battalion Association, 2nd AIF; the Royal Canadian Legion; and the Memorable Order of Tin Hats, South Africa. Thanks also to Lieutenant-Colonel Will Townend of the Royal Artillery Historical Trust for official accounts of the artillery at Alamein, to C. W. Hollies for permission to use his memoirs of the desert war, and to the editorial staff of the New Zealand *RSL Review*. The staff at the Imperial War Museum, the National Army Museum and the El Alamein Military Museum in Egypt were also extremely helpful in answering queries and tracking down veterans.

Finally and most of all, my thanks go to the most important people concerned with this book: the Eighth Army veterans – especially those who answered my appeal for personal accounts.

The veterans are always helpful and generous with their time and memories, and once again a vast number of accounts, tapes, poems, books, pamphlets, letters and memoirs flooded in. Many accounts were sent in by the widows or children of veterans, rightly proud of what their husbands or fathers had done while serving in Eighth Army. My only regret is that I could not use more of them or include any of them in full – there simply isn't the space. I have done my best to reproduce as many as possible, and those that are included speak for all the rest. Every account is valuable – not least in checking the accuracy of the others – and all will be sent on to a suitable archive for the benefit of future historians of the Second World War. Among these valued contributors are:

Harry Addison, 17th Railway Company, 2nd New Zealand Division; A. W. Allaway, the Rats of Tobruk Association, Queensland, Australia; Sam Anderson, who sent a tape on his time with the Black Watch; Joan Aston, *Rats of Tobruk*, Toowoomba, Australia; Peter Banks, Essex; Graham Barry, editor, *RSL Reveille*, Sydney, Australia; John Bell, on behalf of his father, Bill Bell, 27th New Zealand Machine Gun Battalion, Alamein; John A. Black, 27th New Zealand Machine Gun Battalion; Howard Bradley, on behalf of his RAF father; Cyril Brian, RAF New Zealand; Fred. J. Brooks, the Rifle Brigade; Peter Brooks, who found the words to 'D-Day Dodgers'; Eric Brown, MC, who helped with both this and my Normandy book; Lieutenant-Colonel Kelly Brown, DSO, who sent a splendid account of a New Zealand infantry attack at Alam Halfa; Lord Bruntisfield, OBE, MC, the Scots Greys; George Edward Buchanan, MM, 30th Battery, E Troop, 2nd NZEF; Victor J. Bulger, 1st Royal Canadian Horse Artillery; Edward (Ted) Butler, who provided information on the AIF in the UK and on the Rats of Tobruk; John Butler of Canada, who helped with Canadian accounts; Charles Butt, who allowed me to use accounts from the papers of his father, C. H. Butt;

William Charles Carree, Royal Engineers, 'a British Rat of Tobruk'; the late Field Marshal Lord Carver, 7th Armoured Division; Allan Cawsey of Canada; Gay Collington, on behalf of Roland Collington, RASC; Ray Comfort, 2nd New Zealand Division, who supplied an excellent account and photos; L. H. T. Court, the Queen's Royal Regiment, Tunisia; W. H. E. Cousins,

GCC, JP, Queensland; Ron Culbert of Queensland, who sent poems – especially 'Twenty Thousand Thieves'; Alf Curtis, 9th Australian Division Ammunition Company, who provided an account of the siege of Tobruk; Charles Delworth, RASC; Doug Denton, 3rd Battalion the Coldstream Guards; Bob Douglas on behalf of his father, Dr Bob Douglas, 2/2nd Machine Gun Battalion, AIF; S. D. and P. M. Dudley, Victoria, Australia; John Easton; Hugh Eastwood, on behalf of his father, Captain Eric Eastwood; Paul Edwards, 2/8th Australian Field Regiment; Lyndon Evans, 16th New Zealand Railway Operating Company; James Falck, 3rd Battalion the Welsh Guards; E. T. Farley, 7th Hussars; Bert Ferres, MM, 2/13th Battalion AIF; David. L. Garven, 19th Battalion Armoured Regiment, 2nd New Zealand Division;

Cyril Gaylard, 2/7th Australian Field Company, Royal Australian Engineers; Jack Geddes, 22nd Armoured Brigade, 7th Armoured Division; Ernie George, 16th Railway Operating Company, New Zealand Engineers, who allowed me to use extracts from his book *The Fighting 16th*; Robert (Bob) Gill, 2/8th Field Regiment, 9th Australian Division; Neville Gillman, 4th County of London Yeomanry; Frank Grainger, Fleet Air Arm; Bruce Griffin, 2/15th Battalion, Queensland, Australia, who allowed me to quote from his memoirs; Christopher Hadfield, on behalf of Jim Sewell; W. Hadfield, 65th Field Regiment, 44th Division; Pete Hammond, 26th New Zealand Infantry Battalion; Jane Harney, on behalf of her father, Corporal Ernest Hartman, 2/48th Battalion; Denis Hart, 7th Armoured Division; Bill Hawkins, 4th Battalion the Essex Regiment, 4th Indian Division; Maurice Hendry, 2nd New Zealand Division; Douglas W. Hodge, 4th New Zealand Infantry Brigade; C. W. Hollies, who allowed me to quote from his memoir of the desert war; Bill Hopper, editor, *RSL Review,* New Zealand; Mrs Gillian Howard, who sent me letters on her father, Corporal Arthur Smith, 8th RTR, killed at Sidi Rezegh; John and Lorraine Hyland, Arkles Bay, New Zealand;

Gerald Jackson, of Jersey, C.I., who allowed me to use extracts from his book *A Long Parting*; W. H. (Bill) Jenkins, Anti-Tank Platoon, 2/1st Battalion, 6th Australian Division; Lieutenant-Colonel A. E. Johnson, Royal Signals; Dr Mark Johnston of Victoria, Australia, who provided help in locating Australian veterans; Philip Jones, on behalf of his father, Norman, 23rd Battalion, New Zealand Infantry; Ray Jordan, New Zealand; Ray Kennedy, 4th New Zealand Infantry Brigade; D. King of Suffolk, England, who sent the taped memoirs of Spencer Seadon; Robert James Kirk Jr, on behalf of his father; S. C. W. Knight, REME; West Knowles, 6th New Zealand Artillery Regiment; Norman and Audrey Leaf, Auckland, New Zealand; Stan Legion in Canada; G. S. Levien, New Zealand Army Medical Corps;

Ned Maxwell 2/12th Infantry Battalion, AIF; Genevieve Millette, on behalf of her grandfather, Antoine Dingwall; Marie Millette on behalf of her father, Douglas Dingwall; Mrs Grace Moore of Brookfield, Australia, on behalf of her husband, who served at Tobruk; G. H. Morgan, on behalf of his brother, Rifleman Gwyn Morgan, MM, the Rifle Brigade; J. S. Morgan, on behalf of his late brother, G. Morgan, MM; Vic Moulder, on behalf of his uncle, Lieutenant Victor Moulder, 2/2nd Machine Gun Battalion, 9th Division; Mrs B. Muir, on behalf of her husband, Maurice Muir, MM, 24th New Zealand Battalion; Harold Nilson, the Middle East Forces Veterans Association; Cyril W. O'Brian, 2nd New Zealand Division; W. J. (Bill) O'Neill, 1st Battalion the Gordon Highlanders, 51st Highland Division; Max Parsons, 2/12th Australian Field Regiment; Gordon Planner, HMS *Circe*; Paul Pregnolato, South Africa; Ben Price, 18th Infantry Brigade, AIF; Arthur Prosser, now of Waitkanae, New Zealand, formerly of the Royal Gloucestershire Hussars; Keith Reid, RAASC, 9th Australian Division; J. J. Richards, 26th New Zealand Battalion, Cassino; Kenneth Riley, MM, 48th RTR, for his account of action on the Gothic Line; Geoffery Robinson, 9th Australian Division; Norman Roulston of Ebbw Vale, Queensland, on behalf of his late father-in-law, Albert Fletcher, REME X Corps; Bill Rudd, 2/24th Battalion, AIF;

Major Eric Schmidt, Royal Engineers; Jim Sewell, 7th Armoured Division; John Sheenhan, state secretary, the Returned Services League of Australia, Sydney; Keith Simcock, 34th New Zealand Anti-Tank Battery; John Sinclair, HMS *Kipling*; Harold Skipper, Dulverton, Somerset; Ernest Smallridge, V Corps Signals; E. J. (Ted) Smith, 'A' Battery, 11th (HAC) Regiment, RHA; Peter Smythe, 25th New Zealand Battalion, 6th New Zealand Infantry Brigade; Barbara Snel, Carignbah, Australia, on behalf of her father, Arthur Spencer; John Statham, 11th Regiment,

Royal Horse Artillery; Phyllis Sturmfels, Rotorau, New Zealand, on behalf of Staff Sergeant James Huston; Bill Sutherland, RSL, New South Wales, Australia; Garth Suthers, 2/9th Battalion, AIF; Lloyd Tann, 18th Infantry Brigade, 2nd AIF, who allowed me to use extracts from his unit history of the 2/5th Australian Field Ambulance; Henry Tranter, 9th Australian Division; David Troop, 3rd Battalion the Coldstream Guards; Sir William (Bill) Vines, 2/23rd Battalion, AIF; Sapper Reg Wheatley, 754th Army Field Company, Royal Engineers; Jack Wilkinson, 9th Australian Division Cavalry (Mechanized); John E. Williams, Royal Artillery, Cassino; W. A. Wood, Queensland, Australia.

And finally, to any of my correspondents whose name I have inadvertently left out, *mea culpa* and my apologies.

Index